THE EXPERIENCES OF TIRESIAS

NICOLE LORAUX

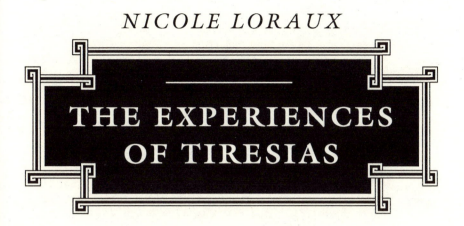

THE EXPERIENCES
OF TIRESIAS

THE FEMININE
AND THE GREEK MAN

Translated by Paula Wissing

PRINCETON UNIVERSITY PRESS

PRINCETON, NEW JERSEY

Chapter 7, "Herakles: The Supermale and the Feminine," is adapted from an
English translation by Robert Lamberton. This translation was originally published in
David M. Halperin, John J. Winkler, and Froma Zeitlin, eds., *Before Sexuality:
The Construction of Erotic Experience in the Ancient Greek World* (Princeton, NJ:
Princeton University Press, 1990). Copyright © 1990
Princeton University Press.

Chapter 8, "Therefore, Socrates Is Immortal," is adapted from an English translation by
Janet Lloyd. This translation was originally published in ZONE 4: *Fragments for a History
of the Human Body, part 2*. Copyright © 1989 Zone Books. Reprinted with permission.

Published by Princeton University Press, 41 William Street,
Princeton, New Jersey 08540
In the United Kingdom: Princeton University Press, Chichester, West Sussex

Library of Congress Cataloging-in-Publication Data

Loraux, Nicole.
[Expériences de Tirésias. English]
The experiences of Tiresias : the feminine and the Greek man /
Nicole Loraux : translated by Paula Wissing.
p.   cm.
Includes bibliographical references and index.
ISBN 0-691-02985-7 (CL)
1.   Sex role—Greece.   2. Greece—Civilization—To 146 B.C.
3.   Femininity (Psychology)   4. Masculinity (Psychology)   I.   Title.
HQ1073.5.G8L6713   1995
155.3′3—dc20   94-36789

This book has been composed in Postscript Galliard

Princeton University Press books are printed on acid-free paper,
and meet the guidelines for permanence and durability of the
Committee on Production Guidelines for Book Longevity of the
Council on Library Resources

Printed in the United States of America

1 3 5 7 9 10 8 6 4 2

CONTENTS

ABBREVIATIONS AND KEYWORDS

ad "at" (line no., etc.)

Allen: Allen, T. W., and D. B. Monro, eds. *Homeri Opera*. Oxford: Clarendon Press, 1975–79. 5 vols.

Austin: Austin, C., ed. *Nova Fragmenta Euripidea*. Berlin: de Gruyter, 1968.

Bergk: Bergk, Theodor, ed. *Poetae Lyrici Graeci*, 5th ed. Leipzig: Teubner, 1900–1914. 3 vols.

Bollack: Bollack, J., ed. *Empédocle*. Paris: Minuit, 1965–69. 3 vols.

Campbell: Campbell, David A. *Greek Lyric Poetry: A Selection of Early Greek Lyric, Elegiac, and Iambic Poetry*. London: Macmillan; New York: St. Martin's, 1967.

CUF: Collection des Universités de France (Paris: Les Belles Lettres).

DK: Diels, Hermann, and Walther Kranz, eds. *Die Fragmente der Vorsokratiker*. 6th ed. 3 vols. Berlin: Weidmann, 1951.

Edmonds: Edmonds, J. M., ed. and trans., et al. *The Fragments of Attic Comedy*. . . . Leiden: E. J. Brill, 1957–61. 4 vols.

Edmonds: Edmonds, J. M., ed. and trans. *Elegy and Iambus*. London: W. Heinemann; New York: G. P. Putnam, 1931–. The Loeb Classical Library. 2 vols.

fr. "fragment"

fr. incert. "uncertain fragment"

IG *Inscriptiones Graecae*. Berlin, 1873–.

Kern: Kern, Otto, ed. *Orphicorum Fragmenta*. Berlin: Weidmann, 1922.

Kock: Kock, Theodor, ed. *Comicorum Atticorum Fragmenta*. Leipzig: Teubner, 1880–88. 3 vols.

Littré: Littré, Emile. *Oeuvres complètes d'Hippocrate*. Rpt. of Paris 1839 ed. Translation and Greek text. Amsterdam: Hakkert, 1973–.

MDAI(A): *Mitteilungen des Deutschen Archäologischen Instituts.*

MW: Merkelbach, R., and M. L. West, eds. *Fragmenta selecta*. New York: Oxford, 1983.

Nauck[2]: Nauck, August, ed. *Tragicorum Graecorum Fragmenta*. Göttingen: Vandenhoeck and Ruprecht, rpt. 1964.

Page: Page, Denys L., ed. *Poetae Melici Graeci*. Oxford: Clarendon Press, 1962.

Pfeiffer: Pfeiffer, R., ed. *Callimachus*. Oxford: Clarendon Press, 1949.

Rev. Arch.   *Revue Archéologique*

SEG: Hondius, J.J.E., et al., eds. *Supplementum Epigraphicum Graecum*. Leiden, 1923–.

s.v.   "under the word"

von Arnim: Arnim, Hans von, ed. *Stoicorum Veterum fragmenta*. Leipzig: Teubner, 1903–24.

West: West, M. L., ed. *Iambi et Elegi ante Alexandrum Cantati*. Oxford: Clarendon Press, 1971–72. 2 vols.

THE EXPERIENCES OF TIRESIAS

THE FEMININE OPERATOR

THIS IS NOT a book about women, though well before the final chapters, devoted to the study of a few paradoxical feminine figures, Greek women are often discussed.

It is a book about men or about the feminine.

Already this *or* requires some explanation. I will come to it. Now is the time for a few clarifications.

"Men are the city": assuming that this oft-repeated *topos* is correct and the Greek city is equivalent to the group of virile men (*andres*)* who inhabit it, modern historians of antiquity (who, for their part, prefer to speak of a "men's club") feel justified instead, when they speak of the *polis*—especially in its democratic form[1]—and the politics that most closely approximates the type "invented by" the Greeks, in saying that the city is founded "on the exclusion of women." Assuredly this brusque formula could be qualified, despite the abundant commentaries it has provoked, but I will consider it to be sufficiently accurate in cases where the institutional reality of the city is of less importance than the representations on which political life is founded. Moreover, I am dealing with the feminine, not with women.

The feminine enters Greek politics (and politics everywhere?) in the form of a hypothesis based on a negation: the repeated—and vivid—denial of the benefits a man might obtain if he were to cultivate a feminine part within himself. Is this a "fear of sexual confusion"? A desire for irreversible separation, all the better to give the *anēr* the consistent purity of a model? For citizenship is ordinarily expressed by way of *andreia*, of virility as the name for courage; and on more than one occasion in the fourth century B.C., political opponents looking for a nasty insult called each other women—witness the "civilities" exchanged between Aeschines and Demosthenes.

But questions that are too quickly put aside because they are self-evident often mask a great deal. Beneath the obvious glorification of the *anēr*, I detect a concern with defining the man/citizen according to a notion of virility that is impermeable to anything feminine. And in this concern I see an enduring political effort to consign an opposing, or at

*A glossary of key terms will be found at the end of this book.

least different, tradition to marginality—another tradition that is equally Greek, a tradition that, from Homeric epic to heroic legend, postulates that a man worthy of the name is all the more virile precisely because he harbors within himself something of the feminine.

It is likely that more than one discriminating factor differentiates the citizen from his other, or others. But if one does not regard the opposition between likeness and difference—even if it is "radical"—as the last word in Greek thinking (after all, Plato knew better than anyone else that the Same participates in the Other), one is forced to admit that the richest of discriminating factors is the feminine, the operator par excellence that makes it possible to conceive of identity as fashioned, in practical terms, by otherness. This means that a Greek man, or anyone who wishes to read the Greeks, must perform mental operations that are more complex than merely verifying a table of antithetical categories again and again.

Before I go any further, an example: Aristophanes' Socrates, in a face-off with the lout Strepsiades, who aspires to be his disciple. The sage's first lesson consists of an exercise on grammatical gender and the form, feminine or masculine, of words as they agree—and agree they must—with the thing that they designate. The question concerns the masculine, and the word under discussion is *alektruōn*, the term for "rooster," which Strepsiades has put under the category of the masculine. Socrates then exclaims: "You see what happens? You call the female "cock" just as you do the male, since you say *alektruōn* in each case." And the buffaloed Strepsiades learns that he must use *alektruaina* to refer to the female, a word that Socrates has just forged for the occasion.[2] No doubt the Athenian spectator was supposed to laugh loud and hard, but one would wager that he was laughing less at Strepsiades' thickheadedness than at the absurdity of a philosopher who wishes to give a feminine form to the *word* for cock. A number of words pertaining to the animal world have a masculine form that may be used to designate a female if preceded by a feminine article: e.g., *kuōn*, "dog," to which in this case the extremely negative values of the bitch may be attached[3]—and indeed, Strepsiades has mentioned *kuōn* in his list of masculines. But no feminine form can exist for males that are always referred to in the masculine—the cock, like the ram, the billygoat, and the bull. Now Socrates has rejected *kuōn*, which effectively admits a disparity between the gender of the word and the animal's sex, in favor of *alektruōn*, thereby pairing the cock with a "cockette," which amounts to undoing the idea that a cock is a cock. Of course Aristophanes wants to give the Athenian public a laugh at the expense of such a nonsensical sage, and the recipe is an effective one. But a reader desirous of greater understanding, with the perspective brought by time, will perhaps detect a theoretical issue of an altogether different stripe underneath the comedy: the authentically Socratic debate that pits feminine against masculine, playing it out as far as possible. Certainly Plato recalled it.

It is true that Greek discourse on the difference between the sexes allows us to settle for perfectly clear formulations. Those wary of ambivalence will be content with an explanation, on the subject of a passage from *The Clouds*, in the form of a comedian's simple joke. And readers are often content to ascertain that the table of opposites functions without exceptions. In fact, since so many texts reiterate this antithesis in a pure and simple form, there is nothing to prevent one from saying that the Greeks were able to maintain the division between the sexes down to the last degree, especially if, as it has been proposed, they saw sex "not only [as] . . . an organ fulfilling a determined function, but also as a sign indicating what role(s) an individual endowed with it may play within a given system."[4] Call this system society: at once the way is paved for sexuality, as perceived in its physiological dimension, to be totally and immediately invested with the social. Foucault is not far off, with his "principle of isomorphism between sexual and social relations" that for him was the key to the sexual behavior of the ancient Greeks.[5] But anthropologists of Greece in particular have breathed a sigh of relief that social roles arrived just in time to spare them from having to view sexuality as a *terra incognita*. It is enough to paper over the difference between the sexes with the social division of roles. Once this has been accomplished, everything, it is said, will be clear. Perhaps a bit too clear.

By selecting and organizing the sources in the appropriate way, the investigator wishing to sort out these roles will always be able to detect the dominance of the masculine, even in Greek ideas about biology. Perhaps then there is no further need for surprise that women, who "ought to be drier than men,"[6] are damp and cool. Basing her argument on her own field, the Africanist who made the preceding remark reconstructed the logic that claims that the male incontestably remains in his warm and dry body. But the Hellenist immersed in canonical oppositions *knows* that for the Greeks the male is warm, and each new reading offers the pleasures of further verification. Similarly, in discussions about the existence of a feminine seed, Aristotle, following the Apollo of the *Eumenides*— who denies women any active role in conception—will always win out over the Hippocratic physicians who give equal roles to male and female.[7] Therefore, when it comes to sexual behavior in society, the emphasis may fall, depending on individual choice, on studying male self-mastery and the "practices of the self" or on condemning the Greeks' confusing misogyny.[8] Interpretations diverge; dominance is assigned the same place.

This insistence on the principle of separation as an open-and-shut case offers the advantage of reaching the obvious by avoiding trouble—a risky intellectual business, for then the most edifying discourses may be taken at their word: for example, Xenophon's *Oikonomikos* that, by duly allotting each sex its position, has fueled so many discussions about Greek women or about the *anēr*.[9] But once separation is the issue, even the least ideological texts—such as the *Iliad* or the heroic epics—can be read by applying the drastic interpretative grid of social roles. And Achilles can be the "heroic individual," without granting this paradigmatic individual the tears shed by the hero of the *Iliad* or the overwhelming despair that would have driven him, had it not been for the intervention of one of his companions, to slit his throat when he heard of Patroclus's death. And the epic hero is credited with the abstract "beautiful death" of the Athenian citizen-soldier, a death deprived of any corporeality because his body is merely on loan from the city, while everything about the dead Iliadic champion's body is beautiful. Last, if it is true, as Jean-Pierre Vernant has recently argued, that the heroic individual lends eminent solidity to the social values that he sublimates in his death,[10] can Achilles really be considered a model, Achilles whose own fundamental core so lacks this very solidity?

In fact, the sorting process that takes place in the epic is never over. Here masculine and feminine function are two essential determinants, alternatively predominating and all the while inseparable. Convincing evidence for this can be found by listing all the attributes that secretly link Achilles to Helen, or by examining Andromache, the "ideal woman of the *Iliad*," who nonetheless is endowed with the fearsome name of an Amazon and who in her mourning will suffer as a warrior suffers in death.[11] This is the moment to recall "the ongoing exchanges" evinced in Indo-European tradition from Vedic India to Greece "in religion as in legend, between the domain of war and that of femininity,"[12] from Arjuna's feminine ornaments to the robes of Herakles or the "tender skin" of the warriors of the *Iliad*.

There comes a day when historians, seeking a cure for this fascination with the "classical city"—which means achieving a certain distance from it—find it necessary to venture afield, taking the low road or the high, if only, once they return, to bring some play into the well-oiled gears of the system. My choice, if I have to put it in so many words, was to go back to the world of the epic. After studying the funeral oration as a civic genre in which *andres* and *andreia* coincide because a citizen's duty toward the city lies in this coincidence, after reflecting on the thought processes by which an autochthon of Athena's city tackles the subject of the exclusion of women, I have followed Dumézil's advice and returned to the *Iliad* once a year. This annual return to the *Iliad*, in which a warrior worthy of the name of *anēr* inevitably fears, trembles, weeps, and allows himself to be called a woman without any loss to his virility,[13] has convinced me that Greek formulations of the difference between the sexes must be approached via the notion of exchange: *all* exchanges between the sexes, and not only inversion—for everything, in the end, will fall into place, for the greater glory of the city (I will return to this point)— or even the exchange that operates by the mixing of opposites and the blurring of all boundaries.

Mixture and inversion do not begin to exhaust the Greek register of exchange between the sexes.

In the case of mixture, a strictly corporeal notion of bisexuality provides the context for ambiguous figures who display a mixture of virility and femininity. It is worth noting that this notion is just as explicitly stated in the field of medicine, and as the result of observation, as postulated in the fictions of mythology. Hippocrates, for example, considers sterile women to be masculine, while sterile men exhibit feminine characteristics. Another example, from Hippocrates again: depending on the way in which the seeds are mixed during conception, there exist men who are pure *andres*, as well as *andres* who are still virile of soul (*andreioi*) but whose bodies lack the strength of the first, and *androgunoi* (men-women); while among women there are those who are the most female and the best formed, others who are already somewhat bolder (*thrasuterai*), and finally those who, because of their audacity, are called *andreiai*, "virile ones." And then there is Plato, legislating on sexuality from a civic perspective in which it is necessary, no matter what the cost, to separate the sexes and to protect the citizenry from unlawful love affairs, "for children, both boys and girls, and for the women-men and men-women (*gunaikōn andrōn kai andrōn gunaikōn*)."[14] In mythology one finds the primordial Androgyne, the Orphic Zeus, or the Hermaphrodite of the poets and sculptors, all grouped by the moderns under the heading "bisexuality": an imaginary bisexuality, of course, still envisioned only from the standpoint of the body—which limits the notion from the outset—and defined as "the possession of both sexes by one and the same being" or as an "accumulation of sexes."[15]

No doubt the Greeks have employed these figures, and a few others, in an attempt to "envision the sexual body of mortals," in an "anatomy of the impossible" that produces "autarchic" units.[16] But it is equally likely that such inwardly turned figures lead only to a "litany of limitations" while locking the mind into a single, ossified vision. Perhaps it is impossible to think about the body by confining oneself to the body alone. I propose that the Greeks, who have imagined these blocked bodies, which are the product of mixtures and a type of short circuit, also understood that a double register—that of metaphor, for example—offers the mind more possibilities than does the simultaneously disparate and overly homogeneous notion of monstrosity. With that, I would wager that it is in line with the Greeks that Freud, starting with the idea of "the anatomical distinction between the sexes," created the theory of an "enlarged" sexuality extending into the realm of the psyche and a bisexuality that is at once generalized and basic to the human species, "so that the contents of theoretical constructions of pure masculinity and pure femininity remain uncertain."[17]

The mixture of the sexes was a Greek question. The moderns have interpreted the exchange between the sexes by placing it under the heading of inversion, and they see this exchange enacted in social rites such as religious festivals and initiatory practices: in the Argive festival of the *Hubristika*, in which men and women trade clothes; in the transvestism of the ephebe who, on the eve of his accession into the state of *anēr*, dramatizes his passage into full virility by momentarily playing the woman; in Spartan marriage customs in which the young bride, giving up her hair, masculinizes herself to welcome the bridegroom who will consequently be less reluctant to rejoin the society of his fellow men— these are the most frequently mentioned examples in the arguments of the partisans of initiatory interpretation. It will be observed that the notion of inversion satisfies the mind insofar as it does not introduce any breach in the binary division of Greek categories. Once applied to these always transitional practices, the canonical distribution is reformed, unblemished, and the regulated functioning of the civic order is fully capable of controlling provisional reversals, which are unable to shake its foundations. But theoretical difficulties immediately arise when one attempts to generalize and makes inversion into the only figure of the Greek imagination and then tries, at the risk of simplification,[18] to apply a similar key to the texts. And how, especially in the case of rites in which inversion is marked by a basic asymmetry that always redounds to men's benefit, could everything be subsumed under a "law of symmetrical inversion"?[19]

It is necessary to consider the work of Froma Zeitlin, whose efforts to challenge this overly mechanical process have led her to analyze transvestism in the high classical period and in the space of the city within the institutional genres of Greek theater. Tranvestism is central to both tragedy and comedy since, by definition, female roles are taken by men, but also because the plot can introduce transvestism as a mechanism of the action—except that in the second case symmetry is not guaranteed (supposedly temporary exchanges end badly in tragedy, succeed only for women in comedy, and can always be assigned to the level of metatheater: how can one avoid thoughts about the interplay of reality and fiction when an actor with a female part must play a woman who disguises herself as a man?). Assuredly, *andres* do everything in Athenian theater: play, listen, judge. But the feminine garments donned by the actor-citizen, the highly marked accessories, such as the long traditional dress, that make up the theatrical costume offer striking manifestations of the relationship between the theater and femininity, a relationship made visible in many ways, beginning with the "androgyny" of its tutelary deity Dionysos.[20] And once again, men are the ones who will find pleasure and benefit here, by virtue of the "final paradox . . . that the theater employs the feminine to imagine a more complete model of the masculine self."

Here I will interrupt this quotation to interject that it is also possible to stress the importance of the deed that introduces a feminine enclave into the virile world; this disturbs the immutable table of oppositions somewhat. Men undoubtedly remain the recipients of social practices and mental operations, but during dramatic performances the feminine realm is revealed to be essential, for it is there to modulate and at the same time support the necessary virility of the *andres*. Now I can continue with the quotation and accept the idea that "to play the other" opens the citizen's masculine identity "to the often banished emotions of terror and pity."[21]

Let us leave the theater for a moment. But later on in these pages, we will again encounter this essential witness, the privileged site for a *logos* that, in the great days of the classical city and in civic legitimacy, speaks a language that is not the political parlance, with its rigid taxonomy of roles and positions.

It is time to state what the reader will have already guessed from this preamble, in which I had to list the roads not taken and my reasons for choosing others that still need to be explored. Simply put, my concern is the feminine as the most desired object of the Greek male.

This leads me without further ado onto the track of mental operations intended to appropriate some of the great experiences of femininity, in hopes that this also (or above all?) will shed light on the body. In other words the operations studied here are linked to incorporation and encirclement—in short, they pertain to a logic of inclusion. This is so not only because these operations serve to interiorize the feminine but because inclusion is the theoretical operation par excellence, which makes it possible to think of transcending the tables of oppositions. Similarly, in another field and on a totally different subject, Charles Malamoud studies the relationship between village and forest in Vedic practices and thought and reflects on the function of sacrifice, which is not "to definitively separate the village from everything that is not the village" or "to set the villager apart so that he can manifest his superiority to the forestal world that surrounds him, his talent . . . for capturing, for *encompassing* the forest," "but also to propitiate it by giving it its own share inside the village."[22] Put *anēr* in place of *village* and replace *forest* with *the feminine*: now we are at the heart of the matter. And when Malamoud bases the whole of his approach on the "intolerable" character of opposition, which prompts the "encompassing order" to integrate the other within it, "even if it entails being subjected to its influence, having to *adopt its language in part*,"[23] his words offer the best expression of what, throughout this long inquiry, I believe I have detected concerning the operations carried out by the Greek male mind to undermine the constituent opposition of his being. Certainly it is a profitable opposition, in that it assures him of his dominance, but one could postulate that it is unbearable because it reserves for the other sex the intensity of pleasure and pain.

In Malamoud's view of Brahmanism, the grandeur of the *dharma* requires the integration of the essence of the forest into the village. I would like to convince the reader that the Greeks, even those who most conform to the civic order, vied with one another to imagine what the feminine brings to the *anēr*.

Ideally, the exemplary *anēr* is the model of virility. But when *andreia* has no other meaning than "courage," by virtue of his exemplary nature the man-citizen is perceived as being asexual. In the language of the Prague School, one could say that man is the unmarked element of the pair man/woman. Let us say at least that the disincarnated male model exalted by the Athenian funeral oration has no body. A simple support for civic behavior, the *sōma* was the city's due, and the debt was paid with the combatant's death.

Unless it meets the other, the masculine man—this political subject— has no body. Could it be that the body—even sexual being—belongs entirely to the realm of women, as if there were "only one sex, the female sex"? As if women were "all sex and men all gender" (the men are human, and women would be "the very representation of the difference between the sexes"); and this is indeed what mortals, so recently separated from the gods, saw in their bedazzlement at the catastrophe in the form of a young bride named Pandora.[24]

I see at least two levels—pleasure and pain—on which these questions, recently asked on the subject of a period still close to us,[25] can be verified in ancient Greece.

So is it necessary to speak of pleasure in the feminine? This is not, of course, what we have learned from the studies devoted to the dominant Greek ideas on the subject. In the cities a complete ideology aims, officially, to prove that sexual pleasure is men's lot by right; women, destined to bear children and to prepare themselves for that goal, must be content with the carefully limited marital portion that the austere Hera concedes in a whisper to Aphrodite.[26] But this is not the version of the problem that is presented in the myth of Tiresias.

The story is well known. Before he became the seer whose story intersects with that of Oedipus, Tiresias—in one version of the myth—was a woman. Or, at least, for a time and because of having struck, wounded, or killed (or at least separated) a pair of copulating snakes, he inhabited a woman's body. Of course, one day, by again attacking a pair of snakes, Tiresias regains his male form. But this passage through femininity leaves him with the *experiences* of both sexes (two "characters," "natures," "pleasures," or "forms"), the subject of endless speculation on the part of Greek and Latin authors.[27] Here is what happens next:

> One day, as Zeus was quarreling with Hera, maintaining that the woman had more pleasure in the sexual act than the man while Hera insisted that the contrary was so, they resolved to send for Tiresias to ask him, since he had experienced both conditions. Responding to the question that he was asked, Tiresias said that if there were ten parts (to pleasure) the man enjoyed only one and the woman nine.[28]

Hera, the guardian of the orthodoxy of marriage, is enraged when faced with the evidence of how little attention women pay her in comparison to Aphrodite. In revenge she blinds Tiresias, but Zeus, who found the answer entirely to his liking, makes him into a seer.

Since it is not the blind seer who interests me here, I will forgo the end of the story to remain with the Tiresias whose experience of both sexes gives him knowledge about feminine pleasure, even if it contradicts official certitudes. As the protectress of civil marriage, Hera had every reason to be furious. It only took one man, formerly a woman, to destroy the reassuring view that placed wives beyond the influence of pleasure and brought *andres* to a simple and straightforward virility. But like the Athenian comic poets (e.g., Aristophanes in *Lysistrata*), the mythical Tiresias thought—and knew from experience—that when it comes to the pleasures of the bed women are excellent "riders," less passive than might be thought from the remarks of all those who saw Greek sexuality in terms of the opposition between activity (always masculine) and passivity (belonging to women).[29]

Of greater interest is the Tiresias who, in another version by the Hellenistic poet Callimachus, was blinded and made a seer by Athena for having trespassed all bounds when he beheld the goddess's naked body.[30] Assuredly, feminine secrets are well guarded and must remain so. In each case Tiresias's dead eyes had witnessed what he no longer needs to see, since he knows.

This is the Tiresias I take as an eponym, not the generalized mediator to which some have reduced him.[31] In placing this book under the sign of Tiresias, I am not unaware that more often the paradigm of the *anēr* in the thrall of the feminine is Herakles, with his gowns and his powerful body wracked with acute suffering. Certainly it is gratifying that for once the feminine is not immediately associated with suffering, for ordinarily women are more readily associated with suffering than pleasure—besides, patience! suffering will have its day before long, and there will be plenty of it. But my choice is dictated by another, perhaps more "serious" and certainly more purely theoretical reason. Because of what he has experienced and his ultimate function as a seer, Tiresias is intimately connected with knowledge. Book 11 of the *Odyssey* clearly states that after Tiresias died Persephone made an exception and spared his intellectual faculties, which means that he alone among the forgetful shades has memory and consciousness—and these are precious commodities for introducing a series of studies about the feminine operator. For I am less concerned here with compiling a list of acts or effective practices than with pursuing a line of thought about the difference between the sexes as reflected in the intellectual (or shall I say psychic?) operations that it accomplishes with the feminine element.

It might be suggested that suffering is more classically feminine than pleasure—particularly the tearing pains of childbirth, imagined by some to be near pleasure, which women must experience in order to achieve the social fulfillment of reproduction, a matter that their constitutions and the city concur is the preeminent quality of their sex. The Greek male dreams of this penetrating pain (*odunē*), of the rending of labor (*ōdis*), and not simply, as has been said and as I myself have argued, in order to "dispense with women in the bearing of children"—unless it is understood that one dispenses with women only to incorporate their femininity. For in suffering like a woman, even the super-virile Herakles is able to increase that virility to its highest pitch. This is not inconsistent. *Andreia* requires the heroic test of pain, and childbirth, not war, is the cause of the most intense pain.[32] The conclusion is self-evident, supposing that there was actually a need to state it.

In the same way, the *anēr* adopts maternal qualities. This does not have legal ramifications in Greece, as is the case in Rome, where "the technical term for mother as the one who gives birth, *parens*, takes . . . the opposite meaning of 'father' or the ascendant in the paternal line";[33] the appropriation of the feminine happens discretely, without extending to the use of delicate phrases such as the medieval fantasy of "Jesus our mother."[34] Nevertheless, in Alipheira in Arcadia Pausanias saw an altar to Zeus *Lekheates* (of childbirth), for it is there, the inhabitants told him, that the sovereign god gave birth to Athena.[35]

Zeus's "maternities" are well known: he swallows Metis to give birth to the warrior goddess or to complete the Orphic cosmogony.[36] The Hesiodic story of Metis (spelled with a lower case, *mētis* is often the attribute of feminine conduct) is almost an apologia, in which Metis is swallowed by a Zeus fearful that she would give birth to a child more powerful than he. For everything fulfills the Father's desires. With the pregnant Metis, Zeus reenacts, albeit more successfully, the deed of his father Kronos who, driven by a similar fear, swallowed his children, whom he stored in his *nēdus* (his belly, but the word can and often does refer to the womb).[37] By incorporating the mother into himself, Zeus bypasses the son, who is replaced by a daughter totally devoted to the rights of the *anēr*. It is worth pausing to consider Zeus's gestation, so often represented by the Athenian vase painters. One is easily convinced that while, from the standpoint of a sexuality limited to "acts," penetration passes for the "model act" in the eyes of the Greeks,[38] the feminine modality of the completeness of a body enclosing the child that it carries[39] —in this case, that of Zeus, who has absorbed a female divinity—offers the Greeks a way around a power mightier than that of the strong god.

To be certain, this account may be briefly compared with the Vedic story of how Indra averted the birth of a being stronger than he, the product of the love between Sacrifice and Word. It is "by slipping into the embrace of the two lovers" that Indra, "making himself into an embryo, penetrates into the womb and occupies it. At the end of a year, he is born and takes care when leaving to tear out the womb that enveloped him." Word will bear no more children. "Her only child"—comments Malamoud, from whom I have taken this account—"is this divine embryo who secretly raped her and who chose to be reborn in her only to mutilate her."[40] The comparison is instructive. Certainly the Greeks were not the ones who imagined penetration (accompanied by a mutilation that after all is its brutal opposite). Zeus's method is more gentle, or more subtle: incorporation. Metis, the feminine entity, now exists only inside him, and by virtue of the alchemy of the divine belly, the dreaded son will be born a virile daughter.

Considering this story from an analytical perspective, my goal is certainly not "to blame the masculine god because he usurps childbirth."[41] To this reproach, voiced by Marcel Detienne, who was noting that one can, under the circumstances, speak of the "denial of women's maternity" (which it is, whether one chooses to mention it or not), one can respond by saying that whenever the key actor is the father of gods and men, it is always constructive to take an interest in the workings of the imagination. And the fantasy of male childbirth is eminently Greek, even if its ultimate aim is not always to keep (or ensure) the power to give birth.[42] And for the hearer of the myth, this fantasy, even if not an act of "usurpation," amounts to appropriating, as Zeus does, one of the most widely recognized manifestations of femininity in order to strengthen the notion of virility, which is probably more threatened than would appear.

At the other pole of the horizon of this book, I would like to situate Plato and the use he makes of the feminine metaphor of reproduction, and with it the paradox created when he displaces reproduction to the side of the philosopher's mental creativity, making pregnancy the cause or at least the obligatory preliminary of love. M. F. Burnyeat, who has judiciously pointed out this oddity concerning a passage from the *Symposium*, adds that in this as well as other developments, conception always seems to have already taken place, without any other origin than itself, without any preceding metaphorical sexual union inside the soul.[43] It is certainly significant that Plato refuses to imagine the coupling between masculine and feminine in the philosopher's soul, but I do not aim to explain this gap by mentioning Plato's homosexuality. It is better to examine—and this will only be suggested in the following pages—his fairly literal use of the word *ōdis*, the word for childbirth and not, as the dictionaries have it, "anguish," in the *Symposium* and in *Phaedrus* or, in the latter dialogue, the conditions under which the soul suffers from the seed buried deep within it and finally gives birth, stirred by desire.[44] It would be better to reread the *Theaetetus* and attend to the pains of unfruitful birth of the namesake of the dialogue.

In any case, I will observe that Plato is neither the first nor the only Greek thinker to reorient the metaphorical network of the feminine toward the male in this way and for his benefit, even if he is the only one to devote himself to it in such a systematic fashion. This is why I will hesitate to find the roots, as others have done, of Aristotle and the representation of the female as a defective male in the Platonic operation of the "metonymic installation of the woman in the philosopher."[45] But it is true that the Platonic strategy is a complicated one, for with a perpetual oscillation in some texts it is bent on absorbing the feminine into the philosophizing *anēr*, while in other dialogues the entire effort seems to lie in shifting all the representations away from the political, including the exclusion of the feminine and the rigorous separation of the sexes, to the benefit of the male philosopher. The fact that this second operation takes place in the *Phaedo*, the dialogue about the soul, is undoubtedly no accident. But I will attempt to show that Plato's use of the hero Herakles—misogynistic, supermale, and yet closely allied to the feminine—as the paradigm for the "purely" masculine is yet another tactic in his convoluted strategy.[46]

Does this operation, which was Greek before it was Western, ultimately consist of moving the feminine from the woman's body to the man's soul so that it may be absorbed into his mind? If one speaks of displacement and not "replacement,"[47] such a move can indeed be reconstructed. The man gains in complexity, while the woman loses substance. And in fact, in Greek poetic tradition women's bodies, even while celebrated for their physical beauty, have something of the *adunaton*: from the first Hesiodic woman, who is all exteriority, to the goddess Athena, constituted by her wrappings (*peplos*, breastplate, shield) and whose incongruous nudity is blinding because it is unthinkable, not to mention Helen, so dazzling as to be wraithlike. This elusive silhouette is all that remains of feminine figures, while the cavity within them—their *nēdus* in both the generic and specific sense of the term—easily nourishes male dreams of interiority.[48]

Fine. But, to state as some (male and female) scholars have done that this automatically means that the woman is forgotten and the man is readied for a role of uncontested mastery would be to seriously mistake the nature of psychic operations, in which nothing is ever achieved without a cost; everything leaves a trace, something always remains, something is always lost. If the mortal body, in *erōs* and reproduction,[49] is felt in a feminine modality, and the soul is lived in the mode of the body, the reason is that something of the body is always and forever lodged in the soul. And therefore, without his knowing it, the philosopher's soul contains something of the woman who, before finding a respite from the pains of childbirth of which the *Republic* also speaks,[50] wanders like Io, pregnant by Zeus's doing and hounded by the gadfly that pursues her. Plato can indeed forbid his guardians the theater and proscribe any imitations of women, especially if she is "sick, in love, or with child";[51] didn't their philosophers' souls forestall them on this point?

It is high time to leave Plato. But not without noting that the definition of the city as "the community of pleasure and pain" ("when . . . all citizens equally rejoice at or suffer from the same events") immediately follows the discussion of the community of women, which provides its foundation.[52]

Let us leave the soul and return one last time to the city, to observe that the strict separation between feminine and masculine truly has no other place, no other boundaries than politics—or, more exactly, the *ideology* of politics. For, in ancient Greece, politics is probably more extensive than is suggested in the singularly edifying official parlance that speaks of the peaceful functioning of the city of the *andres*. If the pertinence of this language is challenged at all,[53] it becomes clear that this inner conflict represents, if not an adverse definition, at least an essential side to politics, even though politics in the form of *stasis* (sedition) is endlessly refused and rejected from the city just as it takes place in its midst. In a word, it is *denied*. Clearly, each of these negatives must be permitted to play against the other: conflict, the feminine (in each case it is the marked term of the pair), both working on behalf of men and civil order.

And in fact, the moment that civil order breaks down, women arise—virile women like Clytemnestra "the tyrant," who embodies the only conceivable version of a woman's assimilation of the masculine, which always occurs—is it surprising?—with the potential threat of a seizure of power. In short, it is the time of gynecocracy,[54] unless the division, which has become widespread, splits the *polis* in two. When civil war rages, the women erupt, often in a group, into the breach that has been opened in this fine totality. They fight on the rooftops in service of a faction, throwing stones and tiles at the opposition. And the Greek historian who must give them a place in his account wonders about women's true nature:[55] bold and audacious like the women-men in the treatise *On Regimen*, or fearful, as females must be when *andreia* belongs to men? In both examples, when real women make it imperative to abandon the imaginary feminine and grapple with the notion in the midst of a troubled city, there is urgent pressure to connect the difference between the sexes with politics on the terrain of conflict.

This amounts to saying that between reproduction and battle, between pleasure and pain and a courage that can have no name, the feminine has a dual nature, as if it has been split in two. It is complex, even contradictory, as any rich operator should be—an operator that can be expected to provide some distance on the civil taxonomies and to join politics with what it wishes to ignore.

The thirteen chapters of this work were initially conceived, often in very different form, between 1977 and 1985, in the course of a single project—gradually, as it should be, coming to be honed, modified, and even reworked (and I have made no systematic attempt to eliminate the traces of this evolution). These articles were written in reference to one another and reflect ongoing investigations and many questions. Four chapters were originally intended for psychoanalytic journals, while the others implicitly deal with the questions raised by that discipline. I will close by attempting to clarify this deliberate reference.

Historians and anthropologists concerned with ancient Greece generally avoid references to psychoanalysis in their work, and while they each have their own reasons for this distrust, the statement that "our" notion of sexuality is not Greek is a deciding factor in their eyes. They look to Foucault for support, because his last book is an attempt to "shape the familiar evidence" of "this everyday notion that is so recent" and because he declares that the Greeks had no "notion akin to sexuality."[56] I confess that I find such statements more surprising than enlightening, because while I do not consider sexuality as an invariable, one of the constants of sexuality is the fact that at any moment in history it is composed, to a considerable extent, of the thoughts of each individual or group about his or her sexual being. And the study of the Greek man and the feminine quickly leads to the hypothesis that an entire range of Greek thought focused on sexual differences (or, at least, that the Greeks thought a great deal about them) and ways to put them to male advantage, much more than on the endless verification of man's active role in the opposition between passive and active—for let us not forget that one of the definitions of the citizen is to alternate between commander and commanded, without this, however, leading to the feminization of the *anēr*.

Furthermore, if politics is often considered to be the covert mission of psychoanalysis, it is not without interest, inversely, to focus on the problems that sexual difference (which Freud certainly did not invent, although he formulated decisive questions that have aided us in understanding it) poses to politics, from the presumed invention of the latter by the Greeks. Treating the feminine as an operator of difference does not presuppose adhering to or attacking Freudian hypotheses about feminine sexuality, as my investigations principally concern the relationship between the Greek man and the other. Moreover, instead of penis envy, the recurring issue has been the Greek male's longing, which must be given its correct name, "pregnancy envy,"[57] to weigh himself down with penetrating sensations whose utterly feminine intensity is supposed to place them out of the reach of the paradigmatically virile citizen. In other words, this attempt to understand what the *anēr*, as a political subject, could imagine about the feminine has perhaps unearthed an ancient version of the reflection on "the catastrophe . . . of being a man" mentioned by Lou Andreas-Salomé in one of her letters to Freud.[58] This does not mean, however, that I have sought to verify the idea of a "fulfillment" that would lead each sex "to the boundaries of the other."[59] This is undoubtedly a lofty goal, but the historian works with what is at hand, and in representations of Greek women, the feminine, while coveted by the other sex, nonetheless is revealed to be more divided and amorphous than might be expected, and lacking any real positive opening toward the masculine. Furthermore, could it have been any other way? In a universe of representations suited to the *andres*, could one hope for anything more than a peek behind the curtains of the official language, with a generic speaker on each side who speaks for and to his fellows?[60]

Such, then, are the necessary constraints of my task. I will leave it up to the reader to judge the results. In methodological terms at least, I viewed the reference to psychoanalysis as offering additional liberty, less because it provides a set of arguments that can be applied no matter what the cost than because it offers an invitation to imagine, as a way of satisfying the compulsion to understand and to attain a sense of the specificity of the object—to reconstruct Greek mental operations on the subject of the indissociably psychic and corporeal condition of the sexual being. I hope in this way that I have made room for both history and the invariable.

It is possible—and this is a risk that anyone working on the edges of a discipline must incur—that neither historians nor psychoanalysts will find their due here—the latter because they prefer Hellenists prudently ensconced on their own turf who thus leave the glorious *ponos* of interpretation to them; the former, because they are suspicious of any work that relies on constructions and requires the full engagement by the investigator in the research—first of all, in the form of the choices that he or she has made. Nevertheless, I would wager that the risk is worth taking.

Before letting the book have its say, one further remark is necessary. I have avoided applied psychoanalysis in these studies (thus I am not interested in Herakles in his relationship with Hera, but in understanding what the Greek imagination of the *anēr* could fashion on the basis of this rebellious submission), which also means that I have chosen not to interpret plots from the standpoint of the actors involved in them. Friendly pressure notwithstanding, I did not believe that I had to say what Tiresias had "really" seen, because Callimachus's poem is discreet enough only to suggest that he saw the "unseeable." Despite the suggestion made to me, I did not find it necessary to argue that by seeing Athena's nudity Tiresias believed he saw the naked Mother,[61] because Tiresias's mother was one of the goddess's close companions and the young man, projecting the maternal figure onto Athena, would have thereby discerned her nakedness. There is nothing to know about Tiresias's unconscious, but the Greeks have a great deal to say about his blinding. And there is much food for thought for a Greek reader (listener) concerning Athena's femininity. Therefore I have not interpreted these elements, eschewing the "It's . . ." method, which one should be so careful to avoid: it's the mother, it's the Greeks' homosexuality, etc., and then one stops, already overwhelmed.

While the workings of the mind occasionally short-circuit, especially when focused on the differences between the sexes, these latter can be traced only by following the slow rhythm of experiment and error, and by refraining from indulgence in one's own interpretative impulses. I am speaking here as a (female) historian of the Greek male, whom I see as he constructs himself, through the workings of imagination, in his relationship to the feminine.

Intellectual and friendly support was precious to me during the entire course of this project. In addition to the dedications made for given chapters, which mark a particular debt, I would like to express particular gratitude to Marcel Detienne, for having encouraged me to work, doubtful as I was, those many years ago, that such a thing as a specifically masculine imaginative realm existed; to Laurence Kahn, Hélène Monsacré, Marie Moscovici, Maurice Olender, and Yan Thomas, who by their own research as well as their questions and suggestions have never ceased to help me surmount barriers; to Froma Zeitlin, for our ongoing dialogue, as fruitful as it has been intense, which continues to draw our paths ever closer together; to Patrice Loraux, listener and reader, kind and always accurate critic; and last, to Eric Vigne, who for many years believed in this book and knew how to wait for it to be written, all the while giving me the courage to write it.

August 1989

PART ONE

WOMEN, MEN, AND AFFLICTION

Chapter 1

BED AND WAR

EN POLEMŌI, LEKHOĪ: Ainetos, dead in battle; Aghippia, dead in childbirth. Two inscriptions on a stele, naming two unknown but illustrious figures from Sparta.

The Spartans who engraved their tombs with these and other suitably terse but sufficiently revealing inscriptions were obeying a regulation of their funeral legislation according to which, Plutarch says, "it was not permitted to engrave the names of the dead on tombs, except those of men fallen in battle and women who died in childbirth."[1]

Bed and war, equal value to the hoplite and the woman in labor: the extent of the equivalence can be ascertained by recalling that in the eyes of all Greece Sparta was reputed to have invented the hoplitic ideal of the beautiful death sung by Tyrtaeus: that of the citizen fallen like a soldier in the front line.[2] Of course, unlike the masculine model, the feminine version of the beautiful death barely extended beyond the boundaries of Lacedaemon; at least it left no traces in the accounts of the Greek historians—but history, it is true, has little use for women and their labor pains.[3] In short, the high value placed on death in childbirth, generally considered to be a Spartan attitude, must seemingly be explained in purely Spartan terms. We know that in Sparta motherhood, or rather, the procreation of beautiful children destined to become robust citizens, was a woman's greatest occupation.[4] Well before Plutarch, Critias and Xenophon speak of the curious Spartan custom of requiring athletic training for young girls and even pregnant women.[5] In the case of the *parthenos*, of course, it is the future wife, the procreatress of citizens, who exercises in order that "the man's seed, strongly rooted in a robust body, fully sprouts and that she herself is strong enough to bear labor and easily and successfully struggle against the pains of childbirth"—to bear labor the way that the hoplite bears the enemy's assault, to struggle against pain: labor is a battle.[6] Critias mentions training pregnant women, and nothing indicates that the Sophist has succumbed to the Spartan mirage when he mentions the exercise that his kinsman Plato will make into an essential component of his educational program for the city in the *Laws*.[7] According to an edifying tradition, this cultivation of women's courage and bodies bore fruit, and Gorgo, the wife of the hero of Thermopylae, has the honor of proudly proclaiming that if Lacedaemonian women alone command males, the reason is that they alone give birth to males.[8]

But it is the nature of the historian to challenge well-established traditions. Therefore, I will look beyond Sparta and Spartan tradition for evidence of the equivalence between childbirth and war.

When it comes to Athens, the search seems doomed to failure: how could the death of a woman be measured against the paradigmatic scale of the citizen-soldier's death? In fact, in Athens the only institutional opposition to be found is between the "beautiful death" celebrated during official and collective funerals,[9] and all other deaths: private deaths, the deaths of both men and women. So be it. But it is precisely on private tombs that, utterly unexpectedly, one encounters something of a symmetry between war and labor, and even though it is not institutionalized, this phenomenon nonetheless serves as an important reflection of attitudes. On the funerary reliefs in Athenian cemeteries, the dead person, it is known, is represented by his or her life. No allusion is made to his or her death, except in two cases: the death of a soldier and the death of a woman in childbirth.[10] Of course, the Athenian marbles do not violate the censorship that everywhere in the Greek world forbids representations of the moment of birth. On the steles, time is frozen in the moment before or after the child's delivery. Her girdle untied, her hair undone, the suffering woman falls into the arms of her attendants before giving birth and dying as a result; or else, in the intemporality of an already-vanished presence, the dead woman, seated in a chair, casts a vacant eye upon the newborn placed in her arms by a servant.[11] But the essential is there. Just like the soldier, whose face is forever that of a warrior, the woman in childbirth has achieved *aretē* in death. To be sure, this symmetry is not expressed in language but is conveyed in images. Does this mean that is it any less significant?

Lovers of words, however, will take consolation in the epitaph of a woman who died in childbirth in the second half of the fourth century and who was buried in the Kerameikos. She is named Kratista, and her death is celebrated in verse:

> Here the dust has welcomed the courageous daughter of Damainetos, Kratista, the beloved wife of Arkhemakhos: she who perished one day in childbirth, in the throes of suffering, leaving for her husband an orphan child in his abode.[12]

As in the case of citizens buried further away in the official cemetery, who are celebrated like Homeric *kouroi*, the vocabulary is that of the epic, from the groaning "throes of death" (*stonoenti potmōi*) to the *megaron* (the palace, here "abode"), and the expression of courage through strength (*iphthiman*: "courageous") to the designation of the wife as the "companion of the bed" (*eunin*), by way of the indeterminative *pote* (one day).[13] Furthermore, the woman's name is prophetic—she is called "the very strong one"—and contrary to all expectations, the language of the epitaph in the Athenian Kerameikos is Doric. Whether or not the young woman's family wished to bestow the title of honorary Spartan on her is something that we will never know.[14] But obviously the text conveys the symmetry between war and childbed. And more than symmetry—the words suggest something of an exchange, or at least the presence of war during the labor of giving birth.

This evidence is sufficient to beckon one to extend the search beyond the institutions of Sparta and Athens to note everything the Greek imagination has to say about the equivalence between the mother and the hoplite, these two civic roles.

MOTHER, HOPLITE

A remark by Jean-Pierre Vernant will serve as my starting point—a remark that is often quoted, if not always considered in its full implications. Stating that "marriage is to the girl what war is to the boy,"[15] Vernant forgets neither that marriage is also a necessity for the boy who wishes to attain his full stature as citizen[16] nor that for a woman marriage is realized only through motherhood. The fact that there is a delay between the wedding night and conception, as Plato prescribes in his *Laws*, or that the poets like to condense the two nights into one[17] is, after all, of no importance. Sooner or later, the married woman will be brought to completion by motherhood, for she only acquires the full status of legitimate wife once she has given birth, leaving behind her the formidable delights of the *numphē* for the measured continence of the mother of the family, the Thesmophoros who alone merits the name of *alokhos*.[18]

Alokhos: one who shares the same bed, *lekhos*, or rather she who is attached to the bed of the husband, this institution.[19] *Alokhos, lekhos*: in the Greece of the cities, the conjugal bed is not the subject of jokes, for it is the legitimate—not to say civic—place of reproduction. It will be recalled that the word for the woman who gives birth is *lekhō*[20] and that for the most part the vocabulary of childbirth, beginning with the word *lokhos* (childbirth, delivery) is derived from the root *legh*—"to lie down": e.g., the verb *lokheuō* or *Lokhia*, epiclesis for Artemis. An etymology that is practically universally accepted (at least since the time of the lexicographer Hesychius)[21] confirms the identity between *lokhos* as a word for childbirth and *lokhos* denoting, as early as Homer, an ambush and then the armed troop.[22] Thus, Pierre Chantraine can write of *lokhos* that all its derivatives "refer either to the notion of childbed or to military uses."[23]

Assuredly, this is too pat. The historian's joyous surprise at the encounter between war and childbirth in the same word is followed by doubt, as the price of imprudently trusting etymology becomes evident. Philologists themselves hasten to take on the case. To reduce the disparity between meanings—"an ambush is not a bed," says one of them—and to spare themselves what they consider to be "verbal acrobatics," some conclude that "there is not one but two words, *lokhos*, which are simply homonyms."[24] A linguist's solution, which even Benveniste has occasionally used: to reduce the "opposite meaning" or even diversity, postulate two roots that are strictly separate from one another. All the same, linguists ought to read anthropologists. Perhaps then they would reflect on the strange and recurrent associations, far from ancient Greece, linking ambush to childbed—for example, in Burgundy, where the husband, during the time of his wife's delivery, carouses with his companions in what is called an "ambush."[25] A coincidence, the philologist undoubtedly would say—but it happens that under the circumstances the similarity is noteworthy. And what is to be said when a Greek, and furthermore, a highly authoritative Greek, plays on the word *lokhos*? Such is the case in Hesiod's account, in the *Theogony*, of Kronos's "ambush" to spy on his father Ouranos. His father has secreted him in his mother's lap (*Gaiēs en keuthmōni*: in the Earth's "hidden place"), like all the other children to be born of Gaia;[26] Kronos is sent to wait in ambush by Earth herself, who has grown tired of Heaven's embraces. From this post, in a delivery that Ouranos certainly had not foreseen, Kronos emerges *ek lokheoio*—understood as the maternal orifice—to slit his insatiable sire's scrotum.[27] A strange business, no doubt, but how can one deny that Kronos here is the "child of double meaning"?[28] By insisting once again that the word is a simple homonym? One would still have to note that in spite of all Hesiod, as a well-informed Greek, makes an effort to reunite the two words *lokhos* under the sign of ambivalence. It is better to take the word—and the Greeks—literally.

Next it is necessary to answer the objections of the historians of antiquity. Let us admit that there is only one word, they say (as they have said to me), but in the classical period—the time of orthodox representations—the ambush is the fate of lightly armed combatants, who are held in infinitely lower esteem than hoplites. Consequently, how can one use this quirk of language to support the notion of the similarity between the woman in labor and the hoplite—for, after all, the valorous citizen-soldiers of Sparta are by definition hoplites? The objection is sensible, but one cannot be too careful about the abuses of good sense in history. This time I will take my answer from Homer. If the Iliadic ambush (*lokhos*, therefore) is the absolute criterion of bravery because that is where the value of the warriors can be discerned, "where the cowards and the brave are revealed,"[29] the reason is that, from the first, the notion of valor has linked childbed to war: in words—which bear the traces of Homer's Greek—showing the contiguity of childbirth and ambush, and in classical ideology, with the allusiveness of the hoplitic model.

And here, with renewed zest, I will resume the survey of images of the warrior in the representations of motherhood.

The association between motherhood and war in the cities is apparently straightforward: mothers produce hoplites. This is what Gorgo used to say; in Sparta it is the aim of *paideia* for women. No curse is more damning to a community than the wish to annihilate it, down to "the boychild in his mother's belly"—the city-to-come in the bellies of women—and inversely, the blessings that Aeschylus has the Danaids implore for Argos combine the happy delivery of mothers with the domestication of Ares, the murderer of young men.[30] To give birth, then, is to produce boys for the city, and in Euripides' *Suppliants*, the tragedy of motherhood in mourning, the mothers of the Seven against Thebes weep for what had once been their pride: as *kourotokoi*, bearers of children, the seven mothers had given birth to seven *kouroi*.[31] The birth of daughters is rarely discussed, as if the city could get along without these future childbearers. It is true that by giving sons to mothers the Greek imagination symbolically accomplishes the ever problematic integration of women into the city: a fine tactic, which forever assigns them the place of mediation between men and all the while banishes the ever threatening fantasy that the *genos gynaikōn* (the race of women) reproduces itself in a closed circuit.[32] In short, according to the literature—comedies of course, but tragedies as well—one would believe that Greek women, whether named Andromache or Lysistrata, give birth only to sons,[33] and the parabasis of the *Thesmophoriazousae* expresses the only appropriate challenge that the women of Athens can make, by demanding a place of honor for the mothers of good citizens—who not surprisingly are found on the side of the hoplites.[34]

Two texts—a fragment from a tragedy, a passage from a comedy—clearly express the civic idea of motherhood. The fragment is a famous excerpt from Euripides' *Erechtheus*, quoted by Lycurgus in his speech *Contra Leocrates*. Because he wished to accuse Leocrates of *lipotaxia*, of leaving the ranks, the Athenian orator multiplies the edifying examples of hoplitic conduct before mentioning a woman who dared sacrifice her daughter for the salvation of the city. A mother, a daughter: this conjunction, which could be a pure anomaly embedded in Lycurgus's patriotic eloquence, in reality contributes to the greater glory of orthodoxy. The mother, it is true, is the wife of the autochthonous Erechtheus. She affirms that he comes back to the city to use women's confinements (*lokheumasin*) as he pleases, condemns the tears that mothers shed on the hoplite's departure, and makes this confession, worth the most lengthy of speeches:

> If, in my house, instead of daughters, a male sapling had grown, at the time when the enemy fires would have threatened the city, wouldn't I, confronting his death in advance, have given this son a spear to send him into combat? Ah! if only I had children capable of fighting and gaining renown among warriors, and who were not born to be useless adornments to the city.[35]

In short, for want of a single son, she would use one of her daughters like a hoplite pledged to die: this is Praxithea's solution. Although less tragic, the declarations of the coryphaeus in *Lysistrata* are no less instructive. Speaking to the male audience of citizens assembled to laugh at women, she mentions "paying one's share" in the form of a tax made up of men[36] and contrasts her civic spirit to the detestable conduct of the old men of the chorus who have wasted the funds collected by the ancestors in the days of the Medic wars, without paying their war taxes in exchange. *Eisphora* is the war tax, and the ancestors' fund is known as *eranos*. But the same word, *eranos*, is used to denote the women's quota, and the verb *eispherein* to refer to their contribution in the form of men. It is a way, of course, of juxtaposing two opposing behaviors: women produce sons, old men despoil the ancestral heritage. But also (for in *Lysistrata*, there is nary a word in which the ordinary sense is not doubled by a second, equivocal but clear meaning) it is a way of saying that if there are men, the reason is women, since the old men are no longer capable of making their manly contributions. But the textual polysemy does not end here, and what gives these lines their full meaning is perhaps what is not said: that the word *eranos*, in Athens, is also used to refer to the citizen's gracious gift of himself to the city[37] when he offers his life in a beautiful death.[38]

Men give their lives, women give their sons. A simple parallel, perhaps too simple. A tragic heroine will help us go beyond it.

A heroine named Medea, who will sacrifice her sons to her vengeance as an abandoned woman, nonetheless knows the burden of motherhood. We are familiar with her exclamation, at the end of her formal exposition on the sufferings of being a woman:

> It is said of us that we lead a life without peril in the house, while they fight in battle. Mad reasoning. I would rather go to the front of battle three times, my shield on my side, than give birth once.[39]

In short, referring to the traditional Greek division of labor between the sexes, Medea objects that childbirth is a battle more dangerous than the one faced by the hoplite. Her only innovation is her excess, for with respect to Greek tradition as a whole, childbirth is a battle, or at least a trial worthy of the name of *ponos*.[40] And indeed, *ponos* is one of the terms used to refer to the pain of childbirth, in poetry as well as prose, and especially in the Hippocratic corpus, which does not disguise its dangers.[41] Clearly, the author of the treatise *On Regimen* reserves for men a way of life based on pain (*epiponos*);[42] clearly, transcending all distinctions between the sexes, the author of the fourth book of *Maladies* employs the word *ponos* to refer to any profound and extended suffering. But the same theoretician also knows that women suffer (*poneontai*) in childbirth, especially the first time;[43] and another gynecologist mentions *ōdines kai ponoi*, the sufferings of labor and childbirth.[44]

Ponos is ordinarily associated with the masculine universe, where it denotes what the male must be able to bear in order to be a man—thus in Sparta the young man learns to steel himself against *ponos*,[45] *ponos*, the word for lengthy effort, for affliction; the pain of the Achaian warriors of the *Iliad*, engaged in the interminable work of war; the toil of the Hesiodic man, forever separated from the gods and condemned to the peasant's harsh life of effort.[46] In the classical period *ponos* is again used to refer to the hero's labors—the labors of Herakles, traditionally designated as *athloi* but known as *ponoi* in the works of Sophocles and Euripides; the labors of Athens, the city-hero in the funeral oration uttered by Pericles in Thucydides.[47] Is giving birth undergoing "the highest manly trial of womanhood"?[48] In that case, the extreme height of femininity would be to transcend it, and if childbirth really seals the marriage,[49] it also brings women some of men's glory.

Of course, in this feminine battle some of the signs of manhood are reversed. To go into war as well as to accede to his status as citizen, the Greek male girds his loins.[50] The woman in childbed, on the contrary, unties her girdle,[51] beneath which, the texts say, she has carried her child, the girdle that she will again knot to celebrate her rising from childbed[52] —to mention only a few of the expressions denoting "this subtle play of the wearing and lifting of the *zōnē* that punctuates the sexual life of the Greek woman."[53] Nonetheless, even when it is reversed, the sign that relates childbearing to battle is there. And when Euripides' Suppliants state that they have carried their children "beneath their livers,"[54] again, perhaps it is fitting to see this as more than a physiological depiction—it is a way for women to position themselves with respect to the universe of the warrior. A vital organ, the liver would protect the child. While Greek gynecological texts say nothing of the sort, medical writings refer to the critical state of the woman who has been wounded in the liver during childbirth, because wounds to the liver are included among those that bring death.[55] A wound to the liver is first and foremost a man's wound.

The Homeric warrior, the strength of his knees broken, is wounded in the liver, beneath the diaphragm; adversaries are likely to aim their blows at the liver; and a man or a woman who kills herself in a manly way thrusts the blade into the liver.[56] Thus, even when reversed or displaced, the signs of war are at the heart of what the Greeks have to say about motherhood.

This feminine war is waged under the redoubtable protection of Artemis, a "goddess-woman" but a virgin goddess whose rejection of marriage readily associates her with the universe of warfare, in which she sometimes appears next to Ares.[57] However, Artemis also takes a decisive role in the lives of women. She is *Lokhia*, the Midwife; and because she works with the Eileithuias, the divine protectresses of childbirth,[58] it happens that she is given the name of Eileithuia.[59] As mentioned earlier, the protection offered by Artemis is of a fearsome nature, and with the mention of her name, one enters into a disquieting zone where childbirth is less glory than defilement,[60] where more than once the child's birth means the murder of the mother. Because the goddess is for the cities of men both the Savioress (*Sōteira*) and the Pure One (*Hagnē*),[61] she is for women *Soōdinē*, the one who is "called on to assist in the bitter pains" of childbirth and who succors them; but in the same hymn, Callimachus indicates that by her own accord, "in the cities of the wicked, women die in childbirth as if struck by a sudden blow" (*blētai*: struck by an arrow).[62] For Artemis slays women in labor, as she strikes women generally, with sudden death dealt by her archer's arrows.[63] Still, it would be advisable to be certain that she is terrible only when she chooses to be, as Callimachus claims. Like everything else surrounding her, this matter is shrouded in mystery. If sudden death is sometimes celebrated for its gentleness, death in childbirth inspires nothing but terror in the pregnant woman, who fears the arrows of the goddess,[64] and in the *Iliad* Hera, the protectress of marriage, authoritatively remarks that Zeus has made Artemis into "a lion" (*leonta*) for women, permitting her to "kill the one that pleases her."[65]

A lion? The word is usually translated as "lioness": as one of the scholia for this line of the *Iliad* suggests, and it is known that in the epic many animal names lack a feminine form.[66] Still, let us admit that she is indeed a lion—since once a hypothesis has been conceived it must be tested, and for reasons of textual consistency (if she is a lioness, an animal normally endowed with a reputation for her maternal qualities, Artemis would be a strange mother indeed for women). If Artemis is a lion—that is, a warrior[67]—how are we to understand Hera's assertion that her bow categorically lacks all authentic martial value in the world of men (and indeed, in this world the bow is the sign of bastards, traitors, and for-

eigners)?[68] The uncertain glory of dealing with women is reserved for
Artemis, and it is only in her confrontations with women that the goddess, neither truly maternal nor comparable to a regular warrior, reveals
herself to be a lion—war again, but war in a feminine mode. Often helpful, always a potential adversary, the virgin Artemis leads women into
combat, a combat completely unlike that between equal forces fought by
the hoplites. At its best, this battle departs from the hoplitic model because nothing is farther from the beautiful death, the death that is taken
on, chosen, or conquered, than sudden death, a death given and received
without the victim's knowledge, a death that is paradoxically gentle but
without glory. At its worst, it is something like all-out war[69] appearing
on the horizon of womanly *ponos*. The specter of Artemis's arrows extends beyond the manly and civic model of honorable combat and freely
chosen trials.

This leads us at last, perhaps, toward a universe unlike the paradigmatic and unambiguously masculine world of hoplitic confrontation—
toward the suffering of women. However, before penetrating the conti-
nent of "black suffering," it is a good idea to note that on occasion the
relationship between war and childbed is reversed.

Such is the case in a passage from the *Iliad* in which, to the reader's
astonishment, Menelaus stands beside Patroclus's corpse to defend it
"like a lowing cow, who yesterday still knew nothing of motherhood,
[lies] at the side of a newborn calf." And the poet adds, "so at Patroclus's
side the blond Menelaus stood."[70] Patroclus has just fallen and his soul
has fled, weeping for his youth; Menelaus immediately hurls himself into
the turmoil of battle to save the hero's body. What reader would expect
this melancholy and tender image of birth? Is this a way of expressing the
danger surrounding Menelaus? The first labor pains of a woman are, it is
true, an ordeal much to be feared;[71] but between this *ponos* and the frenzy
of the son of Atreus, "burning to kill whomever he meets," there remains
a distance, never to be bridged. Must we, like the scholiasts, emphasize
the symbolic figure of the mother, whose moans of pain and tenderly
attentive love exalt the warrior's devotion to the dead hero? Most certainly there is another Homeric warrior, one of the bravest, who behaves
like a mother in the midst of battle. I refer to Ajax, whose shield, in
an odd passage from book 8, is like a mother's belly for Teucer.[72] Still,
Teucer is an archer, Ajax's shadow, and for this reason he can "like a
child dive under his mother." But who would think to compare Patroclus, the soldier fallen in front of the ranks and the prototype of the
beautiful dead man whose corpse is the most precious of goods,[73] to the
fragility of a newborn calf? It is probably advisable to consider this comparison as an inseparable whole; then one would note that the attentively
protective relationship between Menelaus and Patroclus is like that of

mother to child. Nevertheless, after all this discussion, one term of the analogy is death, and the other, birth. One is forced to recognize—and perhaps it is better this way—that the text retains its strangeness. Perhaps more light could be shed on it by assaying other comparisons between representations of combat and those of childbirth.[74] To avoid wandering into overly conjectural territory, I will stop here for the moment, not without observing that these confused trails quickly lead away from the beauty of war to the war that causes pain.

But patience! Now it is time, first, to speak of the suffering of women.

THE FEMININE WORD FOR "SUFFERING"

After pregnancy, which many texts make into a burden, there is suffering, which is under the auspices of the Eileithuias *mogostokoi* (of difficult childbirth),[75] cries,[76] and always that pain that is "exactly like fire."[77] This searing pain, said to be indescribable,[78] can nevertheless be conveyed with words: *ōdines* is the general term, which vividly describes labor and which, even in the child, makes the woman's suffering present.[79] But to describe the tearing intensity of the pain, the language of poets, along with that of the physicians, habitually uses the word *odunē*.[80] The extension of this term is certainly not limited to the field of feminine suffering, but because of its dark connotations and because it applies to the hurt that penetrates and cuts through the flesh[81]—often localized in the thorax and the belly[82]—this generic name for the "pain of body," as the English translate it, has a privileged place in the gynecological literature[83] and, more exactly, in the evocation of childbirth. Furthermore, *odunē* sounds somewhat like *ōdines*, which facilitates the shift from one word to the other[84] and makes childbearing the specific locus of these "pains that cut through the body."

Therefore, women suffer and bear children. When the child ceases to be the exclusive continuation of the father, it simply takes the name of the suffering of the mother who bore it. For the Jocasta of the *Phoenician Women*, *ponos* is a name for Oedipus, while to convey the idea that Agamemnon, in his sacrifice, killed Clytemnestra's own daughter, her mother gives Iphigenia no other name than *ōdis*[85]—as if the mother's relationship to the child were frozen for all time into an unending childbirth. This temporal suspension gives rise to a certain apprehension about femininity, and all the discussions pinpointing the "misogyny" of the Greeks are inadequate to conceal the fact that there were Greeks—and, to top it all, Greek men—willing to undergo the experience.

The femininity of which midwives (*maiai*) are the privileged but silent witnesses[86] is sometimes categorized by men in medical writings under the heading of "women's ailments,"[87] those complaints that women dare mention only to other women and that doctors, incapable of correct diagnosis in this case, too often treat just as they treat men's diseases.[88] However, more than any other man, a doctor must know how to listen to women, which he can do, provided that he silences his own masculine discourse to accept that of his patients, which is persuasive, articulate, and decisive when they speak of their bodies and what is happening to them, a subject that they obviously know better than anyone else in the world.[89] And because he has a clinical viewpoint, the doctor has some chance of avoiding the normative dominance of male models; thus it may happen that a medical prescription runs counter to the legislator's injunctions.[90] This is how the exercise that in Sparta is supposed to harden women for procreation enables one of Hippocrates' patients who did not wish to conceive to reject the sperm she had carried for six days.[91] Because the Spartan legislator sees women as "half of the city"—the half that reproduces the other—the law promoting the strengthening of the body prevails over all other considerations; but for doctors who are interested less in the city's constitution than the reality of the female constitution, women are first of all bodies to be treated.

However, once again it is in tragedy—especially Euripidean tragedy—that the greatest departure from the orthodoxy of childbirth as a manly trial is to be found. In the feminine arena of childbirth, *ponos* is eclipsed by *nosos*, "sickness," *anagkē*, "constraint," and *amēkhania*, a term for "helplessness,"[92] not to mention the derangements of madness. At least one passage from *Hippolytus* suggests that childbirth is another form of insanity. How may the sickness that "crushes Phaedra on her sickbed" be interpreted? After having successfully envisaged possession by a divinity—Pan or Hecate[93]—and the sufferings of the soul, the chorus of the women of Troezen add their provisional conclusion:

> There is wont to dwell with women's natural ill-tuned blend (*dustropos harmonia*) an evil unhappy helplessness in pains of childbirth and delirium. One day this storm will be unleashed in my belly. But I will cry out to the heavenly protectress of childbed, Artemis the Archer, and she, the one that I venerate, each time, thanks to the gods, will come to my aid.[94]

A surprising text in which women's *dustropos harmonia*, a constitution that is at such odds with itself,[95] cohabits, as if in a marriage, with the helplessness that is indissociably the pain of labor and loss of sanity.

Ōdinōn te kai aphrosunas: "childbirth and madness." This—the pain of the woman in labor and the loss of sanity (*ōdis kai phrenōn kataphthora*)—is also what Electra suffers in the *Choephoroi*, as she deciphers Orestes' tracks, matching the hair and footprints of the lost brother to her own.[96] It is a metaphor, people say, and hurry to domesticate the contentious word beneath a decent translation (*ōdis*? but that means "pain"). Still, the association of the two semantic fields of madness and childbirth, even in metaphor, would be noteworthy. But one can also take the text seriously. "From the smallest germ (*sperma*) can spring the immense tree of salvation," Electra said a few lines earlier. And indeed, her mind led astray in the confusion of reading signs, she gives birth to the hope named Orestes.[97] Childbirth and madness: again and above all this is the indecisive state reflected in Aeschylus's portrayal of Io, victim of the goad of an *odunē* in which madness blends with interminable pangs of childbirth.[98] Childbirth *or* madness:[99] the physicians' highly realistic language presents these as alternate solutions to the ailments of young women. The erratic fevers of *mania*, suicidal madness, are sometimes followed by recovery, and then the women, as a way of celebrating the young girl's return to reason, consecrate clothes to Artemis as they would in the case of childbirth. But still, the best solution for a young woman is to marry as soon as possible; once she is pregnant, she will recover her health.[100] Though lost in lovelorn reveries, Phaedra is no longer a *parthenos*, and the women of Troezen are mistaken in interpreting her languor. The queen's "secret ill" in the tragedy is no pregnancy, even if the Cretan woman is reputed to have brought with her to Athens two statues of Eileithuia, the Cretan goddess;[101] and a funerary relief from Thasos employs the dual model of Phaedra's sufferings and that of the woman in childbirth to express the dying woman's pain.[102] Quite simply, Phaedra loves. It is true that the height of a woman's femininity is summed up by its equivalence to sickness, love, or childbirth: this equivalence, given dramatic form in the opening of the *Hippolytus*, is expressed with dazzling clarity in a text from the *Republic*, in which Plato, proscribing every kind of mimesis to the guardians, specifically forbids them to imitate any woman, especially, "to imitate her sick, in love, or in the pangs of childbirth."[103]

And yet Greek men, including and above all—o irony of ironies—the characters of Plato, never cease in their suffering to imitate the woman in childbirth, whether by aping her with their bodies or borrowing her language of suffering. Thus the name for the labor of giving birth (*ōdines*) becomes the generic designation for searing pain: Platonic pains, that of the soul sick of the body, of the soul tormented by desire, bounding madly like Io beneath the gadfly, the soul that, in the presence of the beautiful object, gives birth; or the dereliction of a mutilated Kyklops, abandoned by his fellows and caught in the trap made by a man of *mētis* who said he was "Nobody."[104] The model for suffering is feminine; women's physical suffering is used to express moral pain.

It is also used to express—which is even more interesting—the suffering of men afflicted in body. Dead in childbirth, women were like hoplites. In a just turnaround, a passage in the *Iliad* methodically and without a trace of ambiguity compares the suffering of the wounded warrior to that of the woman in childbed.

In book 11, Koön's spear has wounded Agamemnon. The son of Atreus is subjected to carnage

> as long as the warm blood still spurts from his wound. But when the wound dries, and the blood ceases to flow, despite his ardor, searing pains penetrate the son of Atreus. They are like the piercing and cruel arrow that strikes a woman in labor, the arrow shot by the Eileithuias, the goddesses of painful childbirth, the daughters of Hera who carry out this bitter work. As piercing as these were the pains that penetrated the son of Atreus, despite his ardor. He leaps onto his chariot

and regains the empty ships.[105]

In the scholiasts' view, this long simile means above all that Agamemnon's wound is enflamed. In medical terms the warrior feels like a sick man whose "blood stagnates and heats up"; the result is suffering (*ponos*).[106] But the scholiasts add that the sharpness of the suffering means that Agamemnon cannot be treated like a coward when he flees the pain in his chariot: to suffer in this way is in itself a battle. Moreover, the wound in his arm, site of the hero's warlike strength, is enough to take a fighter out of the fray.[107] But this is not all: illuminating such a vivid comparison requires one to delve more deeply into the text, flushing out everything that links Agamemnon's *odunai*, these pains that, true to Plato's later description, penetrate and burrow into the flesh, to the *ōdines* of women.

Agamemnon, then, was wounded by a spear. Thus was accomplished the plan of Zeus, who had willed that the son of Atreus be "struck by a spear or hit by an arrow,"[108] to put him out of action. Koön's spear, the manly arm, the weapon of the *anēr*, prevailed perhaps because it wounded like an arrow. For apparently no pain is more intense or "black" than the pain inflicted by an arrow.[109] But if in this case the arrow is the metaphor for the spear, the world of war, where the arrows bearing black suffering come from the archer's quiver, is certainly short-circuited, and in an inextricable condensation of masculine and feminine, Agamemnon's *oxeiai odunai* are compared to the Eileithuias' "sharp arrow"—because perhaps, in matters of the experience of sharp pains, the prize goes to women.[110] In short, the wounded hero and the woman suffering the pangs of birth have enough signs in common for a generalized exchange to take place.[111] The pangs of the woman in childbed are bitter enough to reveal that they are the result of a divine arrow, but inversely, because arrows are laden with suffering, throughout the *Iliad* they are said to be "bitter."[112] And deep wounds, whether real or metaphorical, are exhausting. To convey the intensity of the situation, again in book 11, in which Odysseus, surrounded by Trojans, has his back against the wall, the poet compares the hero to "a stag that a man has wounded with an arrow," who "has fled for as long as his blood remained warm and his legs moved"—but "as soon as he is overcome by the swift arrow," he succumbs.[113] One comparison in particular is important here. *Teiromenē* designates the woman in painful childbirth, and like her, overcome by pain, the man whom Agamemnon's horses carry away to the hollow ships is nothing more than a broken king (*teiromenon basilēa*).[114]

How is one to gauge the weight of such a comparison, unique to book 11 and to the *Iliad* as a whole, in which the most valorous warriors are put out of commission by spears and especially arrows?[115] Of course, there is another leader who has been wounded, this time by an arrow with nothing metaphorical about it, which calls forth a profusion of feminine signifiers. I am thinking of Menelaus, wounded by Pandaros with an arrow "heavy with black pains."[116] Perhaps it is not incidental that Agamemnon's brother is precisely the one in question here. However, most of the arrows unleashed in the *Iliad* cause the warriors pains that receive only a clinical description,[117] and furthermore, many passages assign a highly orthodox division of sexual values.[118] So is the simile in book 11 exceptional? Undoubtedly. And it leads, in any case, to strange interpretations: thus, according to Plutarch, "these lines, women say [what women? the vagueness is appreciated], were written not by Homer but by a Homerid who had given birth or who was about to give birth and who felt the bitter and sharp bite of pain in her bowels."[119] But there is no need to imagine such a strange invention, adding the fiction of a Homerid who wrote these lines to speculations about "the woman who wrote the *Odyssey*." It would be better, instead, to shed light on the passage by investigating evidence of the feminine concealed in the text of the *Iliad*. For, in addition to the orthodox division of tasks, more than one passage in the *Iliad* presents the feminine in the midst of war.[120] Even without a systematic study of the division between masculine and feminine, it may be recalled that when both parties are of equal strength, war itself can have a feminine referent, the celebrated "true worker, holding a scale in her hands,"[121] as if the activity of a woman best expresses what pits men against each other in a fight to the finish.

In other passages of the *Iliad*, Zeus holds the scales. The parallel is striking and should at least invite one to take a second look at accepted notions, such as the supposedly absolute dominance of the virile model in the *Iliad*. Unlike the Trojan universe, which is seen from within— inside the city, the palace, and the chambers, where women hold an important place—and unlike the world of Odysseus, peopled with feminine presences but where the exemplary woman is compared to a wise king before she regains a woman's normal place, her husband's bed,[122] the figures in the male group of fighting Achaians are strongly imbued with feminine elements. The same emblem is assigned to the king of the gods and a humble working woman, while the sufferings of a woman in labor are attributed to the one among heroes who is the most kingly of kings.[123]

Once again, I ask: when, in a poem dedicated to the sufferings of warriors,[124] the king of kings, wounded in battle, suffers the pains of an anonymous woman, is it appropriate to cling to the word *misogyny* to describe Greek thinking about femininity? One might object that the Homeric epic belongs to one period and classical Greece to another, and that between Homer and the classical period one finds, for example, Hesiod with his Pandora and Semonides with his *Diatribe against Women*[125] —the foundations for a solid tradition of blaming women. Most importantly, between the time of Homer and the classical period, the manly model of war incontestably grew in strength, perhaps because of the famous hoplitic reform, and it culminated in the Athenian funeral oration, with its *topos* of a beautiful death—a civic, abstract death that barely touches the body of the citizen, for in the final analysis the citizen has no body.[126] During the classical period, finally, death is a paradigm, and in a hierarchy of different types of deaths, one can compare the death of the woman in labor to that of the hoplite; the epic, which places all value on life, on the contrary makes the warrior's body into the locus of all suffering, including the most painful torments of all, which devolve on women.

To suffer like a woman, die like a man: these two poles would frame the course of the history of Greek thought on sexual roles. But one must also abandon the belief in linear evolutions and be open to setbacks, returns, advances, and tensions and finally be willing to focus on the specificity of each discourse.

On Tragedy, Women, and Herakles' Body

During the classical period one discourse resists the imperious suggestion of virile models because its function is to question all civic representations:[127] masculine victory is at its most ambiguous in tragedy.

Not that the reality of the division of sexual roles is questioned onstage. That is a matter for the philosopher, and Plato and Aristotle each pose the problem in his own way, the first by refusing any differences between men and women in their aptitude for war,[128] and the second by contesting the idea that childbirth must necessarily be a *ponos*, since this is not the case in societies where a woman's way of life is always governed by toil.[129] The tragic universe is not greatly concerned with reapportioning what is found in reality but instead offers a reflection on how these values are distributed by subjecting them to all kinds of possible distortions. Once again the issue of the equivalence between the warrior's *ponos* and that of the woman in childbirth should be raised. Tragedy has more than one way of thinking about the matter by throwing it off balance.

The first model of this tragic reflection is found in the *Oresteia* and consists of denying the very existence of feminine *ponos*. Only men suffer, because only men fight, and the bond between mother and child created by gestation, childbirth, and infancy must give way to the law of the father. "You accuse the one who suffers (*ton ponounta*)—you, who sit at home?" This is Orestes' only answer to Clytemnestra who, to exculpate herself of her crime, was naming Agamemnon's faults—in particular, the sacrifice of Iphigenia. After Clytemnestra's murder, when the investigation for Orestes' trial is underway, Apollo will top all the others when he says that "the death of noble hero" killed after his return from battle "is something different" than the murder of a woman who does not even deserve the name of child-bearer, *tokeus*.[130] Clytemnestra can always try to soften her son by recalling how she fed him. But earlier Orestes' nurse had belied the queen's remarks, for it was she who received the infant when it left its mother's womb and raised it for its father.[131] Clytemnestra's dream was premonitory. The male child that she had nourished was indeed a serpent, born fully armed,[132] who would turn his weapons against her, until he denied any bond of kinship between them. "Am I then, of my mother's blood?" he asks during his trial, wresting this indignant response from the Erinyes: "Didn't she nourish you beneath her girdle, assassin? Do you reject your mother's sweet blood?"[133] Nonetheless, Orestes' victory is not the last word of the trilogy, and the feminine principle finally conquers a place in the city. Tragedy is not a tribune for propaganda.

The second expression takes the form of men who dream of reproduction without women: Hippolytus, of course, whose *hubris* is to fail to recognize in Artemis the goddess of women in childbirth; Jason, too, who does not want to be in arrears to Medea; Eteocles, already, who refused all cohabitation with the race of women and wished to forget that he came out of a mother.[134] Their failures correspond to the extent of their misreading of the situation.

The third representation once again features Hippolytus, the Amazon's son. This time the preceding perspective is turned around, and the male undergoes sufferings that are unnamed except in the world of women, giving a negative twist to his initial misjudgment of feminine values— *ponos* in the feminine, reproduction and pain. Because of this he will die, though not without discovering that he has a body. The dying Hippolytus finds his physical being—at the beginning of the play only Phaedra, who suffered from it and destroyed it, had a body.[135] If physical pain mimics the sufferings of women, it is not without importance that the dying Hippolytus is wracked by spasms and cries described as *odunai*.[136] To be sure, his head is the locus for the sufferings of the chaste Hippolytus, follower of Orpheus,[137] whose torn flesh the messenger had just mentioned.[138] But in his agony, his head and body crushed,[139] Hippolytus experiences unto death the duality of being human, which is not only *psukhē*.[140] The shy adolescent, rejected by his father, had already discovered the law of reproduction, finally accepting the bitterness of childbirth (*pikrai gonai*), but this remained a way of feeling sorry for himself, the issue of his mother the Amazon's sad delivery.[141] He will go no further, too engaged in his rejection of women to recognize that he has given a feminine name to his pain.

I must turn to Herakles, Sophocles' Herakles, to make further headway in the interpretation of physical suffering. Herakles, hero of strength, reduced, in a final catastrophe, to the stature of *athlion demas*, a miserable body.[142] Herakles who weeps and moans, and who notes, "under such a blow I discover myself, unhappy that I am, a mere female."[143] Herakles, the hero of multiple exploits, but also the supermale who enters an *oikos* only to plow the feminine furrow before setting off for distant parts. Herakles whose wives, the legitimate Deianeira and Iole, who is almost that,[144] are first of all childbearers, which the text of the *Trachiniae* states in typically Sophoclean fashion, both precise and discreet: Deianeira is, has been, a field to be plowed. A foster mother, she bears nothing but fear in her bosom, or more exactly, she carries inside her the paradoxical and painful birthing of Herakles. She grows heavier and heavier, like a pregnant woman, but her burden is one of misfortune. Inversely, the *ponos* that is brought in one night and removed in another has two meanings, for Herakles' return removes her cares, bringing with it the conception and trials of childbirth. A young woman who is no longer a virgin, Iole, too, is surrounded by images of fecundity, ever since the innocent Deianeira asked of her, "Is she without a man or is she with child?" Nearly a young woman, she seems to be still a child, long ago conceived by her parents, but she is in labor with all the weight of unhappiness.[145]

And here Herakles, who knew only the *nosos* of desire, is beaten by a "female woman"[146] and crushed by a cruel sickness with searing pains.[147] More exactly, the pain is the result of the weapon that Deianeira used, as if it were a dagger[148]—she reserves the sword for herself—to destroy Herakles in his body. The warrior's fortune and misfortune: indeed, Sophocles' Herakles owes much to the heroic figure of Herakles the son of Zeus, which began with the Homeric epic and more generally reflects the influence of the traditional image of the warrior, an incarnation of force subject to exhaustion because he is the "triumphant victim" of his strength.[149] Engaged in the "groaning labors" in which blame is a source of glory, the epic Herakles suffers and weeps,[150] and in cults devoted to him as well as among the mythographers, the hero of endurance displays his close complicity with sickness and femininity.[151] But Sophocles is not so faithful to tradition that he refuses to reinterpret it to include Herakles' sufferings among the "sicknesses" that figure in his work as so many expressions of tragic heroism. Because death, the ultimate and first *nosos*, is what enables the tragic Herakles to be born to himself, Sophocles renews and displaces the theme of the weeping and suffering hero so that Herakles, once "robust, alive, and flourishing," at last finds himself crushed, weeping,[152] and in pain.

To these sufferings, which bring an end to his heroic *ponoi* but which are also a *ponos* in themselves,[153] the defeated supermale gives the name of *odunai*, and his description is a precise summary of what the Greeks have to say about women's diseases. Spasms and wrenching, insidious constrictions torturing his sides, bursts of delirium, unbearable heat[154]—in a word, Herakles is wracked by suffering equal only to that of a woman in childbirth.[155] One might well respond that this is crediting Sophocles with a wild idea that would only occur to a female reader with a fertile imagination. Perhaps. Tragic ambiguity, the essence of which is to tell without naming,[156] always, it is true, leaves it up to the reader to decide. Whoever fears to plunge into the text can remain deaf to the suggestions of words, but whoever pays attention to the signifiers is drawn into one surprise after another. Thus respectable commentators have already noted that the same words are used to express Herakles' physical sufferings and the parturition of the desiring soul in the *Phaedrus*. One could probably object at this point that Herakles does not suffer in his belly, the feminine site of the *odunai*, but in his side, from an intolerable pain shooting through his ribs, like the mortally wounded Centaur Nessos, and like Deianeira, who dies from a piercing wound in her side.[157] I will answer that in fact Herakles, wounded in his side (or in the lung),[158] feels pain throughout his entire thoracic cavity, a part of the body that is considered to be an indefectible whole, even if a distinction is made between its upper and lower regions in the Hippocratic writings, the *Timaeus*, or Aristotle: it is a man's body.[159] Finally, one might note, the hero's body is devoured by a terrible poison, whose power is more evocative of the Erinyes' mortal net than the wound caused by the Eileithuias' arrows.[160] But Homer, already, was endowing arrows and javelins with a desire "to taste white flesh and to gorge themselves on it until drunk,"[161] and for Herakles, as for Agamemnon in book 11 of the *Iliad*, the spasm is a goad.[162] For the chorus of the *Trachiniae*, there is a conjunction between the arrow and poison: the arrow that Herakles once shot at Nessos to regain Deianeira; the venom a mixture of poisons—the Centaur's blood mixed, around his wound, with the poison from the hydra of Lerna in which Herakles had dipped his arrows.[163] And depicting this ill-omened mixture is a signifier that condenses all the tragic ambiguity. It is a homonym: *ios*, in fact, which happens to be a term for arrow, is also the name of the poison. In the *Trachiniae*, *ios* denotes both the arrow and the poison, and in a remark on this play on words that has led more than one commentator astray,[164] the chorus speaks of "the shadow of the Hydra stuck" to the hero and "the murderous goad" (*phonia kentra*) by which the Centaur drives into panic the one who once was his murderer and is now and henceforth his victim.[165] Signaling both a reappearance of the feminine in the manly hero's broken body[166] and the monster-slayer's reversion to savagery, the *odunai* that tear Herakles apart can be compared to the "arrows" that pierced Agamemnon.

The warrior's fortune and misfortune: to break all the limits, even those of the virility that he ostensibly embodies, to suffer like a woman. While it may not be the death of epic warriors, this is where the tragic hero meets his end.[167]

One could stop right here. But this would mean missing a fourth model, which inverts the third. If tragedy puts men on the stage who suffer and die as women do, it also presents women who die in the manner of men. The price of this reversion to the civic model is a new twist in events. For a tragic heroine, death often means suicide; for example, Deianeira, who, like Ajax, kills herself with a sword and who, though a woman—the text is clear on this point—has died like a hoplite.[168] The reader may rest easy. All the talk of Deianeira's suicide after Herakles' death does not mean that I have forgotten that I began with death in childbirth and the value of the mother who gives birth to sons. I merely wish to point out that even when tragedy puts matters in a new way, it can reflect orthodoxy. The homology of mother and hoplite appears on-stage in the form of this suicide, this disgraceful end. Male suicide is uncommon in Greek tradition, in which women kill themselves in far greater numbers. More importantly, men's suicides are distinct from those of women: the sword is suitable for the male, the rope for the female.[169] But tragedy complicates this distribution by depicting women like Phaedra, who kill themselves in a womanly fashion because they have been far too feminine, and women who kill themselves in a manly way because in their deaths they are exalting their maternal qualities. Thus they conform to a certain orthodox idea of motherhood, even as they resort to the suicide to which their condition as women has driven them. The finest example is Euripides' Jocasta, who survived the discovery of incest to dominate the *Phoenician Women*, this tragedy about mother-hood, and to die on the bodies of her sons, pierced by the very blade that killed them.[170] Sophocles' Jocasta was above all a wife and hanged herself.

Homeric tradition has it so, but in addition, the man whom to the bitter end she wished to believe was her husband had just revealed that he was her son.

But Deianeira? Doesn't she die, it will be said, because she killed Herakles, whom she loved more than all else? I will be careful not to deny it, for in many ways Deianeira, this tender wife known as the man-killer, dies from Herakles' death. She dies because she killed him "without a dagger." A wife in despair, she dies in the hero's chamber on the nuptial bed,[171] inflicting on herself a man's death, the only one that Herakles would have thought worthy of him.[172] But since she is a true tragic heroine, in reality Deianeira's death is doubly determined. She dies in place of her husband and because of her son. Observe that, strictly speaking, Hyllos causes her suicide, and he is the one who lies beside her and shares her bed when she is dead[173]—Hyllos who, before describing the dashed Herakles, violently disowns his mother and continues to disown her when, silent like Eurydice when Haimon's death is announced, the distraught Deianeira rushes through the palace.[174] Like Eurydice, whose son's death kills her, Deianeira, who weeps for a home that is forever empty of a son,[175] will use a dagger to end her life. She takes "the mournful blade that carves into the flesh," she uncovers her side, and stabs herself between the liver and the diaphragm:[176] that part of the body where blows are mortal, where warriors are struck, where Ajax drives his sword, where Euripides' Herakles would like to press his dagger[177]—the place, finally, where a woman carries her child, beneath the liver, beneath the "girdle" that is the diaphragm.[178] Deianeira, the childbearer, who knew no alternative to virginity but pregnancy,[179] had, however, believed that she could be something else for Herakles: an object of his love. One of the meanings of her death is that a woman who has borne children is forever completed and cannot go back in time to the delights of the *numphē*.[180]

This attempt to venture into the infinitely variable landscape of exchanges between masculine and feminine must come to an end. While orthodox Greek thinking about women is marked by a fine, stable unity, no people has better understood than they that the distribution of masculine and feminine is rarely decided once and for all: from Hesiod to Hippocrates by way of Empedocles, not to mention Aristophanes as reexamined by Plato, haven't the Greeks taken delight in dividing humanity into womanly women, virile men, men-women, and women who act like men?[181] However, they have been the most inclined to reflect on the division between the sexes not on the physiological plane but on what may be termed the social level, of the behaviors of men and women that are essential to the city—bearing children and fighting. To say that women die like men and men suffer like women is of course a masculine way of making it clear that death, the unique object of the Greek man's thoughts, must belong to men, and that the body, experienced in suffering—but also, imagine the *andres*, in pleasure[182]—is feminine: a male fantasy, but the fantasy of men who have identified the femininity inside themselves.[183]

Chapter 2

PONOS: SOME DIFFICULTIES REGARDING
THE TERM FOR "LABOR"

PONOS AGAIN.

Ponos offers a way to continue exploring the uneasy balance between war and childbed, by means of which the Greek woman's participation in manly trials makes her the wholly feminine model of suffering for men. Furthermore, it provides a way to enter more thoroughly into the tension inherent in the male paradigm of the heroic exploit. Meanwhile—and is this a surprise?—we will again encounter women—or rather, or already, the feminine—and, once again, Herakles, the suffering hero of virility.

Ponos, then.

It happens that the only possible translation of this word is "work, or labor," which only apparently simplifies the task (there is of course the labor of childbirth, but what Greek would think that a soldier labors?). To be sure, Pierre Chantraine's *Dictionnaire étymologique* lists these terms among many other glosses, including "harsh effort" and "affliction," "struggle," and "physical suffering."* But Chantraine also observes that *ponos* is always distinguished from *lupē*, "sorrow." And in fact, unlike sorrow, which makes time stand still and isolates one from human society, *ponos*, always thought of in terms of duration,[1] is embedded in human temporality, something that has a beginning and end, something that is carried to its conclusion.[2] Therefore, "affliction" is not "sorrow," which is obviously not enough to make *ponos* into the elusive Greek term for "labor." Even stretching the relationship a bit, the contiguity with *lupē* is enough to corroborate the distinction. For, as J.-P. Vernant observed some time ago, "*ponos* is applied to all activities that require painful exertion, not just tasks that produce socially useful values." And he adds, "In the myth of Herakles, the hero must choose between a life of pleasure and ease and a life devoted to *ponos*. Herakles is not a worker."[3] The reader stands warned. Here the emphasis is not on a productive process but on the prolonged effort of the man who struggles: the labors

*Liddell and Scott, *A Greek-English Lexicon*, 9th ed. (Oxford: Clarendon Press, 1985), provides these glosses, among others: work, esp. hard work, toil; bodily exertion, exercise; that which involves much trouble; work, task business; stress, trouble, distress, suffering; pain, esp. physical (s.v. *ponos*).

of the hero, the endurance of the warrior, but also a neutral way of denoting, for example, the long ordeal that a storm represents for a fleet of ships.[4]

If things were this simple, if *ponos* were always a neutral designation, it would offer little to illuminate Greek representations of work. But it happens that in the classical period the value of *ponos* seems perpetually reaffirmed, which encourages us to follow the austere Greek paths of human effort. At the outset of this trajectory, but also at each stage along the way, the anchorage and reference point will be the universe of classical Greece. This does not mean abandoning the idea of going further back to make sense of even more ambiguous representations, even if it entails constantly shifting from Xenophon to Homer and from Hesiod to Diodorus of Sicily.

To begin, then, *ponos* in the classical Greece of the cities.

A CLASSICAL CONFIGURATION

A painful, meritorious activity: this could be a gloss for the word in the fifth and fourth centuries B.C.

When Pericles, in the last speech that Thucydides attributes to him, invites the Athenians "not to flee trials on pain of giving up the pursuit of honors,"[5] he eloquently says that glory—*logos*—is to be had only for those who have known how to struggle. And in Herodotus's *Histories*, *ponos* is ordinarily the criterion for "what is most worthy of discussion."[6] In short, *ponos* goes hand in hand with the *logos* of glory, and no one has better expressed this association than Pindar, the bard of the athletic exploit, always ready with the reminder that *ponoi* need to be put into words if they are to remain memorable, but whose poetic labors, like the object they celebrate, also merit the term *ponos*.[7]

Worthy of *logos*, in the discourse the Greek conducts about himself, *ponos* is a preeminent criterion of value. In fact, in the pairs of opposites that constitute Greek thinking about the city in the classical period,[8] this word is always a positive, a plus in the category in which it occurs.

This is true for Pindar, for whom effort, envisioned as the exploit, this generous expenditure that is the basis of the noble life-style, contrasts with unflattering representations of the common folk.[9] And one will not be too surprised that Thucydides' Pericles made use of the same values, though transposed into the arena of warfare, to praise Athens for "having expended more than all the other cities in human lives and effort (*sōmata kai ponous*)."[10] The classical city, as we know, did not create any value systems to compete with aristocratic representations.

To be more precise, in the table of civic values in which the athlete's exploit merely takes second place, *ponos* is associated with war and agriculture, in contrast to the supposed laziness of artisans, which, according to the ideologue Xenophon, impels them, in case of war, to "remain sedentary, avoiding struggle and danger."[11] Later I will return to the *ponos* of the peasant, which perhaps is less simple than it first appears.[12] Since the time of the Homeric epic, military *ponos*, traditionally associated with danger (*kindunos*), refers to the exertions of combat,[13] and thinkers about war ask the *stratēgoi* to instill desire for it in their troops: what an army, then! and what a leader, with arms as terrible as those of the warriors of the *Iliad*![14] For heroism always looms just over the horizon of military effort. The Trojan war frequently is called *Troikos ponos;*[15] and in the works of fifth-century writers, the city of Athens, noted for martial exploits that are deemed so many labors, is endowed with the glorious character of the city-hero.[16] In Athens effort always means exploit. It is true that the classical period saw only the beautiful side of war: neither groans nor suffering, blood nor tears, always high deeds.

But first of all the citizen is skilled in warfare because he bears the name of the male, *anēr*. And, quite naturally, *ponos* serves to indicate the cardinal opposition between sexual roles that, perhaps more than all others, serves as the basis for Greek society. On the male side is *ponos*: a normative principle for Xenophon, it is used in simple observations by the author of the Hippocratic *Regimen* and the author of the *System of the Glands*, who contrast the manly life, characterized by fatigue and a toughened body, with the "ease" of women's leisurely lives.[17] Would a male renounce the effort that makes him a man? This leads to expostulations about a world turned upside down and allusions to Egypt, where "the males sit weaving cloth, while their female companions, always outdoors, seek their food."[18] But most of the time the world is rightside up, which means that in no case does women's domestic activity deserve the name of *ponos*. Overall the Greek division of sexual roles tends to be constructed on the pure and simple denial of feminine activity. Therefore, the model for women's lives emerges in counterdistinction to men's *ponos* (and I will quickly add, to the efforts of the citizen and the Greek). It is a model in reverse, always mentioned as a foil but one that creates intelligibility, useful for unmasking unmanly ways of life: women are lazy, raised in the shade and sitting in the depths of the house, just as men who do not deserve the name of *anēr* are lazy and sit in the shade— Xenophon's artisans, Herodotus's lazy Ionians, Phaedrus's beloved whom the lover protects from male exertion, the rich man of the *Republic* whose superfluous fat does not impress the poor man whose skin has been burned by the sun.[19] A manly regimen, and a regimen for women: the disparity between the two must be maintained at all costs, and only an excess of virility, due to a life too exclusively devoted to exertion, will lead the Hippocratic doctor to prescribe hot baths, a soft bed, and *rhaithumia* (ease) for his male patient.[20]

And yet there is a place for *ponos* in women's lives, for their one and only qualifying trial. Women must be taken into account, even when imagining a male society. The labor of childbirth is this trial, and women are integrated into the city as childbearers. "Three times in childbirth, I endured feminine suffering (*gunaikeioi ponoi*)," says one of Aeschylus's characters, and no one in Greek tradition refuses the name of *ponos* to childbirth, except perhaps the Apollo of the *Eumenides* and his protégé Orestes, those extremists of patrilineal filiation.[21] Moreover, tradition, with like unanimity, posits a rigorous equivalence between feminine *ponos* and the soldier's activity that epitomizes the masculine ordeal:[22] the supreme honor for Greek women.

The noble and the rest, the warrior and the artisan, man and woman: *ponos* is the determinative criterion in each of these pairs of opposites. All that is needed to complete the list is to oppose the Greek to the barbarian. We won't be disappointed. Plutarch contrasts Alexander's *ponos* to the *truphē* (softness) of the Persians, as philosophical royalty is contrasted to slavery.[23] Herodotus had already depicted the inability of the Ionians, too imbued with the values of their Persian masters, to endure the protracted struggle and sustained effort that would have set them free.[24] It is true that according to this same Herodotus, the Persians, who are incapable of properly appreciating *ponos*, see it only as servile labor because, beginning with the Great King, they associate freedom with *truphē*.[25] But it should be recalled that this is a Greek speaking, putting words in Persian mouths that all the better reflect Greek values.

What is missing from this table of opposites is the slave. In fact, slavery, which can be imagined metaphorically, frequently turns up in inquiries about *ponos*—always as a negative. However, there is no place on either side for the person of the slave—not because he works, sometimes with citizens and at the same tasks, but rather, he lacks the autonomy that solely determines the value of ongoing effort. Thus the register of *ponos* contains scant mention of the slave:[26] he is all obedience, so his job does not depend on merit. Even more importantly, because real struggle is his lot, he could never be contrasted with the citizen with respect to *ponos*. Also, it is true that in classical Athens the chasm dividing liberty and slavery is so wide that it is impossible even to think of the slave as the other, even in an entirely negative fashion. One has to accept the fact: *ponos* takes the historian far away from ideas about production, toward the civic world of quality in which the only effort of value belongs to people whose status does not force them to work. No antimony exists for the citizen between labor and leisure, and seeking to assign within the field of *ponos* a place for the word *skholē*, which in its most banal sense refers to the active leisure of the free man, one fails to encounter any negatives, certainly not the words denoting laziness and the pleasure of existence as a life-style to be condemned: *argia, rhaithumia, malakia, truphē* are regularly opposed to *ponos*,[27] but this is not the case for *skholē*, which offers the citizen all the leisure in which to train himself, like Xenophon's Ischomachos, for the manly labors of war and agriculture.[28]

I have already mentioned Xenophon several times. Indeed, because *ponos* has positive connotations, Xenophon, with his passion for extremely clear values, makes himself its prophet. According to him, the citizen's life is totally devoted to great effort, from adolescence, during which *ponos*, associated with the educational practices of hunting and athletics,[29] tends to become a synonym for *paideusis* (education),[30] up to adulthood, during which unceasing struggle is always rewarded, be it in the conquest of a virtue or in the effort that is its own reward.[31]

No one will deny that the most florid passage in this great hymn in praise of *ponos* is Herakles' apologia at the crossroads in the *Memorabilia*. Nor does anyone deny that ownership of the idea dates back to Prodikos, Xenophon's role being merely to transmit or shape this Sophist example. But Xenophon made it sufficiently his own for this passage to illuminate all his ideas, in light of the choice of the adolescent Herakles who, on the threshold of adulthood, opts for a way of life marked by *ponos* instead of an existence devoted to pleasure (*hēdonē*).[32] And thus, as the result of an edifying twist, Herakles, the "divine glutton," who is endlessly portrayed in comedy as the incontinent one, becomes the symbol of philosophical struggle, in which effort must always defeat enjoyment. An old story, perhaps, since, before Prodikos, the Pythagoreans had already attempted a similar move. However, the apologia was to give a definitive place to the symbolic figure of the hero among philosophers from the Cynics to the Stoics, not to mention Herakles' destiny among the Christians.[33] In this manner, the valorization of *ponos* inside the framework of an evolving "Socratic legend" gradually moves from citizen to philosopher:[34] an important shift that could probably be explained by the political and intellectual context of the fourth century.

My aim here, however, is not to illuminate this process but merely to emphasize how much civic and then philosophical ideas about *ponos* seem to be aimed at avoiding ambiguous representations of effort as exploit— a worthy ideological operation, to be sure. Fortunately, the Greeks were not simply ideologues. Even at the height of the classical period, they could always disrupt the overly consistent systems that they had created, and in this instance they never ceased to consider the ambiguity of *ponos*, this way of referring to exploits by using the word for fatigue.

MATTERS BECOME MORE COMPLICATED

For instance, Pindar again, the bard of *ponos* as lofty deed. Despite his wish to view the exploit in entirely positive terms, he does not shun the word when he wishes to designate the lowest end of the scale of afflictions, the torments of Hades. Moreover, for Pindar *ponos* is simply the lot of the human condition considered in its generality, what lies between the honor of heroes and the ignominy of outcasts.[35] Exploits, torments, and the difficulties of life: *ponos* takes us far from civic certainties in which words have only one meaning.

Those dissatisfied with clearly demarcated polarities will perhaps be interested in the anomalies that sometimes crop up to thwart the established order of traditional values. For example, in one of Demosthenes' speeches, the opponent of a rich propertied landowner, unconcerned with upsetting the tradition that associates *ponos* with agriculture, asserts that he has "paid with his person (*tōi emautou sōmati ponōn*)" in the silver mines "the price of his labor and his fatigue" and then denounces his adversary's *truphē*.[36] However, far from being proof that attitudes in fourth-century Athens have evolved, this example supports the cause of accepted values—a landowner who has the largest fortune in real estate in Attica is no longer a peasant but a rich man who can lay a claim to the civic ideal of effort—and one is left only with the idea that the logic of *ponos* is liable to many twists and turns. Abandoning the security of the table of opposites, I will now focus on the tension between the exploit and struggle, already suggested by Pindar, that subtends all ideas about *ponos*.

Thucydides, for example, writes of *ponos* as the deed of the city-hero, but in both the active and passive voice, the verb *ponein* is used to describe the difficulties that an army encounters in the course of a battle or the trials that weigh on a city.[37] This indicates that one can be either the triumphant subject or the overwhelmed object of *ponos*. Let us return to the *ponoi* of a city, in a perpetual tension between the high deed and the ordeal. In tragedy *ponoi* are glorious for the city that speaks of them and painful for the others, who are silent. And when, in Herodotus, the Lacedaemonians advise the Plataeans to seek Athen's aid to bring *ponos* to the Athenians, it is obviously not to give Athens glory but trouble.[38]

Thucydidean eloquence makes all contortions possible: it is enough to play on the double meaning of *ponos*. Thus the Corinthians can define effort as the Athenians' "festival." This will not prevent Pericles from evoking real festivals, the remedies for the fatigues (*ponōn*) of the city.[39] The same Pericles, now comparing *ponos* to the effort of the piece-worker, further on will contrast Athenian "ease," viewed as aristocratic "leisure," to the coarse inurement to pain that forms the basis of Spartan military effort. Once again the canonical opposition between ease (*rhait-humia*) and *ponos* is reversed.[40] But in the classical period, it is still necessary to master these rhetorical games and maintain them at a certain heroic level. For Athenians smitten with glory and immortality, the time has not yet come to leave to posterity the surprising message offered to all who pass by the epitaph of a Phrygian athlete from the first century A.D. After speaking of the dead man's successes, it continues,

> But that glory comes from struggle; do not forget, for as long as you live, to delight in the sweetness of life (*truphē*).[41]

Let us linger a moment in Thucydides' Athens. One ordeal, and only one, could unseat all values, including honor, and constrain the Athenians to recognize the other side of *ponos*. I mean the plague, which Pericles, after evoking the city's Labors, identifies as the scourge (*ponos*) weighing on the Athenians.[42] *Ponos* used to mean exploit; now it refers to the trials of disease. This is an invitation to take a closer look at it from the physicians' standpoint.

For the author of the *Regimen*, there is no exploit nor ethical perspective, simply *ponoi* considered as physical exercises, *gumnasia* that, when combined with appropriate food, offer the basis for a healthy life.[43] But exercise must not be too tiring, or it is likely to become sheer physical suffering—once again *ponos*.[44] For this is frequently the meaning of the word in the Hippocratic corpus and for all the writers who, from Sophocles to Aristotle and including Thucydides, share the physicians' language.[45] It is even the term that Aristotle applies to sick people, *ponountes* (sufferers), as in this case he does not use the most commonly employed participle of the verb *kamnō*. I will return to this word, which in Homer was close to the verb *poneō* but had evolved so that by the classical period it refers only to disease.[46] *Ponos*, it can be seen, has remained more ambiguous, and one can always play on its double meaning, of suffering as a trial and of labor as effort.

Aristotle's discussion of childbirth is interesting in this respect. It is an accepted fact that women suffer when giving birth. At least Greek women do, for they are sedentary (*hedraiai*, a word that refers to their seated position). And Aristotle contrasts this painful *ponos* with the easy delivery of Egyptian women. In Egypt, it will be recalled, women work. And, like all peoples where the women's life-style requires physical effort (*bios ponētikos*), this *ponos* toughens their bodies and drives away or neutralizes *ponos* as suffering.[47] Labor or suffering: it seems indeed that Diodorus and Strabo had understood the message when, mentioning the peoples who reject the Greek sexual division of tasks to put women to work, they tell the edifying story of a Ligurian woman who, hired for a daily wage (*misthos*) and working with the men, retired to the brush for just long enough to give birth, after which she went back to work. It took the child's cries, or in another version, the master's awareness of her struggles as she worked, to make her agree, once she had received her *misthos*, to go home with her newborn.[48] The *bios ponētikos* has dispelled the labor of childbirth as women's *ponos*.

Assuredly, these things only happen to other people. Nonetheless, it is still a Greek who thinks of the alternative. And, whether *ponos*-exploit or *ponos*-trial, *ponos*-labor or *ponos*-suffering,[49] the two poles are always distinguished clearly enough for there to be the possibility, even the necessity, of choosing one meaning over another.

This is at least how things look in the classical city and afterward. But Greece did not always follow the royal road of contrasts, and the archaic period produced references to *ponos* in which no alternative meanings were offered.

Such is the case for Hesiod, for whom work is the law of men and their suffering. Work as man's pain: the work of the peasant, of course— this has been said again and again.[50] Nonetheless, in the reflection on the human condition expressed throughout the myth of Prometheus or the myth of the five races, the widespread nature of *ponos*, this long and heavy labor, from which men used be shielded in the old days, comes to the fore.[51] We are all of the iron age: this is the lesson that the lyric poets and tragedians will read in Hesiod, as they emulate the idea that the human condition is nothing but one long struggle.[52] Men must work because the golden age is over: only a few traces of it remain, such as the wondrous land of the Egyptians of Memphis, who "perform none of the other labors that other men must struggle to carry out to obtain their harvests," for the Nile floods and fertilizes their fields of its own accord (*automatos*). It is necessary to work, since man derives his subsistence from agricultural labor and not from raising animals like the nomadic Scythians, "the least active of men," who are content to follow the movements of their flocks, a true living field.[53] But above all, men must live, and that alone is a *ponos*—after Hesiodic man, tragic heroes will have their surfeit of this experience.

Let us leave the Egyptians, who have a decidedly strange relationship to *ponos*, let us leave the wandering Scythians, and return to the Hesiodic notion of work. *Ponos*, then, is suffering. While the *Works and Days* tries to reach some kind of accommodation with this idea by inviting one to accept *ponos*, since for man there is no other solution, the *Theogony* offers a more radical view by giving Ponos a genealogy that makes him a son of Eris, odious Strife, the descendant of Night.[54] The peasant's life is marked by a good Eris and a bad one; in the *Theogony*, on the contrary, dark Eris reigns alone, burdening the lives of mortals. But up until the *Works and Days*, Hesiod expresses the happiness of the men of the golden age by isolating them from "struggle and distress," thereby associating *ponos* with Distress (*Oizus*), another descendant of Night, this time her groaning daughter.[55] Clearly, a "veritable valorization of work"[56] is not to be found in Hesiod.

As one goes back into the Homeric universe, it becomes clear that *ponos* as the law of the human condition is not unknown in the epic. There is even a hero who embodies it: Odysseus who endures, "untired by ruses or pain," and whose long series of sufferings the *Odyssey* does not even bring to an end, since it predicts for his future, beyond the narrative, a difficult and measureless *ponos*.[57] But although Odysseus is described as a truly human man, his struggles are also considered a heroic trial. The first lines of the *Odyssey* tell how "from high battle, in the course of trials over which he has triumphed, he won the prize of having saved his life,"[58] and the *Iliad* speaks of his readiness to perform all labors[59] —works of deception, since this is Odysseus; also warrior's work, since this is the world of combat.

In the *Iliad* war, the only human activity possible for the hero, is accompanied by mourning and tears.[60] There one finds *ponos kai oizus*, the eminently Homeric pair.[61] The task at hand is *ponos*, the most generic term for the effort of waging war, suffering and trials, mourning and sorrow: *ponos* is indissociably all of that for Homer.[62] Thus it is not surprising that *ponos* is frequently linked with *kamatos*, the word for "fatigue,"[63] and if one is to understand Homeric "work," one must also consider *kamatos* and the verb *kamnō*, which perhaps even more than *ponos* express the close association between labor and suffering: the exhaustion that brings down the warrior, the labor of the artisan crafting a beautiful object, and, a bond linking artisan and warrior, the exhaustion intermixed with human life to such a degree that the dead are said to be "tired out" from bringing the *ponos* of existence to its conclusion.[64]

Labor and suffering, suffering as labor: imagining such an equation is not easy. A highly unstable notion, Homeric work is equal—this has often been remarked—to the value of the worker.[65] In the *Odyssey* the *kamatos* of the frail maidservant toiling at her millstone and the *kamatos* of Eumaios are pure suffering;[66] on the contrary the work of Odysseus building his marriage bed is highest nobility, and even the hero's crushing exhaustion when he is buffeted by the waves is a sign, in reverse, of his heroic energy. The same is true for *ponos*. Suffering predominates in the *ponos* endured by the Achaians for ten long years in front of Troy, but the *ponos* of Achilles, engaged in book 21 of the *Iliad* in prolonged warfare, is evidence of the hero's intractable strength.

However, in the final analysis, the notion of exertion, whether heroic or simply human, seems to win out over any notion of productive work. Or at least this is what the later evolution of *ponos* and *kamatos*, these Homeric names for work, attest. The two diverge. The history of *ponos* treats the noble side of effort; *kamatos* concerns all of humanity. *Ponos* retained the marks of its close Homeric association with heroic effort, while *kamatos* and *kamnō*, which in war specifically denote fatigue, become specialized terms associated with disease.[67] In the meantime, "work" loses all connection with notions of productivity.

Affliction, then, forever and always. But the adjective derived from *ponos* has another surprise in store, once we leave behind archaic thought and attempt to regain the classical city. In a heroic context, Herakles, son of Zeus, was for Hesiod *ponērōtatos kai aristos*: the most burdened with sufferings and the noblest. In fifth-century Attic comedy, *ponēros* is nothing more than the term for a tramp, a lowborn rascal who wants to play the citizen without being worthy of it.[68] A sign of the acute contradiction that divides Greek thought concerning work: during the classical period[69] derivatives of *ponos* come to be associated with the ill repute of the lowest classes, to the point that a Xenophon has no fear of contrasting *ponēria*, worthlessness, to the citizen's virtuous *ponos*[70]—once again based on the understanding that, in this table of official values, only citizens count, whether good or bad.

Ponos versus *ponēria*: this is only one of the avatars of a root meaning "difficulty," in which the vocalic *e* has given the words for poor man (*penēs*) and poverty (*penia*), while forms with the vocalic *o* refer to labor as effort,[71] even though it means a subdivision into *ponos*, the quality of the good citizen, and *ponēria*, denoting the bad quality of the bad citizen. In short, a narrow margin separates *ponos* as synonym for value from cognate terms describing a notion of work that implies, to quote Lucien Febvre on the subject of seventeenth-century France, "sometimes discomfort, despondency, suffering, or humiliation."[72]

One character in this strange adventure reconciles within himself the heroic *ponos* and the *ponos* of the human condition, eminent dignity and the abject humiliation of *ponēros*: I mean the hero Herakles, the Herakles of cult, myth, tragedy, and comedy, who is more vivid in Greek thought than the edifying constructions that the philosophers attached to his name: Herakles, a representation we have met more than once already; Herakles, the hero of struggle, linked to those Labors by which, to once again cite J.-P. Vernant, "the Greeks expressed in the heroic mode problems linked to human action and its application in the world."[73]

HERAKLES, *PONOS*, AND THE CATEGORY OF THE HEROIC

Herakles' Labors, termed *ponoi* (or *mokhthoi*, one of the more common synonyms for *ponos*),[74] display the essential manifestations of the hero's personality in the texts of the classical period.[75] Two examples, both from

Sophocles, make it possible from the outset to measure the ambiguity of the notion of *ponos* as applied to Herakles. In the *Philoctetes, ponos* is what brought the hero the immortality of valor (*athanatos aretē*); in the *Trachiniae, ponos* describes his exploits as well as his servitude and battered body.[76]

It may be taken for granted that even during the worst of his trials, glory is Herakles' lot, and I will not pursue this question. Instead I wish to consider the spent Herakles,[77] whose deeds the Homeric texts ordinarily associate with misery and ignominy;[78] or the enslaved Herakles,[79] who in the first lines of the *Trachiniae* is described by Sophocles as "always in someone's service," and of whom Aeschylus recalls that "sold, he endured the conditions of slavery."[80] However, because the suffering Herakles is particularly dear to archaic thought, it is undoubtedly better to give his exploits the name that Hesiod and Homer give them, *athloi*, a term that the mythographers of the Roman period will utilize as the canonical designation for the twelve Labors.[81]

Athlos (or *aethlos* in the epic) leads first in the direction of suffering, since the labors are "groaning" and have won Herakles the title of being the unhappiest (*athlios*) of men—of course one must see things this way and not as Dion Chrysostom does, in the first century A.D., when he states that the title of *athliotatos* comes from the custom of referring to the *ponoi* as *athloi*.[82] This is the occasion to observe in passing that the adjectives derived from the terms for exploits—*athlios, ponēros, mokhthēros*—all describe the man as unhappy when they do not refer to him as miserable. But *athlos* also indisputably leads to slavery. The *Iliad* usually refers to the *aethloi* as the "labors of Eurystheus," linking them to the pitiless king who commanded them, and in the *Odyssey*, the hero who has become a shade in the underworld recalls that he was "enslaved beneath the yoke of the worst of humans, who had inflicted terrible labors on him."[83] Even more clearly, in the excursus that Diodorus and Apollodorus devote to the labors of Herakles, everything that happens between Eurystheus and the hero can be summed up in three words: *athlos*, indissociably the exploit and the imposed task; *prostagma*, which refers to the command; *telein* and its compounds, which refer to the accomplishment of the labor. The task that is imposed is thus *athlos*, even more obviously than *ponos*, and if during the classical period the tragedians alternate between the two words without distinction,[84] this synonymous relationship does not imply that apart from Herakles' deed one must seek to give this precise meaning to *ponos*. Whether these usages are purely mimetic[85] or not, they tell us nothing, because, I would venture to say, *ponos* is too well protected by its status as a cardinal term of civic ideology.

Amid pain and servitude, *athlos* as exploit still remains, and only the Pindaric view of athleticism, with its normative tendencies, consistently attempts to dissociate the exploit from suffering and generally remove its ambiguity.[86] The founder of the Olympic and Nemean games, Herakles is certainly the prototype of the athlete, but the remainder of his career hardly warrants the comparison. *Athlos*, therefore, is also the painful trial, the torments of Aeschylus's Prometheus or the forsworn god in Hesiod's *Theogony*, or the Homeric tribulations that the text connects, as in the case of Herakles' labors, with the person responsible for them.[87] Finally, in the *Odyssey* it is the trial of the bow to qualify for Penelope's hand, as much as and more than a contest.[88] Led astray by continuous debate over the word's "original meaning" and anxious to make a choice, philologists have insisted on the dimension of suffering in *athlos* or attempted to keep the notion of struggle as the principal sense of the word that gives rise to athletic terminology.[89] But they have not always paid adequate attention to the recurrence of *athlos*, at the height of the fifth century, to refer to a task that was imposed.[90]

Of course the problem is real, and a difficult one. What category will give unity to a word whose denotation already has shifted, from the *Iliad* to the *Odyssey*, from the Labors of a Herakles striving under the law of Eurystheus to the royal trial of the bow? Instead of privileging one meaning to the detriment of the other, I propose to put *athlos* in the category of that which gives rise to an *athlon*.[91] *Athlon* is the prize, *athlos* the social service that calls for compensation, and that definition must also include the agonistic struggle of the contest[92] and the groaning trials. It is true that in the exact matter of Herakles, this does not put an end to my difficulties, for still no mention has been made of an *athlon* rewarding his labors. Indeed *athlon* appears frequently with reference to contests. It is for an *aethlon* that the horsemen depicted on the Hesiodic shield strive to do their utmost, it is for *aethla* that the Achaians compete in book 23 of the *Iliad*—but in book 22 Hector's life was the *aethlon* for which Achilles and the Trojan hero spent their strength, in a mad race of pursuit—and in the *Odyssey*, *aethlon* refers to Achilles' weapons, the stakes of the confrontation between Odysseus and Ajax, or even Penelope herself, for whom the suitors accept the trial of the bow.[93] But one looks in vain for a clear reference to *athlon* in the matter of Herakles' groaning suffering,[94] and other than admitting that this absent reward is confused with immortality,[95] one must note the silence and not search too hard, for there are no clues, to determine whether it is due to accidents of textual transmission or censorship (the refusal to measure the efforts of a hero who was born a mortal and died a god or, inversely, the refusal to give the honor of an *athlon* to labors that the *Iliad* presents as "ignominious"). Rather than forcing the issue, I will merely stress that in virtually all the sources, assuming that the Labors are the outcome of something other than a logic of pure constraint, Herakles' career is less connected with recompense than retribution (*misthos*). For all that, this retribution is more often refused than granted, as if to emphasize the idea of a service rendered for another in suffering—service for its own sake, without any goal other than to subordinate the hero to a will beyond his own.

The idea of service could use additional clarification. It shows up on the general level of Greek ideas about the heroic as a symbol which attests that "the source and origin of the action, the reason for the triumph, are not found in the hero but outside him."[96] In this perspective (conventionally referred to as historical psychology), it is not without importance that from Homer to Diodorus the Greeks felt a similar repugnance about attributing to human action a source that is also its agent. On another level, returning again to Homer, we should try to understand Herakles' trials in the uncertain light of the research done on the status of work in a world, that of Achilles and of Odysseus, in which the mercenary thete is in fact likened to the slave, where "even a contrast as simple as that between . . . slave and free man is not very clear," since the same word (in this case *drēstēr*, the "servant") can refer to the free man in the service of an aristocrat and the slave whose freedom has been placed in another's power.[97] Then it is time to mention the dual value of *misthos*, a word for retribution that refers in the epic to the reward for a high deed as well as to the thete's salary—and from one book of the *Iliad* to the next, the same task is described either as *aethlos* or the work of a hired thete (serf).[98] If indeed there are tribulations that, lacking an *athlon*, merit a reward, it would be those of Herakles, which Pindar himself attributes, at least this once in the hero's career, to his preoccupation with *misthos*, when he extracted "willy nilly from the insolent Augeas the price for his services (*latrios misthos*)."[99] But nothing is simple when it comes to measuring Herakles' tracks on the field of *athlos*. For when the same Pindar argues within the very real framework of the values of the city, he establishes a clear demarcation between the *misthos* owed the worker who "defends his belly from pernicious hunger" and glory, the necessary recompense for the *athlos*.[100] Does he do this because in order to speak of Herakles, the paradigmatic athlete, it is necessary to resort to a bygone way of thinking and reconcile glory and wages in the epic manner? At least it will be conceded that, in the case of Pindar as well as Homer, the operation is successful if the worker is a hero or, like Poseidon laboring in the service of the Trojan Laomedon, a god.

However, this operation may no longer have been possible for Pindar's contemporaries, and everything suggests that during the classical period *athlos* as the term for service loses ground because it leads to inextricable problems.

We have come a long way from *ponos*—or perhaps not. For the odds are good that the process by which *ponos* replaces *athlos* in the context of the

Labors of Herakles in the fifth and fourth centuries is a fruitful ideological operation. Set apart from clear notions of work as service, weighted with socially positive value, *ponos* dispels a good share of the hero's ambiguity. When *ponos* fully becomes a source of merit, at the outcome of a long social process that makes possible a total distinction between servile work and the occupation of the citizen, when the free man is clearly defined as one who does not depend on another for his subsistence,[101] then *ponos* replaces *athlos*, and Herakles, no longer able to obey, must be free. Then the hero may no longer be subject to external constraints in the form of destiny or a despot. His vocation for difficulty must instead become the fruit of free choice: hence Prodikos, Xenophon, and the crossroads where the son of Alcmene is supposed to have found himself, "at the age where young men are already the masters of themselves (*autokratores*)."[102] Then, of course, to envision Herakles' choice, one chooses, or cuts, or prunes away; one chooses glory (but also inwardness), another tries to eliminate suffering and slavery as much as possible. It is no longer possible to see that through Eurystheus, the simple instrument of Hera's will, Herakles—"glorious by Hera"—was attached to the goddess's service and has nothing of the slave about him. It is no longer possible to see that in the epic Herakles was great in his servitude precisely because he had not chosen his status—unlike the thete who hires himself out voluntarily[103]—but had submitted to it as his fate.

But the cause is understood, and henceforth there will be no escaping this extensive process of salvaging Herakles as symbol of *ponos*. Witness the mythographer Apollodorus, who prefers, however, the detailed account of the mythical hero's vicissitudes to the expurgated versions offered by the philosophers. Returning to Pindar's information on the subject of *misthos*, he asserts that Eurystheus refused to consider the Augean Labor as an *athlos* because heroic effort was rewarded with payment.[104] Whether legendary hero or citizen, the moment one is not a slave, one's personal honor is supposed to be the fruit of struggle. Herakles is not a worker.[105]

Let us return once again to the rupture introduced by Prodikos the Sophist. As master of a science of words that teaches how to distinguish among synonyms, Prodikos entered the annals of history for putting an end to the ambiguity of ideas. Hence, the attribution to Herakles of a *ponos* that is at last relieved of superfluous groans. But there is no Sophist who does not know that words retain their ambiguity. Thus in Aristophanes' *Clouds*, Unjust Speech, representing Sophist education, trips his opponent up in his own definition of *ponos*. Preaching the virtues of the old-time education, Just Speech had condemned the practice of bathing—a perfect occasion for the other to accuse him of blaming hot baths, and therefore Herakles, who is traditionally associated with these baths, known to dispel the fatigue of an athlete and procured for him by Athena (or the Nymphs) as a remedy for his exhaustion.[106] And entangled in an overly restrictive definition of *ponos* in which, as a good ideologue, he has alluded to noble effort without giving fatigue its due, Just Speech finds himself accused of undervaluing Herakles' manhood[107]— comic sophism, no doubt, but comedy itself is not always serious with the hero of *ponos*.

Beyond these ideological attempts at orderliness, the ambiguity of *ponos* takes on a new form. When fatigue is used to refer to work, how can balance be maintained (how can the suffering of a mortal be imagined without losing sight of the quality of effort, or work be envisioned without trying to banish the exhaustion that accompanies it)?

But also, how is it possible to avoid purifying labor that has become so dissociated from service that it requires neither reward nor sanction, that has lost all connection with the exemplary and thus banal figure of the worker? Decidedly, Herakles is not a worker.[108]

PART TWO

THE WEAKNESSES
OF STRENGTH

HAVING SEEN that a woman's "manly trial" is a reflection on men's battered bodies of something that can be experienced only in the feminine mode, that the hero's glory lies in raising himself out of the ignominy into which he has been plunged, we are ready to begin our survey of Greek representations of the masculine, whose essential mechanisms are exchange and ambivalence—a one-way exchange perhaps, working to the greater benefit of the Greek male and resembling an act of appropriation (to apprehend the woman that is in man; to consider virility in terms of its most decisive boundary). The ambivalence, however, is even stronger: for beyond the official paradigms, with their all-too-clear oppositions, Greek reflection about the male figure is always paired with an effort to plumb his internal faults—indeed, his fundamental fault.

The Greeks have much to say on the subject, this people who nonetheless have often been made into miraculous bearers of a positive and untarnished ideal of beauty, the same people who, in the name of structuralism, have been locked by commentators into opposing social roles as a means to avoid mention of sexual roles.

These chapters will probe the disputes concerning the internal nature of the *anēr*, not because I intend to declare war on interpretations accused of "binary" thinking (which—today it is practically a *topos*—must be taxed with all sins), nor because I want to reveal the contours of an extremely ancient line of thought entirely devoid of contradiction. Quite the contrary: because binary thinking ultimately subverts itself and the archaic is at the heart of the contemporary, the masculine profile that gradually emerges is sustained by the fact that the Greeks wholly and openly emulate the exploit that never fails to place men under the sign of a lived contradiction, which is intensified rather than transcended.

Therefore, I would like to reopen the case by beginning with what seems to be the most orthodox representations of the *anēr*: the ideal that will bring to mind how much the certitudes of hoplitic discourse continue to display a fascination with the fortunes and misfortunes of an Achilles or Herakles—Achilles, without whom Troy would not be defeated, who knows it, and who plays the woman at Scyros, but in spite of all chooses war—where he excels; Herakles, the supermale condemned to don the garments of more than one woman. But let's not get ahead of ourselves. . . .

Chapter 3

THE SPARTANS' "BEAUTIFUL DEATH"

THE "BEAUTIFUL DEATH" (*kalos* or *euklees thanatos*):[1] the death of the citizen-soldier fallen on the field of honor.*

A reader of Athenian funeral orations finds this a simple and clear equivalence, limpid like the *topoi* of official speeches.[2] With this expression the orators designated by the city to speak at the Kerameikos refer to the freely chosen death of the citizen who attained valor by giving to the city the life he owed it—he became "a man of valor" (*aner agathos egeneto*)—and immortal glory. The precise conditions of his death, like the actual vicissitudes of combat, are never discussed, and this glorious death generally has an elliptical quality. The citizen's death is never described; at most it is a pretext for a stereotypical piece about hoplitic morals intended for the edification of the audience, in which, however, oarsmen and hoplites sit side by side. But if the "moral" of the funeral oration can seem paradoxical, it is the paradox of the democratic city and not the speech itself.[3] In short, in official Athenian discourse everything is simple, perhaps precisely because everything occurs on the level of *logos*—in other words, of collective imaginary representations. In Athens the "beautiful death" is an abstract model.

However, when considering the Athenian model, one must not forget that the "beautiful death" is a preeminently Spartan theme, which Athenian official discourse has shaped to benefit its democratic regime. Therefore it is necessary to go back to the source and, at the risk of encountering a few surprises, penetrate the universe of the hoplitic city of the *homoioi*.

For instance, tradition about Sparta: there the beautiful death is not only an ideological theme; it is presented as a categorical imperative that must not be violated. "Do not flee the battlefield before the enemy horde but remain *firm at your post and be victorious there or die*":[4] such is the principle governing the Spartans' military behavior, and readers know of the profound psychological shock felt by the Greeks when they heard of the surrender of the hoplites from Sphacteria. According to Thucydides, "it was the most unexpected event of the war in the eyes of the Greeks, for the opinion concerning the Lacedaemonians was that neither hunger

---

*This essay is dedicated to Pierre Vidal-Naquet.

nor any other extremity would make them give up their arms but they would keep them and fight as they could unto death."[5]

In Spartan practice the beautiful death is not always such a clear-cut matter—far from it. Although formulations of the imperative all resemble one another, they are numerous, and this multiplicity is the source of hesitation over its exact content.

The Spartan beautiful death is more complex than the Athenian model, more baffling in its living reality than the hoplitic reputation of the Lacedaemonians would suggest. Thus, limiting one's sights to the sometimes shifting contours of the imperative is not enough. It must also be viewed in the context of the institutions in which it is embodied—the status of the "trembling ones," the *tresantes*, comes to mind. Only then will it be possible to see the tensions of the beautiful death in action, in a narrative completely dominated by the glory of Sparta, the account of the battle at Thermopylae in book 7 of Herodotus's *Histories*.

Meanwhile, it is necessary to take note of a problem inherent in the material, well known to historians of Sparta but particularly acute in this case. The beautiful death is part of Spartan legend, and the vast majority of the sources are not Spartan—not even one, if Tyrtaeus, the bard of the beautiful death, was indeed born in Athens, as ancient tradition states. But the same people who claim the honor of the poet's birth for Athens consider him the authorized spokesman of the Spartan ideal,[6] the one whose poems would inspire the Lacedaemonian warriors to "want to die for their country" (*pro tēs patridos ethelein apothnēiskein*).[7] Therefore Tyrtaeus will serve as a guide in this study of the Spartan beautiful death, with the systematic comparison of his elegies on war with the information provided by the Greeks of the classical period acting as a barrier—at least I hope so—against the pitfalls of the "Spartan mirage."

A HOPLITIC REQUIREMENT

To hold fast: in fact this is the essential precept governing hoplitic combat and the solidarity of the phalanx,[8] and after Tyrtaeus, Herodotus glorified the endurance of the Spartans, "the only people in the world" capable of "waiting resolutely, arms raised," for the Persian army.[9] As corollaries to this precept, a certain number of interdictions are imposed on the soldier: it is forbidden to leave one's rank or to flee,[10] no matter how outnumbered by opposing forces;[11] it is also forbidden, obviously, to surrender.[12] In short, when the outcome of the battle is desperate, the Spartan is supposed to let himself be killed on the spot, and Tyrtaeus exalts the beautiful death of the first warrior fallen in the first rank of troops[13] after being wounded in the front of his body by innumerable blows: a beneficent death, which covers the city and its people with glory and in return grants the hero distinguished funeral honors and immortal glory.[14]

This death, prepared for and anticipated many times in the *agōgē*—the education that the Spartans themselves refer to as "training"—is a means of meeting what Henri Jeanmaire calls "the test of *aretē*."[15] In an echo of Xerxes' question to Demaratus after the Spartan sacrifice at Thermopylae as to whether those who remain are like (*homoioi*) the dead,[16] Thucydides asserts that the Greeks will end up doubting that the prisoners of Sphacteria were "like the dead."[17] This echo is clearly no accident. "Like": in other words, of equal value. In line 424 as in 480, the beautiful death is the absolute criterion of Spartan bravery, and surviving consequently appears all the more problematic. But for Herodotus, in any event, the use of the word *homoioi* is not neutral, nor is it, a fortiori, for Thucydides. Without accepting the correction to this passage of the *Peloponnesian War*, which consists in omitting *tois tethneōsin* to give *homoioi* its political, and specifically Spartan, meaning of "citizens by full rights"—which would amount to transforming the text into a questioning of the survivors' civic status[18]—I will observe that when he employed this term Thucydides, like Herodotus, could not have been unaware of the "Spartan" resonance that it would necessarily have for Greek readers, since in Sparta citizens are those who are like one another.[19]

The beautiful death, then, if not a criterion for citizenship, is at least an eminently civic manifestation. Unlike the Homeric warrior, whose *aretē* is fed by immediate stimuli[20]—the cries of the combatants, the exchange of challenges, the murmurs of admiration from the mass of ignoble bystanders watching the champions confront one another—the hoplitic soldier consciously sacrifices himself for the city, having internalized the values of this absent yet nonetheless omnipresent spectator.[21] Therefore the hoplite's glory is conferred not by the song of the bard nor the buzzing of public clamor (*dēmou phatis*).[22] It comes entirely from the city, whose temporal continuity and perennial status guarantee the fighter immortal renown.

The need for self-mastery (*sōphrōsunē*), even in death, is still a hoplitic and civic virtue. Of course, one must make light of death, "considering life as hateful and the black Keres of death as lovable as the sun's rays."[23] But the city's austere military ethic forbids the soldier to find any fascination in annihilation and the frenzy known as *lussa*. One must *accept* death (*ethelein apothnēiskein*) and not seek it as did Aristodamos, the best Spartan warrior at Plataea, who was deprived of all posthumous honor because he had broken that law.[24]

Death is "beautiful" only under these conditions, and the adjective must not be taken only in its ethical sense, as in the Athenian version of the *kalos thanatos*. For Tyrtaeus, *kalos* retains all the aesthetic resonance that it had for Homer, and the beauty of the dead young warrior is not an empty phrase for the Spartans.[25]

But the beautiful death is not only a representation, a model. It is part of the carefully tempered management of courage, and the Lacedaemonian city backs its exaltation of the brave with rigorous legislation that parcels out praise and blame. Glory goes to the brave, the glory of the dead man and those who return alive and victorious; dishonor goes to the cowardly. Xenophon praises Lycurgus for making his fellow citizens brave men "by openly procuring happiness for the brave and unhappiness for cowards," and according to Plutarch, the celebration of the former and denigration of the latter had an important place in Spartan education.[26]

Then there are the others, such as the "trembling ones" (*hoi tresantes*), whose unhappy existence the texts concur in presenting as the reverse of the beautiful death of the brave. When Xenophon, followed by Plutarch, states that one "still ought to admire Lycurgus for having caused his fellow citizens to value a beautiful death above a shameful existence," he is a direct descendant of Tyrtaeus.[27] We know that the trembling ones receive *oneidos kai atimiē*, opprobrium and dishonor.[28] Victor Ehrenberg has studied the multiple raggings to which these degraded *homoioi* are subjected, and I will simply refer the reader to his work.[29] But a thorough examination of the actual Spartan practice of the hoplitic imperative is essential to my argument, and I will take a moment to consider the meaning of the institutional dishonor assigned to the *tresantes*.

THE BEAUTIFUL DEATH: AN INSTITUTION?

Lacedaemonian propaganda and Spartan legend usually make the beautiful death a *nomos*, a law. "If these feelings must be impressed onto souls in a lasting fashion, must not there first of all be laws that will assure courageous men of an honored and free life and that on the contrary will inflict an abject, painful, invidious existence on the cowardly?"[30] This opinion, uttered by Xenophon's Cyrus, monarch of a Persia that has often been seen as an idealized Sparta, would suggest the actual existence of a legislative body in Sparta organized to handle "the beautiful death." But fiction offers a more codified view of the reality that it claims to present.

While the Spartans, unlike Xerxes' Persians, have no need of whips to compel them to march into combat, their courage can be understood as purely agonistic exaltation as well as constrained submission to the law, a master that, according to Herodotus, they fear more than subjects fear their great king.[31] But to put the question in these terms, as has often been done,[32] would be to forget that *aidōs* or *aiskhunē*, the extremely effective cement of Spartan civic cohesion,[33] is accompanied by a traditional repugnance for written laws.[34] In reality, whether one understands *nomos* in the sense of "custom" or the more technical meaning of "legislation," the result is basically the same. Internalized or rigorously codified, the demand for bravery is perceived to be *the same as a law*, and the famous epigram of those who died at Thermopylae must be understood in this way:

> Stranger, go tell Lacedaemon that we lie here in obedience to her laws (*tois keinōn rhēmasi peithomenoi*).[35]

Written or unwritten laws? In any event, laws that are thought of as a voice that dictates the norm. Such is the "law" of the beautiful death in Sparta, and the essential fact remains that the most tangible effects of *nomos* are felt *in the lives* of Spartan citizens. Unlike the Athenian *epitaphioi*, which have no place for the idea of a beautiful life,[36] the Spartan code provides a whole series of rewards for the victorious courage of the survivors, from the pleasure the young man feels at being admired by men and desired by women[37] to the innumerable delights of the adult and the honors that surround the old man.[38] In keeping with his habitual utilitarianism, Xenophon sees the infamy that weighs over the coward as an effective form of pressure to inspire courage in the soldier and, if fate has it, grant him a life of honor.[39] But in this respect he also agrees with Tyrtaeus, for whom the glorious death is nothing, all things considered, but a necessary last resort. The greatest good for a Spartan is still life, on the condition, of course, that it is a life of honor (*timē*).

This touches on an essential point: the very real pragmatism governing the Spartan code of bravery. When Xenophon asserts that above all it is useful to glorify the beautiful death, for it leads the Spartans to victory and causes fewer casualties than beset those whose fear leads them to prefer flight,[40] again he is the zealous commentator of Tyrtaeus. Does he know that the position he adopts in this instance is almost Iliadic? For despite its ostensibly hoplitic nature, the Spartan ideal is nonetheless very close on this point to declarations that recur in the epic.[41] Much can certainly be said about the coexistence of epic values and civic norms. For the moment let us remain with Tyrtaeus, who declares that if one must accept death, the reason is that the consequences of defeat would be even worse than death; but that inversely, it is by accepting death that one has the best chance of escaping it.

> For those who dare to march in close formation into hand-to-hand combat in the front ranks die in fewer numbers and save the people for the future; but among those who tremble, all valor is lost.[42]

Like *aretē*, of which it is the crown jewel, the beautiful death, the common good of the collectivity,[43] saves the city, but hoplitic discipline and courage save the majority of fighters (*pauroteroi thnēiskousi*) from death. These are the assertions of volunteers, of course, but they are as distant from the abstract model of the funeral oration as from all the morbid exaltations of death.[44] The *Sayings of Spartans* will repeat them in a humorous vein.[45]

Nonetheless, a word of caution to those inclined to speculate about the great wisdom of the Spartans, who see courage as a remedy for oliganthropy: matters become singularly complicated once one has carefully examined what the Spartans call a "trembling one."

One thing is certain. One must win or die, Demaratus said to Xerxes (*epikrateein ē apollusthai*),[46] and Tyrtaeus, while not unaware of the harsh reality of defeat,[47] explicitly situates himself, because of the parenetic nature of his verse, in the unique perspective in which courage leads to victory.[48] In this case the *tresas* is condemned because his flight or cowardice nearly compromises the chances for victory. But in the case of defeat? Must it be said that all one has to do to be condemned is to survive defeat,[49] and that it is better to return dead than alive? In fact, if at times citizens defeated in battle are severely judged because their deaths were useless,[50] more often they are celebrated as if they had been victorious. Is dying at one's post a kind of victory? The pride of the relatives of the dead from Lekhaion (in 390) or Leuctra (in 371) seems to confirm this.[51] Does this mean that all other soldiers are perforce *tresantes*? Some have thought so, perhaps rightly,[52] but such rigidity would totally contradict the pragmatism that I believe I have found in the texts of Tyrtaeus and Xenophon.

Others have reckoned that the mere loss of one's shield was enough to condemn a soldier to degradation: this too is a completely plausible hypothesis—we know how much carrying a shield contributed to the cohesion and solidarity of the phalanx,[53] and a famous Lacedaemonian aphorism, which enjoins the soldier to return "with or upon" his shield, is evidence of this.[54] However, this principle is not applied literally,[55] and the Spartans' reaction was probably the function of precise circumstances of weakness or defeat, as well of the state of affairs in the city. Therefore it seems impossible, even useless, to undertake the sort of reconstruction that Ehrenberg has made of the history of the institution, dominated by the eminently ideological presupposition of Sparta's continued decadence from the time of the Persian wars.[56] In fact, torn between multiple demands and multiple interpretations of the beautiful death, in their everyday lives the Spartans probably lived out the tensions and contradictions using a code of valor in which honor and well-understood interest sometimes became allied only by means of more or less disguised sophisms.

To understand the peculiar status of the *tresantes*, who are degraded but nonetheless integrated into the collectivity, in which they play the role of a living and derisory exhortation to courage,[57] there is no need to imagine a category of Spartans subject to crueler punishment, even if ultimately their fault is minimal.[58] One of these "tremblers" is Aristodamos, who did not have the nerve to die with the Spartans at Thermopylae—who, like the hoplites of Sphacteria, were in fact betrayed because they were ignorant of the treacherous military tactics used against them.

In and of itself, the Spartan attitude toward the prisoners of Sphacteria would suffice to discourage any hasty generalizations. Indeed, the entire affair turns out to be ambiguous, from the official response to the defeated hoplites requesting orders[59] to the degradation of the men imprisoned in Athenian jails despite constant attempts to liberate them.[60] Therefore historians have reached no agreement concerning the real significance of their punishment: Diodorus reckons that the prisoners were blamed for tarnishing the Lacedaemonian reputation while Thucydides sees it as a preventive measure designed to eliminate any thoughts of subversion.[61] But all things considered, the essential is undoubtedly less their degradation than their ultimate reintegration into the civic corps of *homoioi*.

Is this the evidence of hesitation over the meaning of an ambiguous *nomos* or simply the sign of impenitent pragmatism? The two explanations should be considered together. The Spartans, who so severely punish Aristodamos and tolerate the ridiculous insubordination of Amompharetos in Plataea,[62] are aware of at least two reasons that legitimize the beautiful death, one founded on the material interests of combat, the other on the feeling of honor.[63] In Sparta the beautiful is paired with the useful, which should not be surprising. Professionals in war, the *homoioi* have no need for the ideological pledges masking Athenian amateurism to make themselves credible.[64]

They are technicians of the military art, not only for Xenophon, an authority on *tekhnē*,[65] but also for Herodotus: at Plataea[66] and even Thermopylae, where they know how to feign retreat, applying a century in advance the tactical advice that Plato gives in the *Laches*.[67] Therefore, what was said of the sacrifice of Leonidas and his companions can be applied to the degradation of the *tresantes*: the formal prohibition against retreat explains neither the beautiful death nor the institutional punishment of cowards.[68] Perhaps a distinction must be made between an honorable retreat and a desperate situation in which leaving the battlefield would be dishonorable. But even in this last case, pragmatism—or the desire to avoid oliganthropy—can dictate a compromise in which the leader's honor and the men's safety are given equal weight, which allows for retreat.[69] And when Herodotus, praising the Athenians for saving Greece, asserts that without the action of Athens the Lacedaemonians, "all alone, would have gloriously succumbed after accomplishing great

deeds" or "would have concluded a treaty with Xerxes,"[70] one must undoubtedly not be content, as Plutarch was, with attributing this alternative to "Herodotus's malice" or his pro-Athenian bias.[71] All the material
that has been examined up to now indicates that actually Sparta was not
required to adopt a suicidal course of action. It at least had the choice
between two solutions.

Nothing better reveals the complexity of the conditions surrounding
the beautiful death than the famous example of Thermopylae. Heretofore
resigned to abandon the simple certainties of those who love the fine
pages of history, I will attempt, in conclusion, a reading of Herodotus's
account of the battle, a narrative—it is known—in which Spartan tradition overshadows all others.[72] Didn't Herodotus "forget" the presence of
the Thespians and Thebans as a way of reserving the immortal glory of
the freely accepted sacrifice for the Spartans alone,[73] just as the Athenian
orators forgot the Plataeans' role in order to award the glory of Marathon to the Athenians?[74]

THERMOPYLAE: THE BEAUTIFUL DEATH AND THE EPIC

This is not the place to wonder about the profound reasons for
Leonidas's final resolution. Others have done that before me, and like
them, I believe that the king of Sparta and commander in chief of the
Panhellenic forces chose the only solution capable of achieving the necessary retreat of the allied troops and saving Sparta's honor. Without worrying too much about the contradiction raised by some scholars between
the thesis of royal *devotio*, authorized by an oracle with all the characteristics of hindsight, and the acceptance of the need for sacrifice in obedience
to Spartan law, I will consider the second argument, that of the beautiful
death, as the principal official Spartan version of the battle at Thermopylae.[75]

This leads me to note the orthodox hoplitic elements in this narrative.
As could be expected, they are numerous. The theme of endurance, first
of all: at Thermopylae the Spartans waited resolutely at their posts. The
strong resemblance between Demaratus's definition of the Spartan resistance and some of Tyrtaeus's verses has already been noted.[76] I also need
to mention the account of the first two days of combat, in which on two
occasions and at the cost of bloody confrontations, the Persians are
forced to abandon their hopes of seeing the Lacedaemonians flee.[77] Of
course, in Xerxes' eyes, it is either impudence or folly to pit such a small
number against an immense army,[78] but because he did not believe the
Spartan Demaratus, the great king is unaware that in the hoplitic view
this disproportion furnishes yet one more path to glory. It would be
pointless, moreover, to see this as a suicidal compulsion, for as Her-

odotus observes, "only Ephialtes"—the traitor—"caused the loss of the Greeks remaining at their posts."[79] According to the law in which courage necessarily leads to victory, *normally* the Spartans would not be defeated. It took the use of artifice to triumph over the hoplitic order, and this gives Herodotus the opportunity to tacitly contrast Ephialtes' cupidity and deceit with Sparta's desire for glory,[80] the furtive nocturnal march of Hydarnes' men and the audacious sortie of Leonidas's companions, in broad daylight, beyond the pass.[81] Another detail merits attention, for from the standpoint of the hoplitic representations it presents undeniable interest. When the final outcome of the battle is no longer in doubt, when Leonidas is dead and the troops guided by Ephialtes enter the action, then the Spartans form one last phalanx "all together" (*pantes halees*).[82] Nothing remains for them but to die, which they do, but since death, compared to the glory it brings, is but an insignificant thing, Herodotus, using an ellipsis reminiscent of the *epitaphioi*, makes no transition between the final battle to the distribution of prizes for bravery.[83]

However, the glorious version of the beautiful death does not completely disguise Spartan pragmatism. The site for the battle was meticulously chosen, after multiple calculations and previsions,[84] and, far from wishing at all costs to realize the *topos* of the small versus the great, on the contrary the Greeks sought to shift the unequal balance of forces, since they expected to meet the Barbarians in a pass where great numbers would be of no use[85]—a tactic that came close to succeeding. And, confronted with the debacle of the Immortals who, "fighting in a narrower space, with spears shorter than those of the Greeks, could not gain the advantage from their greater numbers,"[86] Herodotus does not fail to recall that the exemplary citizens are also professionals of war: "They made it clear by different qualities that in the midst of men who knew not the art of war, they possessed it in depth."[87] This science culminates in a simulacrum of flight that inflicts heavy losses on the Persian army, and in a significant echo of Tyrtaeus's *pauroteroi thnēiskousi*, extremely light losses for the Spartan troops.[88] Thus everything in this account of the first day of battle recalls that in Sparta courage is linked to military technique. Nothing out of the "ordinary" has occurred up to this point, and from this perspective the beautiful death would be nothing more than a noble and unavoidable blot on the record.[89]

Under these conditions, what can be said about the death of Leonidas's Three Hundred Spartans? Afterward celebrated as a beautiful death for the edification of the citizens of Sparta and all Greece, it presents a completely different face in reality. When the battle turns hopeless, after the allies depart, the beautiful and glorious death is out of the question;[90] what remains is death as a rough, even savage accident. Fierce as the great warriors of the epic, Leonidas's Greeks leave the pass "like men marching to their death."[91] The Spartans fight like madmen, "aware of the death that awaited them."[92] They use all the strength they have against the Barbarians;[93] it is no longer the time for *aretē* or the hoplitic ritual in general. Spears are replaced by swords;[94] then, after the violent melee, with its epic overtones, around Leonidas's body, the Spartans, whose swords have been broken, defend themselves "with their hands and teeth."[95] This savage battle, a "battle of boars,"[96] is more evocative of the warlike frenzy of a Tydeus[97] than the hoplite's *sōphrosunē*. *Parakhreomenoi te kai ateontes*, henceforth indifferent to everything that is not battle,[98] their minds distraught,[99] the Spartans are obviously in a state of *lussa*,[100] the very *lussa* that ten years later the city will not pardon in Aristodamos and that, to his misfortune, he fled in terror at Thermopylae.[101] Herodotus's use of the Homeric *ateontes* is not inadvertent. The hoplitic vocabulary lacks a term for martial frenzy. Therefore the epic tone of this part of the narrative has often been stressed,[102] and in fact, the fight over Leonidas's corpse clearly recalls the Homeric melee over Patroclus's body.[103] As if the Spartans' deaths reached back beyond hoplitic tradition to reenact the mad exploits of mythical warriors, Herodotus selects his vocabulary for the black death from the Homeric register.[104] More straightforwardly than Tyrtaeus, who when telling of Thermopylae was able to cast new thoughts into epic form, Herodotus borrows the language and concepts of the epic.

It will likely be observed that this abrupt plunge into a distant past is explained by the soldiers' hopeless situation, and it is true that before Ephialtes' betrayal the Spartans conformed to the hoplitic norm. But this hopeless quest for death can be explained in another way. If the situation is exceptional, so is the status of the combatants. They are chosen warriors—*logades*—who will probably be compared to the *hippeis* since they number three hundred,[105] and whether they are viewed as an exceptional elite corps or the royal guard, they seem predestined for death.[106] Elite warriors, the chosen ones are bound by the close solidarity of the military confraternities of old,[107] and whether fighting in the front lines or closing ranks to retreat before the enemy,[108] they represent a bygone period in which the elite corps either is victorious or meets its death. The local history of Arcadia and Boeotia retain the memory of similar annihilations,[109] and for Herodotus this elite vocation is the most clearly displayed in Sparta. In addition to the Three Hundred at Thermopylae, the historian mentions two other groups of three hundred that fell to the last man—those in the high classical period who fought the Messenians at Stenyklaros[110] and those who had earlier confronted three hundred Argives in a pitiless *agōn* over Thyreae.[111] This last episode, although it belongs to legend as much as history, is nonetheless essential, for it shows that the maximalist version of the beautiful death only acquires its full meaning when the combatants are an elite. If the chosen ones were not supposed to follow their companions into death, why would Othyradas, the brave survivor of an *agōn* in which no concessions were made, kill himself on the battlefield, ashamed as a *tresas*?[112] As for the *hippeis*, it is known that they were supposed to die with the king,[113] a rigorous imperative that likewise bears the traces of a knightly past in which all discipline was reduced to the unconditional allegiance of the *kouroi* to the *anax*.[114]

Whatever the case, whether chosen ones or *hippeis*, Leonidas's three hundred Spartans, *promakhoi* doubly isolated from the outposts of the Greek battle,[115] equestrian champions faced with deception and the multitude of barbarian troops, had no other way out than death at Leonidas's side. The curious association, within the same passage, of Leonidas's beautiful hoplitic death with the savagery of the battle fought by his men,[116] is thus made clear. Surrounded by his elite warriors, the king of Sparta revives a heroic past to which the hoplitic precepts are unable to adapt unless pushed to the extreme. This also sheds light on the fate of Aristodamos, who while part of the Three Hundred could not use his inflamed eyes as a reason to escape the fate of the elite soldiers.[117] The texts suggest that in Sparta the beautiful hoplitic death is echoed by the death of the epic warrior. This detail might make it possible to shed more light on the stubborn issue of the *tresantes*; for the requirements of the Spartan city were probably not identical for the chosen ones and the simple *homoioi*. However, the vast majority of texts are too imprecise when it comes to the status of the warriors and the various themes of degradation to make verification of this hypothesis possible.

Therefore, I will stress the symbolic importance of the battle of Thermopylae for the Spartans. By viewing this battle, which was exceptional in so many ways, as the paradigm of Spartan valor, the city probably wished to see itself as heroic, but in so doing, it emphasized all the more the profound complexity of its own military code.

Hoplitic discipline and martial frenzy, the union of the most aristocratic desire for glory with the most developed military technique—such are the paradoxes of Thermopylae. They are also the paradoxes of the Spartan ideal of the beautiful death, officially embodied in the battle of Thermopylae.

In conclusion I will mention an episode that, although it takes place on the sidelines of battle, nonetheless has become celebrated since antiquity. Spying on the Spartans shortly before the two armies clashed, one of Xerxes' envoys sees them combing their long hair. Summoned by the astonished king, Demaratus explains that "such is the custom (*nomos*) in Sparta; when they are about to risk their lives, the men groom their hair."[118] The Spartans probably deck themselves out for battle "as if for a party,"[119] unless they are preparing to be beautiful corpses, in anticipation of the funereal *prothesis*. In this sense, the Spartan *nomos* would be a response to Tyrtaeus's lines about the beauty of the young warrior fallen in the first rank. But further explanation of this unusual attention to personal grooming is necessary. According to Xenophon, who obviously attributes the origin of the practice to Lycurgus, this custom makes them "greater, more noble, and more terrible" (*meizous kai eleutheriōterous kai gorgoterous*),[120] and the Spartan hoplites use these terms to evoke the wild Suevi who, according to Tacitus, arranged their hair to make them "taller and . . . more terrible when they enter battle."[121] Even considering the obscure nature of such information,[122] it is likely that this practice was, if not a rite, at least a magico-religious practice intended to make the warrior frightening. Consequently the Spartan *nomos* must be seen in light of the spectacular qualities of the warriors' deeds and the spellbinding mimicry designed to inspire *Phobos*, panic and terror, in the enemy.[123] This is not surprising. We know that there was a temple to Phobos in Sparta.[124] Of course, in the fifth century, the *nomos* Herodotus describes was probably part of the Spartans' military *kosmos*—one custom among many. Nonetheless, such a practice only acquires its full meaning in the context of the heroic days of the hirsute Achaians[125] or the historico-legendary past, in which the Spartans let their hair grow to celebrate their conquest of Thyreae.[126]

This route has taken us a long way, to the antipodes of the hoplitic order and the pragmatism that presides over Spartan courage. Neither austere discipline nor the Spartan's professionalism must be underestimated. They make up the framework, at once rigid and relatively supple, surrounding the *homoioi*. But it is also true that in the most ostensibly hoplitic of all great Greek cities, the traditional values of the citizen-soldier often poorly conceal a heroic past that the Spartan *kosmos* never completely reduced to silence.

Chapter 4

THE WARRIOR'S FEAR AND TREMBLING

THE INVITATION is irresistible to leave the realm of interpretation and go back to the text itself, to move from Spartan courage to the Homeric code of bravery, for instance, epic *andreia*. But—this comes as a surprise to anyone with overly conventional ideas of heroism—one must yield before the evidence: there is not a single epic warrior who has not trembled on some occasion. This does not mean that he forever merits the title of *tresas*. Of course he quaked with fear. And then, always, in the end he overcame himself, all the stronger because of this instant of terror. Or to put it another way, fear can be transcended, but without fear there is no epic.

There is not a single great warrior who has not one day felt terror quake throughout his whole being, as if fear were the hero's qualifying test.

Already the gigantic Achilles (or rather, the monstrous Achilles, *pelōrios* like Ares, the god of murderous war) advances toward the walls of Troy. He bounds across the plain in a brilliant flash of bronze armor. In front of the Skaian gates, Hector awaits him for a duel unto death. Neither his old father Priam nor his tearful mother Hecuba has been able to weaken the Trojan's determination. A steadfast warrior, "he still remains (*mimnei*), awaiting the approach of the gigantic Achilles." But far from being in the thrall of fear, the hero immobilized in expectation is the bearer of terror, as expressed in a simile, the first in the lengthy dramatic movement that, in book 22 of the *Iliad*, at long last puts Hector and Achilles face to face:

> As a serpent in the mountains, on his hole, awaits a man; he has fed on noxious poisons, an abiding fury deep within him; coiled around his hole he casts a baleful eye about him. So Hector, full of an ardor (*menos*) that nothing can quench, remains without flinching, his gleaming shield leaning against the ledge of the rampart.[1]

This passage merits further examination. The frightened man suddenly catches sight of the mountain snake. But obviously this role does not fall to Achilles. Leaving Hector to his waiting, looking far back to book 3 of the epic, the reader finds that Paris is the wretched warrior beset with terror:

His heart is immediately stricken with fright. . . . Like a man who sees a serpent in a mountain gorge, he quickly draws himself up and moves away; his limbs are overtaken by shivering (*tromos*), and he retreats as his cheeks turn pale; so [Paris] plunges back into the mass of haughty Trojans, gripped with fear before the Atreidai.[2]

Only Paris would be this fearful of a confrontation with Menelaus, who, although his natural enemy, has no martial thunder about him. And Hector has an unfair advantage when it comes to insulting his foppish brother, the shame of the Trojans. Achaians and Trojans alike know that the archer Paris is a coward, almost by profession. His panic is certainly disproportionate to the situation (might Hector's likeness to the snake be intended to convey the archer's misreading of the threat of danger that he believes awaits him? After recalling this passage from book 3, perhaps more than one listener of the *Iliad* thought so).

But Paris, as the designated victim of terror, is not the only soldier battling on the Trojan plain who is frightened. In the *Iliad* no one is exempt from fear, for courage and cowardice are not only a matter of social standing—as Odysseus claims during the assembly in book 2, when he systematically calls kings and known heroes brave and men of the people cowards, especially their spokesman Thersites (whose craven nature is revealed elsewhere, for consistency's sake).[3] As the bearer of an aristocratic ideology of rank and virtue, Odysseus intends to put everyone in the Achaian camp in his place. However, now that order has been restored, it is necessary to close this ideological parenthesis to confront the bald facts: in the *Iliad* fear is more widespread than anything else, and only Zeus escapes it.

The coward, then, is afraid (Paris, Thersites, and Dolon when he confronts Diomedes), but so is the man of valor. To be more precise: so is the bravest of men, as if true courage were revealed in the capacity to experience terror, all the better to vanquish it. And it is the brave especially who are afraid. Such is the case of Diomedes,[4] who—as portrayed in book 5—painfully succumbs to terror, and of Ajax, second "best of the Achaians" to confront Hector[5] (but a few books earlier, Hector shook when he faced Ajax). Is Achilles the only one to sow fear without ever feeling it himself? Yet, to dissuade Menelaus from confronting Hector, King Agamemnon does not flinch from saying that Achilles sometimes quaked before the Trojan hero. Perhaps it is a simple rhetorical variation, but in book 20 Achilles, before filling his opponent with terror, for an instant takes fright at the sight of Aeneas's spear.[6]

There is the fear that each person feels and there is collective panic, which each of the two armies experiences in turn (the Achaians, again before Hector; the Trojans before Diomedes, Ajax, and, of course,

Achilles), when both camps do not succumb to it at once (for example, everyone, Trojans and Achaians alike, shudders at the monstrous cry of the wounded Ares).[7] Even off the battlefield, no relative, however unmartial, is spared fear. The child Astyanax is frightened by his father's helmet, the Lycians dread the voice of their master Sarpedon, and Priam's sons cower before the old king's anger. The gods take pleasure in chilling mortal hearts, whether they come in the guise of friends (as in the case of Aphrodite appearing to Helen, Apollo to Hector, Iris or Hermes to Priam) or meet them as opponents (for example, Ares unsettles Diomedes, and Achilles is stricken with fright before the unleashed Scamander). But everyone quakes before Zeus, even the two goddesses who habitually thwart his designs—Athena, his favorite daughter, and Hera, his irreconcilable wife. And when, in book 24, Achilles, welcoming Priam, the father of the slain foe, "takes the old man's hand in his fist, so that the latter no longer has any fear in his heart,"[8] this brief pause, this truce with fear, can be seen as the finest invention of an epic poem that relentlessly subjects gods and mortals to the power of the same terror.

Everyone in the *Iliad* is afraid, and all types of fear are depicted, including terror's aftershock—for example, Aeneas's reaction after barely escaping Achilles' weapon:

> Aeneas escaped the long pike. He remains there, immense sorrow spreading over his eyes in his fright at the spear lodged so near to him.[9]

Homer is able to pinpoint all the nuances of fear on the warrior's body, including the color green, the sign of terror (the "green fear" of the spy Dolon, who was intercepted by Diomedes at night, or that of the routed Trojans). Doubtless it is the nature of the coward for "his complexion to take on all hues," while the brave man, who moves ever forward to present his chest or belly to enemy spears, can be recognized by the fact that "his complexion does not change color."[10] But there is not a hero who does not shudder at one time or another.

It is a surprising truth of the warrior's universe, where no matter how highly the ideology of valor is prized, it never overshadows the awareness that war and fear are linked: a universe in which nothing is more shameful than trembling (*trein; tromos*, the "shudder," also refers to the "rout")[11] but which has no word to blame the "men caught by panic" (*andrōn tressantōn*) when Zeus strikes terror (*phobon*) among them.[12] Thus when Diomedes is forced to back away because of the all-powerful god's thunder, Hector can hurl the supreme insult at him:

> From this day forward [the Danaans] will despise you, since you have turned into a woman. Disappear, you cowardly plaything . . .[13]

Earlier on, the wise Nestor, the routed hero's companion, has already invalidated this speech ("Hector can call you a laggard or coward; no one among the Trojans will believe it"). The brave man's fear, of sole interest to the poet and what alone moves his audience, is the product of a reflection that has nothing simplistic about it. To be sure, the true remedy for a warrior's fright is still to hold fast (*menein*: what Hector does in book 22, when he is, for the moment, more terrifying than he is terrified; what Odysseus and Ajax each are able to do in turn in book 11). Of course, "he who is truly a hero should stand fast and with all his might either wound or be wounded."[14] But all the same the poet recognizes that sometimes the hero is supposed to retreat:

> Thoas, no man today is to blame, as far as I know: all of us know how to fight. None of us has made a cowardly error, no one has given in to fear when he reveals himself in the midst of cruel combat.[15]

What is said here in the voice of the hero Idomeneus is that there is fear and fear.

There is fear and fear—cowardly fear and the fear that, admitting reality, perhaps will allow the fighter to turn a critical situation around; fear as panic and fear as awareness. The distinction is clearly made, this time in action, regarding the same Idomeneus. The hero plunged into the melee and fought bravely. But Aeneas and Deiphobos advance on him, two of the bravest of the valorous Trojans. "Terror (*phobos*) does not take Idomeneus for all that, like a coddled child. He waits for them (*menei*), like a boar. . . ." But at the same time, he calls for help:

> Come to me, friends; I am alone. Help me. I am terribly afraid (*deidia ainōs*) when faced with Aeneas's attack.[16]

Idomeneus is right to be afraid; younger than he, Aeneas has the strength that brings victory. *Phobos* used to mean "terror," or more exactly, "flight"—terror that has already taken the form of flight. The verb *deidia* (and the substantive *deos*) denotes the fear that one feels because one has been able to analyze the disparity between forces. *Deos* can stimulate the hero; *phobos* annihilates him. For *phobos* is what he must be careful not to feel, at the same time that he provokes it so that it spreads perniciously throughout his opponent's heart and body. Thus *phobos* is of particular interest here.

The terror that is always transformed into flight (examples of *phobos* as the word for "flight" are legion in the *Iliad*),[17] is associated in Greek religious thought with the Gorgon's mask, "fright in its pure state, . . . terror as a dimension of the supernatural, . . . primordial fear."[18] But in the *Iliad* Phobos in person is a god, the son of Ares, and when, in book

13, accompanied by the faithful Merion, Idomeneus—once again—advances toward the battle, there is time for a simile:

> Thus one sees Ares, scourge of men, march into combat, followed by Fright (Phobos), his intrepid and strong son, who makes the most resistant warrior flee (*ephobēse*).[19]

Phobos and the Gorgon adorn the heroes' shields (as well as the serpent, which Hector, coiled as he waits, will resemble). Shields, it is true, are designed to imitate the aegis, the supernatural weapon that Zeus ordinarily concedes to Athena or Apollo and that always provokes immediate retreat (*phobos*) because it is ornamented with frightening figures, including, in prominent places, Phobos and the Gorgon with the tangle of serpents on her head.[20] But transcending mere imitation, the warrior has integrated terror into his essence. The simile of book 13 says it well. Institutionally, he is the *mēstōr phoboio*, master of flight, because, possessed by the *menos* that is warlike fury, he has donned the Gorgon's mask; he himself has become Phobos or Ares. If mediocre fighters— Menelaus and Paris before entering single combat, for example—are frightening once they have resolved to risk their all,

> (their gaze is terrible—*deinon derkomenoi*; [likewise, Hector-the-serpent in book 22][21]—and those who see them are stupefied),[22]

what can be said about heroes? The same that is said about Ajax, bounding, full of fury, to do combat with Hector:

> Thus the monstrous (*pelōrios*) Ares hurls himself. . . . Thus the monstrous Ajax hurls himself. . . . A smile is on his terrifying visage; meanwhile beneath him his feet take great steps, and he brandishes his long javelin. Seeing him, the Achaians feel great joy, while an atrocious terror (*tromos ainos*) creeps into the limbs of all the Trojans. Even Hector feels his heart beating in his breast. But it is too late for him to escape.[23]

But patience: *alloprosallos* Ares is such that the terror endlessly moves from one camp to the other.[24] And now here is Hector, in the following book:

> In his eyes shine the look of the Gorgon and Ares, scourge of mortals.[25]

And lost, the Achaians flee. The warrior strikes terror because *phobos* is in him, muted and terrible, throughout his shining bronze-clad body, in his strength and gaze.[26] To describe this phenomenon in psychological terms would be missing the mark: *phobos* is not a feeling. Or, at least, *phobos* is not only this feeling of terror that paralyzes the petrified opponent but also the demonic power inhabiting the warrior in his state of fury. Or again, transcending the man who embodies it as much as the man who feels it, *phobos* is the bond that links the terrorized to the terrorizer at the very moment of his escape.

But by virtue of the harsh warrior's law of reciprocity, the terrorizer will be terrified,[27] because terror is everywhere in battle, terror that will quickly turn on him. The glittering of bronze, the clatter of weapons, piercing or maddened gazes, unrestrained cries: terror does not come without noise (*iakhē te phobos te*), and who in the melee could assign a place to noise? Like the battle, "equal for all,"[28] that generates clamor and fright, it spares no one on either side—especially those who have unleashed it.

This brings us back to the heroes of each camp who most clearly deserve the title "master of flight": Achilles and Hector.

Hector, then, waits, and around him time stands still, the image of his somewhat ostentatious immobility (which is perhaps what the form of the verb *mimnein* conveys, with its repetition of the pure and simple notion of waiting, which a simple *menein* would have suggested). Whoever sees him—the poet, his listeners, we who are irremediably nothing more than readers—sees the terrible personified. Now, in his heart of hearts, Hector chafes—just like the serpent. But the hero chafes at himself, while the serpent's anger awaited the careless passerby. Hector chafes and "speaks to his magnanimous heart." He says to himself that to escape Achilles he would indeed reenter the Trojan gates; but he will not do it, so as to avoid Polydamas's gaze (the reasonable brother whom he did not heed and who advised him to retreat) and the properly severe judgment of the Trojan men and women (by his folly, they would say, Hector has lost his people). Rather than hear himself be blamed, he would prefer to accept a heroic death in front of the walls of Troy. But Hector also tells himself that he would put his weapons down at the foot of the wall and go to Achilles to propose a treaty that resembles surrender. And in this dialogue between Hector and his heart, his heart, the place where honor resides, responds to the element that wishes to live in the hero:

> If I go to him, am I not to fear that he will have neither pity nor respect for me, that he will kill me, as if I were as naked as a woman?[29]

As naked as a woman: it is unwise to be too quick to apply the anachronistic grid of psychological analysis to these words. As he thinks of the monstrous Achilles, Hector does not identify himself—not yet nor, it will be seen, any longer—with a woman.[30] He simply knows that if he lays down his arms he will be naked—*gumnos*, which is functionally the case for the lightly armed warrior, like the archer Paris whom the combatant with his shield habitually likens to a woman, because war, true

warfare, is not a woman's business. A woman? The mere thought is humiliating enough to ward off all temptations to make a treaty, and he
dismisses it as impossible:

> No, no, this is not the time to go back to the oak and the rocks . . .

(which is to say, to lose himself in the chimerical myths of man's origins,
in which man is not born of men but of rocks and trees); so he banishes
it as utterly out of place:

> This is no time for tender talk between young man and maid—as a young
> man and a maid tenderly chat.

In the hero's strange admonishment to himself, who is the young man
and who is the maiden? Does Hector refer to the debate inside himself
between strength and weakness? Or does he see himself as playing the
role of the *parthenos* opposite Achilles? It is more likely that the emphasis
falls on the verb denoting tender conversation: *oarizein*. *Oar* is the title of
the wife as companion; *oaros* and *oaristus* refer to the intimate conversation of two lovers united by Aphrodite; *oarizein* is the verb designating
close relationship (from companionship to the tender interview between
Hector and Andromache in book 6).[31] All the better to condemn the
temptation of a treaty, the fleetingly dominant reverie of peace once
again restored, to reject all hope in the illusory world of fiction, Hector
accuses himself of not knowing that warriors engaged in single combat
are not flirting. But was he as mistaken as he wished to believe? For on
two occasions the language of the *Iliad* refers to battle unto death as a
"rendezvous": the rendezvous of war or of champions (*oaristus polemou,
promakhōn*), to which the heroes "avidly hurl themselves"[32]—amo-
rously?—more avidly, perhaps, than they would approach a romantic
meeting. Now Hector readies himself for such a rendezvous, murderous
but intimate (of the intimacy between two heroes, born out of the long-
ripening hatred fueled by repeated confrontations between equals).[33]

And still the defender of Troy remains motionless. He dreams but
waits.[34] If this "feminine" temptation did occur, the hero named it all the
better to banish it.

But Achilles approaches, and Hector is afraid. Achilles advances, the
paradigm of the strong warrior blazing like fire throughout Indo-European representations of combat. Like Enualios (another name for Ares),
he bursts forth like a flame in a terrifying glitter of bronze.[35]

> And Hector, as soon as he sees him [more precisely, the moment that he is
> aware of him (*enoēsen*)] is overtaken by the desire to flee. He no longer has
> the endurance to remain where he is; . . . he departs and takes flight (*pho-
> bētheis*); and the son of Peleus hurls himself forward, sure of his agile feet.

A simile immediately transforms Achilles into the falcon of the mountains and the fleeing (*trese*) Hector into the timid dove. Such is the overpowering nature of *phobos* that the furious serpent is transformed into the fluttering dove, in other texts the symbol of frightened femininity. Hector flees, Achilles at his heels, and in the meantime, in the memory of long ago days of peace, he sees the springs of the Scamander where the Trojan women and maidens once used to wash brilliant garments.[36] And already the images of the past are far away.

> They rush past, one fleeing, the other, behind, in pursuit. Out in front a brave man flees, but braver still is the one who pursues him with all his might.[37]

The blurred quality of *phobos*: it is as if "a same demonic power of terror encompassed them both, bonding them together."[38] It is as if the terrifying Achilles and the terrified Hector have become a single blur, which is expressed by the dual, the verbal marker that makes two into only one (*paradrametēn*). The two heroes vie for speed. But no mortal has ever dreamed of interpreting this rivalry in agonistic terms. Why does the text specify that they are not fighting for the prize of a contest (*athlon*)[39] but for Hector's life (death)—Hector the former tamer of wild horses, now a racehorse himself running at full tilt? Because this race lacking a stadium, for which there are no rows of seats, has its spectators: the immortal gods whose vision of this human, all-too-human drama had made us forget their existence but who nevertheless are there when men put their lives on the line. Together they watch the heroes making their three circuits of Troy.

Time for a change of scene: on Olympus a few words are exchanged between Zeus, who would like to save the Trojan hero, as he has consistently done up to this point, and Athena who, faithful to her own ends, desires his defeat and the triumph of the Achaian champion. This time Zeus yields, and already Athena has left the gods' abode for the Trojan plain, which Achilles and Hector are rounding for the fourth time.

And the pursuit continues. A new simile suggests how relentless it is:

> Like a dog in the mountains that follows over hill and dale the fawn of a doe that he has flushed from cover. The fawn, out of sight, has crouched under a bush; the dog runs about, sniffing it out until he has found it. So Hector does not succeed in escaping the swift eye of the son of Peleus.[40]

The comparison invites commentary, for in its apparent banality it has much to say about the drama enacted before Troy. It says that in this infinite race in which the two heroes proceed at the same pace, Achilles is the virtual winner because of his fierce determination. It says still more by superposing the mountain and the race on the plains. The site of the

serpent's den and earlier that of the falcon, the mountain is the realm of
the hunter and the place where the wild ephebe takes his exercise (the
young man, the warrior of the future, who in Crete goes by the name of
dromeus, runner).[41] However, compared to a cornered fawn, Hector resembles less the mountain ephebe than the animal offspring, the tender
and unarmed prey that young men enjoy tracking with their hounds. A
fawn flushed from its mother's lair: the hero has forgotten that the warrior is forbidden to hide,[42] and this hero most of all. More lucid, Achilles
had announced at the end of book 20 that from then on the confrontation between Hector and himself would be without mercy ("On the
whole battlefield let us no longer shrink from one another," he cried).[43]
And Achilles, in this race transformed into a hunt, is indeed the dog, but
he already resembled a dog when he appeared in his monstrous beauty at
the beginning of book 22—the celestial dog paired with Orion.[44] Soon
he will be able to hand the body of his enemy over to the dogs that
devour the corpses.

For the moment Hector flees, desperately, and despite his momentum
Achilles does not catch up:

> Just as a man in a dream is unable to pursue one who has fled, and the latter
> in turn cannot flee without the other in pursuit, so on that day no sooner
> does Achilles reach Hector in the race than Hector escapes him.[45]

An immobile race with an impossible outcome? It simply appears this
way. Homer is no Eleatic philosopher, and in the *Iliad* Achilles, who is
the essence of swiftness,[46] must catch up with Hector. If he has not already done so, the reason is that, for the fourth and final pursuit around
Troy, Apollo, not far from his protégé, has endowed the Trojan with
strength. But as Zeus decides against Hector, he disturbs this fallacious
equilibrium, and Apollo withdraws, leaving the field to Athena. It is she,
in form of the arm of the Achaian champion, who will tame Hector—as
Achilles will soon announce to his opponent (but in this epic world of
war where man, in face-to-face encounter with the enemy, is both absolutely alone and given over to the gods, it is Ares—through Achilles,
beyond Athena—who will strike the final blow against the hero).[47]
Achilles again reminds Hector of this:

> One of us, in succumbing, must satisfy Ares the enduring warrior with his
> blood.

Athena, then, advances toward Achilles; with words that promise
glory, she invites him to catch his breath. He stops and waits, while the
goddess, proceeding toward Hector, is set to convince him to make a
stand at last. So great is the power of *phobos* over the brave that the
intervention of a divinity, in whom deception serves the cause of war

(the *mētis* to carve up the monstrous strength of fear), is required to keep him from fleeing. For reminding the hero overwhelmed with fear of his bravery amounts to deceiving him. In her astuteness Athena works for a gain (*kerdosunē*) that is Achilles' victory. A mistress of disguises, she has taken the figure of Deiphobos, the hero's beloved brother, and Hector does not suspect the trick. There he is, entrapped in his bravery, and the gambit in which he stakes his life is the final episode of this long scene. Full of gratitude toward the unexpected ally who has not, like the others, remained trembling behind the ramparts, he believes that he can face his opponent, now that he is not alone and his double, with the name full of *phobos*,[48] marches at his side. "Let us fight with fury," says Athena-Deiphobos, who awakens Hector's *menos*.

> And, perfidiously, she shows him the way. They march toward one another and make contact.

That is the end of Hector's fear, and his greatness will be that, brought back to himself by a divinity's ruse, he is able to rise above himself even as he spots the trap. But let us return to the long-deferred confrontation. Before engaging in combat, the Homeric warrior always addresses his opponent, and generally his words foretell his acts, for he intends to instill *phobos* in the other.[49] The first to speak, Hector refers instead to the past in order to recognize, before Achilles, that he gave in to panic, that three times he fled around the walls because he dared not await (*meinai*) the Greek hero's attack. But he also announces that this is the end of it ("This time, on the contrary, my heart impels me to hold fast before you. I will have you or you will have me"). Everything is in order, then, except that Achilles, in his hatred for Patroclus's killer, refuses beforehand to follow the Greek code of war, which requires that the body of a warrior who has fallen before the ranks be handed over to his kin. And Achilles' exhortation to courage, made as he hurls his javelin, has a sinister ring:

> Remember all your bravery, then. For it is indeed now, if ever, that you must be a fighter, an intrepid warrior. There is no more refuge for you now.

But the blow misses the Trojan hero, offering Hector the occasion to respond in word and deed. Throwing his javelin in turn, he repeats the story of his renewed courage—if his flight had been forgetfulness, his endurance is memory, in the proper meaning of the word: a new encounter with himself, self-possession when brought face-to-face with himself.

> It was your desire that I, overcome by fear, forget my flight and my valor. No, you will not plant your pike in the back of a man fleeing from you. I am walking right into you; drive it straight into my breast.[50]

Athena has already returned Achilles' weapon to him; Hector's javelin, thrown far away when it struck his opponent's shield, is lost. It is time for Hector to turn to the false Deiphobos, who has obviously disappeared, and the hero recognizes Athena's treachery and the death that awaits him. What matters now is that Hector feels not a trace of fear; still, to express his heroic resolution not "to die without a struggle or glory, nor without some high deed, the tale of which will be made known to men to come," one last simile using animal imagery appears, carried by the very momentum of the text:

> He speaks, and draws the sharp sword hanging at his side, the sharp strong blade. Then, drawing himself up, he takes off, like the high-flying eagle that flies toward the plain, across the dark clouds, to swoop down upon a tender lamb or a hare in its burrow, so does Hector swoop, waving his sharp sword.[51]

This is not the least remarkable of the four similes that have measured out the final moments of the hero's life. Like the first of these, in which he was a serpent, this one gives him the initiative (in the other two, as dove or fawn, he was pursued by Achilles). But that is not all. Here Hector is compared to the royal bird, the emblem of Zeus. And this high-flying bird is headed—at last—toward the plain, where the hero's destiny will be accomplished. One can always imagine that he comes from the mountains, but nothing in the text alludes to this: the site of the ambush and hunt has vanished, and what remains is the arena of loyal confrontation (and, to return to the first of the four comparisons, it is now clear how, upon seeing Achilles a moment ago, Hector could not help but feel fear: likened to the serpent coiled on his hole, he was ready for a war of ambush, and in no case a face-to-face confrontation). Better yet, Hector the eagle takes flight to seize its prey—a tender she-lamb or hare in its burrow in which the feminine elements intensify the sense of weakness. Nothing could better say that Hector, formerly a fawn in its lair, has reversed the situation. But he has turned it around for himself alone: the fact that he is no longer afraid does not mean that he makes others afraid, and Achilles, whose lance will soon be compared to the evening star, is not the hare, any more than he was the man of the first simile. The inexact nature of the present analogy quickly becomes apparent: clearly it is no accident that when the Trojan hero has the initiative, the image skirts the reality of the relationship between forces; it is a way of indicating that the Trojan's efforts are doomed from the start. However, there is another way to view this disparity, by crediting the poet with the intention of giving Hector, on the level of words and fiction, the imaginary revenge of victory (just as he gave to this king's son who will never reign the royalty of an eagle; in book 17 Menelaus, himself a king, is more appropriately compared to the eagle who swoops down on the hare).

Once again let Hector spring:

> Like the high-flying eagle, who goes to the plain, across the dark clouds . . . , so Hector hurls himself forward, moving his sharp blade. Achilles too leaps, his heart fills with a savage ardor (*meneos agriou*).

For Hector the worst has arrived. The eagle has reached the plain, but the savagery is completely on Achilles' side. Then, perhaps, before abandoning the hero to his loss, there is time to note a detail in this simile that has been neglected until now: the dark clouds (*nepheōn erebennōn*) that the eagle crosses. Zeus is the king of the clouds, just like his emblematic bird, and this detail would have nothing remarkable about it if the clouds, the color of darkness, the color of Hades, did not portend death, which for the warrior often takes the form of shade, even a dark cloud.[52] Soon Erebos's cloud will envelop Hector.

With the description of Achilles in his *menos*, shining in his glistening weapons, everything is said. Only the trajectory of his javelin will hold our attention, and we will never know what became of Hector's soaring and the sharp blade he brandished that will not wound his adversary (we learn only that he was full of ardor at the moment that Achilles' weapon touched him). Achilles drives his pike into Hector's body, "there where life can be most quickly destroyed," and finishes off the dying man with words, speaking again of the outrageous treatment that he has reserved for the enemy's corpse thrown to the dogs. Hector begs, then gives up and predicts that Achilles will suffer a similar fate before the Skaian gates. And his tearful soul leaves his body and departs for Hades.

Let us leave the Achaians to toil over this lifeless corpse, which they find "truly softer to the touch" than the body that had so frightened them not long ago. The time will come when Achilles, who dreamed of cutting up Hector's body to eat it raw, must return the dead man to the Trojans to bury it. Then he will take Priam's hand so that the old man will no longer be afraid.

It is time to stop, however great the pleasure of rereading the *Iliad*. I have reflected on it at some length, in hopes of conveying, in addition to the perfection of the poet's artistry, the firmness of Homeric thought, unmarred by any concessions or delicacy and far from any edifying intent or pedagogical aim. Without a doubt the bard's Greek audience rejoiced at Achilles' victory for the Greeks; but they must also have been able to understand that Hector was afraid, and to suspend judgment. Then they would know that the hero lost nothing of his heroism, even if his opponent simultaneously gained an additional measure. The most attentive of listeners, perhaps, would then recall Agamemnon's statement that Achilles also trembled before Hector. The warrior's vicissitudes: one day

fear will overtake him. Weakness crouches at the heart of strength, awaiting its moment, and the hero's peers will be able to gauge his bravery by
the extent of his trembling.

But still it is necessary to leave Homer.

It is not certain whether the Greek cities of the classical period, where
the *Iliad* was used to educate the young, truly wished to hear this strong
lesson about weakness. Lyric poets, perhaps, knew how to bear it in
mind, although they made more of weakness than strength. For example,
Bacchylides alters the Homeric vulgate, making the mighty Herakles feel
sudden terror when he descends into Hades, before the shade of
Meleager, whose bright weapons still gleam (in the *Odyssey* it is Herakles'
shade that terrifies the dead, who fly off like birds amid tumult and
shouting).[53] But by the time Bacchylides is writing his poetry, tragedy is
the dominant form, and fear, because perhaps it is more ambivalent than
ambiguous, has no real place in tragedy (except at the side, which is
finally overcome, of the past or barbarianism: the Gorgonesque faces of
the Erinyes, terrifying the spectator; savage warriors evoked from a distance, like the Seven chiefs who, against Thebes, call upon Phobos—the
city knows that it will triumph over all these terrors). And the civic attitude toward war chooses only one side of the twofold nature of Homeric
discourse (the warrior frightens/the warrior is afraid), retaining for its
citizen soldiers only the fighter's intrepid nature; fear, which has obviously been rejected and given to the other side, belongs to the enemy.
This is the case in Selinus, where, among the gods receiving thanks after
a victory—right after Zeus, right before Herakles—we hear of the god
whom Homer called the intrepid son of Ares: Phobos, who has lent a
hand to the citizens in their struggle against the enemy.[54] This is above all
the case in Sparta, where Phobos has his temple,[55] where the army
charges to the disquieting sound of the flute,[56] where elite fighters going
to meet their deaths comb their long hair to appear more beautiful and
more terrifying to the enemy. But the "trembling one" with the Homeric
name (*tresas*) is banished by society, and no *menos* can rid him of the
opprobrium of having one day fled from danger, since warlike fury is
also henceforth proscribed as out of place.[57] The Athenians wish to hear
of nothing but courage, and fear, this undesirable word, has disappeared
from the official phraseology of war (at most they accept its appearance
when their ancestors faced exceptional adversaries, in mythical times
when Theseus made a sacrifice to Phobos to attract him to his camp
against the Amazons, the daughters of Ares).[58] Leaving this civic modesty
far behind, Alexander will not hesitate to offer the nocturnal mystery of a
sacrifice to Phobos in his own name,[59] but like the people of Selinus, his
intention is for the enemy to be crippled by fear. Who ever heard it said
that Alexander was afraid?[60]

Chapter 5

THE WOUNDS OF VIRILITY

MOST DEFINITELY, Greek images of the heroic weakness of strength are found outside the orthodox *logos* of the city.

I am already convinced that epic is the privileged site for investigating the multifaceted nature of the model of what constitutes the masculine. There are many reasons for this; there the *anēr*'s body is living flesh, perceived in its animate materiality, not the pure abstraction conjured up in official speeches, in which *sōma* refers to the life that the citizen must expend because his body is only a loan from the city.

For instance, then, in war—when it is neither beautiful nor monstrous but simply war—the male body, toughened and vulnerable at the same time.

Virility, as expressed by what can be seen on the male's opened body, as if the warrior's wounds speak for the quality of the citizen. At least this would have been the current definition, according to the Greek Plutarch in his account of the life of Coriolanus, in the early days of the Roman republic. Coriolanus, then, currying favor with the consulate [14.2]:

> At that time it was the custom for candidates for the consulate to go down to the forum in a cloak, without a tunic, to solicit and greet the citizens, either to lower themselves further by this dress, which was suitable to their undertaking, or to display to the eyes of all, when they bore scars, the proofs of their valor (*sumbola tēs andreias*).

More than once in Roman history, scars were used as proof, notably during trials: Latin authors called them *cicatrices ostendere*.[1] But in this instance, the evidence of a man's wounds is an institutional way of defining the politician. The practice is a Roman one,[2] even though Plutarch provides the only positive information about it, which is in Greek. The scars of the candidate for the consul are *sumbola tēs andreias*. *Sumbolon* is the word for a sign of recognition, half of which is matched with the remainder to form a whole (just as the warrior's bravery awaits its translation into political form). The word for "courage" as it is identified with manhood, *andreia* in Greek, refers to the quality of the *anēr*, the male, who is indissolubly citizen and soldier—Roman facts couched in Greek words. But it is also true that the Greek translation of Roman deeds has more to say to the Greeks.[3] Indeed, it is probably no accident that Plutarch confines his discussion of this old custom to Coriolanus. The patrician's rigorously martial nature might compel the servant of Mars to endure the fortune and misfortune that are the warrior's destiny. And even more than *vir*, the Latin word for the male, the Greek *anēr* expresses total fidelity to the Indo-European vocabulary referring to the second function—that of the warrior—which denotes "man considered in terms of his heroic disposition."[4]

From wounds as signs of manhood to scars as the marks of the politician. Or, in other words, if politics has tempered the excesses of the warrior function in the Roman city, it is up to the soldier to be a better citizen than the others. During the heroic days when valor prevailed in the republic and, ideally, birth alone was insufficient to confer supreme magistracy, it was necessary for a man to display visible signs of manliness on his person. While he wears neither belt nor tunic (*azōstos, akhitōn*), the consular candidate certainly does not deserve the name of *gumnos* ("naked") that the Greek language reserves for the fighter of the second rank, since hidden beneath his cloak but soon to be revealed to the eyes of all, he bears his wounds. The lofty deeds inscribed in his torn flesh clothe him in bravery.[5]

Much could be learned by comparing Plutarch's Coriolanus (who readily complies with the custom and whose scarred body would have convinced the people had his patrician arrogance not undone him) with Shakespeare's Coriolanus, equally marked but who refuses the test because he loathes the idea of the plebeians "put[ting] their tongues into his wounds." Deviating from a value system in which bloodshed means honor, the behavior of the Shakespearean hero would then perhaps reveal his highly ambivalent relationship to manhood.[6] However, it is not the Roman Coriolanus who interests me here—or Plutarch's or Shakespeare's hero—but his wounds. Or, more exactly, far from Rome and Plutarch, what interests me is the wound as an inscription of manhood, and what becomes of it once this Roman question has been shifted to the perspective of Greek representations of *andreia*.

A CIVIC SILENCE

Wounds cause the body to speak. Is this why the classical Greeks, who put so little trust in the body, speak so little of the wounded? In Athens this silence that bespeaks denial is not unfounded. Since there *andreia* is associated with death in war, official eloquence devotes itself to ignoring those who have survived instead of abandoning their bodies and lives for the greater glory of the city. But while they are less radical than Athens in matters of *andreia*, other Greek cities of the classical period[7] have provided no more information about the consideration given the wounded, probably because they and their wounds were of little interest.[8]

Such an attitude can be seen in the histories of Herodotus, in which only the Athenian definition of *andreia* as the beautiful death applies on the Greek side. The Spartan Leonidas will earn a laudatory mention because he fell at Thermopylae, "revealing himself to be a man of the greatest bravery." What makes a man is his death, which erases the body and inspires the encomium. Thus Herodotus says very little about the wounded, except to note that they were able to prevail over their wounds. For example, at the battle of Plataea, the Greeks dashed the barbarians' hopes that the men riddled with wounds would offer no resistance, and "lined up and grouped by cities, [they] took turns sustaining the battle." So doing, they undoubtedly saved their strength, but one will observe, if one pauses at the words of the account, that "took turns" translates the expression *en merei*, which democratic Athens has assigned the function of characterizing the rotation of duties within the city. The Greeks respond politically to the barbarians, who counted on the growing weakness of Greek bodies. In reading the edifying history of Pytheas of Aegina, it even seems that Greek wounds are signs of *andreia* only when beheld by a foreigner. In this case the onlooker is Persian: aboard his ship, which was captured by the enemy, Pytheas fought until he was "mangled with blows throughout his whole body." He fell and perhaps would have died if Greeks and not Persians had surrounded him. But it happens that the Persians, who march into battle under threat of the lash, admired him and took care of him. The Greeks find him alive when they in turn capture the Sidonian ship that transported him.[9] I would willingly wager that for a fifth-century Greek, valor has no need of being written on the body.[10]

It is true that as an ideological model the "beautiful" war, which is waged against enemies from outside, has nothing to do with broken bodies (or bodies at all, perhaps). Long live the living and the glorious dead! Not surprisingly, it is in the historians' accounts of the most hideous of wars, the *stasis* that pits citizens against one another, that mention is made of wounded, even mutilated or tortured bodies. For the observer, the wounds are horrible because citizens have inflicted them on other citizens.

Thus, only in the political arena—or in the arena controlled by politics—does the paradigm of abstract virility emerge in full institutional form. One "becomes a man" by enrolling one's name on the registry of the deme, but one becomes "a man of valor" by giving one's life to the city; and then one exchanges one's body for the glory of which the city is the guardian.

But by limiting this inquiry to official representations, one fails to recognize that the Greeks, even in the high classical period, knew better than anyone else how problematic virility was. Some discourses are revealing, such as tragedy, which highlight ambiguity. And above all there is the voice of a distant past, present in the memory of the citizens who tirelessly repeat, invoke, and reinterpret it: the tradition of epic, in which heroes are manly because they have known suffering, in which the warrior's body is exposed to all manner of wounds.

Wounds Given, Wounds Received

In the *Iliad* the authentic warrior is the fighter who in one blow is able to tear open his enemy's armor and stab him in the breast. However, because hard battles are not fought without occasional bloodshed, there is not a male body that is not destined sooner or later to suffer the painful gash of a blade cutting into flesh. Or to use Pindar's words, "Whoever strikes a blow receives a blow; that is the rule."[11] One god in the epic embodies the inexorable law of reversibility governing warfare, even in the form of his vulnerable body: I mean Ares. Omnipresent on the battlefield where men are falling, the "ultimate terror" whose spear finishes off dying heroes, the furious Ares is the monstrous god whom the fighters appease with their blood. But as if a law decreed that the murderous melee must turn against the one who rules it, as if the secret destiny of the divine slayer foreordained that one day he would "lie with the dead, in the blood and dust," Ares seems fated to undergo the trial of the law, which he embodies, in the suffering of his gashed body. For more than once in epic, the god of war is wounded by a mortal.[12] It is true that only Athena's protégés, such as Diomedes and Herakles, attack him, so that the initiative for the blow ultimately redounds to the goddess, who is the only one able to wound him. A great deal could be said about these repeated confrontations, which unfailingly end with the crafty goddess-warrior's victory over the murderous god. The vulnerability of the brutal Ares could be contrasted with the "magical" invulnerability of the goddess, she who is never wounded nor indeed ever the target of a mortal weapon.[13] Perhaps then, returning to the classical city that honors Athena and tends to evict Ares, one might better understand why the goddess reigns uncontested over the "beautiful" war. Thus, to illustrate the reversals of war, I prefer the hero Ajax to the god Ares: Ajax *arēios*, the powerful warrior whose strong shield evokes that of the divine Killer.

We know how one day the Achaians chose Odysseus over Ajax, who was considered by Homer to be the "best" after Achilles, and how, overcome by the mad hatred, the hero killed himself. Let Pindar comment on this dark episode:

However these were not the same wounds that they had opened in the warm flesh of the enemy, whose fearsome spears dealt them repeated blows, around the bloody corpse of Achilles or on so many other days of murderous combat.

The enemy's warm flesh . . . the expression was certainly shocking, and from the scholiasts onward, more than one reader set about to weaken its raw power. However, it is better to stay with the text: perhaps wounds are warm, but above all, when the blade plunges deep, the flesh of the virile man is warm, as warm as the bodies of women are cool.[14] The slashed corpse of the enemy, the torn body of the hero: the law of exchange in war claims that one prefigures the other. Ajax has just died, opening his ardent body upon the blade that has so often dug into enemy flesh. The moment has come to recall both his valor and the changing fortunes of war.

A worthy second to Achilles, whose body seems impervious to the blows glancing off of it without a trace, Ajax moved unwounded through the *Iliad*, and his courage made one believe that his body was invulnerable.[15] But the day comes when the warrior's untouched body is opened once and for all to death: aided by Apollo, Paris killed Achilles, and Ajax, throwing himself onto the sword that Hector had once given to him, now impales himself on an enemy blade. Thus, the exchange of death covertly presides over the hero's solitary end, and perhaps it is for this reason—because he dies as a man beneath the deferred blows of another man[16]—that his suicide cannot feminize the warrior.

Pindar was moved by the death of Ajax to evoke his ardent valor in the midst of the bloody fray, and likewise Sophocles will construct his *Ajax* around the reversals of warlike strength that take the blood of the one who sheds the blood of others.[17] But, it has been said, Ajax is only a second Achilles, and Pindar and Sophocles conjure up their version of the hero in vivid relationship to the Homeric figure of the warrior. There is no point in further postponing the questions raised by the *Iliad* concerning the epic value of the slashed body.

VULNERABLE, INVULNERABLE—VIRILE

It is time to take a direct look at the ambivalent attitudes about the virile body. In the *Iliad* they are profound and unsparing.

In the beginning, however, everything is perfectly clear. Lovers of *realia* delight in reading Homer, not knowing which to praise the most, the clinical precision of the descriptions or the attention paid, "for the first time in history," to the transport and treatment of the wounded.[18] But the evidence must not be ignored: when it is a matter of wounded bodies, overdetermination is at its height, and several levels of meaning are inextricably intertwined.

One is no less a man for being a hero, and this means that one is mortal, in other words, vulnerable, since a man's mortality is suggested by the expressions that he "eats Demeter's bread" or "his body can be torn by bronze and stones." Of course, the Homeric epic would like to say, as Pindar will dare to do, that "the children of the gods are invulnerable," but there is not a fighting man in all the *Iliad* who does not know that even Achilles has "like the others a skin that an iron blade can gash and a life like that of others."[19] Vulnerable the man, then, and vulnerable the hero, who is sheltered for a while by a god's protection from blows that tear the flesh. But there is no mortal born who can completely avoid combat. Or rather this man is a dream, a necessary fiction that serves all the better to express the ardor of battle:

> Then he would no longer have anything to criticize in the action, the man as yet unwounded or untouched by the sharp bronze, who would arrive at this moment and move through the pitched battle, whom Pallas Athena would take by the hand and lead, deflecting the rush of arrows. On that day Trojans and Achaians by the hundreds were laid out side by side, face down in the dust.[20]

Is man vulnerable because he is human? Of course, that is part of it, but there is not enough evidence in Homer to make this notion into a theory, or even a fine table of binary oppositions. For, let it be recalled, the body of the god is also vulnerable—some gods, at least, almost all of them in fact, something that in early Christian days will scandalize Clement of Alexandria, who was quick to see the gods' wounds as a sign of pagan error.[21] Here they are, mortal men and immortal gods, all in the same boat. It is impossible to persist in making vulnerability and mortality a unified pair. A different tack is necessary: for example, to start off by noting that all the great heroes of the *Iliad* suffer from a wound at least once.

All the heroes, or almost, except, it has been said, Achilles and Ajax. The *Iliad* never claims that they are invulnerable, but when they are in a fury, arrows and javelins seem to fly by without ever touching their bodies, or at least if they penetrate their flesh, they do not sap their fighting strength. Unbounded fury is the warrior's surest protection.[22] This is how one must understand the passage in book 21, in which Achilles, wounded in the forearm, continues to slay the Trojan foes as if nothing had happened (in any event, one will be wary of realistic readings such as that given by Daremberg, who gravely concludes that wounds to the thoracic limbs are sometimes benign). Another remarkable exception—this time in the *Odyssey*—Neoptolemus, the son of

Achilles, who after the sack of Troy heads home: "without a scratch, whether from the blows of sharp weapons or the wounds of hand-to-hand combat, he had escaped the blind surprises that Ares' fury sows in battle." But contrary to all expectations, the *Odyssey* is more demanding of the hero than the *Iliad*, where he is at least permitted to weep. Indeed, Neoptolemus did not cry for an instant.[23] Let us close the chapter on exceptions and return to the *Iliad*. The evidence is clear: all the great heroes—and Achilles himself—are, one day or the other, more or less seriously wounded. There are even entire books (book 4, book 11) that seem to be devoted to lists of the wounded.

Should one then boldly conclude that wounds are eminent signs of *andreia*? It is worth taking the time beforehand to note that if this is indeed the case, it is true indirectly, because of the narrative requirements of the epic. I will explain. It is not enough to say that all the great heroes are wounded; one must add that they are only wounded, or again, that to be wounded and only wounded is a privilege reserved only for heroes. Arrows, which as they fly kill the humble foot soldier, miss great warriors (and kill others, who are less well known, instead). But it happens nonetheless—because Ares would be untrue to his nature if he did not make the blood flow—that a hero is struck. He has been wounded; within the limits imposed by the epic, verisimilitude has been maintained. In book 11 (384–95) Diomedes, who has been wounded only in the foot by an arrow shot by Paris, wishes to see this "only" as proof that his opponent is not of his stature. Paris is an archer, and Diomedes contrasts the "scratches" his arrows make to the formidable blows dealt by a great warrior—"they make one a dead man right away." It is certainly not to be denied that the archer is a fighter of poor repute, and Diomedes has the ideology of the epic on his side, where the worth of the blow is equal to the man who has dealt it. But what Diomedes does not know, cannot know, is that like Agamemnon, like Odysseus, like Menelaus, like Achilles himself, he is protected by his status as agent of the epic narrative: how can Achilles be killed in the middle of the *Iliad*? The hero does not die because he cannot, unless Zeus—or the poet—decides it. Then Sarpedon falls, Patroclus dies, while the day will come when Achilles will kill Hector, when Paris, outside the scope of the narrative, will kill Achilles. In the meantime, all the other heroes are wounded once.

Does this mean nonetheless that wounds are always substitutes for death? Does considering wounds as small deaths offer a sufficient measure of their full significance? That would certainly be underestimating the complexity of the epic strategy. Yet another point of departure must be attempted. It lies in the tension within Homeric *andreia*, between conflicting values accorded to wounds: the first is apparently negative (to be wounded is truly inglorious), while the second is, ultimately, positive (because it is painful, the wound exalts the warrior's courage) and perhaps even totally positive (clearly, not just anyone is wounded).

In some episodes it seems that being wounded has nothing glorious about it: it is proof that one did not stand fast before the enemy or was not swift enough to make the first strike.[24] Then the narcissistic wound magnifies the body's sufferings, and the diminished hero will go so far as to abandon his position to escape the enemy's gaze. Such was the fate of the Lycian Glaukos, struck in the arm by an arrow:

> Glaukos jumped back from the top of the wall without being seen. He does not wish for one of the Achaians to see him wounded and go off rejoicing.[25]

So Glaukos is hit by an arrow, and he has no more desire than a Diomedes or Odysseus struck by an archer's point to witness the noisy triumph of a fighter from the second rank. Is that what provokes his hasty retreat? However, Glaukos has nothing to blush about over a wound that—the rest of the narrative confirms it—is as rough as Ares himself and, like Ares, painful,[26] unless the Lycian chief is particularly sensitive about his honor because he was visible when the arrow put him out of action. For there are many other heroes whose pains, even when caused by an arrow, have no other function than to offer stirring proof of the endurance by which the true warrior can be recognized. Thus, in book 11, where one after the other the great heroes are struck, it will simply be said, on the subject of the valiant Eurypylos, whom Patroclus finds hit in the thigh with an arrow and who looses black blood from his painful wound, that "his heart remains firm nonetheless."

And so here, far from being the source of disgrace, the wound becomes the most efficacious proof of the hero's virility. It could even be that it is simply glorious, if not to be wounded, then to have one's body assaulted by the penetrating, searing, sharp pain known as *odunē*. This happens to heroes who count—Menelaus in book 4, Agamemnon and Diomedes in book 11—and as if relating a crucial event, the pace of the narrative slows, and courage is likened to endurance.[27] Through this bodily suffering, the battle has moved inside the warrior, who is all the more valorous because he has met danger in the very recesses of his being. This sheds some light on the Homeric fighter's vulnerability: he is close to invulnerable when he surpasses himself in mighty deeds, but with an open gash in his body, he is destined to be seen for what he is, a great hero.

Wounds: a validation of manliness; a way, perhaps as well, for the warrior to relate to the other (to this other warm flesh) as to another self, by means of his knowledge of his body and its danger zones, the precision of which has not failed to draw the attention of readers.[28] Because he feels the threat weighing on his own person, the hero can recognize the "good spots" on his foe's body, where one blow is enough to kill or, when desired, simply wound. But let there be no mistake: this knowledge of the gashed body is not realistic in a clinical sense. Instead, from one book to the next, the poet of the *Iliad* proceeds to create a symbolic cartography of the manly body.

For the manly body is a body to be opened—according to the rules.

The Opened Body

When a man's body is opened, it is—by definition, it seems, in Homer—a living body (the attraction of combat lies in the fact that the fighter risks his life at every turn, and warriors flock to battle as if to a "rendezvous"[29] beyond the lines). Of course, once the hero has been killed, it is necessary to subject his body to a treatment that completely "closes" it to make it a beautiful corpse. In the case of Hector, the gods themselves will oversee this process, and despite the cruelties that Achilles inflicted on his enemy's corpse, Hermes can proudly announce to Priam that his son "is there, completely fresh, . . . all his wounds closed, all that he received—and how many warriors drove their bronze into his body!"[30] But it is the living who interest me here, those whose bodies are to be opened in battle.

In the universe of the epic, the wounded body has been penetrated, cut, or torn. It is always penetrated: weapons lodge in flesh, and with its frequent use of the verb *pēgnumi*, the epic seems to take pleasure in plumbing the depths of the male body. But first and foremost, the warrior's body is to be cut and torn. The verb *temnō* and its derivatives convey images of cutting and carving: pikes are "flesh carvers," and when two men valiant above all, two disciples of Ares, advance toward each other, they "burn to carve up each other's flesh with the implacable bronze."[31] While on a purely descriptive level, tearing may be designated with the verb *diaskhizō*, this is purely an exception, and the language of the *Iliad* greatly prefers the verbs *dēioō* and *daizō*, which are certainly more expressive because they convey the essence of the bloody ritual of warfare. To tear is of course to rip open the breastplate and the flesh lying beneath it; it is also—for most often it is an act involving many people—to massacre; last, it can also refer to the act of the sacrificer, and with Achilles as the subject, the same verb denotes the mangling of Hector's body and the slaughter of the twelve young Trojans on Patroclus's funeral pyre.[32] Etymologically, it is true, the distribution accompanying a sacrifice (*dateomai*) is not far away, and indeed an anomalous division threatens the body of the warrior who has fallen to earth, "torn apart" by the chariot wheels passing over him or whose lifeless flesh will be "divided" by the dogs and birds.[33] These instances of *temnō* make it immediately clear that the vocabulary for sacrificial carving and the cutting and gashing of male bodies is the same—Homer invites such an observation, with his explicit comparisons between the warrior's death and the slaughter of a sacrificed ox.[34]

In short, sacrifice mingles with warfare, with what could be more exactly termed the implacable game that pits warrior against warrior, driving him to cut into his enemy's live flesh. It is a formidable statement, and an awkward one as well. The historian of Greece would like to keep the peace, altering it to preserve the watertight seal on the canonical boundary separating sacrificial rites and the regulated order of battle within the model of the city that he has constructed. And indeed, the classical city seems to support the historian's reservations; its official prose makes no mention of connections between war and sacrifice, as if the suppression of this dangerous proximity were intentional. But the language of poets and tragedians has it otherwise, and the barely disguised contiguity between combat and offering occasionally appears in broad daylight in the works of a Pindar or Aeschylus.[35] Yet nothing is gained by backing off from such a remark, no matter how unprepared I am to take the next step in interpreting it. Perhaps I have indeed wandered into a minefield,[36] and this is probably not the moment to venture any further. At least this incursion has offered me the opportunity to observe that only life-threatening cuts or gashes make a wound into a mark of manhood, for the one who inflicts it as well as the one who receives it. Everything else is merely a scratch, or to use Homer's words, a simple "script" on the skin.[37] The bloody cut, more or less explicitly compared to the sacrificial offering that puts men into communication with the gods, contrasts with the merest mark (or when in spite of all, the blood runs, a slight tint of purple), leaving only a trace on the one who receives it and a reproof to the one who gave it, a sorry fighter whose arrows only glance off his adversary's body.[38]

An arrow, for instance, that was not shot in vain will lodge in the body or even penetrate the entrails;[39] meanwhile very special attention is paid to the moment it tears the skin (*tameein khroa*). Readers of the *Iliad* know that the warrior's living body has no other name than *khrōs*, as though the fragile envelope of skin serves to evoke the depths of its flesh. And to convince the Trojans that the Greeks are not invulnerable, all Apollo has to do is say to them:

> Give no quarter in the battle with the Argives. Their skin (*khrōs*) is neither stone nor iron that would enable it to resist the bronze that carves into the flesh (*khalkon tamesikhroa*) when they are hit.[40]

Instead of merely being content to translate *khrōs* as "flesh" or "skin" interchangeably, we should ask why the manly body is identified with its envelope, its surface. Comparing the innumerable instances in which *khrōs* denotes the body of the living warrior with passages in which the flesh of dead fighters is referred to as "fat,"[41] one would certainly be persuaded that the living body is enclosed in its wrapping of skin because the body's integrity, which is so threatened from the outside, is at stake. Having neither the time nor space to enter into the matter here, however, I will continue pretending to confuse flesh and skin. For in truth the word *khrōs* is less crucial to my argument than the qualifiers associated with it the moment that the enemy blow strikes the warrior's body. Then the skin is "tender," "beautiful," or "white" or "desirable": the beautiful skin of Ares or Hector, the white skin of the fighters that the arrows desire to pierce—arrows that burn to taste it, to glut themselves on it—Ajax's white skin, his tender skin, his desirable skin.[42]

Enough has been said about Ares, and about Ajax, for the reader to be surprised: Ares the murderer, Ajax the invulnerable, the unassailable warrior—how can these two be endowed with skin so soft that it is evoked in terms more fittingly used to describe the complexion of a young girl, or even more generally, of a woman (the skin of Greek women, who bask in the shade indoors, is—perforce must be—white)? Others have asked this question. Pointing to everything in the *Iliad* that eroticizes warfare—this dance, this rendezvous, this melee, in a word, this amorous struggle—such commentators emphasize the femininity latent in the most virile warrior, and that war reveals.[43] I will adopt this argument, with certain qualifications. The hero's femininity is revealed less by war in general than by the bronze point. To be more precise, the very instant that the enemy weapon hews the warrior's body, the fragility—wholly feminine, without a doubt, but also very human[44]—hidden in the body of the virile man appears, tinting the entire surface of his skin at the crucial moment.

For never has the fragility been perceived with so much moving acuity, never has skin appeared more tender than around the edges of the tear made by the spear, when, for example, it moves "straight through the delicate neck" of Euphorbos, Patroclus, or Hector.[45] Realists are certainly correct in observing that this indeed is "a very delicate part of the body that is poorly protected by armor."[46] Still, never is the insistence on the skin's softness so great than at the moment that it is injured. For convincing evidence, one can even leave the battlefield to enter the world of women, when in mourning they mimic on their own bodies the wound that proved fatal to the hero. Thus, weeping over the body of Patroclus, Briseis in her mourning lacerates "her breast, and her tender neck, and her beautiful face."[47] Delicate is the neck, tender is the skin of a woman, and Briseis is beautiful, but of a beauty that can be evoked in a stereotypical formula; and it is not unimportant that the poet feels the need to recall these obvious verities at the precise moment that the weeping woman's fingernails attack the integrity of her body. Without further ado, let us return to Ajax: everything indicates that the surprising, tender, and desirable whiteness of the skin of this indomitable warrior's body can be attributed to the spear that threatens to pierce it.

It is time to draw this survey to a close, and perhaps also to place it within an overarching view of Greek representations of the masculine—where I did not wish to begin, preferring the *sumbolon* of virility to the rhetoric of *andreia*.

From the symbolic scars of Coriolanus to the body of the Homeric hero that is at once virtually invulnerable and ever so fragile, this investigation took an unpredictable course. At any rate, I did not try to compare the incomparable or bridge the irreducible distance that all too obviously lies between an ancient Roman custom of which Plutarch is the herald and the epic universe, in which Achilles and Ajax win renown. But fundamental to this distance were criteria that defined the man endowed with *andreia* by the signs of manhood marking his body. Greek tradition is quick to contrast the wound that opens a man's body with the dangerous closure that in more than one way dooms the female body to strangulation. Perhaps, in fact, Greek thinking about the masculine finds it advantageous to close women's bodies all the better to open those of men[48]—a productive maneuver, to be sure, since even the physicians, whom one would like to think were realists, located wounds only on the bodies of men.[49] This can probably be seen as a way of denying the "simple" evidence that women's bodies are inherently open—slit.[50] For the warrior's blood must have full value, this blood that he sheds "by the decision of his own free will," at the same time that the woman "sees" her blood flow outside her body "without necessarily desiring it nor preventing it."[51] Hence the need for male wounds and the imperative, which weighs over Greek women, to be pregnant—in the service of civic reproduction, of course, but also because pregnancy is a valid way of sealing a woman's body.[52] By considering the heroes' wounds, then, I was hoping to focus on one of the Greek indicators of virility. However, as should be expected the moment that one penetrates into the world of the *Iliad*, with Homer—in other words, with the Greeks, with us, even at the very beginning—things have become singularly complicated.

This complication is certainly not the result of discovering that man has a feminine side, or observing that the feminine element within him is revealed at the very moment in which his quality as a manly hero is painfully inscribed on his flesh. When the historian of the imaginary studies the Greek figure of the hero, following, for example, the adventures of Herakles, the notion is soon apparent that a man is never so much a man as when there is something of the woman in him. So the complication does not rest there, but in the extreme ambivalence in Homeric thought, in which the heroic body must simultaneously be invulnerable and gouged, in which more than once a great warrior is nonetheless spared the qualifying test of the wound. Transposing what Emily Vermeule says of the paradoxical mortality of the epic hero to the Homeric representation of the masculine, I would say that he is "an unstable composite of irreconcilable elements."[53]

Once again: even when the classical city strove to make the masculine the stable category par excellence and a basis for politics, the Greeks had ample opportunity to consider the conflicting nature of virility. But it is not without importance that these investigations were carried out first of all in the epic, and it is the greatness of the *Iliad* to be able to offer such a superb account of the shifting state of the masculine: vulnerable-invulnerable, wounded but intact, strong for being able to welcome the flaw within but, the moment afterward, triumphant for having conquered weakness, the body indomitable and delicate.

This vacillation is troubling, too troubling. Tireless efforts will be made to put order into civic orthodoxy, in the name of a masculinity unmarred by any weakness, which as everyone knows is supposed to be the seat of *logos*.[54]

Chapter 6

THE STRANGLED BODY

ONCE AGAIN, the body. The male body, the female body. Open, closed. Torn, intact. And above all, the body as the subject for the workings of the imagination, for constructions of fantasy.

In the beginning, it is true, I had thought to find something else: the real, all-too-real body of the person condemned to death, subjected to more than one type of violent treatment. A few years ago Romanists and Hellenists gathered to pool their knowledge and questions about physical torture and the death penalty in the ancient city. Suddenly I was confronted with the sorry plight of the Greek historian with regard to this matter and envied the specialists studying Rome for the rich documentation at their disposal. Did this mean resigning myself to understanding the Greek body on only the most abstract level? Happily, the situation turned out to be more complex. Once again, the feminine entered into play, like a screen that reveals more than it hides. The obstacle known as femininity can offer access to the virile being.

It is not too surprising that the classical city has little to say about the tortured body. One need only mention the extremely limited autonomy of evolving juridical thought or the extent of the civic repression of the body in Greece, which is especially evident—unfortunately for us—in texts, like those of the historians, that must fulfill their stated function by mentioning tortures and executions. In addition, the desire of certain cities to set an example solves nothing: does a collectivity base its exemplary status on the types of punishment that it inflicts? This sort of misplaced curiosity is liable to put the Greek historian in the position of the foreigner described by Plutarch, who when asking Lycurgus about the punishment that Lacedaemon reserves for adulterers, received the following nonreply: "How could there be," the legislator objected at last, "any adulterers in Sparta?"[1] Last but not least, this line of inquiry is blocked by the reality that the Greeks tended to euphemize all forms of death.[2] *Kteinō*, "to kill," *thanatoō*, "to cause someone to die": in historians' accounts as well as civic decrees, the idea of execution always overshadows descriptions of the means employed, and the fact of the execution blots out the use of legal violence.[3] Again, it is a good idea to read the philologists: there one learns that the etymology of the verb *kteinō*, "the most common verb in Greek meaning 'to kill,'" only means "to wound."[4] Death is mentioned with great care, and in this world of euphemisms, fortunate is the one who succeeds in learning of the means of punishment.

But, since the difficulty is Greek, I will use Greek ways to find a way around it. Greek is the path of *logos*, in which thinking about a social practice means subjecting it to a highly elaborate discursive process, so that what is stated is illuminated by what is left unsaid. Therefore, in order to give full meaning to the silence generally observed concerning modes of execution, I will focus on recurring sequences in the texts dealing with capital punishment. Even so, the language of these documents requires serious attention: for example, the term *kteinō* which, beyond any clearly drawn mental boundaries, is used to refer to the act of "killing in general, whether men or animals, killing in combat or putting to death"[5]—"to kill" a being of a different or like kind, an animal or a man, an enemy or a fellow citizen, one's neighbor or even oneself; "to kill": on the battlefield, in a civil war, in an execution, or a sacrifice. Perhaps the time has come to unite under the heading of "killing" practices whose specificity led anthropologists studying ancient Greece to treat them in distinct ways. At least I would like to test this as a working hypothesis; it will be a partial test, since I will deliberately blur the line that separates capital punishment from suicide as I examine Greek representations of the strangled body.

The strangled body: the body of those condemned to death, of those who die by their own hand. I am fully aware that I am employing comments on suicide by hanging as a means to decipher the rare and laconic information that we have at our disposal concerning execution by strangulation. In so doing, I do not mean to ignore either the specific nature of suicide and the gravity of the condemnation that in Greece weighs on this "most sinister of acts,"[6] or the distinction that some societies have clearly made between strangulation and hanging. But anyone who takes an interest in Greek representations of the body quickly makes the following observation: the discourse is the same for the suicide and the condemned individual. Along with the image of the rope around the neck the same sequence always recurs. And always the same silence blocks all access to the means and precise instant of death,[7] as if the image of the neck in the noose erased all distinctions between "killing" and "killing oneself," as if all deaths by rope were the same, transcending all differences or oppositions in the way they are carried out.

For Herodotus, the chasm between the act of killing and the act of sacrificing is bridged by the general Scythian practice of strangulation.[8] True, this anomaly can be attributed to the Scythians' barbarian status, and one can point out that in Greece even strangulation is absent from sacrifice.[9] The undeniable fact remains: in the civic universe of the Greeks, where sacrifice and capital execution are (*must be*) separated into watertight compartments, all forms of strangulation, from execution to suicide, are one, to the degree that on more than one occasion the reader hesitates between two possible interpretations of the word *agkhonē*. Certainly there are passages in which *agkhonē*, understood as a reference to hanging, unambiguously denotes suicide, in fact the very model of all suicides.[10] There are others that permit some hesitation between suicide and execution, even if one finally ends up deciding in favor of suicide: such is the case of Orestes' exclamation in the *Eumenides* or of Sophocles' Oedipus.[11] Finally there are others in which one probably has to assume that *agkhonē* refers to execution, even if *andragkhos* (the strangler) is not the most common term for executioner.[12]

STRANGULATION, HANGING, SUFFOCATION

However, to determine the place that Greek cities reserve for strangulation and hanging in their penal systems, I will first consider them only as executions.

Explicit references to *agkhonē* are not to be found in Athens, and after compiling a list of Athenian punishments (throwing the condemned into the Barathron, torture by *apotumpanismos*, poisoning with hemlock), D. M. MacDowell calmly concludes (too calmly, perhaps): "It is remarkable that neither hanging nor decapitation seem to have been used."[13] Had he been more careful, he would doubtless have reserved a special mention for *apotumpanismos*, which for the ancients—the repeated use of the verb *kremannumi* is evidence—was not without some resemblance to hanging, while the moderns tend to see it as a variety of death by strangulation.[14] But in any event, *apotumpanismos* is nothing more than an indirect way of employing hanging or even strangulation.

After Athens, will it be necessary to look to barbarian lands to find unmistakable allusions to hanging or strangulation? The work of Herodotus seems to invite this, as it refers to Babylon or Scythia,[15] but it is not at all certain that, in this case as in many others, the Greekness to which Herodotus refers can be reduced to the Athenian model alone. In fact, it is not necessary to leave the Greek world to follow the tracks of *agkhonē*; however, one must leave the center for the hinterlands or an archaizing, even anomalous city such as Sparta.

First of all, hanging is utilized for executions in Macedonia; or at least it must be said (which is perhaps not exactly the same thing) that on two occasions Alexander rid himself of "philosophers" who hindered him in this fashion.[16] Then there is Locris, whose inhabitants strangled the daughters of the tyrant Dionysios in reprisal;[17] but Locris is famous above all for the conservatism—the Greeks call it *eunomia*—of "Za-leukos's code," by virtue of which the act of proposing new legislation entailed risking one's life. The would-be reformer submitted his proposal with the noose around his neck—or, according to other sources, stand-ing underneath the rope dangling from the gallows. Of one accord, De-mosthenes, Diodorus, Polybius, and Stobaeus ingenuously explain that if the project met with displeasure, the rope was quickly jerked.[18] History does not say whether the Locrians often had to pull the rope, and if Demosthenes' report is to be believed—according to which, in over more than two centuries only one new law was adopted—it is likely that the radical nature of the punishment was enough to discourage any zealous innovators. But there are always the fearless ones ... Whether real or theatrical, it was an exceptional procedure and not a customary penalty. Perhaps the same is true regarding execution by strangulation or hanging in Sparta, since history has preserved the name of only one con-demned man, not the least among men: King Agis IV, executed after a mock trial by the ephors, his enemies.

On the basis of this unique example, the desire for generalization has led historians of Greek law to vie with one another in making the most of a passing mention by Plutarch concerning "the room in the prison where the condemned were put to death by strangulation." And, without wondering overmuch whether Plutarch himself had not proceeded by induction from the case of the lone Agis, they proclaim that Sparta prac-ticed execution by strangling.[19] But the silence of tradition makes it im-possible either to confirm this opinion[20] or truly weaken it—even though, for my part, considering everything that makes Agis's death into an episode of high drama, even tragedy,[21] I would be inclined to see it as an exception.

Slim pickings, one has to admit, richer in exceptions than possibilities for generalizing and where the line between punishment and murder has been blurred more than once. But although this type of execution makes only a furtive appearance in Greek history, it was important to my argu-ment to recall that in some Greek cities certain condemned prisoners were hanged or strangled. For the essential lies within this constantly repeated equivalence, "hanging or strangulation."

Hanging *or* strangulation: I won't hide the fact that this *or* should pre-sent a problem to historians of Rome, if it is true that there persons "strangled or hanged belong to two different universes, the first having a right to funerary honors, and the second belonging to the *insepulti*."[22] But the distinctive nature of the Greek data must be respected. Without being overly preoccupied with the gloss cited above, which designates the executioner with the term for "strangler," all one need do is consult the Macedonian, Locrian, and Spartan data to be convinced that in the language of the Greek historians, strangulation, even when achieved by hanging, is the common element of these practices.[23] Reading Polybius on the subject of the gallows and Diodorus on strangulation in Locris,[24] one could of course conclude that two competing versions existed. But the account of Agis's death makes it necessary to abandon this facile solution. Plutarch mentions suffocation and strangulation when speaking of the young king, but as he is careful when describing Arkhidamia's hanging body and its removal to specify that the king's mother and grandmother suffered the same fate,[25] there is no more room for doubt. "Strangulation by hanging" is the only way to describe Agis's death; this is the only phrase that makes it possible to avoid the hesitations of the commentators who sometimes speak of strangulation, sometimes hanging, as if there were a choice between two penalties.[26]

Matters are no different when it comes to suicide. If the middle voice of the verb *apagkhō* is conventionally used to indicate that hanging took place, no further details are ever given concerning the means by which it is accomplished,[27] and the description always comes to a halt, as if the threshold of the unsayable had been reached, with the vision of the rope around the neck of the hapless man or woman. For example, the premonitory chorus of Euripides' *Hippolytus*, in which the women of Troezen evoke Phaedra's hanging:

> Overcome by her cruel misfortune, she goes to hang a cord from the nuptial roof, which she will adjust around her white neck.

The women will say no more; a maidservant is already shouting that Phaedra has hanged herself. Or, in the *Virtues of Women*, the story of the daughters of a defeated tyrant whom the people condemn to die by their own hand: the elder loosens her virginal belt and ties it into a knot; she shows her younger sister how to slip her neck into the noose; and already she beholds her sister dead.[28] Or the *aition* of the Boeotian cult to Artemis *Apakhomenē*: children playing around a temple find a rope, and tying it around the statue's neck, they say that Artemis "has been hanged/hanged herself" (*hōs apagkhoito*). Once again, one must rely on the verb *apagkhomai* in order to speak of hanging; the tree—dear to historians of religion—from which cohorts of virgins hang is absent from the account, and this *aition* makes no room for the beam in the marriage chamber from which tragic heroines suspend their ropes.[29] Without the epiclesis of the goddess, the story told by Pausanias would also be appropriate for a strangled Artemis.[30]

It would probably be fruitless to seek anything in this gap, which appears countless times in the literature, other than the special silence the ancient Greeks observed concerning the conditions under which death arrives. At least its consequences seem to be inevitable: in cases of suicide as well as execution, hanging is only one variety of strangulation.[31] Once again we encounter *agkhonē*: it is certainly proper to stress, as the philologists do, that while it is a derivative of the verb *agkhō* (to clasp, embrace), this word has become so removed from its root that its primary meaning has lapsed in favor of the specialized sense of strangulation or hanging.[32] But matters are not always as clear-cut as the philologists would like: from Herakles clasping the Nemean lion in his arms to Aristophanes' horrible children, ready to strangle their father, the acceptation of *agkhonē* remains loose, while *agkhō*, closer to *apagkhomai* and *agkhonē* than it seems, ordinarily refers to suffocation or strangulation.[33] Nothing in the Greek documentation, then, seems to forbid the notion that hanging, like strangulation, is a "means of asphyxiation."[34] One merely has to consult the writings of the physicians, in which all forms of asphyxiation are related: hanging is included without any discussion. When a Hippocratic author, listing the ailments that afflict pubescent girls, mentions side by side the desire for death by drowning and death by the noose, the juxtaposition may be more than mere chance.[35] At least the doctor knows that the hanged man is like the epileptic, because the latter, like the former, displays the key symptom of asphyxiation, which is the presence of foam around the mouth.[36]

This semantic field can be further explored by briefly considering suffocation. Instead of dwelling on the synonymy of *apagkhō* and *apopnigō*, or a gloss furnished by Hesychius in which *agkhonē* is likened to *pnigetos*, one might concentrate on a passage in the *Frogs* in which Dionysos, consulting Herakles about the quickest way to Hades, is advised to consider hanging himself:

> There is one way that starts with a rope and a stool: all you have to do is hang yourself.
> Shut up! it is suffocating.[37]

The full meaning of the fainthearted god's abrupt response can be sought in the preceding—or immediately following—lines. Dionysos has asked for "the shortest road," specifying that he wishes it to be "neither too hot nor too cold." And, in fact, after hanging, which is described as suffocating, the objection will be made that hemlock is "cold and icy." There is no doubt about it: as the scholiasts and commentators have seen, *pnigēran* must be understood in the double meaning of the word *pnigos*, which refers to suffocation as well as torrid heat.[38] Let us leave suicide for a moment to return to capital punishment. Is it necessary to recall that the icy hemlock given a condemned man causes a death that is noble in some ways? The ends met by Theramenes and Socrates[39] are sufficient to make it clear. In contrast, strangulation will be considered an ignoble way to die. But before this examination of the order of values goes any further, the physician should speak once more: it is a law of life that the human body must release its heat. In other words it must be "opened," and in the act of breathing an exchange is made between outside and inside.[40] Ultimately suffocation blocks the breath of the hanged or strangled person, whose body is forever closed.

A difficulty remains: doesn't a joint discussion of strangulation and hanging overlook what is really a radical difference between the two ways of dying, namely, the "aerial" aspect of hanging?

Commenting on the Roman taboo that deprived hanged persons of burial, but not those who died of strangulation, Jean-Louis Voisin has shown that only the absence of all contact with the ground is sacrilegious.[41] When they say that strangulation and hanging are equivalent, aren't the Greeks refusing to attach any importance to the fact that the hanged person's feet do not touch the ground? To be sure, one text suggests the opposite: the unfaithful maidservants in book 22 of the *Odyssey* are punished by hanging, and Telemachus takes great care to stretch the cable high enough "so that their feet could not touch the ground." In fact, in a passage that is as fleeting as it is memorable, their feet will move for a very brief instant.[42] But in addition to the fact that one piece of evidence does not make a tradition, perhaps what predominates in Telemachus's preparations is the concern for their efficacy.

At the other end of the chronology, an example from Plutarch suggests to the contrary that it is never too late to lay a corpse out on the ground, even when the person has been hanged. Thus, when Agis's mother loosens the noose that binds Arkhidamia's body, which she stretches out on the ground before covering it up and "hiding" it as if to bury it, she seems to be initiating funeral rites for her kin.[43] In addition to the admittedly latter-day evidence found in Plutarch are the details furnished in the middle of the fifth century by a scene in Euripides' *Hippolytus*. Phaedra has hanged herself.[44] At the moment when action is called for, the chorus, not surprisingly, hesitates ("Will no one then bring a double-edged blade to deliver her throat from the knot and liberate the queen from the noose that strangles her?"). When at last the women of Troezen are convinced that it is too late, they keep watch to see that when this "unhappy cadaver" is raised up, it is laid out "as is due to a dead person."[45] These lines seem to suggest that by laying the body of a hanged person out on the earth, the dead one is repatriated to the bosom of the vast confederation of the dead—in other words, all those who merit funerary rites.[46]

The aerial dimensions of hanging are stressed not in institutional ritual[47] but in the realm—poetic, if not imaginary—of tragic language and metaphor. For Sophocles and Euripides there is, of course, the verb *artaō*, the derivative of *aeirō* in which the action of raising and attaching or suspending are inextricably blended.[48] There is also the derivative *artanē*, the word for the dangling noose, about which Aeschylus takes additional care to specify that it is attached "from above" (*anōthen*).[49] And a series of epithets can be used to qualify *agkhonē*, or again *brokhos*, the most common word for "noose." The tragic poets habitually call the noose used by the hanged person *metarsios* (aerial), *ouranios* (celestial), or *kremastos* (suspended).[50] But inversely, as if to recall that suspension is indissociable from the noose, when Sophocles characterizes Jocasta's death as *aiora*, he is quick to reinforce the notion of a bond, and the hanged woman is "bound by the high braid of a knot" (*plektais eōrais empeplegmenēn*).[51]

But this evidence is fragmentary, and at each moment the textual effect overshadows technical precision and hardly encourages further investigation along these lines. So what then? Perhaps it is time to focus, more systematically than I have done up to now, on the value system linked to hanging as the paradigm of strangulation.

Again, in order to shed light on the matter, the text's silence on execution must be supplemented by an examination of suicide. Still, book 22 of the *Odyssey* is explicit concerning the atrocious, ignobling nature of execution by hanging. Contradicting Odysseus's orders (one time does not a custom make), which had required that the maidservants give up their lives at swordpoint, Telemachus chooses to hang them, "for it will not be said that a pure death (*katharos thanatos*)[52] ended the life" of these women. In a kind of echo, the text goes on to describe the nooses put around their necks, so that they "suffer the most pitiful of ends."[53] In the case of Agis's death, the taboo that forbids the touching of the dead king's body would be enough to render his death impious. One can wonder, however, if the scandalous character of this death[54] must not also be imputed to the means of execution. But the question, as we know, has no answer.

Still, there is suicide by hanging, in Rome an ignoble death with a reputation that fared hardly any better in Greece[55]—a hideous death, which according to Euripides' Helen is shunned even by slaves. The ultimate stain (*lōbē*) that Jocasta inflicted on her life, before Antigone herself finds it to be her last resort,[56] hanging generally punishes dishonor. From Epicaste, who married her son, to the daughter of Mykerinos raped by her father, and from tragedies to the historical narratives of Herodotus, who reports how Pantites, one of the two survivors of Thermopylae, hanged himself to escape his shame—hanging is the lot of desperate people who have lost all *timē*.[57]

Therefore, it is not too surprising that in Thucydides' austere history the only two incidents of strangling or hanging are blamed on the horrors of *stasis*. Civil war abolishes all limits, beginning with those that ordinarily separate killing that is murder from the murder committed by a suicide. Surrounded by their democratic opponents, caught in a trap, reduced to absolute disarray, twice the oligarchs of Corcyra are forced into suicide, either hanging themselves from the trees or strangling themselves with the straps of their bedding or strips torn from their clothing.[58] Hanging as an atrocity of civil war? Decidedly, in a world in which *stasis* is the absolute evil, hanging does not get a good press.

The Woman in the Noose

To shed some light on the discredit weighing on this type of death, my examination of the semantic field of suffocation can be broadened to include the word *brokhos*. *Brokhos*, then, is the noose that has already been knotted, the mesh that is about to tighten—in a word, it is the instrument of strangulation. But there is also much more to see in *brokhos*: it is the symbol par excellence, indeed the exact synonym, for *agkhonē*.[59]

If "bonds are the privileged weapons of *mētis*,"[60] without a doubt death by the noose must pertain to the realm—both so important and so disparged in Greece—of cunning intelligence. One of the characteristics of the bond is its capacity to adjust tightly around the prey that it ensnares. Thus the noose becomes a necklace of death, and from Homer to Euripides, the verb *haptō* expresses the too-perfect adaptation of the *brokhos* to the neck of the one who is going to suffer from it[61]—whether he or she has been condemned by the city, is a candidate for suicide, or again (for the uses of *brokhos* are many) is a sacrificial victim, a bird entangled in a snare or the prey caught in the mortal trap of a metaphorical hunt.[62] With *brokhos* as, in many instances, with *agkhō* and its derivatives,[63] killing depends, even in war, even in hunting, on guile and not on honorable practices of open confrontation. In war *brokhos* becomes the lasso, the truly anomalous weapon, and in the metaphorical hunt that is the murderous ambush, *brokhos*, the net of death, connotes ignominious betrayal.[64]

The evocative power of images of treachery: all is already lost for prey caught in a snare, and there is nothing more can be said about its fate. Hence, perhaps one can better understand the unspoken rule that from Herodotus to Plutarch and from Homer to Euripides dictates that descriptions of strangulation stop before they have begun, blocked at the mention of a neck in the noose. Nothing more will be said of the strangled body. The Greek habit of repressing the body has its part here, but so does the imaginary, which is free to borrow from the rich associative chains evoked by the term *mētis*. One image is particularly striking:

when, in book 22 of the *Odyssey*, the maidservants hanged by Telemachus, "their heads in a row, the noose slipped around all their necks,"
become so many thrushes or doves caught in the "net set on the bush."[65]
Must this metaphor be taken lightly? Must it be seen as the product of
chance or the poet's pure fancy, under the pretext that "the common
element, the only one, is the image of the noose slipped around the
neck"?[66] On the contrary, I am inclined to take this Homeric metaphor
seriously, for the sake of the consistency of Greek representations of
strangulation and because at least one other text suggests the likeness
between a hanged woman and the bird caught in a trap. In Euripides'
Hippolytus Phaedra is twice compared to a bird. Before speaking of her
suicide, the chorus recalls how she, a bird of misfortune (*dusornis*) from
the land of Crete, arrived at the port of Munychia: even then, for her to
set foot on shore, they had solidly attached the "end of the braided ca-
bles"—the knot was already tightening. Beholding his wife's inert
corpse, Theseus in turn will make her into a bird that has flown from his
hands and instantly vanished into Hades.[67] The second image probably
evokes the flight of the dead woman's soul, free at last. At any rate,
Phaedra, who hangs from a noose that the text makes clear is both
braided and aerial, is indeed the poor bird of which the chorus was singing.[68] Once again, the consistency of the image is the result of the painfully precise evocation of the noose.

The hanged woman is like a bird. It is time to add one more item, a
decisive one at that, to the list of dubious values that make hanging or
strangulation into a bad death: *agkhonē* is first of all a feminine death.[69]
One only has to recall the cohort of hanged heroines in mythology and
cult: Phaedra, of course, and the strangled Artemis of Boeotia, but also
Ariadne, Erigone, Kharila, and many others.[70] Must women's affinity
with *agkhonē* be attributed to a "feminine nature" that is "less courageous
and firm"? Before attempting to provide a physiological explanation for
this phenomenon, the author of a Hippocratic treatise, the *Diseases of
Young Women*, employed such a hypothesis in passing, to account for the
epidemics of suicide that periodically afflict young females.[71]

If generalities of this nature seem unsatisfactory, if one deems the
Greeks capable of more subtle reflection, one must look again to the
domain of *mētis*. Then it can be noted that *brokhos*, which is essentially a
woven trap, is the focal point for an ongoing interconnection between
the values of the hunt and the utterly feminine values of weaving.[72]
Moreover, in the tragic universe a woman's garments can always be
transformed into the death knot: Antigone's veil becomes a *brokhos*—
"woven of thread"—with which she hangs herself, and in their evocation
of the fine use (*mēkhanē kalē*) that Aeschylus's suppliant Danaids will

make of their virgins' girdles[73] to hang themselves, one can see that for women the line between clothing and the noose is a fine one indeed.[74]

Is the rope a woman's death? When it comes to suicide, the matter is obvious. And since the Greek imagination knows no universe in which the opposition between masculine and feminine does not obtain, reflections about suicide make death by rope and by sword into two distinct categories, continually juxtaposing and contrasting them.[75] For a man the only honorable death is the one, whether it is accepted or chosen, that is brought about by the blade. Whether the result of blows struck in the heat of battle or the solitude of suicide, the wound that opens the flesh makes a man's body a virile body.[76] And regularly contrasted with the keen blade that slits the throat or pierces the breast is the noose, the insidious bringer of death.[77] This dichotomy pervades the universe of the hunt in the *Sophist*, where Plato differentiates and contrasts two manners of taking one's prey. The first consists of catching it in an enclosure (*herkos*), and obviously Plato includes the *brokhos* among these traps; the second amounts to striking the prey. It is probably no accident that when confronted with the choice between *herkos* and *plēgē*, the philosopher decides to explore the second.[78] One might call it a simple philosopher's diversion. But everything indicates that this is not at all the case: for example, even though the death of Cleombrotos, struck down (*plegeis*) in Leuctra by an enemy spear, violates the taboo forbidding anyone to touch the body of the Spartan king, it is accorded more value than the death of Agis, who was strangled by his ephors.[79]

Let us get down to the essential. Death from a noose around the neck means that no blood has been spilled.[80] When I put it this crudely, I am not unaware that "death without bleeding is not in itself particular to hanging" or strangulation.[81] But here only Greek categories concern me, and the opposition between the rope and the sword, between the body that is imprisoned in the *brokhos* and the gashed body from which blood flows is one and the same. In this instance *agkhonē*, whether or not it is the dominant practice in Greek executions, achieves a certain exemplary status. At least in ancient Greece executions in which blood is shed are generally avoided,[82] perhaps in order to preserve the honor associated with death by the blade.

To shed blood or not: this crucial opposition is clearly more apparent in Rome, where "blood . . . takes on various names depending on whether it remains within the body or acquires its sacrality by being shed,"[83] and Hellenists are entirely correct in deploring that the Greek language has no way of making a distinction similar to that displayed early on in Latin between *sanguis* and *cruor*, between the blood that circulates within the body and spilled or coagulated blood.[84] But beyond these linguistic silences, it is not impossible to reconstruct something like a Greek notion about blood, according to which, from Homer to Hippocrates and beyond,[85] it would be natural for blood to flow, even to flow outside of the body,[86] since *haima* originally refers to bleeding from a wound.

And this is where the question of blood brings us by contrast to strangulation. Once again, it is enough to consider Greek medical ideas. In matters of vocabulary, the word *agktēr* will perhaps be of interest, as it is derived from *agkhō*, which denotes the instrument used to close a wound[87] by preventing the blood, whose violent nature is dangerous under these circumstances, from flowing out of the body. From a nosological standpoint, angina also deserves mention, both the name of the ailment and how it is described. As is well known, the modern word *angina* takes its name indirectly from *agkhonē* by means of the Latin *angina*[88]—the Greeks themselves gave this ailment the name *kunankhos*, which is not far from *agkhō*. And the Hippocratic description states that this sickness "is the result of blood, when this liquid coagulates in the veins of the neck."[89] For all that, *angina* is only a benign foretaste of the *agkhonē* of death. To find more striking analogies and pursue these reflections about the strangled body, again it is necessary to consider the feminine dimension of death in the noose. Thus, in order to finish, I will resolutely turn my attention to the language of the gynecologists and what it has to say concerning strangulation or suffocation as it affects the female body.

The Greek male—so goes the hypothesis—is virile in proportion to the blood he sheds, whether it flows from wounds opened in the enemy's "warm flesh"[90] or his own. In the murderous game of warfare, the male body, nicked or indeed torn apart by the spear, is the site of a bloody "division" that the epic[91] as well as classical tragedies[92] express by means of a language that places combat procedures dangerously close to sacrificial practices—as if, on the level of the signifier, the clearest frontiers are blurred; as if, transcending all taxonomies, the unity of bloody death is framed around the image of the slashed body.[93] In the face of such logic, how can one speak of a female body, at once closed in on itself and periodically opened, so protected but which, owing to the intrinsic laws of womanhood, naturally lets blood periodically flow? Greek imaginings about the body consistently emphasize feminine enclosure (which is positive when the body is enclosed around the infant it carries during pregnancy but otherwise is absolutely disquieting),[94] and women's blood, except when it periodically flows, is believed to be enclosed inside their bodies and is therefore less healthy—which, according to Aristotle, can be readily deduced from its black color.[95] Of course, a woman's menstrual period resembles the "blood of an animal that has just been slaughtered."[96] Likewise, according to one Hippocratic author, a woman's afterbirth flows "like the blood of sacrificial victims if the woman is healthy."[97] But since it is considered part of the same semantic field, the natural flowing that ensures the healthy functioning of a woman's body is put on the same level as the gaping wound in the male body. No doubt about it, the virtues of the gash opened by the blade are preeminent.

What, in this perspective, about the female body that is too closed because its flowing has been blocked? Not too surprisingly, here medical texts utilize the thematics of strangulation to characterize the dangerous states in which a woman's body is choked by her own blood; for instance, a young unmarried girl at the outset of her first period. It seems that things could not go well. "For at that moment the blood is carried to the womb to flow outside of it. . . . And if the orifice of discharge (*stoma*) has not yet been opened, then the blood, having no means of exit, rushes upward, given its quantity, to the heart and the diaphragm." The pressure around the heart causes madness, acute inflammation, and the desire for *agkhonē*. And, in fact, it would not take much for the patient to strangle herself. The solution is to hurry to find her a husband. Then, with nothing blocking the flow of her blood, she will be relieved of her sickness.[98] No text in the Hippocratic corpus better expresses the untoward results of the pressure of blood inside the female body than the treatise *On the Diseases of Young Women*: virgins, it is true, are particularly prone to hang themselves because their blood is disturbed and suffocates them. But more broadly, medical discourse claims that the desire for *agkhonē* is feminine[99] because it is natural for women's blood to be occasionally constricted in the womb. Choked from below, the woman seeks a way out from above by hanging herself. Also, by knotting a rope around her neck, she is content to obey the urges of her wandering uterus, which has risen upward in her body as if in search of the ultimate suffocation.

A strange logic—a body twice bent on strangling itself, from below and above. To be more exact, strangulation from above repeats the strangulation from below, for hanging or the desire for death is always[100] a response to a suffocation of the womb (which moreover is often sufficient in itself to kill the sufferer).[101] This is the answer that gynecological thought brings to a Greek question that one could, like Plutarch, formulate in this way: What drives women, sometimes irresistibly, to hang themselves? A gap certainly exists between the open-ended question in the mythico-religious universe and the answer offered by the physicians, and there is no point in hiding it. But it is important that in this instance the logic of medical thought is based on a representation of the feminine body that recurs in the Greek imaginary,[102] in which women's bodies are conduits, canals, means of passage—from the lower to the upper, from the "mouth" (*stoma*) of the womb to the mouth that speaks or is silent, from the suffocating neck (*trakhēlos*) of the uterus to the neck encircled by the noose.[103]

Caught between these two orifices, poised in two directions, how could a woman escape the experience of *agkhonē*?

It is time to end this survey, which has brought us all the way from the practices of the cities to Greek gynecological discourse. After considering this material, one certainly has a right to think that the Greek practice of execution, which has been examined through the prism of its varied representations, has still not acquired the texture of reality, and I do not intend to deny it. Moreover, in an area of research somewhat neglected by anthropologists of Greece, who seem to display little inclination to venture onto the paths so forcefully opened some time ago by Louis Gernet, any exhaustive study or synthesis would be impossible. However, as is appropriate when making a simple survey, my intent was to question and explore. So this investigation, which started off with cities that practice killing by strangulation and ended with the close bonds between femininity and hanging, was not motivated by a taste for digression. Instead it will be recalled that the study of representations requires the historian to be open enough to give any orientation, even if it is surprising at first glance, enough room to accommodate the suggestions offered by the dynamics of the material, and bring to the task sufficient rigor to take the recurrence of an image or a word seriously. I have attempted to be responsive to these requirements, at the risk of finding myself far indeed from capital punishment. There is no way to tie the ending to the beginning, and I will not hurriedly return to Locris, forcing the silence of the documents in hopes of understanding what, in the last instance, brought the enemies of the law to death by strangulation.

Nor will I attempt to invent a category that is broad enough (for example, rejection from the city) to encompass both the imprudent reformer and the woman that the tragedies depict hanging from a noose. The time has not yet come for such generalizations—and it is not at all certain that they are desirable. But by setting out everything that makes death by strangulation, which is indisputably feminine in cases of suicide, the exact opposite of a death inflicted by the blade,[104] perhaps I have taken a step toward elucidating Greek practices of killing. Perhaps, as a consequence, strangulation may be seen to have a certain paradigmatic status, capable of clarifying the civic values that govern punishment. In this case, a rare and as if furtive way of killing would cast a bright light on the repugnance of the Greeks to shed blood at executions.

This is not my point. But this recurrent avoidance of blood, even in legal killings, is important to me. When the city reserves for condemned men a death that they are supposed to share with women, it is proclaiming that they are already dead to the citizenry, for they no longer belong to the community of *andres*.

Thus is preserved the dichotomy—artificial and at the same time utterly necessary, like an ideology—by which legitimately shed blood is seen as opposite to the blood that flows completely "naturally" from the paradoxical bodies of women,[105] bodies that are at once too open and always too closed.[106]

Chapter 7

HERAKLES: THE SUPERMALE
AND THE FEMININE

You were born for that virile excellence which is the
glory of man, *aretē*; you must conquer it, and it is won
only at the cost of life itself.
—Wilamowitz

There is a sanctuary dedicated to mortal man in his
female aspect (*thēluprepēs phōs*), undoubtedly Herakles.
—T. Wiegand[1]

THE OPPOSITION between the body of women and the virile body has
taken shape again in all its clarity—an operational clarity, no doubt? Let
us hope so. Nothing, however, is less clear. For it might be that this
opposition, this conceptual tool, is most in evidence when it is necessary
to transcend it: when imbalance takes over, blurring even well-established antitheses, confusing the very certainties that must, all the same, be
mobilized in order to find our way. It is a risky step, but to proceed with
the inquiry, we have no choice. We must therefore take one of these
configurations in which, to enhance his virility the Greek male appropriates all or some part of the feminine, as if, to remain a criterion of intelligibility, the difference between the sexes would demand something resembling—this is not known, merely said—the regulated practice of its
irregularity.

At this point in our survey, Herakles once again emerges as the paradigm of transgression that ought to consolidate the norm. Once again,
we are brought face to face with this hero. And if this encounter took
place for the first time on the occasion of a meeting between Hellenists
and psychoanalysts, chance played only a small role and the logic of the
undertaking a much greater one. It is not with impunity that one questions the collective speaker postulated under the name "the Greeks." Still,
what did they stand to gain by telling each other myths that endlessly
returned to the immensely galling recognition that there are two sexes
and not one, and by overcoming this disappointment in subverting the
canonical opposition between masculinity and femininity?

It is up to Herakles, then, the hero of manhood, to reveal the close and many-sided relations he has with attributes and behaviors normally classified as feminine.

Herakles, then. More than just one hero, say historians of religion, who enjoy duplicating, even multiplying him[2] (and, faced with all these varied Herakleses, the discourse tends to become fragmented into a simple enumeration of each case). For my part, I will take the opposite tack, treating Herakles as a unified whole, because I define the heroic temperament as unified in its contradictions and, indeed, as constituted by those contradictions. The unity of Herakles, then, should be sought less in biographical narrative—in spite of the interesting work Dumézil has done along these lines[3]—than in an *ethos*: a character, or better, a figure. Not an interior whose hidden deviations might simply be exposed to the light, but an actor constituted by his acts, the external form of an exceptional body. By insisting on this definition, I mean to exclude from the start the facile tendency to endow the mythic hero with a character in order better to analyze him.

There are two reasons for such insistence. First, because to impose on the hero an "excess of psychology" is to do violence to the facts and to be guilty of what Jean Starobinski has rightly called "interpretive supplementation."[4] Starobinski was discussing the role of character in tragedy and was warning us against the temptation to treat dramatic characters as "actual beings . . . endowed with actual childhoods . . . , whereas they have no existence beyond the words attributed to them"—I would rephrase this warning about the "words" attributed to the tragic hero to say that in the case of the mythic hero (and specifically in the case of Herakles), he has no existence beyond the acts he performs.[5] Second, in deciphering the psychic life of a hero, one should proceed as if setting out to interpret the thoughts of the persons who figure in a dream, persons endowed with the inner life of the dreamer. If myth is actually something like the collective equivalent of a dream, Herakles is not the proper object of our analysis; we should rather be analyzing the workings of the Greek imagination that produced the figure of the hero. Because I am convinced that there are other questions for psychoanalysis to ask about myth besides the interpretation of the inner life of Oedipus, I have chosen to discuss a figure whose principal characteristic is the fact that he is constituted from the outside. Identified with his body and specifically with his invincible strength, Herakles has no interior. Even when he appears in tragedy, it would be sheer fantasy to attempt to endow him with one. Existing exclusively in the fortunes of his career as a warrior, from birth to death he is delivered over to the will of others, subject to a destiny that was imposed on him in his mother's womb.

One last remark before I make my point: it is essential to my interpretation that no Greek hero was more popular than Herakles. This means that, from archaic epic to the Hellenistic period, the figure of Herakles underwent constant reevaluation. But because no one city was able to appropriate him definitively, the process of reevaluation took place not in the political field, with its multiple identifications and inevitable distortions,[6] but rather within the logic that presides over the Greek concept of the powerful hero.

No politics, no inner life? Here is a golden opportunity for psychoanalysts and historians of the imaginary to meet on neutral ground. . . .

THE CONTRADICTIONS OF HERAKLES

Let us begin with the essential ambivalence of Herakles: even laid low by suffering and drowned in tears, the hero is invincible. The matter can just as well be put the other way round by saying, for example, that "the radiant hero is simultaneously slave, woman, and madman."[7]

Drawing up the list of the contradictions inherent in the figure of Herakles, G. S. Kirk recently pointed to the opposition between the civilized and the bestial, the serious and the burlesque, the sane and the insane, the savior and the destroyer, free and slave, divine and human.[8] I propose to add to this list the virile and the feminine. But we must not leap ahead of ourselves; the list makes no claim to be exhaustive. To add yet one more contradiction to it, we may recall at this point that Greek thinkers had equally credible traditions of a Herakles who is the hero of *ponos*, that is, of pain as glory, and of a Herakles who is the hero of pleasure, the great marrier of virgins, the great fatherer of children, fond of warm baths and soft couches.[9]

More generally, ever since the Homeric epic, the primary ambivalence of Herakles resides in the fact that the powerful hero of many exploits is inseparable from the hero who suffers, who is reduced to helplessness, to that *amēkhania* from which, in Homer and Aeschylus, Athena and even Zeus come to save him at the last minute. With the fondness for the gloss characteristic of Hellenistic literature, the poet Lykophron evokes one of the most spectacular of these inversions of power when he lingers over the adventures of Herakles (himself a shameless swallower) swallowed up by a sea monster, in whose stomach he spends three days before returning to the light of the living. When he does return, he has lost the hair that was the symbol of his power.[10] Here, for once faithful to the Indo-European ideology of war, the heroic thought of the Greeks represents strength as intrinsically ambivalent. The hero is constantly on the brink of ruin from an excess of this strength that gives him his identity,[11] except when he is experiencing madness, his body driven to delirium by the effects of "melancholy" or black bile.[12]

In the Greek world of war and adventure, power is in essence and by definition virility. This brings me back to the contradiction that emerges in the relationship of Herakles—"compulsively masculine" Herakles[13]—to women and to femininity.

What one sees first in Herakles is the assertion of the most virile sexuality: the very type of the supermale, he eagerly deflowers virgins—fifty in a single night, according to the most enthusiastic version of the story. In his wanderings he marries along the way, begets offspring, and then goes off; the huge number of his wives earns him the title *philogunēs* (lover of women).[14] The female body as an object of conquest and pleasure is continually new for him, and allegorizing erotic interpretations of his amorous career were current in the banquets of the Hellenistic period. For example, when someone was bragging about his own sexual prowess, a standard deflationary tactic was to point out that Herakles had done better, moving on as he did from Omphale to Hebe. Omphale is the queen of Lydia who reduced the hero to slavery, Hebe (Youth) the divine spouse he obtained on his apotheosis. But in colloquial speech *hēbē* was also used to refer to the sexual organs, and the name Omphale was connected to *omphalos* (navel) as well as to the umbilical cord and the source of procreative force.[15] Thus the life of Herakles is turned into a journey across the female body.

But this *philogunēs* hero is also—to the great delight of austere classicists such as Wilamowitz—a determined misogynist.[16] He has this institutional title at Delphi, where no woman is allowed to enter his temple, and in more than one Greek city the exclusion of women figures among the specific traits of the cult of Herakles.[17] The Hellenistic period endows this misogynistic Herakles, who lends religious sanction to the rigorous segregation of the sexes, with a literary dimension. In the *Argonautica* of Apollonius of Rhodes, the hero keeps his distance from women and, on Lemnos, refuses to give himself up to the debilitating pleasures of love, while summoning his companions to return to a fiercer, virile valor.[18] There is another tradition that avoids this explicit misogyny and takes an indirect approach—it lists only the sons in the (vast) catalog of the hero's offspring, as if the male must engender only the male. But there is also another more powerful and more ingenious version where the exception confirms the rule, where Herakles has one daughter, one alone, as against seventy-two sons—the singular exception, the absolute anomaly.[19]

This is not the last of the paradoxes. Herakles has another surprise in store for those who are already amazed that this lover of women should be such a misogynist. Herakles, the advocate of the separation of the sexes, has a strong bond with marriage, both in life and in cult, and anyone who does not resolve the difficulty by postulating the existence of two radically different Herakleses must give some explanation of why the hero is so compulsively matrimonial. George Dumézil has recently emphasized the fact that the recurrence of marriage in the career of Herakles is structural.[20] For my part, I will be satisfied merely to mention this point, preferring for the moment to continue to disclose the hero's principle features.

We come now to another dimension that needs to be added to the portrait of Herakles. The myths take insistent delight in putting Herakles at the service of women, or at least at the service of a female will. One thinks first of Hera, of course, but there is Omphale as well—all the texts agree in making him her slave, though they differ on the question of whether or not this servitude is erotic (which comes back to assigning to the hero of marriage the bride's role).[21] Let us stop for a moment at this image of Herakles, slave of women, placed under the yoke of tyrannical female power, an image that thrills certain anthropologists of Greece who, in search of a primitive gynecocracy or matriarchy, latch onto this precious news as an irrefutable piece of evidence.[22] But the comic poets of the age of Pericles, fond of devaluing the authority of a chief of state who was subject to the will of a woman, had already thought this out, and they had gone further. When they see in Aspasia a "new Omphale," a Deianeira and even a Hera, all at once, they reveal the logic by virtue of which, from birth to death, women presided over the destiny of the hero.[23] But the gynecocratic theme is not enough. It permits only a partial interpretation of this aspect of Herakles: in fact, every bit as much as he was the slave of women, he was their faithful champion, as Kerényi, among others, has emphasized.[24] For example, he once served Deianeira, this woman who kills him, his fatal spouse, by saving her from a monstrous suitor.

It is essential here to be able to generalize without succumbing to the vertigo of limitless assimilation: to establish a link among all the women in this hero's life does not entail an obligation to extract at all costs a single female paradigm from this multiplicity. One must loudly remind Hellenists as well as mythologists devoted to psychoanalytic patterns—I am thinking of Philip Slater, whose book *The Glory of Hera* has had a tremendous impact on American classicists—that Greek mythology is, in the powerful phrase of Marie Delcourt, "a language without synonyms."[25] Omphale is herself: she is not an incarnation either of Hera, or of the great chthonic goddess, the Asiatic Great Goddess, or the seductive demoness in the form of a snake; Deianeira is not a reflection of Hera or Hebe, the last wife of Herakles—she *is* the *daughter* of the goddess of marriage, but for all that she is not the double of her mother.[26] Once again, the stakes are high, because it is the very possibility of reading a myth, for psychoanalysts no less than for Hellenists, that is in question. Hera dominates the story of Herakles, to be sure, but one need not, therefore, find in every female figure, right back to his earthly mother Alcmene, an avatar of the bitchy wife of Zeus.[27] What would happen to the family romance of the hero? What would happen to the very idea of a life, fundamental to any heroic quest? No, one must recognize that there is some necessity that drives Herakles and requires that he receive everything from women, even his heroic stature. The sophist Prodikos understood this. In his famous portrait of Herakles at the crossroads, in which the hero is freed from his traditional servitude and transformed into the paradigm of free will, the choice that Prodikos confronts is not between work and pleasure, but between two women named Valor and Luxury. "Herakles had just grown out of childhood into youth; he had reached the age when the young have become masters of themselves and reveal whether they will enter life along the path of virtue or that of vice. He had left home and was sitting in a lonely place wondering which of these paths he was going to take, when he saw two stately women approaching. . . ."[28] In these opening lines of the text, everything indicates that, as an adolescent on the verge of transition,[29] Herakles is waiting for his identity; if the final decision is his, it nevertheless comes from outside— he will have to meet two women in order to choose his identity.

Last but not least in this constellation of paradoxes is the spectacle of Herakles feminized. The step from women to femininity is certainly a big one, but mythic thinking bridges this gap for the hero. When a serious epigrapher publishing the inscriptions of Didyma attaches the name Herakles to the "mortal man in his female aspect," whose sanctuary houses a cult of Hera, the historian with little experience of myth will be amazed. His amazement would certainly be less if he had paid attention to those convulsive moments when suddenly, in the literary tradition, the virility of the hero is shaken. I am thinking of the madness of Herakles. I am also thinking of the description of his death. I shall not discuss here the suffering of Herakles, entangled in "the cloak of Nessos," or his sudden feminine apprehension of his body, but let me simply recall that in Sophocles' *Trachiniae* Herakles suffers like a woman before resolving to die like a man.[30] As for the hero's madness—a *mania* or *lussa* sent by Hera— it can surely be interpreted, beyond the particular destiny of Herakles, as the generic fate of the Indo-European warrior whose excessive *menos*,[31] or "surge of combativeness," is converted into an insane rage. Finally, the murder of his sons is a woman's crime and, in the fit of madness in which he kills them, Herakles equates his suffering to that of infanticidal mothers—a connection Euripides underscores by means of the chorus.[32]

When he returns to himself, the devastated hero (according to Diodorus) stays "idle for a long time inside his house," like a woman, before facing once again the perils through which a man wins glory; but Euripides had already portrayed him as desolate, seated like a woman and veiled like a woman so as to escape any other's glance.[33]

In Herakles, therefore, we have one of the Greek figures representing femininity in man. Of course, when we use the word *femininity*, we restrict it to its sociological sense and define the feminine conventionally in terms of certain roles. Perhaps we shall often have to be content with this, since there is no real hope of finding a dimension of feminine sexuality in the relationship of the virile hero to his own body. The Greeks were extremely discreet on this score, and it was left for Jarry to dream of the bisexuality of the supermale, "passive now as a man, now as a woman."[34] But the cause is not entirely lost. If, as the myth of Tiresias asserts, women's pleasure must remain a secret, there is nevertheless another kind of female experience that Greek discourse does leave open to men—namely, the very suffering that Herakles undergoes in his agony, which constitutes a means of experiencing femininity in his body.

Thus, in addition to his innumerable relationships to women throughout his heroic career, Herakles has a relationship to femininity itself. This observation is important, and we must dwell on it for a moment before the destiny of the hero draws our attention to that element in his family romance which pits him against a certain representation of woman. By insisting on the feminine in Herakles, I want to suggest that only such a focus allows us to go beyond the pure and simple repetition of the Greek catalog of oppositions that structure the world of men, where, as it is generally agreed, the opposition of male and female is predominant. The only question the Sphinx did not ask Oedipus was that of the relationship of the sexes,[35] precisely because in their myths the Greeks never represent the rapprochement of the sexes—though in the reality of their social life they have ways of coming to terms with this.[36] What the myths give us, however, is a systematic disruption of the "normal" distribution of the characteristics of man and woman, expressing the experience of the feminine lived out by man,[37] or the terrifying conquest of the masculine by woman.[38]

Without insisting on the clear imbalance between these two elements in the Greek economy of sexual difference, I shall concentrate on the first of them, on the male experience of femininity, and more specifically I shall attempt to decipher the femininity of Herakles the Strong by way of a few Greek signs or emblems of the female—because, with Starobinski, I believe that in the case of the mythic hero, "the impersonal burden of names and things" counts for as much as "the virtual psychological background."[39]

HERAKLES AND THE FEMININE

To attempt to study the femininity of a Greek hero at the level of his sexual identity requires defining femininity in the framework of what, from Hesiod on, constitutes woman: a body, reduced essentially to a belly; and finery, which is often a veil. The belly is "the bitchery within," which in the economy of the appetites is the erotic, but it is also what brings the children of man into the world.[40] The finery is what (in the *Theogony*) makes woman into a beautiful surface, an exterior.[41] These contradictory definitions have an element of parallelism, but for the most part they simply coexist—like the depths of the hollow within and the exteriority of the surface.

It so happens that Herakles is also a belly, and as far as his clothing is concerned, the woman's *peplos* often competes with the lion's skin that is his official garment.

The Belly of the Glutton

The monstrous appetite of Herakles is a mainstay of the Greek comic poets, and simply to evoke his *boulimia* is automatically to provoke laughter.[42] Mythic and religious tradition attributes to him the ability to devour an entire steer, either in the course of a monstrous contest of gluttony or simply at the urging of his own hunger.[43] Thus in his *Hymn to Artemis* (159–61) the Hellenistic poet Callimachus evokes Herakles on Olympus waiting impatiently for the goddess to return from her hunt:

> Quickly he closes in on the animal. The apothesis of his body on the Phrygian pyre has not ended his gluttony[44]—he has the same gut he had the day he found Theiodamas at his plough.

On that occasion Herakles had consumed the farmer's ox . . . raw. One word in this text is particularly striking: Callimachus uses one of the Greek words for "belly" (*nēdus*) to refer to Herakles' hunger.

In comedy—not that laughter is foreign to this passage of Callimachus—Herakles' voraciousness is explicitly understood as equivalent to vigorous male sexuality. This is the sense of a comic fragment in which the hero tells of his journey to Corinth, land of pleasure, where he "ate" Okimon-Basil (a prostitute whose name is that of an aphrodisiac plant) and lost his shirt—as if the choice between belly and clothing were in fact a necessary one. This is why in *Lysistrata* the husband screams in a frenzy of desire, "My cock is Herakles invited to dinner."[45] Finally, giving in to the *nēdus* is not necessarily seen as a victory, as we see in a Euripidean tirade against the "race of athletes . . . enslaved to the jaw, defeated by the belly (*nēdus*)"[46]—and of course Herakles is the paradigm of the

Greek athlete. If we look at another Greek word for "belly," *gastēr*, along with its derivatives, we find a similar situation. In Aristophanes the ambiguities of this vocabulary are obvious. As a gluttonous slob Herakles is called *gastris*, while in another comedy the word *gastris* seems to be used only for women. Moreover, the word *gastron* (potbelly), which is applied to Dionysos, elsewhere clearly denotes the effeminacy of the obese rich.[47]

This discussion of vocabulary has taken us some distance from the subject of male sexuality. From Homer to the tragedians and beyond, *gastēr* and *nēdus* refer ambiguously to the stomach and to sexuality, but the same words also refer to the belly as the seat of hunger, as the location of the viscera, and as the womb.[48] Moreover, it is not only in the physiology of the Hippocratic doctors that the belly takes on feminine associations.[49] There is at least one passage in Homer that supports the Hesiodic texts in indicating that, within a man, the belly draws the male toward the female, and, more specifically, that the belly in man is feminine. The passage in question is the introduction of the beggar in book 18 of the *Odyssey*, "famous among the people of Ithaca for his gluttonous gut that never stopped eating and drinking" (18.2–3), but who is also "without strength or vigor" (*oude is oude biē*) and is called "Iros" by the young. The text says the reason is that he serves as their messenger. He is a sort of male counterpart of Iris—Iris in the masculine—but his very masculinity is problematic. If we add one more level of meaning, the joke takes on its full force: etymologically, *Iros* is derived from *is* and means "The Strong" or "The Virile"—the young noblemen of Ithaca must have laughed for a long time.[50]

What does the *nēdus* of Herakles have to do with all this? Even if we can take it no further, we can at least observe that the tradition knows of two other devourers distinguished by their *nēdus*: the Kyklops and Kronos. Homer uses the word to refer to the stomach of the Kyklops—a stomach that has just engulfed several men, with the result that this cannibalism has removed the Kyklops from the sphere of humanity, and so, in a sense, from that of masculinity.[51] Hesiod says that Kronos devoured his children as they left the *nēdus* of their mother and swallowed them up in his own *nēdus*. Of course, *nēdus* means "womb" in the case of Rhea and "stomach" in that of Kronos,[52] but it is impossible to imagine that the ambiguity of *nēdus* could have escaped a Greek reader, when the word recurs after only twenty-five lines. Zeus himself, long before he begat Herakles, his last child, in Alcmene's belly, had already more than once been endowed with a *nēdus*. The one in which he swallowed up the pregnant Metis, before giving birth to Athena by way of his head, may still pass for a stomach, but the thigh in which he enclosed the infant Dionysos after the latter was driven from his mother's womb is unambiguously called a "male *nēdus*" by Euripides.[53]

My aim in devising this catalog of the strange uses of *nēdus* is not to turn Herakles' belly into a womb—there is nothing in the texts to permit this. What I would like to do—over the objections of the philologists who will hold up plenty of passages of Homer or of Euripides where *nēdus* is simply a man's stomach with no feminine connotation—is to call attention to a rich chain of associations rooted in signifiers that are ambiguous in their relation to male and female.

The status of Herakles' belly must remain unclear, but it may have been worth casting a certain doubt on its all-too-apparent masculinity. As far as his clothing is concerned, however, the evidence is clearer from the start—though this does not mean that the interpretation of such evidence is obvious.

The Peplos *of Herakles*

We do not need deep mythological analysis of Herakles to find that clothing is a highly suggestive topic[54] in the case of a hero whose cloak and symbol is the skin of the Nemean lion.[55] But when we describe the problem in these terms, we have not gotten very far, and it may be helpful to place Herakles under the sign of the female. I knew the story of Herakles' deadly cloak and that of his transvestism in the palace of Omphale before I became interested in the femininity of Herakles, but even if the idea had occurred to me, I am sure I would have been reluctant to establish any link between the two stories. Then as I was rereading Diodorus Siculus' account of the life of Herakles, I came on a strange piece of evidence, one that is all the more disconcerting because it is unique and occurs in no other text.

According to Diodorus, when Herakles returned from war to a life of festivals and games, each of the gods gave him a gift in some way connected to the divine benefactor's own attributes. Hephaistos gave him a club and a cuirass, Poseidon gave horses, Hermes a sword, Apollo a bow and arrows. Demeter initiated him into the mysteries. I have saved until the end what the text mentions first: the gift of Athena was a *peplos*. Since up to this point Herakles had nothing to wear but his lion's skin, the gods' intention was apparently to dress him up properly. In any case, the *peplos* must be taken to be an integral part of the hero's gear. The problem is that the *peplos* does not appear again in the text and that Diodorus uses the word *khitōn* for the much more famous cloak that adheres to the battered body of the hero in his death-throes.[56]

It will be pointed out that the *peplos* is festive clothing and that Athena (the goddess of weaving, whose cult at Athens involves the *peplos*) gives one to Herakles for the times of relaxation between heroic exploits. Be this as it may, it is surprising that Athena the warrior can find no better gift for her protégé, whereas Hephaistos supplies him with his fighter's cuirass. Of course, the *peplos* is virtually an attribute of Athena, and the one that the city of Athens presented to the goddess every four years, decorated with a Gigantomachy, was a symbol of protection and victory, a sort of talisman. Still, the goddess presents the hero with *a peplos*, not with her own—there is nothing to suggest that the reader is to identify the *peplos* of Herakles with that of his protectress. In short, Athena's *peplos* simply does not provide the key to this passage.

An obvious question arises: what on earth can Herakles do with a *peplos*? Throughout Greek tradition, the *peplos* (piece of cloth, veil, dress) is a woman's garment—and sometimes a barbarian's garment—no contradiction, as far as a Greek is concerned. The woman's *peplos* corresponds to the man's *khitōn*, and although there is some fluctuation down through the long history of the word, from Homer to Plutarch the contrast of *peplos* and *khitōn* remains consistent. In the *Iliad*, when Athena is leaving Olympus for the battlefield and arming herself for war, she takes off her *peplos* to put on her father Zeus's *khitōn*, since it is more appropriate for warfare.[57] At the other end of the tradition, Plutarch provides the information that in the Argive festival called the *Hybristika*, women put on the men's *khitōn* and *chlamys*, the men the *peplos* and veil. In between, Euripides (though elsewhere he uses the word *peplos* in a male context in its original sense of "veil") emphasizes the femininity of the garment in the famous scene of the transvestism of Pentheus in the *Bacchae*.[58]

It is possible to look for an explanation of the hero's strange feminine finery in the principle of inversion that is called into play in rites of passage in the Greek world—particularly those of passage from childhood to adulthood. There is a comparison to be drawn with the female disguise of Achilles on Skyros or with the long robe of the adolescent Theseus, interpreted as a woman's garment because the transvestism paradoxically emphasizes the moment when the young man "stops being a woman."[59] But whatever the connections of Herakles with the ephebes in the state cults,[60] nothing in the text of Diodorus gives us a basis for interpreting his *peplos* as an ephebic garment. When the divine gifts are mentioned, Herakles has already experienced marriage and madness, faced the Centaurs, and completed his major labors. Now the rhythm of the story slows for a time to accommodate the theme of the founding of the Olympic Games. It is possible that Diodorus is giving us a flashback to the time of the war the adolescent Herakles fought at the head of an army of ephebes for the liberation of Thebes. Even so, the fact remains that the *peplos* seems to be presented to Herakles with a view to the future, presumably a long future; it is not intended for a moment of transition.[61] Short of violating the silence of the text or vaguely interpreting this *peplos* as an initiate's robe, we cannot remove the difficulty.

To make sense of the *peplos* of Herakles, then, we must compare the information provided by Diodorus with other traditions that portray Herakles wearing women's clothes at various points in his career. The episode of Herakles in the palace of Omphale and their exchange of clothing is a familiar one. There is another story, told by Plutarch in answer to the question, "Why does the priest of Herakles at Antimacheia on the island of Kos put on a woman's dress and wear a ribbon on his head when he sacrifices?" The story tells how, driven ashore with his ships on the island of Kos, Herakles was attacked by the Meropes, and alone against his attackers, for once he got the worst of it. He escaped only by hiding in the home of a Thracian woman, having disguised himself as a woman. Finally, after defeating his adversaries, he again put on a robe, this time with flowers, in order to marry the daughter of the king. This brings us back to the priest's costume. To add a final detail, Plutarch tells us that in the locality in question, when bridegrooms receive their brides, they dress up in women's clothes. Stepping outside of myth and of Greece, we may mention in this connection one of the Roman manifestations of Herakles, *Hercules Victor*, who is clad in a long woman's dress and is served by transvestite priests.[62]

Historians of religion who have wanted to protect the masculinity of Herakles have claimed that the episode of his stay with Omphale was a Hellenistic addition to his saga. Until recently, the pictorial evidence, which for the most part is late, seemed to support their position; but a new reinterpretation of a number of images has suggested that this tale of transvestism was well known from the classical period.[63] The partisans of an austerely virile Herakles will get out of this by insisting loudly that it is the theme of servitude that predominates here—and that this removes the problem of the exchange of clothing. Others will explain the hero's dress by emphasizing the softening effects of love which, as everyone knows,[64] makes warriors effeminate.[65] A closer look is nevertheless called for, along with a clear focus on the garments of Herakles.

As Omphale's slave, Herakles exchanges clothing with his mistress. She wears the lion's skin and carries the club; he spins wool, wearing the saffron tunic appropriate to women, the *krokotos*. On Kos the hero wore a flowered dress for his wedding, and his priest added to this feminine attire the ribbon around his hair, the *mitra*. Whether or not (like the historians of religion) they simply conflated the two episodes, the Roman poets mention the *mitra* in their descriptions of Herakles in the palace of Omphale and provide the further information that all of these events took place to the accompaniment of the oriental, effeminate sound of the tambourine.[66] Let us consider this list: *krokotos*, flowered dress, *mitra*. The *krokotos* is essentially feminine (or, from its origin, barbarian). The decorated dress is normally reserved for women, and only the pursuit of certain clearly defined professions (or the performance of certain activities) can give men a right to it.[67] The *mitra* also belongs to feminine or barbarian finery and is explicitly presented as a Lydian invention, from that land of luxury and ease over which Omphale ruled. It is true that certain categories of men are permitted to wear it, most conspicuously athletes, but Herakles is not an athlete for the purposes of this story.[68]

Historians of religion and anthropologists of Greece have suggested many explanations in their attempt to understand these instances of transvestism. Frazer spoke of "imitation of . . . [the] goddess" by the priest at Antimacheia, but the priest in question is a priest of Herakles until proved otherwise.[69] Such an explanation would seem to require transplanting Omphale to Kos—hardly an efficient solution—in order to make her into a manifestation of the Great Goddess. Herakles' homosexuality has of course been brought forward as an explanatory hypothesis.[70] Homosexuality is certainly not alien to the tradition of Herakles, but Greek homosexual behavior (including that of Herakles) is essentially pederastic, and transvestism has little to do with it.[71]

Moreover, in the mythic repertory, Herakles loses nothing of his masculinity, even when he is wearing a *peplos*, and the variants that develop his effeminacy are largely Roman. Marie Delcourt's research on the virile, indeed ithyphallic, male figure in woman's dress—a figure rich in meaning in the context of mythico-religious ideas concerning sexuality—has a great deal to contribute to the elucidation of this representation of Herakles.[72] This transvestism also lends itself to interpretation as a nuptial ritual, as Delcourt, among others, suggests, for the *peplos* is the marriage gift par excellence and is often accompanied by a crown or ribbon. By way of Herakles as god of marriage, worshiped through a *hieros gamos* ("sacred marriage rite"), we come back after a long detour to Dumézil's remarks on the importance of the matrimonial career of the hero. His remarks contain a weighty anthropological hypothesis, built on serious argumentation.[73]

Nevertheless, in order to explore all the connotations of the portrayal of a male figure in a *peplos*, we must take the further step of setting Herakles next to Dionysos, the god who wears the *krokotos* and the *mitra* and is institutionalized as such throughout Greek tradition.[74] Dionysos "the Lydian" was officially feminized—at least after a certain point—in contrast to Herakles, who is only an occasional transvestite. In his festivals he presides over a joyous transvestism that carries with it none of the tragic consequences of Pentheus's experience.[75] To strengthen the comparison, one might point to the numerous links between Herakles and Dionysos, in myth, in cult, and in art, where the two sons of Zeus are shown specially united at the banquet of immortality that celebrates the apotheosis of the hero.[76] Once again, however, it is in comedy that the true meaning of the comparison becomes clear.

In the *Frogs* of Aristophanes, Dionysos sets out to go to the underworld and in order to do so decides to make himself look like Herakles, whose descent into Hades was well known. And so he puts on a lion's skin over his *krokotos*. Dressed up this way he meets the real Herakles, who bursts into laughter—deathless laughter.[77] This scene may be taken to indicate that Herakles did not yet have anything to do with women's dress in Aristophanes' time (nor, for that matter, did Dionysos with the lion's skin, though it is sometimes associated with him later). Another possibility is that Dionysos-Herakles produces laughter of two sorts: first, there is the laughter internal to the comedy, the laughter of Herakles who, from the heights of his affirmed masculinity, is amused at the heroic getup of Dionysos the Wimp;[78] and then there is the secondary laughter of the spectator, who knows that Herakles has more to do with the wearing of the *krokotos* than he admits. There is no denying, however, that for the moment Herakles is the strong hero, and in either case, Dionysos the Effeminate only puts his impregnable virility into higher relief by the attempt to mimic Herakles. To come back to the myths of transvestism, then, it seems that the *peplos* and the *krokotos* of the hero paradoxically emphasize his virility, which remains untouched by his wearing what is, with the exception of the veil, the most feminine disguise imaginable.

Herakles' *peplos* is surely in the same category as the warm baths associated with him. Although warm baths suggest the lazy life of women, this does not mean that the hero/athlete who takes his strained muscles to the relaxation of the bath is thereby turned into a woman. The logic that sees in a hero wearing a *peplos* or in an athlete relaxing in the heat of the bath a man transformed into a woman turns out to be a facile one, against which we must hold up the logic of polarity that is second nature to Herakles.[79] An excess of virility leaves Herakles' strength in constant danger of being exhausted, and so it is appropriate for him periodically to return to a more reasonable level of male energy. Given Herakles' own ambivalence, such equilibrium will always be unstable, and he can only acquire it by balancing one excess against another—a surplus of femininity against an excess of masculinity. The feminine element in Herakles is essential, in that it is a major factor in keeping him within the human limits of *andreia* (maleness/masculinity). Herakles is all the more the human figure of the masculine hero for being dressed as a woman and performing women's tasks.

There remains the most famous of all the tales of Herakles' clothing—that of his fatal shirt—and with it a final surprise. In the *Trachiniae*, Sophocles dramatizes the process that led Deianeira to give Herakles a cloak permeated with the blood of Nessos. He has her call it a sacrificial garment, but the effect she anticipates is one of erotic magic, since this gift is intended to seal once again her union with the hero (though in the process he is implicitly placed in the position of the bride, as the recipient of beautiful clothing). Deianeira calls this gift a *peplos*, and not a *khitōn*, though the latter term seems more appropriate.[80] The lexicons brand this as imprecise tragic language, because they generally prefer to reduce "anomalies" to "approximations" rather than come to terms with them. This sort of argument is unacceptable because it does not do justice to the precision and rigor of Sophocles' language. In the *Trachiniae*, the lethal *peplos* is simultaneously a winding sheet, a woman's trick like the sheet in which Clytemnestra caught Agamemnon, and an ambiguous garment that will make Herakles into a "woman" before he gains control of himself in his death agony.[81]

As anthropologists of Greece know, the wearing and giving of clothing plays a very important role in the balance of the relationship between the sexes. The example of Herakles indicates that it serves as well to dramatize the exchange between masculine and feminine that takes place within the hero. The *peplos* of Herakles is at once a revelation of weakness hidden in strength and a chance for strength to circumscribe the feminine contained within it.

In Diodorus it is Athena, the hero's faithful protectress, who gives him the *peplos*—Athena, whose links to bisexuality are famous. She is a warrior goddess and the cherished daughter of Zeus, but she still presides over weaving and other women's work, and in Athens the young women weave the *peplos* for her. In the family life of the Olympians, she can stand her ground even in the periodic conflicts between Zeus and Hera on Olympus. She is a virgin who refuses marriage and supports the paternal cause, but in the *Iliad* she is the faithful ally of Hera. This brings us to the divine family of Herakles.

This subject has been put off deliberately, in order to avoid saddling the hero of strength with an excess of psychology by complacently deriving his relation to the feminine from his relation to the wife of Zeus. Herakles' behavior had to be considered independent of any connection to his family romance in order to avoid obscuring along the way the exteriority that serves as the character of the hero (an exteriority whose methodological importance I have emphasized). His femininity had to be deciphered by means of the network of specific characteristics that, in Greek mythical thinking, furnish the clues to interpretation, because they are able to cast light on the figure of the hero more reliably than could an appeal to his infancy. We can now try to define Herakles' relation to Hera, which indeed is essential to understanding him. But we must again take the precaution of orienting our search by means of signs—points of reference that will turn out to be as crucially important as they are superficially insignificant.

OF THE NAME OF HERAKLES AND THE BREAST OF HERA

From the moment of his delayed birth, the bastard Herakles finds himself in the middle of the "eternal conjugal conflict of philandering Zeus and unresigned Hera."[82] As soon as Herakles is born, Zeus must abandon him to his mortal destiny and can only try to lighten his brave son's burden by placing him under the protection of Athena. Athena herself must give way from time to time before Hera's unrelenting hostility, which has complete power over the hero. This subjection is clearly expressed in a passage of Euripides, in which Herakles, having just come to himself after his homicidal madness, names his enemy:

> Let the famous wife of Zeus dance and make the floor of Olympus resound.
> She has accomplished her will. She has smashed the first man of Greece right
> to his foundations. Who would pray to such a goddess? Jealous of Zeus on
> account of a woman's bed, she's killed the innocent benefactor of Greece.
> (*Herakles*, 1303–10)

Hera is malevolent and all-powerful; it is not by chance that the text says she wears the solid shoes of the men of Argos (and it may in fact be saying that she simply puts on Zeus's boots for the occasion).[83] The hero will nevertheless need this infinite power, converted into benevolence, in order to be accepted on Olympus after his death. It is the goddess herself who offers him her own daughter Hebe for a bride. That event marks the end of a career in which Herakles has been constantly linked to Hera, sometimes by way of her offspring, the legitimate children of Zeus[84]—a career extending from his birth (deliberately delayed by Eileithuia), down through his countless confrontations, direct and indirect, with Ares.[85]

Once the pyre on Mt. Oeta is consumed, Hera receives Herakles without malevolence. Callimachus tells of the goddess's tremendous laughter at the spectacle of the voraciousness of Olympos's new resident. She does even more than that; she mimics the motions of giving birth in order to adopt him.[86] It would be going too far to claim (as a few have done ever since antiquity[87]) that the hero is "really" the offspring of Zeus and Hera. We would be forgetting that the link between Hera and Zeus is no more positive than that between Hera and Herakles; to reconcile all parties at the outset would fail to take into consideration the friction characteristic of the royal couple. That is sufficient reason to continue to embrace the position that Hera simply adopted this son of Zeus.

When the immortalization of Herakles is described as an adoption, the theme of simulated childbirth is largely eclipsed by another tradition that is much better documented among the Greeks and in the ancient world generally. This is the story that Zeus's wife nursed his bastard son in order to make him immortal. The oldest literary sources go no further back than the fourth century B.C. and locate this event in the early childhood of the hero. The pictorial evidence is generally late and more often Etruscan than Greek, but it includes not only the literary version but also the bizarre spectacle of an adult and bearded Herakles being suckled by the goddess.[88] The first version represents a curious suspension, on Hera's part, of a hostility that has already been activated and that will not cease again until the hero's death (though it is true that in this instance Zeus's spouse has been tricked by Athena.) The second version, for all its strangeness, must certainly be placed after the death of Herakles; the symbolic nursing integrates him definitively into the Olympian pantheon.

The picture of the infant Herakles at Hera's breast is an attractive one for those who attempt, in one way or another, to understand the connection between the hero and the goddess as that of son to mother. This is the basis for the interpretation of Diodorus, who claims that the terrified Alcmene exposed the newborn child. Diodorus elaborates further on the "unexpected reversal": the mother who should have loved her child abandoned it and "she who bore a stepmother's hatred toward it saved her natural enemy, inadvertently."[89] Modern interpreters who are anxious to read the relationship of Herakles to Hera as an ambivalent parent-child relationship enthusiastically embrace this lone positive episode in order to balance it against so much that is negative. They see in it the "missing psychological link" that makes it possible to construct a continuous narrative of the mother, alternatively destructive and benevolent, and the son, who is embraced before he is threatened.[90] Those who favor such an interpretation should be warned that the precise Greek facts resist it. First of all, such direct depictions of physical contact between nursing mother and child are rare. One must accept it: adoption and not maternity is to be read in this bizarre image.[91] Furthermore, although Hera represents the married woman in the realm of the gods, she is not very much of a mother with her dubious progeny, on whom she bestows an affection that is indifferent at best.[92]

The second version remains a strange image, a *lectio difficilior*, unambiguously proclaiming the adoption of the hero by the goddess, and thus conferring on Hera the full scope of her role as divine maintainer of sovereignty.[93] This calls to mind the name of Herakles, which translates

equally well into "Glory of Hera" and "Glory through Hera."[94] Either
way the very name of the hero expresses a tight link with his faithful
persecutress. Those who refuse to follow Slater in seeing here "the bitter
irony of the Greek mother-son relationship" have often shied away from
this fact. Historians of religion, who in general have little truck with
ambiguities, have tried to resolve the situation by making it disappear.
The procedure is simple. You begin by listing the episodes and elements
of ritual that argue for harmony between Hera and the hero—there are,
in fact, a few.[95] Then you invent a forgotten prehistory in which the hero
in fact owes his name to his role as consort of the goddess.[96] The restora-
tion of a lost pedigree is an amusingly simple (and unverifiable) solution.
It eliminates all the tensions that clearly constitute Greek mythic thought
in the historic period, when we can observe it in action. The historian of
the imaginary is concerned with the lived experience of the Greeks, not
with the mirage of a past that seems all the more precious for being
irretrievably lost.

Philological analysis has likewise gone off in search of a prehistory,
though along slightly different paths. According to the dubious infer-
ences typically drawn from etymology, Hera presides over that ideal of
youthful accomplishment whose representative in every city in remote
Mycenaean times was simply called *hērōs*. Herakles then emerged as a
privileged specimen for these heroes, who were already closely associated
with the goddess.[97] But this analysis must be confined within its limits,
which are precisely those of etymology. Even if linguistic phenomena
actually do preserve the traces of a lost state of society, there is no justification for treating the complex of myths surrounding Herakles as a
"religious misinterpretation" that turned the original solidarity of the
two protagonists into hostility.[98] We would end up trying to support the
untenable hypothesis that everything that has been said of Herakles from
Homer to our own time is nothing but misinterpretation. But with reference to what truth?

We must accept the fact that by clinging to the idea of the reconcilia-
tion of the two adversaries or by postulating an underlying truth betrayed by history, we forget what is really important. We forget that one
of the recurrent themes of Greek myth and religion is the antagonism,
for better or worse, between a hero and a divinity, against a complex
background of affinity and hostility. Achilles makes no sense without
Apollo, and in that same way Herakles is a figure who, both in dejection
and in triumph, is simultaneously linked to the wife of Zeus and to
glory.[99] Let us look again at the name of the hero. The very reversibility
of the name of Herakles argues for maintaining that ambivalence: he is
simultaneously "glorious through Hera" and "he through whom glory
comes to Hera."[100]

We are obliged, then, to treat the tension between the two translations as richly meaningful for the Greeks. Any alternative would be simplistic, in that it would risk forgetting along the way that neither Hera nor Herakles is a simple figure: the goddess, a strange and disturbing spouse,[101] embodies the ambivalence of the Greek male toward his wife (a necessary but terrible evil, frequently pictured in fantasy as possessing masculine power); the hero, whose surface constitutes his being, has experienced all the reversals of strength and its opposite.

We must accept that there is a tight bond, expressed primarily as hostility, between the goddess of marriage and the divine bastard with his vast matrimonial experience. There is just one text that suggests that this bond of hostility was all the more powerful for having been reciprocal. Let us turn finally to the episode in which Herakles attacks Hera, as if to throw back in her face the dependence in which she has him trapped. In book 5 of the *Iliad*, Diomedes, encouraged by Athena, has wounded Aphrodite. Weeping, Aphrodite comes to her mother Dione for help and consolation. Dione explains to her that she must bear up just as other Olympians have in the past when mortals brought suffering on them. Of the three examples she gives, two involve Herakles turning his arrows against the gods, with Hera conspicuous among his targets:[102]

> Hera suffered, when the powerful son of Amphitryon shot her in the right breast with a three-barbed arrow. Incurable pain gripped her then. (*Il.* 5.392–94)

And so Herakles attacks the breast of Hera, where another tradition tells us he was nursed. Although Homer never mentions this other story, many historians of religion have made the link between them. In order to do this, they emphasize a detail that I have not mentioned thus far: the baby Herakles, already in infancy excessively strong or energetic, seems to have pulled on the goddess's breast so powerfully that she pushed him away in pain.[103] The ancients, however, had already (though long after Homer) established the link between this aggressive hunger and the arrow with three barbs that Herakles shot at Hera. For the poet Lykophron, the two episodes coexist in the life of the hero, by way of a significant recapitulation: Herakles is designated as the one "who struck in the breast with a painful arrow the goddess who had given him birth for the second time, the invincible one."[104]

Hera the invulnerable is wounded by Herakles, producing pain that Homer calls "incurable." The comparison is striking and has inspired all sorts of explanations, from the scholiast on the *Iliad* who claims that Herakles attacked the goddess because she had once refused him her breast, to Philip Slater, obsessed with the theme of venomous malignancy, who dwells on the milk of the bad mother, poisoned in the breast by the arrow dipped in the venom of the Lernaean Hydra.[105] Here more than ever, we must keep a clear head; once again, we will stick close to the indications we have, to the "burden of names and things." In this case, we have the arrow and the breast, along with the images that a Greek might associate with them. We shall not look into the various associations that make the archer an ambiguous, devalued, and even effeminate creature, albeit one who is simultaneously feared as a super-warrior.[106] We shall look more closely at Hera's breast.

The female breast (especially when it is Helen's) can of course have erotic value for the Greek imagination—Hecuba in *Iliad* 22 describes it strikingly as the place "where cares are forgotten" (*lathikēdēs mazos*). It nevertheless remains primarily an emblem of maternity. Hecuba in vain shows her breast to her son Hector in order to deter him from fighting Achilles; the sight of Clytemnestra's breast nearly breaks the murderous determination of Orestes; the breast of Jocasta is evoked obsessively in Euripides' *Phoenician Women*, that tragedy of maternal love. Never is a woman's breast more fascinating than when it belongs to a mother.[107] But despite this habitual representation, that fascination always breaks down, and for Jocasta as well as for Hecuba or Clytemnestra, it is finally the son's rejection, even his hatred, that takes the place of an expected seduction. Men, it seems, are not willing to forgo men's concerns, and above all, it seems, the maternal figure is as much hated as she is an object of desire. Thus when Herakles wounds Hera in the breast, it is really her maternity that he attacks.

Nevertheless, the text adds a detail to which Homer's readers have not always given sufficient attention.[108] It is the *right* breast of Hera that Herakles shoots. It is well known that the Greeks established a close correlation between the right side and the male, the left side and the female. The right belonged to the warrior, the left to women, and in Hippocratic physiology the gestation of a male infant inside the female body is systematically associated with the right side of the womb and with the right breast.[109] By taking aim at the masculine side of Hera,[110] what is Herakles attacking? One possibility is that it is masculinity in woman, and clearly the goddess is not lacking in virility. Hera does not refuse to be identified as a warrior, and when she is hit in the right breast, she is wounded like a warrior—not that she "really" takes on such a role in the elliptical narrative of book 5.[111] Can we bring the warrior one step closer to his mother by pointing out that the wound to the right breast strikes the woman who gives birth to sons?[112] We can, and the Greek tradition on the associations of right and left is so wholly consistent that I am inclined to say, we *must*. But the historian of the imaginary must stop at this point, unless he or she is bold enough to call this son Herakles, based on the iconography that always depicts the hero sucking the milk of imortality from Hera's right breast.[113] Nevertheless, the historian of the imaginary may have doubts about the legitimacy of interpreting the text of Homer by way of later images, in which one is reluctant to see anything but the influence of Homer. Are we to imagine some sort of hostility on the part of the son of Zeus toward the goddess who gave birth to Ares? None of this is crazy, but none of it can be verified. Homer unfortunately does not provide the reader with a book of instructions, and so, even at best, this sort of reasoning reproduces the procedures of the Hellenistic scholars. The temptation to interpret progressively further can become irresistible when we have such precise details, certainly meaningful and yet framed in silence. But where texts are concerned, we must bear in mind that if there is no possible verification, the interpretive impulse may leave one talking in a void. We run such risks, at least, unless we orient ourselves solidly to the text and in its own context—that is, to the system of signifiers, and yes, to the chains of associations, if the association among these signifiers in Greek were not so imperiously programmed (but it is true, after all, that what we call "free" association is first and foremost driven association)—and to the unity of the text from which the reader, myself, has unashamedly extracted the information that interested her.

It is better to go back to the Homeric text to determine what it says. I shall keep close to the development of the episode, which begins on the battlefield and ends in the Olympian home of Dione. At the outset, Athena gives the hero Diomedes the mission of wounding Aphrodite, and only Aphrodite, out of all the deities that are mixed in among the mortal warriors in savage combat. He wounds her arm, taking aim at the goddess who knows nothing of war, but what he strikes is the tender mother trying to snatch her son Aeneas from the bloody melee. In "terrible" pain she returns to Olympus with the help of Ares (elsewhere, her lover or her husband) and flees to the protective embrace of her mother Dione, former wife of Zeus, who gives her daughter the help that Aphrodite herself has been unable to provide Aeneas. The helpless mother learns from the lips of her own mother the sufferings that heroes have inflicted on gods. The first god mentioned in this story within the story is again Ares, Hera's son, saved at the point of death by the goddess, in this case considered a stepmother by Ares' human adversaries (again, mother by marriage, hostile to her stepsons and gentle on the shackled god—as if every maternal figure must be evoked here at once). Then it is Hera's turn, and persecutress becomes persecuted. As her adversary, and later as adversary of Hades, Herakles is identified by his paternal genealogy. In a subsequent passage, Homer will mention Zeus, but for the time being he makes Herakles the son of Amphitryon, as if to deprive the hero of any motive derived from Hera's famous jealousy; this is a discreet way of keeping that theme out of the picture. The truth will come out again in the passage on Hades, but in the tale of Dione, it seems to have been important to leave all the initiative in the hostilities against the gods and Hera to Herakles. Hades suffers as well, when Herakles wounds him in the shoulder, but the brother of Zeus is healed, just as Aphrodite will be healed through her mother's care, once the tale is over. This is the end of the episode. Still guided by Athena, Diomedes will later succeed in adding Ares to the list of the wounded.

No particular lesson emerges at the end of this text, which depicts the family of the Olympians living out its divinity in wounds given and received. The *Iliad* is first and foremost a tale, a narrative. But there are a few things to say. There is a secret structural homology between the real battlefield and the clashes between gods and mortals in Dione's tale, if only because in both, mothers face warriors. In both cases, moreover, sons of Zeus face Hera and her son Ares. Herakles shoots his arrows at Hera; Athena arms Diomedes against Ares and his accomplice Aphrodite. The son of Zeus and the protégé of his favorite daughter are pitted against the supreme goddess and against her son, whose epithet "scourge of mortals" cannot protect him. Is Hera deemed a mother when Herakles shoots her, in this episode where the arms of the mother give way to the arms of the warrior? Yes, she is—enough so to be wounded, so that the arrow may tear the breast, the emblem of maternity, of that mother's body. She is too little of a warrior to stand up to the hero of endurance. She pays the price through the incurable pain in her right breast, the pain of the mother stricken in her body, and perhaps also through the suffering of the masculine element within her.

Throughout the long history of this myth, the relationship between Hera and Herakles is constantly played out in such a way that each of them is placed in confrontation with the element of the *other* sex that is contained within the adversary. Hera generally takes the initiative, persecuting the hero in perpetual defiance of his masculinity and prepared to visit on him the criminal insanity that belongs to women. But the son of Zeus is capable of using his arrows to remind his stepmother that she is a far from perfect warrior—she, the divine model of the wife, whose vocation in the world of men is to realize herself as a mother.

We shall end our inquiry with this last version of the exchange that constantly disrupts the equilibrium of masculine and feminine. It has taken us from the contradictory relationships of Herakles with women to the intimate link between the hero and the feminine. We have had to realize that the feminine element is part of the ambivalence of virile strength, and that it serves in many ways to amplify that strength. Finally, we have addressed the classic question of Herakles and the aggression of Hera—a confrontation between adversaries who are too well matched to get along without each other.

Along the way we have taken a vast amount of material into account—epic texts, tragic and comic plays, Hellenistic poetry, the visual arts, and cult phenomena. The risk, of course, was to lose sight of the myth, which I will follow others in defining by way of its "commitment to narrative."[114] But we have no preserved epic of Herakles, no *Herakleid*, and so we have had to try to synthesize one. One justification for the enterprise is the popularity of Herakles in the Greek imagination, an eminently Panhellenic hero. The cities and the poets never stopped reworking the figure of Herakles, all the time respecting its internal logic, which is to embody the idea of strength put to the test. We have had to take care to preserve the historicity of each bit of evidence and the specificity of its own mode of significance, ranging from Homer to Plutarch and, within a single period, from tragedy to comedy (which, for once, shows itself in this context to be as important as its more prestigious rival). There are many ways of presenting the same mythic hero.

I have also attempted to clarify the nature of the questions that historians and anthropologists of Greece ask, as well as those questions they deem it unnecessary to ask, at risk of wandering off the track of the Greek imagination. One of the most delicate matters is certainly that of interpretation. If, in the end, I do not propose a comprehensive interpretation of Herakles in his struggle with the female, and if all along the way I have stopped interpreting at those points where it would have been necessary to go beyond the limits of a text that was itself incapable of contradicting the chain of associations forged by the interpreter, the reason is that I am not absolutely sure we have any business, when dealing with a heroic figure, to start off by interpreting it—if by interpretation we mean the evidence of a "family resemblance" between our position as moderns and Greek discourse. Because nothing is more difficult to imagine than such a resemblance (how to find a place between anthropologists who, by definition, refuse to accept the idea and psychoanalysts who feel "at home" with Greek myths[115]—how, indeed, except once again to take a position at the boundary), I have tried to follow the Greek chain of associations. I have refused to bring down Herakles to a "virtual psychological ground" whose very generality might give a plausible impression of immediacy, and I have undertaken this exploration at the surface level of the signifiers, dipping only little by little, detail by detail, into the paradoxical substance of a mythic figure.

At this point perhaps each of us, anthropologist, historian, and psychoanalyst, must choose his or her own approach to the hero, with or without the Greeks, who used their story of Herakles to explore the problem of their status as sexed creatures endowed with political power.

Nevertheless, no feeling of supposed closeness could ever justify our failure to consider what the Greeks could have understood by their own associative material, to ask what was at stake when they endowed the *peplos* of Herakles or the right breast of Hera with meaning. There are modes of Greek discourse that invite us into the role of addressee because they are explicitly directed at that other which is posterity. But can we be sure that the same is true of everything that, generally speaking, derives from myth? To put it differently, when we inquire into the Greek "reception" of a myth, perhaps we will always be unsure whether we can ever really occupy the position of the intended audience of this discourse and enter into a dialogue, hearing it as intended by the Greek speaker who told it in the confidence that his Greek audience would immediately make sense of his tale, because he, too, is its audience. I have tried not to betray either this doubt or this inquiry.

And still, I will not deny that to postulate, as I have done, that there is something called Greek sexuality (by which I mean an autonomy of the sexual sphere that cannot be systematically reduced to a taxonomy of social roles), and by crossing the boundary prudently guarded by anthropologists of Greece, I have implicitly taken on the position of interpreter, which amounts to reducing the distance so carefully maintained between "them" and "us" (as if it were not always we who question the Greeks!).

Astounding Herakles: he is pure surface, but his figure has led us to the most intimate encounter with the presence of the feminine in man, unmasking a sexuality barely concealed in social practices, compelling the reader to become an interpreter, and thereby, like it or not, to become engaged in the object under interpretation.

Will we ever be able leave the son of Zeus, a hero strong in his weakness?[116]

PART THREE

SOCRATES IS A MAN

(Philosophical Interlude)

IF THE INSTITUTIONS of classical Athens serve as points of anchorage for the official paradigm of the citizen as a "pure" *anēr*, inherently or permanently devoid of femininity, even corporeality,[1] these studies extend the invitation to modify the import of such a model. At least this model should be considered a localized phenomenon, which is realized where the domain of politics is subject to abstract thinking but competes everywhere else with representations—adopted from the epic or inherited from heroic exploits but nonetheless current—in which virility, in order to be complete, must incorporate within it something of the feminine.

Other orthodoxies begin to emerge, in which rivals (that is, other models for the *anēr*) disrupt the peaceful coexistence between citizen and hero. One of the most highly developed of these is the figure of the philosopher, and even though the multiplicity of schools during the Hellenistic period assigns him varied forms, some of which are mutually antagonistic, overall consistency prevails: a consistency indelibly marked by qualities that Plato, along with others, endeavors to shape into the model for man (virile *anēr* in his achievement, but also mortal like an *anthrōpos*) and philosopher.

What happens when the philosopher replaces the citizen as the paradigmatic *anēr*? When a thinker such as Plato presides over this substitution, the issue is the outcome of a complex strategy. To proceed most quickly, I intend to consider his tactics along two parallel, indeed contiguous or blurred axes: the status of the body and relationship of this model to femininity.

Pledged to give up his *sōma*, this irreplaceable basis for life that he nonetheless owes the city because the city is the source of all life,[2] the citizen had, so to speak, only the loan of his body. The philosophical *anēr*, on the contrary, is the possessor of a body. More exactly, he has something of a body, or again, he needs a body if only in order better to choose to separate himself from it via a well-considered and controlled practice of asceticism. Such is the goal of this corporeality, a goal that ultimately has the same expropriating effect as the view that dismisses the citizen's claim to identify with his *sōma*. But in the meantime, philosophical thought abandons itself to great joy, as it attributes the most feminine of experiences, which it associates with the philosopher's body, to the *anēr* and invents maieutics to offer men the initiatory pains of childbirth[3] —or in matters of *psukhē*, it delights in lingering on the searing pleasures felt by the soul, drunk, mad, or impregnated by the sight of a beautiful object.[4] And what can be said about the dissertations in the *Phaedo* concerning the soul's fragility, which the body's agitations threaten to contaminate?[5]

Taking another step, one discovers Herakles behind Socrates. It might be possible to explain the recurrent allusions to the hero in the dialogues in terms of a single paradoxical reevaluation of the body and a heroism regulated by the disconcerting vicissitudes of strength. But that would be going too far. For the Socratic Herakles knows femininity to the same extent that the authentic philosopher is subjected to the sufferings of childbirth: in the maieutic scene of the *Theaetetus*, the philosophical apprentice is the one who gives birth, and his child is neither viable nor legitimate. Socrates is the midwife, and in no case the soul in labor; and under the heading of *ponos*, the Herakles with whom he identifies, ignorant of excess, experiences only the relaxation of hot baths.

Here the very representations that Plato so readily employs are set at a distance. Or, to be more exact, when the body and femininity are involved, the time will always come when this removal is irrevocably confirmed.

Banish the body, banish the woman; they immediately return. This is probably the first Platonic maneuver (if not his only tactic, at least the ultimate of his gambits, or so I persisted for a long time in thinking): first to exclude,[6] and second, almost simultaneously, by means of a generalized metaphorization, to reappropriate what has been rejected; and the vocabulary and representations of what had initially been denied are swept up into the philosopher's quest for definition. The feminine is incorporated, the body moves into the very substance of the soul. But at the end it has to be admitted: Herakles takes part in the process that follows, in which the woman and the body are finally challenged, and after being absorbed to the point at which they become invisible, they are set apart from the edification that is the outcome of the philosophical paradigm. A portrait of the philosopher as hero: the comedian's lion's skin covering a flawless interior.

The ultimate paradox: if Socrates has a body, like the soul it must ply itself to the enterprise of immortality, for it is its tangible foundation. And Platonic immortality forever claims to be based on separation: reducing what has been mixed to produce pure elements.

Would the statement "Socrates is a man" announce the end of all ambiguities besetting the paradigm of the *anēr*?

Chapter 8

THEREFORE, SOCRATES IS IMMORTAL

To SPEAK OF THE SOUL is to speak of immortality, for the Western soul is immortal (that statement could be considered a tautology). This soul was born in the *Phaedo*; in fact, it provides the dialogue's subtitle. So if we are to discuss the soul, we must reread the *Phaedo*.
—Reread the *Phaedo*: Whatever for? It's such a bore and so spiritualistic.
—Reread the *Phaedo*? Maybe. But there is nothing left to say about it. Tradition—and what a tradition it is—has already said it all.

Two reactions: on the one hand, an outright rejection of what is seen as an edifying text; on the other, a reverential reiteration of a long tradition of spiritualistic commentaries.[1] Both attitudes tend to distance us from this once much-read dialogue. But between the two extremes, is there no other possible approach to the *Phaedo*?

One effect of this double warning might be to prompt us to look further, in the hope of devising a new strategy for coping with the enormous prestige of this dialogue, a prestige based, first, on its supposedly authentic account of Socrates' death; second on its purely philosophical speculation (some developments of which are dauntingly difficult); and third, of course, on the immortality of the soul—for which the *Phaedo* is said to contain more than one proof.

This study will attempt a new reading of the *Phaedo*, not by calling on philology, philosophy, or theology,[2] but by turning, for once, to history. However, there is no point in pondering the historicity of the account of Socrates' death: this question has been left behind by now, as it always has been for readers alive to the role that fiction plays in Plato's work. Rather, let us concentrate on the new departure that the *Phaedo* represents in Greek (and, more generally, Western) representations of immortality. To claim that in this dialogue the immortality of the soul made its official entry into Greek thought is not to forget all that the subject owes to the mysticism of the Orphic and Pythagorean sects, long before Plato:[3] that is something the text of the *Phaedo* itself acknowledges, frequently justifying its initiatory concept of philosophy with appeals to "ancient discourse (*palaios logos*). But the important point is that with the *Phaedo* and the institutionalization of philosophy as a literary genre, a line of thinking, hitherto marginal to the life of the city, acquired a legitimacy that was never again disputed.

But to note this new departure is only half the battle: we must still find out what it is about this text that made such a turning point possible in the Greek representations of immortality. The *Phaedo* may be a seminal text, but in order to discover a reading of it that does more than just reiterate the tradition, let us try to analyze the discursive tactics adopted by this daring promotion of immortality. The aim of the present study will be to seize both on the ways in which dialogue breaks new ground and on the features that established it as a tradition.

A PRACTICE OF SEPARATION

From Homer down to the classical period, Greek man had a body (*sōma*) and a *psukhē* (a word that I shall not translate at this point for fear of identifying it prematurely with "soul"). This *psukhē* was liberated by death. Let us see what a Greek would make of these two notions in the three consecutive, or at times concurrent, figures with which he identified: the epic hero, the soldier-hero of the classical period, and the philosopher. As it happens, these three images correspond to three models of death, and this correspondence imbues them with their exemplary importance.

Consider the death of the Homeric hero: if the collectivity to which he belongs treats the inert corpse in the appropriate fashion, the deceased warrior will attain the social status of death, the bard will be able to sing of his undying glory (*kleos aphthiton*) for the edification of posterity, and his *psukhē* will join the dim, fleeting shades of the dead from the past, in Hades.[4] This last stage is certainly a crucial moment, and yet for Homer, the body seems infinitely more real than the insubstantial *psukhē* that upon death flees, weeping, from the warrior, at last to become a shade among other shades. Gently mocking Socrates' questioners, Plato recalls this: "You seem to have a childish fear that the wind literally blows a soul to bits when it quits the body and scatters in all directions, more especially if one happens to die when it's blowing a full gale."[5]

Now let us consider the death in battle of the soldier-citizen of classical Athens. He has given his life (*bios*) for the city—but equally, the texts sometimes say that he has given his body (*sōma*) or his *psukhē*, which was his breath of life. In exchange the city gives him immortal glory beyond death and a place in the memory of the living. He may go to Hades (always supposing that something remains of him to make that journey, apart from his name, which now belongs to the collective memory of the living); but that is not the essential point. The civic tradition does not have much to say about what becomes of this glorious dead warrior, for the full meaning of his death now belongs to the city. The citizen's life was of scant importance; the collectivity bestowed it on him. Nor did his body matter: already cremated on the field of battle, it has been reduced to bones, an abstract basis on which to construct the political ceremony of the public funeral rites. The official orator steps forward to celebrate the city through its dead; all that matters now are his words.[6]

Socrates is about to die, and as he awaits death, he speaks of immortality—the death of his body and the immortality of the soul (and since the essence of the Western soul lies in its immortality, we need no longer translate that term, *psukhē*). In other words, according to Socrates, body and soul are already irrevocably separated, just as are the visible and the invisible, that which is destined to lose its identity and that which keeps it forever, the dissoluble and the indissoluble, the mortal and the divine. But he explains to his disciples that this dialectical division preexists whatever death will bring about: namely, *lusis kai khōrismos*, the detachment and separation of the soul, which death liberates from the body. Sentenced by the city to die, the model philosopher awaits his death. He does not anticipate it by suicide: he has already done so far better in his lifetime, since he knows that "to philosophize is to learn to die." He has trained himself to reject all the pleasures of the body so that, even in the here and now, his life resembles as closely as possible the existence of one who is dead. Socrates' disciples will have to part from him, bidding him that same farewell (*khaire*) that the funeral *stēlai* in the Athenian cemeteries repeat over and over again. And Socrates, for his part, bids a serene and seemingly joyful farewell to all that he is leaving, all that he has already left: the mass of Athenians, the life of a man and a citizen, the body. Hence, the series of exits—not to say expulsions—and leavetakings, all rehearsals for the farewell to the body, that punctuate the *Phaedo*.[7] Because all life is in the soul, the philosopher, at last liberated from his body, will know the bliss of Hades, the last abode of every soul delivered from its *sōma* but endowed with thought (*phronēsis*)[8]—indeed, assimilated into the very activity of thinking. Socrates the *atopos*, disconcerting as he was in having no place of his own in his lifetime, prepares himself for the only journey conceivable, for even the affirmation of immortality does not preclude the need to "organize one's space in the beyond."[9] He will die so as to philosophize in the underworld . . . meanwhile, the poison is already being prepared for him.

While the text of the *Phaedo* is well known, this brief summary will at least have helped us grasp the full extent of Plato's innovations and to assess the consequences of his shifting the emphasis from the body to the soul, which is now regarded as immortal. From the age of the epic to the world of the city, death was a matter for the society of the living. In Plato the individual philosopher sets out to reappropriate it for himself, laying claim to the blessed status of death. Society dealt with the bodies of its members after the event; the individual is concerned about his soul in advance. For the Homeric hero and the citizen of Athens, death, the threshold of glory, came about in a last battle of warriors; the philosopher, in contrast, has rehearsed the annihilation of his *sōma* throughout his life, and because for him the battle with the body began with his philosophical life, the battle with death is neither a beginning nor an end. So if we speak of immortality in both cases, we must be clear about our terms: as used to qualify glory, immortality came after death; but in the *Phaedo* the soul, immortal in its essence, must be prepared for its autonomy before death takes place. As for the body, its fate is of no concern.

Phaedo the narrator recalls the scene: his long locks tumbled about his neck and, as the discussion seemed to be grinding to a halt, Socrates stroked his head:

> "Tomorrow, I daresay, Phaedo, you will clip these fair tresses."
> "I suppose so, Socrates," I replied.
> "But if you take my advice, you won't."
> "Oh, but why not?" I asked.
> "Because this very day we will both of us clip our hair if our talk [*logos*] comes to a dead end and we can't bring it back to life!" (89b)

For the next of kin, mourning involved imitating with one's own body the loss of life that the passing of the loved one represented. Wailing and beating her breast, Socrates' wife, Xanthippe, has already anticipated the mourning for Socrates, and she has been firmly removed from the group of philosophers right at the beginning of the dialogue. Phaedo, overly faithful to the city's customs, intends to crop his hair in mourning for Socrates. But the philosopher teaches him the uselessness of such funerary rites: at this point all that counts is the *logos*, for it concerns the immortality of the soul.

The same goes for the way in which a corpse is treated. From the age of the epic to classical Athens, society exorcised death with rites of passage. Between dying and being dead, rituals took place, and no one had the right to be called dead unless the funerary rites had been performed in his honor, authorizing his *psukhē* to enter the misty kingdom of the underworld.[10] But the philosopher has telescoped the natural order of time, anticipating dying by practicing death:[11] he has no need of a transition managed by society; once liberated, his soul needs no authorization to move on to Hades without more ado. The complete philosopher, at least, is convinced of the inanity of the rites, even if his timorous disciples need his reassurance; for while they are certainly eager to believe in the immortality of the soul, they continue, swayed as they are by social practice, to attribute too much reality to "what is visible of man, the body, lying there for all to see—what we call the corpse." So Socrates has to comfort the Theban Cebes, who is afraid that the soul will be dispersed and annihilated as it leaves the body and is overly impressed by how long a corpse lasts and even by the seeming "immortality" of some of its parts, such as the sinews and tendons.[12]

Once he has produced his arguments, Socrates proceeds to implement his conclusions: having convinced his disciples, Socrates can use his own body to subvert the funerary ritual. He draws on all the resources of his cunning intelligence. First, he undermines the canonical temporal sequence of the rites. Custom dictates that the body be bathed and prepared soon after death, after which the corpse is laid out (*prothesis*); then the funeral procession (*ekphora*) and burial take place. By dying already bathed[13] and reclining, Socrates compels the whole first stage of the ritual while still alive. To be sure, he has ready justification to account for this bath which, in itself, is an anomaly: "I really think it is better to have a bath than to give the women the trouble of washing a dead body" (115a)—a creditable gesture of consideration that is somewhat disconcerting coming from one whom Aristophanes accused of never washing. But Socrates' words are unlikely to satisfy any thinking reader. Any number of interpretations have been suggested for this bath: the partisans of initiations have seen it as a ritual purification in the strictest Orphic tradition, while philosophers have not failed to point out that by bathing Socrates himself commences the funerary rituals, as if he were already dead. I would only add that, by acting this way, Socrates is not only denying his dead body any influence over the future fate of his soul: by depriving the women of their traditional intervention with the corpse, which they consider their concern, he denies them their essential ritual role. In a similar fashion, Crito later takes the women's place when, on the philosopher's death, he hurries to close his mouth and eyes: the group of disciples replaces the dead man's kin; his companions in thought take the place of the women.[14]

Thus transferring to friends what seemed due to his family is the second means of subversion that Socrates adopts, and it is altogether consistent with his overall attitude. His third and last ploy consists of proclaiming not the basic pointlessness of funerary rituals, but the sage's indifference toward practices that are all equally worthless, since none of them has the slightest bearing on what is essential, and he leaves the choice among them to others. Socrates is no Diogenes: he does not arrange to have his corpse thrown to the dogs and birds of prey,[15] and to Crito's question, "How are we to bury you?" he simply replies, "However you like." Never mind if the illustrious Cynic, his overzealous imitator, freezes Socratic indifference toward the body into a rigid code. Socrates himself, who is more truly detached from life—and probably less critical of the city—leaves everything to do with his funeral rites up to

Crito. It is a good choice. Crito, the long-standing companion and orthodox double of the unorthodox Socrates, has throughout the dialogue held a special place in the little group gathered to attend the philosopher on the threshold of death. He is the only Athenian not confined to the role of a speechless interlocutor, although, locked in his distress and totally absorbed by his preoccupation with all that concerns the body and life of his friend, he has taken no part in the dialectical discussion. But as he quite rightly entrusts the care of his body to Crito, Socrates cannot resist teaching his undialectical companion a lesson on the immortality of the soul: "Bury me however you like," he says, then adds "provided you can catch me and prevent my escaping you." If Socrates, while still alive, truly exists entirely in his *logos*, as he claims, Crito should understand that "Socrates" is nothing but his soul, a soul that, at the moment of death, will immediately flee the lifeless body: so the corpse that Crito will shortly see burned or buried no longer deserves the name "Socrates," and "he won't have to distress himself on my behalf, as though I were being outraged."[16] And "with a quiet laugh," the philosopher exhorts his friend (and through him, the rest of his sorrowful companions) to perform the funeral rites as no more than what Pascal was to call "an afterthought" (*une pensée de derrière*): "And he won't have to say, at the funeral, that it is Socrates whom he is laying out or carrying to the grave or burying" (115c–e).

Socrates is leaving, going to "some happy land of the blessed" (115d): the philosopher's lot is that which Hesiod reserved for the elite of the heroes of the Trojan War, and which Pindar, in his second *Olympian*, kept for the favorites of the gods:[17] for his body, rites now rendered devoid of meaning; for the philosopher, identified with his soul, immortal life. It is up to his disciples to decipher the traces of the soul's immortality upon his inert, silent, opaque corpse. It is a difficult lesson, and one only Socrates' still-living voice can convey in the face of all the accepted ideas of the city. But if we are to gauge the full extent of the originality that the *Phaedo* introduces into Greek thought about death, we must examine how it is that assimilating Socrates to his soul immediately procures Phaedo a philosophic life among the Blessed in Hades.

THE PHILOSOPHER'S COURAGE

All men are mortal.
Socrates is a man.
Therefore, Socrates is mortal.

This well-known argument is a favorite scholastic illustration of an Aristotelian syllogism.[18] Whether or not it is truly demonstrative, the exemplary quality of this model demonstration is founded on the exemplary mortality of Socrates, and that fact is probably not without significance. But is the Socrates of the *Phaedo* a man (*anthrōpos*)? Or rather: is he *just* a man?

One point must be made immediately. In the *Phaedo*, Plato presents Socrates as being in many respects the model philosopher, and the text of his dialogue is a linguistic monument designed to celebrate Socrates the philosopher. Similarly, in archaic poetry, the prologue of the *Theogony* and Aesop's *Life* provided an identity and name for the model (or "generic") poet Hesiod or Aesop. That may seem a surprising comparison until one remembers that in the interval between his sentence and his execution, Socrates turned poet with an imitation of Aesop, who was, like him, both a servant of Apollo and a victim sacrificed to the god. It is with a mention of Aesop's name that Cebes opens the dialogue at the beginning of the *Phaedo*, and for just a moment the image of the *therapōn* of Apollo takes the place of that of the philosopher. Of course, the comparison between Socrates and Aesop goes no further: the poet may be presented as an alternative to the image of the philosopher, but Socrates the philosopher was never to be the object of a heroic cult as was the poet Aesop;[19] nevertheless, the text of the *Phaedo*, which condenses the life of Socrates into his last moments, is the founding text for a discourse on immortal glory, a discourse with many traditional features whose well-known themes provide a contrapuntal accompaniment to Plato's innovative theory of the immortality of the soul.

But it is not in the domain of the poet, explicitly mentioned in the text, but in the domain of the warrior where I will seek an answer to the question, "Is Socrates only a man?" Greek language and thought accommodate men of more than one kind: on the one hand, there is the human being (*anthrōpos*), and on the other, there is the virile man (*anēr*), endowed with great qualities and valor, whom the texts delight in distinguishing from the common run of passive human beings. The epic hero is an *anēr*; so too is the soldier-citizen of the Athenian funeral speech, that bit of civic ideology. Now at the very heart of the *Phaedo*, we find an image of the virile man, the *anēr philosophos*, repeatedly set in opposition to the common run of mortals (*anthrōpoi*). This opposition is essential to the dialogue and is introduced at a crucial point in it (64a–65a): if we are to understand the meaning of this acclimatization to death that the philosophic life constitutes, we must dismiss the multitude from our minds (and along with it, its spokesman, the comic poet), that multitude which regards philosophers as "moribund"[20] because they entertain, in their lifetimes, a morbid love of death. "Philosophers desire death [*thanatōsi*]," declares the multitude, promptly offering them the fate to which they aspire. So it is that the Athenians condemn Socrates to death, emulating Aristophanes's Strepsiades who, in the *Clouds*, ends up by burning down the "thinking-house" of the intellectuals. Meanwhile, however, the philosopher calmly takes leave of the multitude and all its opinions; and only at this point does the text present the opposition between soul and body, an opposition beyond the comprehension of the Athenian multitude. It is also at this point that the soul is allowed to escape symbolically from the body, since it could not escape earlier from this human life from which no *anthrōpos* has the right to flee by means of suicide.

And what of the *anēr philosophos*? He is not far away. If, from Achilles through to the hoplite, and from the hoplite through to the citizen, the virile man has been characterized by the fact that he enters willingly on the "paths that lead to his chosen death" ("les voies de la mort choisie"),[21] it is significant that throughout the *Phaedo* the philosopher's choice is defined as an acceptance of death. It is a deliberate acceptance, the recognition of a law, rather than a quest for annihilation. And this reasoned rather than impulsive desire is expressed by the verb *ethelein*. The word itself suggests the hoplite tradition behind the philosophy and behind Socrates' choice, the choice of the soldier-citizen who accepts (*ethelei*) death for the sake of the city.[22] The philosopher is an *anēr*, just as are the hoplite and the citizen and, like the hero and the soldier-citizen, he knows how to die. In other words, if Plato borrows his language from the civic tradition, the reason is that he intends to replace one model with another—the soldier-citizen with the *anēr philosophos*. The funeral speech views the Athenians as "true citizens" (*gnēsioi politai*); the *Phaedo* prefers true philosophers (*gnēsioi philosophoi*: 66b2). With the twist of language, Plato records something that he was largely responsible for bringing about: the fourth-century victory of the philosopher over the citizen as the model of the virile man.

All virile men confront danger, and the philosophic life is based on that fine risk (*kalos kindunos*) which consists in taking a chance on the immortality of the soul. This is just what the truly philosophic risk involves: believing in the immortality of the soul, conforming to that idea through one's actions, and convincing reluctant questioners, whose objections may at any moment deal a "death blow" to the *logos*. And it is a much graver risk than that faced by Socrates when he confronted his judges. The philosopher's *Apology* did not save his life because it did not win over the city; but it would have been far worse if he had failed to instill in his disciples the idea that the soul truly is immortal: that is why we should regard the *Phaedo* as Socrates' real "apology" (defense).

But both the beginning and the end of the *Phaedo* also contain something akin to a funeral speech for a philosopher who has known how to die nobly (*gennaiōs*) and who was acknowledged as the most courageous (*aristos*), wise, and righteous man of his time. Really, a funeral speech? . . . Yes, really. The attentive reader will perhaps remember that Plato did, in fact, take an interest in the literary genre of the funeral speech, to which he even devoted a dialogue that is named, significantly enough, after one of the silent interlocutors of the *Phaedo*.[23] If the list of those friends gathered around Socrates is symbolic—and there is every reason to suppose that it is, considering both those who are present and those who are not, and those mentioned and those not mentioned[24]—then the fact that Menexenus is one of those present is probably no mere chance: Menexenus, whose name appeared last among all the Athenians present on that day, and for whom Socrates produced his brilliant parody of the civic funeral speech.

We should read the *Menexenus* alongside the *Phaedo*. It is an exercise all the more justifiable since the two dialogues appear to have been written around the same date. When we do so, we notice that the *Phaedo* stands in opposition to the collective funeral speech, a social pronouncement that is misguided (if not positively dangerous) in that it apportions to the good man (*agathos*) and the bad man an equal share of glory in the city. The *Phaedo* implicitly praises a man who did not wait for death to reveal his value/valor and who will find bliss in an afterlife, where all clearly know how to distinguish the good from the bad. We might also do well to ponder the hidden resemblance that relates the beginning of the critique of the funeral speech in the *Menexenus* to the formulation of the philosophical ideal of the fine risk. On the one hand, we find *kinduneuei kalon* ("death in battle may be fine indeed"), on the other, *kalos kindunos*; on the one hand, an overtly expressed doubt about the value/ valor of the "fine death" of the soldier-citizen, on the other, the calculated heroism of the philosophical life, with which Socrates closes his discussion. But we should also note another, even more important reversal of the *Menexenus* in the *Phaedo*, one that affects the philosopher as an individual. The *Menexenus* explores the effects of the civic discourse of glory on Socrates; the *Phaedo* creates its effect by presenting the *anēr philosophos* in all his glory. Spellbound by the funeral speech, Socrates reveled in his own immediate sensation of greater nobility (*gennaiōteros*) and in appearing more admirable (*thaumasiōteros*) in the eyes of strangers. But it is a borrowed nobility that disappears as the memory of the orator's words fades away. In the *Phaedo*, in contrast, what we have is the force of the true conviction that emanates from the philosopher's person and that is felt by all, his close companions and the prison jailor alike. The admiration evinced by those around him reaches its peak when he rescues them from a dialectical rout and is able to inspire them with renewed ardor (88e–89a). But it falls to the prison jailor to declare that the highest degree of true nobility (*gennaiōteros*) has been reached by Socrates (116c). There is every justification for admiring the Socrates of the *Phaedo*, for here he is preparing himself for the journey that will take him to the last abode of philosophers, the blessed place of bliss. We cannot help but recall the *Menexenus* and smile at the imaginary journey that Socrates, under the spell of civic eloquence, believed himself to have made to the Islands of the Blessed.

Of course, to appreciate the difference between the Socratic *logos* and the eloquence of the official civic speech, we must be aware of the pitfalls of resemblance. As Plato is always telling us, nothing looks more like the truth than that which is false—which is why he so often labels as "false" a thought whose language he nevertheless tries to twist to his own advantage. Thus, the reader's task is to detect in that very terminology a clash between alternative models. We should note with amusement that in the *Menexenus* the mention of courage (*andreia*) is accompanied by an astonishing juxtaposition of appearance and truth (247d8), but we should pay serious attention when the *Phaedo* declares that "true friends of knowledge are virtuous and brave" (*andreioi*: 83e).

The philosopher thus appropriates *andreia*,[25] which is the word for both "courage" and "virility" and is also the password of the city's ideology. However, it is not only with reference to the *Menexenus* but also more generally that Plato marshalls his forces against the civic language of immortality by systematically dispossessing the funeral speech of its key words. Pericles, in his funeral speech, claims that the Athenians are in love (*erastai*) with the city; moving one step further, and passing from the city itself to what it considers to be immortality, Diotima in the *Symposium* regards glory as the object of love suitable for most people; finally, in the *Phaedo*, the only kind of love is love of thought (*erōs phronēseōs*). For the *anthrōpoi*, then, the city and its glory; for the *anēr philosophos*, the practice of reflection, which feeds the soul. The funeral speech makes no distinction between life, the soul, and the body. Thus it says interchangeably of citizens that they have given their persons (*sōma*) for the city or that they have decided not to cherish life (*philopsukhein*); the philosopher cherishes life no more than the model citizen, but for Plato the word *philopsukhein* will not suffice to express philosophical detachment, since his entire purpose is to wrest the soul from the life of the body. Therefore he forges a new word and sets the philosopher in opposition to the *philosōmatos*, one who loves the body. With his "fine death," the citizen gave all that he had—his life—but according to Lysias in his funeral speech, that life did not belong to him (*psukhē allotria*) anyway. By dismissing all forms of prestige attached to the body, the philosopher of the *Phaedo* rejects them as alien (*allotrious*) to his being, but he retains what is essential, namely thought, which feeds his soul, is truly his own, and will accompany him beyond death. The incalculable advantage of Plato's strategy is that while the words remain the same, an unbridgeable gap is created between glory, on the one hand, and the immortality of the soul, on the other.[26] To return to the point that most interests us, it is small wonder that Plato, who classifies political virtue on the side of the body (82a–b), is anxious to put the civic mechanism of *andreioi* out of action: in order to show that only philosophers are worthy enough to be called *andreioi*, all he need do is declare that "all men are brave out of fear, except philosophers." What the funeral speech is prone to mask is thereby brought to light, namely, the fashion in which civic virtue is treated as an item for barter: for the orators, the "fine death" involved the incommensurable exchange of a life in return for glory, but Socrates regards that as simply swapping one fear for another, albeit one of a different kind.[27]

Exit civic courage, enter the *andreia* of the philosopher, which involves not an exchange but a purification.

This is certainly a strange kind of *andreia* in comparison with the hoplite morality, whose values Socrates delights in subverting. He sets about doing so by incongruously praising flight—the noble flight of the soul—which, as death advances on a man, jubilantly abandons the field to it. A hoplite never takes flight (that is precisely what defines him as such), but even in the *Laches*, Plato, reflecting on courage, has already set a value on retreat: and it was on the occasion of a retreat in the last stages of the battle of Delium that Socrates the hoplite showed the paradoxical courage that Alcibiades praised in the *Symposium*. And as Socrates repeatedly mixes up the vocabulary of war (in which one takes flight) and that of slavery (in which one makes one's escape), we also sense that what he really intends to do is subvert civic courage.

Now we come to the most famous and most frequently discussed passage in the *Phaedo*. When Socrates declares, to justify the prohibition against suicide, that "we men are in a sort of *phroura*" from which we should not free ourselves or escape (62b), how should that word *phroura* be translated? Tradition has a ready reply: without worrying unduly about the fact that this is a noun denoting an action (generally that of "guarding") or that at this point in the dialogue the separation of man into a body and soul has not been introduced or even suggested, it declares that Plato is simply alluding to the Orphic-Pythagorean theory of the body-prison. It is true that the *Gorgias* contains a passage in which it would be hard to avoid translating *phroura* as "prison," but that is an exceptional meaning of the word—not that this is of much concern to the commentators. Of as little concern is the reversal that Plato introduces in the *Phaedo*, when what he likens to a prison is the world of the living and not the world of Hades, which is traditionally seen as one. There is little doubt that the idea of prison is contained in *phroura*; but if we pay closer attention to the passage where Socrates says that this expression "is not easy to get to the bottom of," we will not accept a univocal translation of the word. The fact is that *phroura* is connected not only to the idea of a prison but also with that of a jail for slaves, since the image that follows develops the idea that men are the property of the gods, who mount guard over them. But in the *Phaedo* the word *phroura* also has its most common meaning, the one that Plato gives it in the *Laws*, the one—above all—that his contemporaries gave it quite naturally: *phroura* also means "garrison service," the guards that ephebes mounted along the frontiers of the civic territory, under the surveillance of magistrates. *Phroura* means "surveillance under surveillance." Thus it must be recognized that the word condenses three separate images: first, the image of a prison; second, that of a pen in which slaves—in this case the whole human race—are confined, with the gods as their masters; and third, that of a garrison service that cannot be avoided by taking flight in suicide. Men, who are slaves under the guards set upon them, cannot escape from life. Moreover, being themselves guardians of this life over which the gods preside, they have no right to flee. Those unwilling to recognize the polysemy of the term have tried to exclude the military sense,[28] without noticing that in the *Phaedo* warfare is constantly intertwined with slavery. Furthermore, the warfare in question is not of the standard type. *Phroura* is the correct word for the operations of ephebes or a siege garrison, while *taxis*, "order in the ranks," is the term used in the *Menexenus* for the discipline under which hoplites fight. Historians of philosophy tend to pay insufficient attention to the background of warfare in Plato (presumably because they do not consider warfare a philosophical subject worthy of the great Plato and his discourse on the soul). However, to do so is to miss the contrast, essential to the dialogue, between the general run of humanity and the philosopher: on the one hand, ordinary human beings are forbidden to escape from the *phroura* because men whose bodies and souls are tied together annihilate all that they are when they commit suicide; on the other, the *anēr philosophos*, subjected though he is to the human condition, is able to free his soul so that it can free the body.[29]

In our reading of the *Phaedo*, we shall clearly have to reflect on the virile courage of the philosopher.

Socrates, the model philosopher, faces death without a moment of fear, and that calm proves the soul to be immortal better than any dialectical argument could. He drinks the poison "quite calmly, without a tremor or any change of expression," a worthy descendant of the Homeric heroes among whom a brave man was recognized by the fact that he "never changes color at all and is not . . . perturbed."[30] But when his disciples can contain their grief no longer and burst into tears, lamenting for themselves even as they lament for their companion (as do the mourning women of the *Iliad*), Socrates' reaction is that of a citizen of Athens, where tears, which are essentially feminine, are forbidden to virile men, and it is as hoplite that he speaks, as he recalls his friends to fortitude ("Do not give way!" *karareite*: 117c–e).

In the first part of the dialogue, Socrates dispossessed the multitude of *andreia* by refuting or reversing its accepted values. He countered the funeral speech with his declaration that only philosophers are courageous; as for Aristophanes, who in the *Clouds* compared his pale, emaciated disciples to the Laconian prisoners from Pylos, Socrates refutes him by imprisoning the entire human race in a *phroura*. His calm in the face of death is manifest proof that he is the very embodiment of the philosophical nature to which books 6–7 of the *Republic* attribute the essential quality of *andreia*. Philosophers in general are courageous because they do not give way (*karterei*) to their bodies or their desires (82c), but Socrates in particular is brave in that, in the dialectical discussion, he is a war leader to his disciples. I have already mentioned the admiration that he arouses in his companions when, acting both as a healer and as a good general, he is able to inspire his "routed and beaten" troops with new ardor: Asclepius, the god of medicine, will have truly deserved the cock (the emblem of victory) that Socrates, with his last words, dedicates to him on behalf of the group of philosophers (88e–89a, 118a).[31] But to overcome the defeatism of his followers, he also has had to evoke the part-historic, part-legendary Thyreatid war, a ritual and initiatory battle,[32] and he has promised Phaedo assistance that, in the last analysis, closely resembles the strength of Herakles (89b–c).[33] The point here is that the philosopher's courage is evident in his speech even more than in his life.

The edifying example of Socrates' serenity may be the ultimate proof of the immortality of the soul, but we must also follow the argument to the end. And there is every indication that courage is necessary for the practice of dialectical discussion. This is particularly the case when it concerns the effects of death on the soul—for then childish fears of bogeys must be stilled among the disciples—or when, in the course of a discussion on the opposition of contraries, some hesitant speaker puts forward an objection that terrifies him. Furthermore, one must remain calm when some anonymous fighter from the ranks, bursting with an unthinking courage that smacks of foolhardiness, rekindles the debate (77e, 101a–d, 103a–b). In short, dialectical discussion is a battle, and although the *Phaedo* is not the only dialogue of Plato to make that point,[34] the language of warfare in it breaks through in an exceptionally coherent fashion. One can argue "in Homeric fashion," in other words, waste no time in coming into close quarters with one's adversary (in testing out a theory, that is: 95b); one can stand firm in what one takes to be a strong position (the verb *diiskhurizomai* is repeatedly used in this sense), but in either case one should always "manfully exert oneself" (90e) in tackling the *logos*, because even the process of reasoning out the arguments involves fierce fighting, which, when the ultimate is at stake—namely, the immortality of the soul—sometimes looks very much like a fight to the death (102d–104b).

Thus, whether as epic hero or new-style hoplite, the philosopher stands firm[35] in *logos* as in life, and the masterly dexterity that the philosopher Plato demonstrates throughout the dialogue as he undertakes to appropriate the current values of the city for his tutelary hero cannot fail to command the highest admiration. By irreversibly separating the soul from the body, Plato once and for all detaches the idea of immortality from the civic glory with which it has hitherto been associated. This is where the long Western history of the soul begins. But whether through philosophical cunning or as a result of the unconscious influence of the rich language bequeathed by a glorious past, the *logos* on immortality continues to be accompanied by a displaced and reversed discourse on courage and deliberate death. Perhaps this is one reason, the *Greek* reason, for the *Phaedo*'s brilliant reputation. After all, the innovations that proved successful were perhaps the very ones that on the face of it looked repetitious.

Nevertheless, that is surely not the ultimate reason for the *Phaedo*'s astonishing success. For tradition, as well as for us, this dialogue surely owes its great force to the fact that the model philosopher is here given both a name and a body and claims to have a soul. Since the presence of Socrates animates the model figure of the philosopher, to ponder the originality of the *Phaedo* is almost to reflect on its subtly orchestrated effect of realism. Of course, it is all for the greater glory of the soul in general, but without the slightest doubt, it is also for the particular glory of this mortal Socrates, now immortalized forever.

ON SOCRATES' *LOGOS* AND HIS MEMORABLE BODY

Nothing is left to chance when it comes to authenticating the *Phaedo* as the "historical" account of the death of Socrates: the narrator was present in person (*autos* is the very first word of the dialogue),[36] a fact that guarantees the accuracy of what he says and thereby validates it. This is probably also the function of the calculated vagueness (in the list of Socrates' friends, for example) and even of the memory lapse that causes Phaedo to forget the name of one speaker more zealous than enlightened. As for the famous "Plato was, I believe, not strong enough to attend,"[37] this initially takes the reader's breath away. Before he has had time to recover enough to realize that behind this narrator with the faulty memory stands Plato the writer (who certainly did know how things stood, on this score at least), he has already been carried deeper into the dialogue. But he will probably have to read further before it occurs to him to raise the problem of fiction itself and wonder how this account can possibly claim to be authentic, if Plato himself was absent.

However, as I have already suggested, it is Socrates himself who does the most to persuade us of the truth of the *Phaedo*: the truth of the philosopher's last moments, which this dialogue stages so imaginatively that the reader feels he is actually present; also, the truth of the arguments in favor of the immortality of the soul, which rather depend on Socrates' presence to carry conviction. Of course, one could set out to list the "proofs" of the immortality of the soul, as indeed all too many commentators have done (finding five, or seven, or eleven, or more or fewer such "proofs"). Or, like certain Anglo-Saxon scholars, one might embark on endless discussions of the validity of this or that proof. But to steer us in the right direction, our reading must recognize that the long dialogue of the *Phaedo* is constructed around the process through which the person and the *logos* of Socrates mutually reinforce one another, in order to give credence to the idea that the soul is immortal.[38] Right from the beginning of the dialogue, we learn that "proof is not its primary object,"[39] and even toward the end, we may still be in doubt as to the persuasive power of the *logos* since, to allay the last fears of his disciples, Socrates has to resort to no less than a wager on moral life, following up with a myth (107a–114c). There can be no doubt that, were it not for the active presence of Socrates, the discourse would be in danger of foundering, much to the consternation of the apprentice philosophers so anxious to confirm their wavering beliefs. On the other hand, Socrates needs the *logos* to convince his companions that his serenity is well-founded: the discussion must not "die," because the philosopher is in need of its aid. That is why Socrates is bent on "rescuing the *logos*, breathing new life into it [*eboēthei tōi logōi, anabiōsasthai*]" (88c–89c), after which, with the philosopher's and the argument's combined victory over death assured, it is only fitting to give thanks to Asclepius.[40] In the meantime the solidarity established between the man and the argument that is proclaimed in the passage on "misology" (89d–90d) is so closely maintained throughout the dialogue that particular key words are interchangeable between the two, applying now to Socrates, now the *logos*.[41]

But one question can be put off no longer, for it is one that the *Phaedo* asks forthrightly: Who is Socrates? The answer seems obvious if we do not look beyond the text's explicit message, which elaborates what appears to be a theory of individuality:[42] Socrates is, of course, his soul. In any event, we first learn that, generally speaking, the personality of a philosopher must be identified with his *psukhē*. We pick this up from the phrases in which, in order to avoid any association with the body, the generic "we" of philosophers in general is used, instead of *psukhē*, as the subject of the action (67a). And the reason why Socrates, having defined Hades as the dwelling-place of souls, ends up installing "the dead" there, is that it is at the moment of death that the essence of a man ideally passes into his soul: the dead man no longer has a body, but then again the body is no longer anything at all. . . . This general lesson may lead clearly enough to the personality who is Socrates, but for Crito, who is not much of a philosopher, it needs to be spelled out. So, when his friend suggests that he should put off the moment of drinking the hemlock, like condemned men who seize one last chance to eat, drink, and make love—those very activities that, at the beginning of the discussion, have been defined as pleasures suitable only for a soul too much attached to its body (81b, 116e)—Socrates explains that he is already on his way and that this Socrates who is leaving is a soul that no longer has anything to do with the individual thing that Socrates' body used to be.

All the same, it is important to note that this lesson comes very late in the day, after (and only after) Socrates has upheld his *logos* with all the living force of his physical presence. Until his discourse had won the day, Socrates still needed to be the mixture of body and soul that constitutes a man.[43] Thus, during a pause in the discussion, the text says, "Socrates himself [*autos*] was entirely given over to pondering the argument that had just been set out" ("Socrate était tout entier à l'argument qui venait d'etre exposé") (84b–c). Léon Robin translates this as "You could see at a glance that Socrates' *mind was entirely preoccupied* by the argument that had just been set out" ("*Socrate, cela se voyait à le regarder*, avait l'esprit tout entier *à l'argument qui venait d'etre exposé*"). But this anticipates the direction that the dialogue is about to take. *Autos ho Sōkratēs*: Socrates himself, the person of Socrates, is not yet just a soul, is not just a mind but an entity there to be seen—and we know how keenly his disciples watched him—despite the fact that, in the earlier stages of the discussion, he has concentrated on attacking whatever is visible and all its misleading charms.

Who is Socrates? His soul, according to him. In the flesh-and-blood discussion, however, Socrates' self has a lot to do with his body, that Silenus-like body that Alcibiades describes in the *Symposium*, a body that masks the internal man and the beauty of his soul yet is indisputably charged with an emotive attraction that his disciples connect with the philosopher's personality. So, despite the authority of the *Phaedo* and the lesson it teaches, not just to Crito but to the reader too, we must go against the grain of the text, or at least its apparent content, and return to the body of Socrates. At another level, to do so comes down to paying due attention to the flesh-and-blood discussion and the language it uses.

In the opening pages of *Psyche*, Erwin Rohde points out that, generally speaking, the *psukhē* is mentioned only when its separation from the living man is either imminent or has already taken place. In the *Phaedo* Socrates is on the point of taking leave of life and much is said about the *psukhē*, his *psukhē*. But his body, too, by no means goes unmentioned, that very body from which his soul must frequently have detached itself if he has himself engaged in the *meletē thanatou*, that practice of death that Socrates recommends to philosophers. (And if we read the *Symposium*, in which he falls into a catalepsy several times, we know that he did indeed engage in it, and often.) Therefore, we must make a detour to take in this *meletē thanatou*, the ascetic practice whose aim, from the archaic shamans down to the philosopher of the *Phaedo*, has always been to separate the soul from the body.

According to Socrates, the practice involves anticipating the state of death, which is first defined here as "the body having been parted from the soul and come to be by itself; and . . . the soul having been parted from the body, and being by itself" (64c). The order adopted here is a strange one: the separation is first envisaged from the point of view of the body, and only then from the soul's point of view. To be sure it is no sooner suggested than rejected; from then on nothing more is said of the body's role in this separation: henceforth only the soul is entitled to isolate itself. However, it would be reasonable for anyone reading the text attentively to suppose that the body does not allow itself to be abandoned in this fashion, since it is to the language of the body that Plato the writer turns to describe the soul engaged in the process of separation.

The soul certainly appears to be alone, which means that, like the body, it needs nurturing (*trophē*, 81d, 84b, 107d). The fact remains that one cannot but be struck by the physicality of the soul's movements as it seeks to leave the body, making an effort to "gather itself together from every region of the body" (67c). In a word the soul does exactly what the chorus in the *Clouds* orders Strepsiades to bring about within himself by concentrating, or to be more precise, by "densifying himself" (*puknōsas*) in order to think better. Nor should we seek to justify such language by recalling the soul that is too attached to the body, with the result that it "wanders in a sort of dizzy, drunken confusion" or, following death, roams about tombs as a ghostly phantom, an image both visible yet illusory (*eidōlon*).[44] Rather, it is the soul of the sage that concerns us here, a soul striving, in all the purity of its philosophical motivation, to effect its separation. Of course Plato has been at pains to forestall the reader's astonishment by underlining the "terrible power" of the enclosure represented by the body to which the soul is shackled and, as it were, adheres, in such a way that the philosopher is obliged to undertake a kind of education of the senses in reverse, teaching the soul to shed every dimension of the body, one by one, in order to concentrate itself within itself.[45] Nevertheless, it is by means of this "technical" vocabulary (which is used throughout the *Phaedo* to convey the soul's efforts at concentration) that Plato manages better than anyone to underline the paradoxical fact that, at the very moment of separation, "it is at the level of the body that the being appears to experience its identity."[46] But now we must return to Socrates, to his soul and his body, to Socrates who has passed beyond the need to practice being dead and now faces death itself, a death clearly no longer in any sense metaphorical—unless, that is, in these last moments of the philosopher's life his body has become a metaphor for his soul, whose liberation it makes manifest just as, at the beginning of the dialogue, Socrates' unshackled body looked forward to the deliverance of his *psukhē*.

So let us return to Socrates and his symbolic or, at the very least, extremely significant body, to this *sōma* that is the clearest indicator provided by the dialogue of how to read it, which makes us consider the importance of the body in a text totally devoted to getting rid of it.

Throughout most of the dialogue, Socrates is seated. Until his disciples arrive, he has been lying down, but he sits up as soon as he sees Xanthippe leave and, at first in a hunched position, lowers his feet to the ground. Thus, Socrates is seated and will rise to his feet only to go take a bath. He will be seated as he drinks the poison, after which, heeding the instructions given to him, he will take no more than a few steps before lying down again, this time for good. Socrates is seated and his position is eminently symbolic, being both that of a man under sentence of death and that of an initiate,[47] as the philosopher himself points out: refuting the analyses of materialist thinkers who, obsessed by physical causes, would think they were explaining the position by describing the interaction of bones and flesh, muscles, nerves, and tendons, he declares that he is seated because he has accepted the judgment of the Athenians (98c–99b). Socrates is seated, and the few movements he makes in the course of the dialectical conversation serve to redirect the discussion from time to time. He took his body as the starting point for the dialogue, when his remarks about pleasure and pain were prompted by the painful numbness of his leg, but this soon led on to reflections on the interrelations of contraries.

When Crito, as instructed by the man responsible for administering the hemlock, advises him to speak (actually, to dialogue: *dialegesthai*) as little as possible so as not to become heated—for this would counteract the action of the poison, which achieves its effect through coldness—the philosopher rejects such a mundane consideration. The fact is that it is absolutely necessary for the hot and the cold, like pleasure and pain, to clash within Socrates' body, since this body is a mirror for the dialectical discussion, particularly the part about the clash of contraries.[48] Only when the discussion is completed and the day comes to an end will Socrates drink the poison. At that point, Plato will turn the inquiry that is suited to dialectical argument (*skopein*: 64d) toward Socrates' body, which must now be examined by the man responsible for administering the poison. The purpose of that examination is to determine the progress made by the hemlock. In this way Plato suggests to the reader an inverted image of the withdrawal of the soul.[49]

In conclusion I offer a few words on the action of the hemlock as it affects the philosopher's body, since it is a process into which Plato seeks to condense the entire meaning of the dialogue. In calling this poison "hemlock," I am following a convention that postdates the *Phaedo* (but is historically well founded), but I am not unaware that in referring to this death draft simply as a *pharmakon*, Plato's intention was to turn it into a drink of immortality.[50] Hemlock, a *pharmakon* of immortality? How can that be? But that is certainly how Socrates regards it since, when the time comes, the philosopher decides to drink it of his own accord, without having to be told to do so.[51] In fact, it is the hemlock, seen by Aristophanes as the shortest path (*atrapos*) to death, that gives material form to what is described in the *Phaedo* as the *atrapos* of the philosopher—the practice of death by which one frees oneself, while still alive, from the constraints of the body. The hemlock, as the material counterpart of the *logos* on the liberation of the soul, effects what Socrates has already virtually accomplished.[52] The hemlock liberates, all the more so since it gives Socrates the chance for an exemplary death in which he can display that calm serenity that generations of readers have so admired. Now it is precisely with this serene death that the realism of the dialogue—that is to say, the effectiveness of the fiction—reaches its peak. And Plato is certainly counting on the persuasiveness of the description to make the reader forget to wonder what death by hemlock must really be like.

But let us once again shatter the paralyzing spell of the sublime moment and see what other ancient authors (not only Aristophanes and Theophrastus, but also Nicander, the doctor) have to say about hemlock. All of them speak of sensations of cold and numbness (and they also agree about the speed with which this poison causes death). But Nicander mentions further details that are at considerable variance with what is suggested in the *Phaedo*. According to him, not only does the subject who has drunk the hemlock become agitated as well as numb but, with his mind wandering, his intelligence and consciousness appear to be affected first.[53] Now the reader must look again at the *Phaedo*. A prudent conclusion would be that Plato simply chose one version in preference to another—that of the poison's gentle effects rather than that of its violence. But one might press on further and accept the consequences of a less reverential inquiry, in which case the death of Socrates, which seems so very genuine, becomes a pure and simple philosophical construction.[54] In fact, the dispersion of the hemlock through the philosopher's body must be symbolic: his head is never affected. It is true that in the *Timaeus*, the head is where whatever is divine in man is rooted, and the philosopher, of all men, is the most capable of cultivating those divine roots. The poison spreads upward, from the feet that have trampled the earth to the heart, whose heat is extinguished by the cold of the hemlock. But for Socrates the battle is over once his feet and legs are paralyzed and the cold grips his abdomen—the seat of the desires that the philosopher has managed to overcome. The rest is silence, silence concerning the nobler part of the body and the liberation of the soul, which the reader must try to imagine for himself or herself.

In freeing Socrates from the body forever, the *Phaedo* thus concentrates on the very thing from which, it seems, Socrates must be liberated: the mortal body of Socrates that, by rooting the man to the ground, makes him an earthly plant. But is it that easy to get rid of Socrates' body? In the last lines of the dialogue, the body—cold and petrified as it is, the body of that Socrates who has already left it—continues effectively enough to sustain the role of an archaic *kolossos*, the dead man's double and a memorial to him.[55] The force of Plato's text is such that it turns his stiffened corpse into a statue. It is reasonable to suppose that Crito will find it very difficult not to seek Socrates in that frozen presence, that he will hardly believe that the Socrates lying there is no longer anything at all, since Socrates-the-soul has already reached the Islands of the Blessed. The *Gorgias*, in Orphic fashion, declared the body to be a *sēma*. But for this tomb-body, which throughout the dialogue has been first and foremost a sign-body, the *Phaedo* itself stands as a *sēma*, in the sense of a commemorative *stēlē*.

The strategy that Plato adopts in the *Phaedo* is truly astonishing: he sets out to expunge the city from the dialogue, even as he borrows civic language and values; to banish the body, even as he uses the language of the body itself. The first of those two operations must have taken the Greek reader by surprise, for without realizing it he found himself won over to a new way of thinking expressed in traditional words. The second may well have disturbed Plato's contemporaries, but it has most certainly fascinated generations of later readers (and after all, that is what tradition means in the case of a text, so it truly was a tradition that was inaugurated by the account of Socrates' death).

To use the body to banish the body is not as unjustifiable as it may appear. The body, it could be said, is simply an image used to speak of the soul; and how can one possibly speak of the soul without resorting to imagery? In the dialogue itself, Cebes begs pardon for resorting to a "comparison." But Plato is a master of the image—and of the image within an image—all the better to win approval from the readers he wishes to bring over to his side.[56]

In this inquiry we have tried not to be too easily swayed by the text's suggestiveness, to be attentive but not mesmerized readers. We have tried to be readers who must be won over. The only hope of coming close to the immortality of the soul seemed to lie in exploring all the paths that led to it in this text, which for a long tradition has provided a veritable storehouse of arguments favoring that immortality. But if we have thereby been led to the paradox of a body rejected, depreciated, and banished, yet more present than ever, how should we now speak of the immortality brought about in the *Phaedo*? If it is Socrates' memorable body that also constitutes a memorial, that makes us believe in the survival of his soul (just as, in the *Symposium*, it was his Silenus-like ugliness that vouched for his internal beauty), what are we to do with that body of Socrates? Now that we have rashly committed ourselves to reflecting on the effectiveness of the dialogue, let us risk the following hypothesis: the *Phaedo* owes its success not only to the brilliance with which it supplants one immortality by another, replacing words of glory with the survival of the soul; but that success also has much to do with the immense unconscious impact made by the play of double meanings. Clearly, Plato is simultaneously playing on two levels when he proclaims that the body is nothing, yet he uses the language of the body to speak of the soul.

Plato resorts to many cunning ploys: he outlaws *mimēsis* from the city in a dialogue where the writing depends on a masterly use of that very *mimēsis*; he condemns cunning intelligence even as he manipulates the technique of *mētis* with marvelous skill; he argues the annihilation of the body in a language where the body dominates. Furthermore, Plato expects the reader to accept these exclusions—and the reader is all the more prepared to do so since, without realizing it, whatever is excluded (*mimēsis*, the city or the body, as the case may be) then bounces back to the reader. Like a perverse child, Plato's reader continues to enjoy the very things that philosophy is repressing: the text is full of hints of them, and these work (silently, secretly and, as it were, innocuously) on the irreproachable champion of knowledge that he believes himself to be.[57] And this is how the tradition of a spiritualistic reading of the *Phaedo* has quietly established itself.

We have tried to read Plato's dialogue on immortality as an argument playing on two levels: the soul is immortal, but that immortality is upheld chiefly by the memorial that was Socrates' unforgettable body.[58]

Chapter 9

SOCRATES, PLATO, HERAKLES: A HEROIC PARADIGM OF THE PHILOSOPHER

"Socrates, Plato, Herakles . . .": two philosophers, one hero. Two historical figures and Zeus's son. An incongruous group, most unsatisfactory to those fond of homogeneity. However, one should not be too hasty in correcting this strange list that Plutarch, faithful to the overall outline of an Aristotelian *Problem*,[1] offers in support of the statement that "all great natures are melancholy."[2] Tradition does not always distinguish between what the Greeks call "the sickness of Herakles" and melancholy, the "wise man's madness,"[3] and this alone would legitimize the hero's presence next to the two philosophers. A historian of culture might add that in Plutarch's day this trio would surprise no one, since Herakles had long been naturalized as a philosopher. But melancholy is not my subject here, and I have hazarded this quotation only for the pleasure of mentioning a Herakles who has been definitively ensconced among the philosophers. Or, to be more exact, I quoted Plutarch as a way of bringing up this threesome, so disconcerting to the modern reader.

Therefore I will discuss Socrates, Plato, and Herakles. That is, I will explore reasons for putting them together, or the place assigned to Plato between Socrates and Herakles, which appears to create a bond between sage and hero. In short, I will concern myself with Plato as he plays the figure of Herakles upon that of Socrates—and perhaps, inversely, the figure of the sage upon that of the hero: Plato as he "compares" Socrates to Herakles, for instance, and all that entails. But this problematic opening brings us face to face with another Platonic figure, the incomparable Socrates.

SOCRATES "COMPARED"?

Compare Socrates? A celebrated passage from the *Symposium*, in which Alcibiades sings the praises of the philosopher, suggests that this is impossible. Socrates is *atopos*, for he resembles no man, past or present, and this information interferes with the "game of portraits"[4] in which one figure is employed to reveal another, Achilles paired with Brasidas, Nestor with Pericles.[5]

The incomparable Socrates: but at the same time, Socrates the paradigm. No better guide exists than Victor Goldschmidt to illuminate this paradox, essential to Plato's undertaking, and with him I will observe from the outset how the Platonic *paideia* both discourages the imitation of heroes in the name of a demanding definition of heroism and installs Socrates at its center as the sole *exemplum* of virtue worthy of emulation.[6]

But I am not finished with this passage from the *Symposium*, for the awesome clarity of Alcibiades' acclaim of Socrates raises more questions than the orator admits. By stating that Socrates cannot be compared to any man, Alcibiades, faithful to the theme of the dialogue, certainly means to suggest that in order to make an image (*apeikazein*) of the *daimōn* Socrates, one must search among beings of the same nature— "not among men," since humans, in Platonic theology, occupy the last place in the hierarchy,[7] but among intermediary beings, the Silenes and Satyrs. Still, by excluding Socrates from the game of comparison that consists in likening a contemporary man to a "man from the past," Alcibiades implicitly treats Achilles and Nestor as simple *anthrōpoi*, illustrious but mortal men and not "heroes"—which is what tradition makes them out to be, although distinct, it is true, from a cultural hero like Herakles.[8] Therefore, Socrates would be incomparable only with respect to the category of human beings. To be sure, nothing in the *Symposium* explicitly prohibits seeking his image among heroes—provided perhaps that the notion of the hero be elaborated, which is no small matter in Greek tradition. Nonetheless, in this passage Alcibiades avoids all reference to heroes, as if to defuse accepted rules of thought about the uses of comparison. Without a doubt, Plato finds this to his advantage here.

However, the stakes of the practice of comparison, which was fashionable in intellectual circles during the classical period,[9] were high, since they are based on a definition of *paideia* as a relationship to Homer—to Homeric texts, but especially to epic as the universal source of education.[10] They are also, more essentially, based on a way of defining the exercise of thought: from Homer to Socrates' contemporaries, comparison is a form of knowledge, which functions indirectly, to be sure, but one that has proved itself throughout a long tradition without any loss of vitality.[11] Through Alcibiades, Plato intends to exclude the Socratic figure from this mode of thought, in which comparison is "meaningful" or "revealing." Such a rejection carries a clear message. If the cohort of mythical and cultural heroes furnishes an inexhaustible supply of images (*eikones*) to those who believe they are able to "understand the nature of an object by means of the relationship that unites it with another object . . . more firmly implanted in the system of collective representations,"[12] the presentation of the paradigmatic philosopher has nothing to do with the game of comparison because the paradigm is incomparable, because philosophy is not satisfied with objects that please the crowd.

The lesson, I was saying, is a clear one. Perhaps even too clear. For things are never that simple with Plato, and on all levels of Platonic thought the choice of an image is the result of a double strategy. The image is a last resort, perhaps, when it is used to replace the impossible narrative (*diēgēsis*)—but we know that, even in the fictional case of a successful *diēgēsis*, there is a passage in the *Republic* that permits "imitation" to break the thread of the "tale," on the condition that the imitated object have incontestable value.[13] A last resort again is the use of the image in the *Phaedo* as a means via discourse to suggest the need for mediating the relationship to being—unless it is simply impossible to take the shortcut of the *eikōn* to express the ideal.[14] Everything suggests that the image is not a gratuitous adornment of dialectical argument, and when, in book 6 of the *Republic*, Adimantos is surprised that Socrates resorts to the *eikōn* "contrary to his habit," this is a Platonic bit of trickery that should be taken with a grain of salt. What reader of Plato would be so ingenuous as to assert that Socrates forgoes the aid of the image? Not to worry: the dialectician, sole legitimate master of paradigm and metaphor, is able to arm the reader against the insidious influence of this manipulation of the senses.[15]

So it is not too surprising that in the work of Plato the incomparable Socrates is himself subjected to the law of comparison, and that his interlocutors, beginning with Alcibiades in the *Symposium*, compare him, as is fitting, to this or that hero—and not to the least of them, since along with Achilles and Odysseus, the official paradigms of the *paideia*,[16] one must include Herakles.

. . . So once again we encounter the Strength of Herakles.

SOCRATES AMONG THE HEROES

Odysseus takes first place, since Alcibiades, barely a few moments before he declares that Socrates is incomparable—the declaration of a man in love, which therefore must not be taken completely seriously—in fact evoked the Homeric hero as the model philosopher, without however giving his name and instead simply reciting a verse from the *Odyssey* to Socrates' advantage. But Alcibiades' listeners and Plato's readers were familiar enough with Homer to know what to think. There is something of Odysseus in the Socrates seen standing transfixed in Potidaea, the very figure of enduring thought, and he is described as *karteros anēr*.[17] Of the endurance and *mētis* that characterize Odysseus in the *Odyssey*, Plato, moreover, always selects the first when he mentions the Homeric hero[18]—it is true that the *polutropos Odusseus*[19] is also *polutlas*, and that the Odysseus of the thousand wiles is echoed by a suffering Odysseus who competes with Herakles for the title of hero of endurance—and when, at the conclusion of the *Republic*, the tale of Er promotes Odysseus, alone among epic heroes, to the rank of sage by attributing to his soul the choice of a philosophical life, Homeric ambivalence about *mētis* is quickly forgotten.[20]

After the hero of the *Odyssey*, there is the hero of the *Iliad*, also reduced by Plato to one of the key dimensions of his character, in this case his choice of a glorious death, which Socrates cites as the authority, explicitly in the *Apology* and implicitly in the *Crito*, justifying his own philosophical engagement in life and death.[21] Confronted with those who reproach him for leading a life that puts him in danger of death, Socrates recalls "the demigods that had perished before Troy, and particularly the son of Thetis, who . . . took peril so lightly." The serenity of the *Crito* is largely due to the dream of Socrates and to the prediction, made by the woman clad in white, of his arrival in fertile Phthia. This time Plato's use of Homer is sufficient to the task. In the *Iliad* the description of Phthia crystallized for Achilles the contradiction in the hero's heart between two ideas of life and death—the too-brief life in Troy and the imperishable glory (*kleos aphthiton*) of a fine death, or the too-human return to the country of one's ancestors and a long but obscure life in a fertile land bearing a name redolent of death (*Phthiē*).[22] Reconciled with etymology, Socrates bestows the name of Phthia on his mortal destination, and in the prediction of his dream, he hears the announcement of the last voyage toward the land of the dead, the fertile place of true life.

In the civic imagination that forms the horizon of the Platonic dialogues, Herakles appears to be infinitely more autonomous than Odysseus and Achilles, who are both rooted in the Homeric text[23] and whom Plato easily reduces to a single dimension. Since Herakles, the "god-hero" of myth and cult, is neither linked to a single text nor associated with a particular city, his paradigmatic figure has been represented on innumerable occasions, from the tragic stage to comedy, from the palaestra to the potter's workshop, from Pindaric poetry to philosophy.[24]

While the hero has long been associated with a rich and complex history, Plato knows how to set it down in his own way, and his dialogues present more than one Herakles. The Herakles of the genealogies, of course: Herakles the ancestor that the aristocratic *genē* seek to appropriate for themselves in an attempt that amuses Plato the philosopher of the *Theaetetus* because in his eyes it is simply a result of the "noise" of the city.[25] There is the already intellectualized Herakles whom the "Sophists of quality" and above all Prodikos have set about praising; the one who incarnates the force of nature for Kallikles and the Sophistic hero transformed in the *Theaetetus* into the representative of the impenitent dialecticians[26]—in these various, even contradictory guises, the Sophistic Herakles has his place in the "tribe of heroes," ironically identified in the *Cratylus* with a "race of rhetoricians and sophists."[27]

An ancestral and conformist Herakles, a Sophist Herakles; a valiant hero and a rhetorician. Without reducing the vast complexity of this hero to these two avatars, it can be noted that in Socrates' day both figures are well formed and so much in competition that, in the famous paraphrase from the *Clouds*, the hero is hailed as a model both by the old education and the one claiming to be new.[28] In fact, it seems that his essential plasticity means that the hero of strength may find himself straddling both sides of an intellectual debate: witness Aristophanes' treatment of him when the comic poet, reflecting on his art, challenges "the dough-kneading and starved Herakles" of his predecessors but likens his own vigorous struggle for true poetry with "the ardor of Herakles."[29] Similarly (but perhaps it is in recollection of Aristophanes), Herakles is found on both sides in the Platonic metaphorization of the mind's battles: on one side the dedicated Sophist of the *Theaetetus*, and thus Socrates' adversary; on the other he is identified with Socrates when pitted against the two Sophists in the *Euthydemus*.[30]

Socrates, Herakles: since the meeting between sage and hero is finally brought about in the work of Plato, this pair will orient my search for what becomes of the Socrates compared to Herakles—and perhaps, inversely, what becomes of Herakles for having helped to think about Socrates.

Socrates in a Lion's Skin

Faithful to the lessons of Prodikos, Xenophon's Socrates made Herakles into the paradigm of the immortality that is acquired after the soul has been tested.[31] Instead of theorizing about Zeus's son, Plato's Socrates prefers to be closely associated with him in his philosophical engagement and dialectical battles.

Before getting down to the essential and distinguishing between explicit references to the hero and the sometimes obvious allusions to him, I will consider for a moment the banal practice, for Socrates and his interlocutors, of swearing oaths to Herakles—not in order to situate these interjections amid the variegated range of oaths available to the Platonic protagonists and those reflecting the philosopher's everyday pantheon. The art of swearing calls for a differential study, which if systematically undertaken would undoubtedly shed a great deal of light on the procedures utilized in the dialogues: obviously, such a task is beyond the scope of this chapter. But it is not without importance for those who take an interest in the Socratic Herakles that the hero, by means of the familiar and agreeable, not to say Aristophanic,[32] means of the interjection, is often included in the ups and downs of the dialogue; his name

accompanies theatrically horrified astonishment, comic fright, or osten-
tatiously admiring surprise. It will be added—which is not inconsequen-
tial, either—that for Plato as for Aristophanes, interjections in the name
of Herakles are made in the vocative (*Hērakleis*), as if to call upon the
hero to intervene in person: "To me, Herakles." In these situations it is
more than an oath (of the sort, *nē ton Dia, nē ton kuna*), and it should be
understood as a summons, something like a call for help. "To me, Herakles!" a Sophist's oath, a Socratic oath—in this respect the savior hero
again appears on both sides of the competition. Whether it is Socrates or
one of the Sophists, the interlocutor often calls on Herakles for help
when one of the antagonists comes dangerously close to scoring a point.
In this way, which is less neutral than it first appears, the stakes of the
dialectic are ironically emphasized.[33]

More important—which does not always mean that it is more serious—is the forceful hero's metaphorical presence behind Socrates; for
example, in the *Apology*, the justification of the long Socratic search to
make the answer of the Delphic oracle irrefutable: in this *epideixis* of a
wandering that resembles the accomplishment of the successive Labors,
more than one reader believes he has detected an allusion to the *ponoi* of
Herakles,[34] tacitly evoked in its most traditional form of Herakles as hero
of endurance. But perhaps the essential is precisely that Herakles is not
named. Any comparison to Socratic strength, even if it were flattering, is
thereby circumvented. Such at least is the strategy of the *Symposium*,
where Socrates' resistance to pain is exalted at length, with no need for a
model in deeds. Quite the contrary, it is an aspect of Socrates' own constitution as the autonomous embodiment of the *bios philosophikos*. Thus,
as the incarnation of *ponos*, the philosopher enters into competition with
the hero, and the ultimate result is that the hero is ousted from the discourse on endurance. When one reads the life of Diogenes, it would
seem that the operation has met with lasting success, since the Cynic's
habit of walking barefoot in the snow is a codification of the qualities
that characterized Socrates during a military campaign in Potidaea.[35]

However, when Socrates asserts in the *Cratylus* that he "had donned a
lion's skin," the reference to Herakles is clear. Still, it should be added
that the allusion is shaped and, as it were, distanced by humor:

> You bring up, my friend, a type of words quite out of the ordinary. How-
> ever, since I have donned the lion's skin, it is not for me to back away; but it
> is necessary, it seems, to examine . . . [all] the . . . fine names of which you
> speak.[36]

Socrates replies to Hermogenes, who has just called on the authority
of etymologies of the different terms for *aretē*, as if his interlocutor,
dubbed here with the Homeric title of *hetairos*, were inviting him to face a

lineage of formidable monsters. The emblem of courage is not enough to make one courageous, and Socrates, galvanizing himself to live up to the promises of the outfit that he is wearing, without a doubt is thinking of the misadventures of Aesop's ass or Aristophanes' Dionysos, both garbed in the lion's skin but quickly unmasked in their cowardice, both wretched counterfeits of the mythical monster killer.[37] But comic distance will have protected Socrates for a time against the growing irritation of a reader who is in a hurry to get to the point, while at the same time underlining the importance of the philosophical stakes involved in discussing the words for *aretē*.

When the traps of dialectic become threatening—as is the case in the *Euthydemus*, the *Phaedo*, and the *Theaetetus*[38]—Socrates has a great need for Herakles in person to give him a hand, and the comparison becomes explicit, which however does not exclude the use, in another register, of the strategy of distancing.

There are a number of ways to achieve this. Sometimes Socrates compares himself to Herakles, as in the *Euthydemus*, but to a Herakles who is not at all up to the task—a Herakles in a tight spot, facing two opponents, who sorely misses an Iolaos. Sometimes, and it is the *Phaedo* where once again there is an extra opponent (here Simmias and Cebes, like Euthydemus and Dionysodorus in the preceding example), Socrates plays at being Iolaos, and Phaedo will repay the compliment, contenting himself with the role of supernumerary to better identify the philosopher with the strong hero.[39] Still at other times, in a context of warfare mixed with the palaestra in which the athlete-hero is utterly at home, Socrates, snatching one of his interlocutor's comparisons, presents himself as the impenitent adversary of all the "Herakleses and Theseuses," "powerful (*karteroi*) in the exercise of discourse" and who more than once have knocked him down.

But—this last example shows it in reverse—these varied techniques always permit the philosopher's identification with the hero to be divined; and in a maneuver that the Sophistic Socrates of the *Clouds* would not have disdained, the declarations focusing on Socrates' "weakness" actually convey his superiority over Herakles the strong. Of course, by making Theodorus responsible for the "athletic" comparison, by leaving to Phaedo the task of designating the true Herakles, by attributing to Socrates in the *Euthydemus* the falsely humble conviction of his incommensurable inferiority with respect to the hero, Plato seeks to cover his tracks. But more is needed to fool the attentive reader. In the *Euthydemus* or the *Phaedo*, Socrates *is* Herakles—it is in this guise that he can refer to Ctesippus as "my very own Iolaos" or that Phaedo calls on him for help, thereby reversing the logic of the myth in which Herakles so sorely needed Iolaos's assistance.[40] And in the *Theaetetus*, the philosopher is only the most resistant antagonist of the hero—or of his disciples, "the Herakleses"; multiplied by this plural, it is as if Herakles is deprived of his singularity. Here he attains a strength that no one can challenge: stronger (*iskhurōteros*)[41] than all Herakles' mythical opponents, his models, but also and above all absolutely strong for having ceaselessly hurled himself against the official representatives of the dialectical *karteria*— such is Socrates, because he never budged.

It is up to Plato's readers to choose—each according to his taste—up to what point he wishes to interpret these comparisons. Taken in by the game of the philosophical portrait, he will be happy to see in Socrates a Herakles; clever in sorting out the aims of the Platonic strategy, he will be able to understand that the dialectics of a Socrates, stronger than the *Biē hērakleiē* of the mythical accounts, is strength itself, which is blended with the courage that lies in philosophizing with no concessions.[42] But in either case, it should not be forgotten that with Plato, the history of a heroic Socrates and a Socratized Herakles is only in its infancy in Greek philosophical thought. I will not venture to tell this long story—which would lead up to the Stoics and beyond. I would merely like to situate it, to give the Platonic use of the paradigm its full value, at the dawn of the history that it inaugurates—a history that will continue, however, only at the cost of a displacement or a return in the direction of more traditional representations, where no one, even Socrates, can win out over Herakles.

SOCRATIC HERAKLES

Because Plato shifted the strength that Socrates derived from Herakles from physical to mental prowess, the hero was intellectualized, a rare occurrence in his long career as a paradigmatic figure.[43] The rest of the story moves into more familiar territory, whether this new direction should be attributed to a philosophical choice or the inherent logic of the hero, which is above all identified with his endurance (that of the body but also the soul). Less accustomed to the game of reversals than Plato, or perhaps more Socratic than he,[44] the Cynics seem to prefer, in Herakles as moreover in Socrates, moral strength to dialectical power. Therefore their discussions contain not a trace of rivalry between the sage and the hero: Socrates and Herakles coexist without tension as models of the philosopher, both of them essentially characterized by the endurance of *aretē*.

Witness to the fact already is one Antisthenes, who all the while defining himself, like the Socrates of the *Theaetetus*, as a "fighter,"[45] places "Socratic strength" (*sōkratikē iskhus*) in service of the sole autarchy of virtue.[46] And once again it is Socrates and his serene death that must be detected in the identification of the "happy death" with the supreme happiness of humanity.[47] But as Socratic as he is, Herakles, the cherished hero of Antisthenes, who devotes at least one book to him,[48] is nonetheless undiminished in strength. While in some of his practices Diogenes enjoys imitating Socrates—as we have already seen—according to him he leads "the sort of life that had characterized Herakles when he held liberty above everything."[49] Thus, in the thought of the Cynics there projects a well-regulated exchange between the heroic philosopher and the philosophical hero. From Socrates to Herakles and Herakles to Socrates: if Antisthenes, traveling from Piraeus to Athens each day to hear Socrates, achieved endurance (*to karterikon*), according to Diogenes Laertes, this Socratic experience led him to write a *Herakles*. And just as naturally, the lesson of this Herakles is a Socratic one, since the sovereign good consists in living virtuously, and this virtue is self-taught.[50]

This history of the paradigms of the philosopher closes with the Socratized Herakles. For such a figure—a Cynic's way of expressing Socrates' "strength"—serves as the emblem of the profound transformations that occurred in the mental universe of the Greeks in the fourth century. Herakles, of course, was a philosopher before Socrates got mixed up in the matter: it is known that he was a Pythagorean,[51] even before Prodikos set him at the crossroads of Vice and Virtue and gave him a lasting new dimension, henceforth of an ethical nature, of the hero of freely chosen effort.[52] But because he was a model of *andreia*—the virility that gives courage its name—he still had to undergo the effects of a major ideological event. In this case I am referring to the substitution of the philosopher for the citizen as the paradigm of the accomplished man. Plato labored tirelessly to effect this transformation,[53] but its consequences regarding Herakles would be elaborated by others. The Cynics, in fact, made this son of Zeus into a Socratic philosopher.

Throughout this history, the hero of affliction undoubtedly lost much of his initial ambiguity.[54] By the time of the Cynics, the drunken, gluttonous, skirt-chasing hero who was the delight of Old Comedy[55] was definitively out of the picture, and the strength of Herakles' arms was eclipsed by the forbearance of his soul. It was also the end of the essential weakness of the strong hero, who from Homer to the tragic poets moaned and wept, struggling against a too onerous fate. Afterward Herakles suffers but endures and, no more than the Socrates of the *Phaedo*, knows the bitter joy of tears.

This survey would end here if Socrates and Herakles were the only subjects. But care must be taken not to forget Plato at the last minute. Such a lapse seems unavoidable, to be sure, and as if they were bent on finding that Prodikos and the Cynics had no intermediaries separating them, historians of Herakles the Philosopher are generally eager to deny that Plato has any part in the reelaboration of this heroic figure.[56]

This leads to the risk of underestimating the effect of reciprocal influences, beyond the rivalry—not to say opposition—that, in Socrates' name, pit the philosophical schools against each other. Still, my intention here has not been to turn this perspective upside down. It is a simpler task: I have tried to account for what transpires between Socrates and Herakles in Plato's work, a dynamic that is nothing more than a paradigmatic staging of the setbacks and grandeurs of dialectics. The fact that this staging repeats the dialectician's victory over his heroic model from one dialogue to the next is undoubtedly the originality of Plato the philosopher. But it can also be seen as an all-too-obvious trademark, which forever confines the interplay between sage and hero, played out in Platonic rivalry, within the boundaries of the dialogue. In fact, the Cynics will restore the initiative to Herakles—a Socratic Herakles, to be sure, but one who is merely enduring and who at this time already is no longer intellectualized.

Does this amount to saying that ultimately Plato's contribution to the philosophical history of Herakles must be seen as negligible? I would not be too hasty to make such a statement, even if it is true that the hero does not permanently assume the dialectician's mantle. For Platonic *mētis* functions on several levels, and there is a Plato who, it could reasonably be supposed, has worked, if not on the reelaboration of a philosophical model of Herakles, at least on the enactment of an idea of heroism irrevocably divorced from all ambiguity—not the Plato of the *Theaetetus* but the Plato of the *Republic*: he who speaks in Socrates' voice to condemn Homer's groaning Achilles and demands that only great men's acts of *karteria* be remembered.[57] This is the Plato who invites the sage not to imitate the hero "if he sees him stumble in sickness, love, drunkenness, or some other disgrace."[58] Reading such statements, who could deny that Plato has at least indirectly contributed to establishing the features of an ascetic Herakles?

The fact that this edifying Plato has been more widely heard than Plato the dialectician is another story, which is interwoven with the history of philosophy. Furthermore, the moment of reasoning via comparison had undoubtedly passed, and Herakles as a paradigm called for imitation more than metaphor.

This is how, reinforcing what Platonic thought had joined, a trick of history shifted the heroic paradigm of the philosopher from dialectics toward the theory of action.[59]

Above all, this is how Herakles' link with femininity came to an end in philosophical discourse, while the influence of this discourse continued to wax. Undoubtedly, the poets are still fond of evoking Herakles dressed in women's clothing beside Omphale—but all in all, the theme of exchanged clothing is so transparent that it did not truly imply that the essence of the hero's destiny required that he live in a feminine way.

Herakles is a manly hero, Socrates is an *anēr*. Under the sign of division (*diairesis*), the philosopher cuts and separates the genders: women have the feminine; men, virility—the masculine superego that the Greeks call *andreia*.

PART FOUR

WHAT WOMAN?

FEMININITY for women, virility for men? This Platonic division is too blatant to be meaningful in the long run, and if Plato were the object of this discussion, the task would remain to examine the crafty strategy that makes it possible for the language of the dialogues to appropriate—for the greater benefit of philosophy overall—the femininity that the male mind claimed to restore (and with such condescension!) to women. But afterward the action takes place far from the field of explicit representations, and thus the philosopher will be left to his fate.

For it is high time to examine what the feminine means from the women's side; or rather, to examine what remains of the feminine for women.

Negativity, certainly. The capacity to terrify, but also to seduce and to beguile. Terrifying is the eminently feminine craving for power, the indisputable prerogative of males: Hera and Clytemnestra loom as fearsome indeed. But the imagination is resourceful, and women are credited with this desire primarily because they already lack all power, and this is a way of retroactively putting them in their places, which might lead to an understanding of how it is women's nature to covet what rightly and incontestably belongs to men. Herein lies a way for the Greek male to forget—or tacitly justify—everything that he has taken from female "nature" by envisioning the manly aspect of the other sex solely as a usurper.

And then—all the same—there is the inherent femininity of women. But men have appropriated the "natural" for themselves, so all that remains is artifice, the fascination of Athena, the goddess with the improbable body; all that remains is seduction, the beautiful scourge in the form of the ravishing Helen.

Chapter 10

AND THE MOTHERS' CASE DISMISSED

> My prayer makes a place of honor first among the gods
> for the first prophetess, Gaia (Earth); after her, for
> Themis, who succeeded her on the prophetic throne
> left by her mother, as legend confirms. The third, in
> turn, with Themis' approval, not violent resistance,
> another Titan daughter of the Earth is seated next,
> Phoibe, and it is she who offers it, as a gift for his
> joyous birth, to Phoibos, who owes this surname to
> Phoibe. Then leaving Delos, its pond and its rocky
> crest, he comes to the shores of Pallas, familiar to
> ships, to reach this land and Parnassus, his new abode.
> There he finds an escort and blazing honors; the
> children of Hephaistos clear his way, taming the wild
> earth for him. He arrives and here he receives the
> open homage of the people, with their king Delphos,
> at the helm of the land. And Zeus, filling his heart
> with divine knowledge, seats him on the throne,
> the fourth prophet.
> Loxias speaks here for Zeus his father. These are the
> gods with whom I begin my prayer.
> Aeschylus *Eumenides* 1–20

AESCHYLUS has the Pythia speak to open the third act of the *Oresteia*. Of course the words that issue from her mouth are not her own. Truly the Pythia knows no other way: the servant of the oracular god, the prophetess has no *logos* but that of Apollo, the prophetic word that must be uttered through her virgin's body.[1] And what is pronounced in Apollo's name in the Pythia's voice, the god's "musical instrument," is nothing else than a greeting in the form of a story—a greeting to the ancient feminine powers, the detailed story of a succession. Now it happens that this succession from mother to daughter—begun, continued, and confirmed in the feminine—comes to an end (and is completed) with Apollo, the prophet of his Father. Thus Phoibe, the daughter of Earth and sister of Themis, would have only awaited the triumphal arrival of a young god born in Delos, who when he reached the Athenian shores of Pallas Athena, Zeus's cherished daughter, knew to look for a worthy escort under the sign of his paternal filiation.[2]

Gaia, Themis, Phoibe, and then Phoibos Apollo—a history in four parts but two times: the before and the now, the feminine time of origins and the time of Apollo, without which the cities of men would have no history. Three feminine powers, then the god, the son of the father: this bears a decided resemblance to certain modern historical accounts in which historians of Greece, such as Marie Delcourt or Georges Roux, narrate the history of the Delphic oracle.[3] It is true that reflecting on the Delphic oracle stirs up difficult questions. During the reign of Apollo, the first prophetess, Gaia Protomantis, continues to be venerated inside the sanctuary: how could the god place the goddess he had just dispossessed alongside him? To prophesy in the name of Phoibos, the Pythia must sit on the tripod, which opens onto the "breath issued from the mouth of the shadows of the earth." How can Apollonian *logos* be reconciled with the chthonian depths? The myth answers these questions in the nick of time because it has taken the form of history.

Myth that passes itself off as history? That is the point. The historian and archaeologist no doubt find the situation to their advantage. ("With Apollo's arrival," writes G. Roux, "there was one more god at Delphi, a god who became primary but permitted earlier religious life to flourish in his shadow.")[4] Resistant to the archaeological impulse, for my part I do not intend to forget that this highly consistent story is a myth. I will explain: it should not be too surprising that the match between this mythical "history" and the questions posed by archaeologists in search of history is nearly perfect. For nothing provides a better answer to the questions about origins than myth, perhaps because its unique aim is to foresee, even suggest such queries. So in turn I would like to ask a question of myth: What if this "history" were a trick, myth's very deception?

Let us suppose that the mythic operation consists in presenting as history what in truth is nothing but a way of taking full advantage of the present (in this case, the reign of the son of Zeus). It follows that if one is a Greek male one is the instant beneficiary of an archaeology of power based on Apollo: a single historicizing concession, only one (yes, the god came late), is the cost of legitimizing the latecomer god (the last to arrive, but awaited in joy; dominant but welcoming; generous because he is the only one endowed—at last—with an incontestable *logos*). Glory to Apollo. And what of the feminine in this history? Certainly it has its place, and not the least, since it came first. But it could indeed be that assigning the feminine the place of origin amounts to simply denying it from the outset.[5] The feminine: the primitive, the obscure, the completed, the time that has passed and therefore is always past, or better, that has been assimilated by what came after. It was in the order of things that Apollo incorporated Earth's divinatory power just as Zeus in the *Theogony* was able to take on the power of Hecate, who came earlier but whose power he confirmed and as it were reinstituted. And here is Hecate, even closer to the origin because Zeus brought her back, with all her privileges[6]—it is true that the Most High is the one without whom nothing can be completed. Let us return to Delphi: the Pythia concludes her invocation in line 28 of the *Eumenides*[7] with this Zeus Teleios, who brings everything into fulfillment. The end of the story gives meaning to the beginning, and in his magnanimity Apollo exalted the powers of ancient Gaia at the very instant that he absorbed them. Without any violence. Utterly naturally.

However, less conciliatory versions of the tale exist, in which harmonious succession is replaced by murder and dispossession. In the *Homeric Hymn* devoted to him, the son of Zeus must kill "the female Dragon, the enormous and giant Beast" who guards the sacred spring. And when Euripides in turn takes up the myth, he tells how the newborn infant killed the snake, the son of Earth, to place himself on the oracular tripod. In this account, however, the feminine divinities do not allow themselves to be dispossessed without resisting:

> Now, since with his coming he had driven the daughter of Gaia, Themis, away from the most divine oracles, Earth gave birth to nocturnal visions of dreams that for many mortals signified in their dark sleep the past, the present, and everything that would happen afterward. And Gaia, irritated because of her daughter, took the honor of prophesying away from Phoibos.

Of course then the child-god calls on his father for help, and Zeus will put an end to the nighttime oracles. This is how humans, freed from shadowy divinatory practices, will henceforth and forever honor the song of the oracles.[8]

A strange tale, as ambiguous as could be desired: it seems that the resistance to feminine powers is only included in the story to confirm the full victory of Apollonianism, but it is just as obvious that without his father's assistance the young god would not have prevailed. By means of this struggle for influence, men began to dream, and these dreams are prophetic, indeed truthful (in order to give his son the victory, Zeus will have to refuse humanity the "nocturnal truth" [*alathosunan nuktōpon*]— the word is a weighty one); but if Gaia's anger makes mortals dream, they must place their trust and honor in Apollo; henceforth dreams prophesy in vain. The notion that the shadowy Gaia gave birth to dreams will certainly not surprise Freudians, who will not wonder why, at the end of this story, men believe less in their dreams than in the oracles of Apollo. "The interpretation," it might be thought, "is rather obvious."[9]

On the other hand, the historian of religions will ask how it happens that the tale, which embroils the sacrosanct succession of divine reigns and forms of divination, introduces the oracle only by means of dreams—which tradition ordinarily places "in the beginning"—as if in the form of a reply to Apollo's installation in the temple. Perhaps an answer to that question would account for the way in which the origin is endowed with a twofold nature. In fact, the text has added the prophecy of dreams to the dark primordial royalty of a vaguely evoked "chthonian oracle" as an aftereffect linked to Themis's defeat. What is gained by doubling the *arkhē*? Perhaps it is a way of forestalling the defeat of the feminine, but surely this rout is all the more complete because of the repetitious quality of what has gone before it: the original and secondary origins constitute two defeats (for the feminine in the form of Themis and Gaia), as opposed to two victories for the Olympian order (for Apollo and Zeus). The daughter is defeated, as is the mother, while the son's victory reinforces his father's power. Once again, everything is there.

The feminine had to be vanquished, neutralized with the help of a legend. There is more than one site in Greece where this story can take place, but none is more applicable than Delphi, womb of the earth and navel of the world. And stories are told of how the Earth's omnipotence gives way (serenely or under duress, what does it matter after all?) before the god, his father's prophet.

But if only the ending of the story truly counts, I would like to foil the tricks played by myth by beginning my account of it at the end, with the all-powerful order of the father of the gods and men. In this history there is no doubt that only power counts. Indeed, it was necessary for the feminine to possess it at first, so that it could be quickly relieved of all claims to it.

Ever in need of legitimacy, power is first a matter of naming. And myth says that in very ancient times the feminine was the giver of names. Provided that the end is assured, one can even derive Apollo's name—or at least his most established surname—from a feminine designation. Thus the Pythia used to tell how Phoibe, the sister of Themis and the third occupant of the Delphic temple, relinquished possession of the tripod, and even her name, to the young god. With a few exceptions Greek tradition forgot Phoibe, a vague figure like all the primordial goddesses,[10] but no one is ignorant of the glory of Phoibos. Phoibe was nothing but a name; she gave this name to Apollo; she vanishes from the memory of the Greeks. Perversely I ask myself whether this process was so successful because in reality it begins with Phoibos, even though that would require telling the story in the usual order (the "good," and reassuring, order of chronology). And because nothing is as fundamental as a tale of origins, the process covers its own tracks: the construction and legitimation are forgotten, and all that remains is the memory of the myth, above all suspicion.

With these considerations I will leave Delphi and the theogonic thought of the Greeks for the Athenian city. It will be recalled that Athens is where Apollo first set foot on terra firma. It was a good choice: for Athenian myths have made a substantial contribution to the "history" of the dispossession of the feminine gender. More exactly, it will be said that in Athens the trickery perpetuated by the myth becomes more elaborate, by means of the introduction of a division within what had remained undivided at Delphi. First there is the dual effect of the myth of autochthony, which denies the maternity of women in favor of that of the Earth (*Gē*) and casts over Ge the shadow of the *patria*, the land of the fathers, the land of Athena, the daughter of the Father.[11] Is this a denial of women in favor of femininity? It is something like that, but only something. For in this history the feminine is irreversibly duplicated, since the undifferentiated fecundity of the chthonian womb is both isolated and placed in the service of another femininity:[12] a femininity that is at once enclosed upon itself and, to quote the Athena of the *Eumenides*, "entirely given over to the male, except in bed." There is Ge and there is the virgin, Zeus's daughter, born without a mother, the outcome of a metallurgical genesis and who always takes her father's side—as well as that of Orestes, Apollo's protégé, against the Erinyes.[13] The men of Athens are grateful to the goddess, they who derive their name from her.

A second myth speaks precisely of the name of Athens: of the name of Athens and the lost power of women. This happened in the far-off time when the gods were dividing up the honors. Athena and Poseidon were arguing about the favors of the city of Kekrops. Now it happens that women, just like men, had the vote. So the women voted for Athena, a goddess, while the male votes went to Poseidon. But the women outnumbered the men by one. Athena won, and Athens took her name. It was necessary to compensate the defeated god, and this happened, of course, to the women's disadvantage. They lost all participation in power, and the authority to name as well as be named. They lost the right to name their own children, and even the title of Athenian, which they had just invented.[14] The women of Athens probably were unaware that there is the feminine, and then there is the feminine. . . . But there is no need for further speculation about what happened in the myth: how could the women have known, since the aim of myth is precisely to divide the feminine into a good side (which is for men to acquire) and a bad (the feminine version of the feminine)?

In short, once again it is necessary to begin at the end—in other words, at the present time of the city: there are no female Athenians, but Athena reigns over the Acropolis. So a story tells how the women of Athens were banished into their silent motherhood: punished for using their share of power—defeated, in a word, by their victory. For when they chose Athena, they were voting (for the last time) for the father's cause, which amounts to saying—supreme trickery, admirable denial— that the women voted against themselves. In fact, in Delphi as in Athens, it seems that the masculine principle cannot achieve its splendid victory without the gracious contribution of the very thing that it intends to put in its proper place—the feminine, women. The Athenian version of the story is certainly more refined, since at the end the feminine silhouette of the warrior-virgin alone holds the Acropolis. Thus, to give this myth a meaning in an Athenian milieu undoubtedly means completely reversing Bachofen's reading, in which he associated Athena with maternal rights— the Athenians would have been quite surprised at this—and Poseidon with the law of the father, which was victorious but only thanks to the daughter of Zeus and her alone. Bachofen, it is true, believed in the historicity of an original matriarchy and the eminent value of myth as the "faithful reflection" of a primordial time.[15] Therefore he was looking to myth for the history for which he had become the prophet, a history that he undoubtedly thought was entirely worth the price of a few narrative distortions. Leaving the modern myth of the matriarchy to those (male and female) for whom Greek myths are not enough, I will return to the crucial match played between Athena and the feminine in the Athenian accounts.

Victorious, and therefore defeated: such were the women. Nonetheless, it is still necessary to ascertain whether the opposite statement—the ultimate denial—was indeed upheld. In fact, once again this takes place in the *Eumenides,* when the action is transported from Delphi to Athens. Once again, one vote made the difference in the constant debate between the feminine and the father's law. The women had voted for Athena, except for one; to compensate for that one vote, Athena now equalizes the count in favor of Orestes. The murderous son has won his case. The cause has been heard, and justice done to the father's logic, and civic history can begin. Without further ado Apollo returned to Delphi—Orestes having already departed—while the Erinyes and Athena remain on the scene: the daughters of Night and the daughter of Zeus. Faced with the fury of the Vengeful Daughters, whose case has been forever decided against them, the goddess Athena must now resort to the muffled violence of *peithō* (persuasion):

> Believe me, in order not to endure the pain of heavy sorrow. You have not been beaten. The voices have been divided by a fair ballot, not to dishonor you. (Aeschylus *Eumenides* 794–96)

"You have not been beaten": no explanation—and Aeschylus obviously alludes to solid ones supported by Athenian law[16]—has ever succeeded in convincing me that this declaration is not a denial, the simplest, least elaborate form of denial: "You have not been beaten." And again, "You are not dishonored" (l. 824). Of course Athena has *logos* on her side, which has the power to argue in favor of the superior interest of the Olympian order. But the spectator (perhaps) and the reader (for certain) do not forget the rule that the goddess had promulgated at the moment of the vote:

> For Orestes to be the victor, it will be enough for the votes to be even (l. 741).

And the votes are even. Rejected by the humans, Orestes owed his victory to Athena's participation. There were two sides and one victory. Could there be a victor when no one has been defeated?[17] A strange logic, even if the victory lays claim to the authority of "truth." Decidedly, Athena's declaration leaves me wondering, even though I have read and reread the play to the end, even though I know that the Erinyes will be integrated into the Athenian city under the name of the Kindly Ones and in the service of an "authentic victory" (l. 903). For I also know that Athena will speak again to attribute the *kratos* to Zeus and the victory (*nikē*) to her own engagement in service of values.[18]

Therefore, the case is understood. To think the way a Greek man would of the place of women, it is better to start off by endowing women with an ancient and primordial power. Then it will be all the easier to speak of their defeat and enjoy the luxury of denying its reality at the last minute. Defeat is victorious, since the end justifies the tale, and in the end the city of males is rooted in the order that has Zeus as its guarantor.

One point still needs clarification: why, for the ancient Greeks—to speak only of them[19]—is this mythic script endlessly reenacted in the arena of power? This is a crucial question, which I do not claim to answer. I will offer at most a few remarks, taking as my starting point Clytemnestra, whose shadow, at the end of the *Oresteia*, is irremediably condemned to shame, even unto the world of the dead.

Clytemnestra killed Agamemnon. Because she committed adultery—say the people and the chorus of misogynistic old men. Because she is the man in the pair of tyrants that she forms with Aegisthus. And the spectators shudder at the very mention of the male woman. But if they had paid more attention to what Clytemnestra said, they would have heard something else entirely: the implacable anger of a mother whose daughter had been taken away from her to be sacrificed, a woman who tirelessly repeats that she in turn sacrificed her husband to the Erinyes— the Erinyes of Iphigenia, the "cherished daughter of her entrails."[20] Beyond the shadow of a doubt, a mother's wrath is a terrible thing, since its violence is bearable only when it is masked by the more clearly negative figures of adultery and gynecocracy. Fundamentally, it is reassuring to credit women with a desire for power, whether it leads to victory or defeat. This at least makes them speak a comprehensible language. But when they lay claim to a more ancient authority or a more essential wrong, what status can their resentment be given, within what limits can their anger be contained? Then it is decided simply that Clytemnestra loves power.

Now it happens that from the beginning of the *Oresteia* the chorus, unwittingly prophetic, had detected this maternal wrath and called it by its proper name. Speaking of the "perfidious matron" who guards the house, ready to rise up one day, the elders of the chorus had not named Clytemnestra—to whom they were unambiguously referring—but Anger, "the Anger that does not forget (*mnamōn Mēnis*) and avenges the child."[21] *Mēnis*: anger as memory, the most fearsome name for fury, an ill-omened word that even the gods (and Zeus himself) do not dare to call by its proper name,[22] since perhaps only the Erinyes do not hesitate to speak of their own *mēnis*.[23] Clytemnestra wholly became *mēnis*.

Memory that takes the form of wrath poses a danger for all others. It is something to be feared and avoided, which one tries to neutralize.[24] Clytemnestra is transformed into the female tyrant so that her maternal *mēnis* does not have to be confronted. And then, if one has the courage or the means to do so, one can try to stop her. But it is not an easy thing to do: because it feeds on itself, *mēnis* is endlessly nourished by the resistance that it offers to everything other than itself, and only the person in whom it is lodged can choose to abandon it. To bring this about, then, trickery is necessary, or persuasion (which amounts to the same thing). The *logos* that Athena addressed to the Erinyes opened with a denial, but to convince the Fearful Ones to reject their *mēnis*, nothing less is needed than the solemn promise that the Athenian city will make a cult to them.[25]

Clytemnestra's *mēnis*—converted into murder. The *mēnis* of the Erinyes, which Athena appeases with the promise of a sojourn "sheltered from all distress"; Gaia's *mēnis*, which Apollo is powerless to fight and Zeus will know how to foil; Demeter's *mēnis*, which only the sight of Persephone reascending from Hades will be able to calm.[26] Demeter's daughter had been carried off with the consent of Zeus (who was the father, however); Clytemnestra's daughter was sacrificed by her father, Gaia's daughter dispossessed by Zeus's son. The Erinyes had aligned their wrath with the cause of a mother killed by her son. There seems to be a pattern here. Clearly this attribution of *mēnis* to mothers and ancient goddesses is a way of attempting to imagine the danger incurred by scoffing at the feminine, struck less in its power—though implicit, this avowal is nonetheless important—than in its very flesh: in its progeny, as if by a feminine accident, that is, in the sort of reproductive closed circuit that belongs to the "race of women" and whose specter is so troubling to Greek men. And meanwhile *mēnis* has been brought to an end. It had to happen, for the order of the world, and myth has the task of telling this story. Since nothing is more feared than the implacable memory attributed to mothers, a memory that is not just made up of recollections but also of their obstinate self-possession in their distress and outrage, both the duration and fatal effects of *mēnis* must be told, as well as how it is concluded each time.

To tell of *mēnis* and how to appease it: a fine discursive operation with a double benefit. In one move, primordial mothers are endowed with a strength of passion and a mourning which are understood to be reserved for them, and when the mourning is forgotten, overcome, and resolved, one is eager to bring the tale to a close. At least that is the hope.

"All this is well and good. But what are you to do with the irrefutable statement that *mēnis*, as the 'first' word of Greek literature, for it is the first word of the *Iliad*, refers to the wrath of a man? 'Sing, goddess, of the wrath of Achilles, son of Peleus . . .' Achilles, the 'best of the Achaians.' The hero that is manly unto excess, and nevertheless ripened in his anger, like a woman."

First I would answer that because he is manly unto excess, Achilles can naturally and without danger join the women in their extreme sufferings: Achilles weeps, Achilles fasts like Demeter, and above all because, in his wrath, he hears the curses of the Erinyes more than the Olympian appeal of the Prayers (*Litai*), Achilles dooms the Achaians to mourning.[27]

I could also answer with no further hesitation that it is precisely because the first occurrence of *mēnis* refers to the wrath of a man that I find it interesting. I would probably add that the difference between epic and myth is the difference between a rousing speech and an argument bent on legitimation. Since the epic leaves the difficulties unresolved, allowing tensions to exist without seeking at all costs to dispel them, I am inclined to see it as a truly heroic language. Moreover, I would not be at all surprised that the *Iliad* begins under the sign of the masculine—the masculine that all the myths agree to make a *telos*. But perhaps I would be going too fast; it would be better to examine matters more closely.

A thorough answer to this question would require an extensive study of the strategy of the *Iliad* from the perspective of Achilles' mother, which Laura Slatkin has recently completed. Time here does not permit an examination of how the epic, while multiplying clues suggestive of the goddess's *mēnis*, never gives this "wrath of Thetis" a name or shape.[28] At

this point another question arises: Why does this unseen, unnamed anger, absorbed into Achilles' wrath, assume so much importance periodically throughout the *Iliad*? Of course one hypothesis would be that
the epic has absorbed mythological material outside of (or prior to) the
Iliad in service of its own ends. For my part I see it as a production of
the text, an epic way of including the feminine at the beginning of the
text without naming it, all the while indicating that it is inevitably repressed or at least displaced. The anger of Thetis would therefore be
both necessary (since the *Iliad* suggests its [re]construction) and blotted
out in the very instant in which it is postulated, because the epic tells of
Achilles' *mēnis*. Clothed in her dark veil, Thetis must weep over the
wrong Zeus has done her by giving her a human for a husband and a
mortal for a son. For this mortal is Achilles, who chose immortal glory.

Is it truly necessary to offer a conclusion? In this case I would be wary of
doing so, for I have no desire to lead others to believe that there is
anything in these pages other than highly obscure questions, which are
murky even to the one who asks them. At least I have attempted to delve
into a few Greek myths—which as privileged witnesses to the time of
origins have sparked unending fascination among psychoanalysts—to
uncover a few tricks of the archeological trade. Basically, origins are
never so carefully constructed as when it is important to build on them,
no matter what the cost. One has the advantage of being in the position
of *telos* and assigning a prehistoric place to whatever should not be in the
history.
   Of course, I have made generalizations along the way. I discussed
some myths as myth, and in order to proceed more quickly to the *mēnis*
that the mothers share, I pretended for a moment to forget that even
against a relatively undifferentiated backdrop, each primordial mother
has her own specific characteristics. By focusing on *mēnis* and it alone, I
made an effort not to succumb to the essentialist vertigo of comparison:[29]
not to make Demeter into a kind of Gaia, nor to reduce the character of
Clytemnestra exclusively to a mother-Fury. On the contrary, I believed
that it was necessary to generalize about the highly homogeneous area of
imaginary processes, which are strongly similar from one myth to the next
because no matter how different the tale, the stakes are always the same.
Beyond the diversity of myths is indeed *the* myth constituting the feminine, the myth that pleads for the irreversible dismissal of the mothers'
complaint.[30]

There is certainly no further need to demonstrate that the Greek strategy
of thinking about the differences between the sexes is elaborate and subtle. But the breadth of the operation that aims to dispossess women of

the feminine is more clearly perceived where women are depicted. In the city of men, the only complete women are mothers, women who are officially reassuring to the imagination because they have been domesticated by marriage and toughened by maternity. But believing that the imagination of the *andres* stops here would be the height of naiveté. Of course there are the mothers' "political" claims in Aristophanes, perfectly fictitious all the same, and the institutional practice that protects the political arena from uncontrolled displays of female emotion—for example, in ceremonies of mourning.[31] Above all there is the fantastic recurrence of the frightening Mother, postulated by some[32] in a manner that is undoubtedly too systematic but confirmed in a striking fashion in the maternal figures of myth and religion—one only has to think of a wrathful Demeter, a murderous Clytemnestra—and especially apparent in narrative operations that posit the primordial mothers' power only to undermine it immediately thereafter. The business about the origin was only a smoke screen; everything really begins with the power of the *andres*.

So much for the mother and the mothers. What about other feminine figures? The woman in her femininity? The virgin? The woman in her femininity is named Pandora, or Helen. The virgin will be divine, and once again I will call her Athena.

Helen and Athena: two incarnations of the feminine? Two ways in which one can clearly banish the corporeality of women. Helen is usually spoken of in the neuter, and seeing Athena in her femininity is so distracting to the eye as to blind the one incautious enough to behold her.

Chapter 11

THE PHANTOM OF SEXUALITY

Nor the sweet pity, nor the sorrowful tear
Have lent you your name: Greek, your
   name means to slay,
Ravish, kill, pillage, carry off. . . .
         Ronsard, *Sonnets for Helen* (2.9)

To SEEK a Greek way of reflecting on sexuality, so lightly concealed in the myths that even the evidence for it is like a screen, one may always approach matters indirectly, via Plato. Then perhaps one will reread the *Phaedrus*, which exhibits the perfected Platonic strategy of offering to the soul the excitements forbidden to the body.[1] For instance, imagine a reader absently skimming through the opening of the dialogue, impatient to get to the essential, who pauses, however, at the start of Socrates' second speech, at the opening of the myth of the soul from which he expects so much, because a name had chanced to catch his eye—Helen: Helen whose flight with the handsome Paris caused the Trojan War; at least that is the tradition since Homer. But in the *Phaedrus* Socrates is dealing only with mythological tradition, particularly when he pronounces the second discourse on Eros, which is intended to purify him for having sinned against the god in the preceding dialogue. Therefore, dedicating to Eros a *logos* in the form of a palinode, Socrates lays claim to the authority of the poet Stesichorus, blinded for having, like Homer, "cursed" Helen and who will recover his sight after inventing the fiction of a chaste Helen who followed Paris only in the form of a wraith.[2]

So here is Socrates hiding behind Stesichorus, and here is Helen introducing Eros. I will not linger overmuch on the meaning of the first gambit (inventing a ghost to replace a desirable body? A fine occasion for Socrates-Stesichorus, that is, for Plato, to put the body in its place again, perhaps once and for all). The reader has already slipped away, following Helen's tracks, since by following Helen, from Homer to Stesichorus and Sappho to Aeschylus, it is Eros that one finds—all manifestations of Eros, even the one who, as in the *Phaedrus*, speaks to a handsome youth and not to the most beautiful of women.[3]

For Helen is much more than a woman, even if the woman is Zeus's daughter, and "Helen" is much more than a woman's name. At least that will be my hypothesis: that "Helen" can serve as a Greek term for sexuality—taking this word in its largest, almost limitless meaning, a meaning that is of course neuter, far transcending all sexual differences. Or more exactly (for it is not a question of identifying Helen with sexuality[4] but of using "Helen" as an aid to my reflections on the Greek notion of sexuality): the Greeks too consider the sexuality that surrounds the name of Helen to be a primal force. That is, for one must dare to give the Greeks their due, the Greeks were the first to do so.

HELEN ONCE REMOVED

So in the beginning there was Helen. If human history always begins for the Greeks with the rape of a woman, without a doubt Helen's kidnapping is the model for all that follows—as a prelude to the Trojan War, the dawn of History, which the Greeks so like to recall in the legendary mode of the epic. Their historians, such as Thucydides, can indeed dismiss Zeus's daughter and assign graver causes to this fundamental conflict. Then, arriving on the comic stage, Helen as the motive for the war lends her name to Aspasia, and I would be willing to wager that in the Athenians' eyes Pericles' girlfriend was a more credible "cause" of the Peloponnesian war than the reasons determined by Thucydides.[5] If in the beginning there is war, at the beginning of the war there is always Helen and the "painful lewdness" that Paris chose one fine morning in a cool vale of Ida.

What do the rape of a single woman and a bloody ten-year war have in common? It seems that the first answer to a question insistently posed by the tragic poets in the Athens of Thucydides and Old Comedy was provided by Homer: nothing, if Helen is seen only as a woman, no matter how beautiful. Or again, of course the two are disproportionate, but only for those who do not wish to understand that Helen is herself and more than herself.

Sheltered by the walls of Troy, Helen shares Paris's bed; meanwhile, on the battlefield, Trojans and Achaians kill one another for "Helen." Must it be concluded that she is nothing but a name, this Helen for whom, because of whom, around whom (the Greek language does not always make a distinction between these expressions) men die? Perhaps; on the condition, however, that one immediately adds that in every case the name has immeasurably more weight than the all-too-womanly woman inside the Trojan walls: certainly for the combatants, and for Menelaus and Paris, but also, more surprisingly, for Helen herself. As if her sole identity consisted in being an object for someone else (the object of pleasure or suffering—is there any difference?), the Helen of the *Iliad* is to herself what she is to others: the stakes of the conflict, the enemy enclave inside Priam's palace. The ultimate name for the warriors' suffering, "Helen" is also used to refer to the relationship that Zeus's daughter, as if transcended by the thing that she bears, has with herself.

Helen first appears in the poem seated at her loom, and the figures that she traces into the purple of the cloth say it all in the silent language of her weaving: "There she draws the trials that [Trojans and Achaians] have undergone for her under the blows of Ares."[6] Later, Helen speaks on seven occasions, and with one exception,[7] each time will mark—in an unreal mode, it is true—an attempt to create a distance between the woman speaking and the woman that others see. Like a refrain, three themes govern these speeches: first, the wish for death, "Ah, if I were dead!" (or again, speaking of Paris, "Ah, you should have died!"); then the evocation of the ignominious words that weigh and will continue to weigh on her, uttered by Trojans as well as Achaians; last, to cap it all, the blame that because of "Helen," Helen heaps on herself when she imagines being under the eyes of her brother-in-law, this double of her husband (now Hector and formerly Agamemnon): "I, with this bitch's face," "I, this dismal bitch." Wracked by the perpetual tension between her selves, the Helen of the *Iliad* does not enjoy the tranquil sexuality with which Giroudoux will endow his Helen, a sleek creature untouched by blame.[8] Sheltered by the walls of Troy, Helen's defenses are penetrated by "Helen."

"Helen" is greater than Helen, but it is true that "Helen" is less than Helen, and a coveted or dishonored thing, she is usually referred to in the neuter. Thus, among the tragic poets, she is *agalma* (precious thing) and *kallisteuma* (thing of beauty), along with *teras* (monster). But already in the epic, she was a *thauma* (marvel) for mortals, at the same time as a *pēma* (a scourge) for the city of Troy.[9]

What, then, is Helen, for herself as well as for others? An object? A subject? Indeed it seems that at times all thoughts of making a distinction between the two must be abandoned[10]—when it comes to the theme of tears, for example. Helen's connection with tears is obvious, and in the epic a distinction can generally be made between the tears that she sheds and those which she causes the combatants in the war to shed, who like her are a source of tears—it is Ares or *polemos* who, in the *Iliad*, is *poludakrus*, but Euripides will have no trouble moving back from the effect to the cause, to liken Helen herself to the tears and blood of battle.[11] Still one hesitates, unable to choose between subject and object. How is the reader to understand the comment, made twice in book 2 of the *Iliad*, that the Achaians or Menelaus desire to "avenge the shocks of revolt and Helen's sobs" (*tisasthai d'Helenēs hormēmata te stonakhas te*)?[12] Are the Achaians supposed to redeem Helen's tears, or the tears she causes others to shed? The first solution, chosen by Paul Mazon, whose French translation is the basis for my remark, is tempting for those who, moving like the reader from the Greek camp to inside the walls of Troy, will indeed see Helen's tears flow in the following book. It is equally plausible if one considers, like the listeners of the Homeric recitations, the status of the speakers. Nestor, a good speech-maker who knows how to stir the ardor of his troops at will, and Menelaus, the spurned husband, have an interest in believing or convincing others to believe in the sobs of a Helen carried off against her will. But the second solution, making the warriors, Menelaus first of all, shudder and weep because of or about Helen, is as well founded, on the very context of book 2 as well as on tradition and had already won the favor of the Hellenistic critics. Who, then, could ever choose between Helen-subject and Helen-object?

Helen and "Helen": the inadequacy of the self, the name that overpowers the being it represents, the indecision between subject and object. Before we leave the *Iliad* and the relationship between the daughter of Zeus and herself, yet another figure can be included among these distant images:[13] Helen under the sign of Aphrodite, whose body, paradoxically, is barely present.

   This absence is all the more startling because, for historians of Greek religion, Aphrodite incarnates the immediacy of realized desire, the very image of "love made flesh." And indeed, the body of the goddess, "her marvelous throat, her desirable bosom, her flashing eyes," is how Helen, in book 3, recognizes Aphrodite in her disguise as an old spinster, which ought to have better concealed her (it is true that Aphrodite, unlike Athena, is unpracticed at the game of disguises;[14] more powerful than all appearances, her body is always visible).[15] Helen, though, has no body. Or at least the poet never offers the slightest physical description of her, as if she were merely the depository of her beauty, as if the name "Helen" dispensed him from depicting her. To affirm, with the elders of Troy, that "when she is before one she resembles the goddesses" is not a depiction of the *femme fatale* but simply a recognition that the meaning of the all-divine mortal is found outside herself. Helen's close association with Aphrodite likely means that she is surrounded with *himeros*, the irresistible desire vividly present in the body that, with Eros, leads the goddess's procession in the *Theogony*. Readers of the *Iliad* have not failed to remark that the "sweet desire" that Paris feels for Helen is only equaled by the desire that Zeus, manipulated by Aphrodite, will feel for Hera.[16] But in matters of desire, unlike tears, things are clearer. Helen's *himeros* is always the desire that she incites, rarely the desire that she feels. If Paris has realized the dream of the suitors who at one time all desired (*himeiron*) to be her husband, he is not so clear regarding Helen's *himeros*, which is stronger for him in Troy than it was the day of their first union, on the rocky isle of Kranae. But Helen responds to this burning desire and the discourse that utters it with a silent obedience that could not be taken for anything other than submission to Aphrodite. It is true that Menelaus's "sweet desire" had entered the defenses of her heart just a short while before. Will he experience a man's *himeros* on his own behalf? Perhaps Homer means to suggest that with Helen things are never that simple. For in the very exercise of desire, the beautiful Helen commits a solecism by confusing presence and absence. If the words are to be used with any rigor, in this case *himeros* is not what would direct her heart toward the husband from whom she is separated by everything, but rather *pothos*, the nostalgic desire for what is absent.[17]

Without dwelling on this extremely revealing displacement, I will, however, hazard an interpretation. Helen, who desires what is absent as if it were there, is like a stranger to—or at least is absent from—the desire that she provokes, and anyone who has read book 3 of the *Iliad* will not forget the vision of the beautiful silent woman who, in Aphrodite's footsteps, pensively crosses the city of Troy, wrapped in a white cloak like Hesiod's Aidos and Nemesis as they leave the corrupted world of humanity.[18] Helen has transformed Aphrodite's presence into something strongly resembling distance.

And far from Aphrodite's works,[19] the war wages, where men die for Helen.

EROS, ERIS, ARES

To die for Helen?

> Some, by bringing Helen back, had the opportunity to overcome their troubles; others, while caring little about her fate, would have the chance to live out the rest of their days in security. Neither side accepted these solutions: the first impassively watched their cities destroyed, their territory overrun, as long as they were not forced to abandon Helen to the Greeks; the Greeks preferred growing old in a foreign land, never seeing their families again, to going home if they abandoned Helen.

Isocrates' praise of Helen is fluently eloquent. Ronsard will say the same thing with a poet's concision:

> Your eye is worth ten years' combat with Ilion.

Or again, to conclude the famous sonnet about the "elders/On the Trojan wall, seeing Helen pass":

> For her, body and goods and city risk:
> Menelaus was wise, and Paris too, it seems:
> One for asking for her, the other for keeping her.[20]

Indeed, it was premature to think I had finished with the *Iliad*. With Ronsard in mind, it is worth the time to reread the Homeric lines that served him as a model and clearly see that, as it should be, the epic text is more ambiguous than its imitations.

So, the elders of Troy watch Helen climb the ramparts and, voices lowered, exchange winged words:

> No, there is no blame for the Trojans or the fleet-limbed Achaians if, for such a woman, they suffer such enduring hardship. When she is before you, she is terribly like the immortal goddesses. . . . But, in spite of all, just as she is, let her embark and leave! Don't let her stay here, a scourge (*pēma*) for us and for our sons later on![21]

The mention of *pēma*—the penultimate of these "winged words"—provides the conclusion for these old men. Of course Priam will speak kindly to Helen at that time, but in the Homeric text no Ronsard will continue the conversation to attenuate or reverse the order of the words that have just been uttered: no matter how beautiful, a *pēma* is nonetheless a scourge.[22] The upshot is this: two lines expressing the legitimacy of this war "for such a woman"; two more stating, in strong opposition, the need to be rid of the scourge; and bridging the two distiches, a line that conveys in a simile, the most common rhetorical device used in the *Iliad*, Helen's exceptional beauty:

When she is before you, she is terribly like the immortal goddesses.

An essential line, in that it simultaneously sheds light on the verses before and after it (beauty alone justifies the war but one must be wary of the terrible). This line deserves attention, beginning with the word that opens it (and so forcefully): *ainōs*, "terribly." Similarly, in Aeschylus's *Agamemnon*, the calamity out of which Helen emerges is *phōs ainolampes*, "the light that radiates horror."[23] It is better, truly, to avoid direct confrontations with the divine, where the terrible can always intervene;[24] when one looks her straight in the face (*eis ōpa*), Helen bears too close a resemblance to a goddess.

And yet Helen sees in her own face not a goddess but a bitch: "I, with this bitch's face," she replies to Priam's gentle words. Similarly, speaking of the fighting that was the subject of the *Iliad*, the Helen of the *Odyssey* will repeat, "because of me, with the face of a bitch"—and Aphrodite will again be *kunōpis* in the song of the bard Demodokos just like Aspasia on the eve of the Peloponnesian War for the comic Kratinos.[25] *Kunōpis*: whoever sees the woman sees the bitch. The emblem of a shamelessness (*anaideia*), reinforced by relentless evildoing (for the Trojans, whom Menelaus terms *kakai kunes* (evil bitches), feminine bitchiness becomes obscenity: the polar opposite of the dignity that the world demands of women.[26] A "woman with more than one man," immodest and obscene, thus Helen is a "bitch": the word that Helen aims at herself as the expression of outrage in the *Iliad* will be turned against her by others after Homer, Euripides one of the first among them. For the tragic poet, it is true, lasciviousness clings to Helen like fate, and even when Menelaus's wife, protected by the fiction of the *eidōlon*, remains chaste, her cry of mourning, resembling the moaning of the violated Nymph, continues to ring like an erotic lament.[27] That is not all: because, as a famous chorus of the *Choephoroi* says, feminine desire is limitless, women's bitchiness makes men's blood run. Lubricious and murderous as her sister Clytemnestra, Helen will be the Erinyes for the tragic poets, a hideous bitch in the likeness of these divine Bitches.[28]

Is this Helen-Fury the tragedian's invention? Hardly. For in the *Iliad*, Helen had already heaped enough adjectives on herself to make her into a deathly power. For example, she called herself *stugerē*, "detestable" (like the Furies, like Hades, like Ares the killer, like—for Hesiod—fearsome Discord [*Eris*]). A bitch, she was *kakomēkhanos* (of evil intent), as only Eris—she again—knows how to be, and *okruoessē* (blood-chilling) like civil war, but also like terror, the moans of mourning, and war (*polemos*).[29] As a mirror of Helen and, like her, a master of *eris*, Achilles confirms in Homer what Zeus's daughter repeats—frozen, icy, Helen makes one turn cold, he says; Helen frightens one—and Ronsard will recall this, evoking what it means to see Helen:

> My heart beats in my breast, my natural warmth
> Chills in fear.[30]

To find the series—Eris, Ares, Helen—satisfactory, however, and to refuse first place in this list to Eros would mean misreading Ronsard as he meditates on his Helen ("Mars as well as Love is joyous with tears"). Above all, it would mean misreading the Greeks, from Homer to tragedy by way of the lyric poets. For by endowing Helen with this faculty of breaking men's knees, which in the *Iliad* is the nature of war, the poet of the *Odyssey* and the author of the *Agamemnon* know how to do justice to Eros.[31] They do not forget that Eros, viewed by Theognis as the only party responsible for the fall of Troy, is, with Hypnos and Thanatos but ahead of them in his quality of primordial principle, the great Breaker of Limbs, *Lusimelēs*.[32] Caught between Eros and Ares, Helen with the beautiful tresses is the cursed spouse who brings a dowry of death to Ilion; or what amounts to the same thing, she bears Ares *miaiphonos* in the curls of her "treacherous locks."[33] This is a way of saying that sexual pleasure—the "painful lewdness" that Aphrodite gave Paris as a gift[34]—is indissociably linked to suffering because, as Plato comments, with respect to true pleasure it is, like the phantom of Helen, "a sketch that only acquires its coloration when pleasures and pains are juxtaposed to reinforce each other."[35]

Eros, Ares. Let us not forget Eris now. Hideous Eris, with whom the beautiful Helen is so often associated, and even identified. Eris, the most fearsome daughter of Night, for she is the last to be named in the Hesiodic catalog.[36] Eris, the founder of the human condition,[37] she who threw the apple of discord on the fine day of the wedding of Thetis and Peleus, to set the goddesses to quarreling, so that Paris would choose Aphrodite (and thus Helen) and mortals would slaughter one another. In other words, as told in the *Cypria*, so that Zeus's plan would be fulfilled.

HELEN'S MODESTY IS THE DAUGHTER OF NEMESIS

O Zeus the King, and Night, his ally . . .

Aeschylus, singing of the siege of Troy, has good reason to associate the Father of the gods and men with the dark power of solitary childbirth.[38] For indeed, such an alliance presided over the production of the *pēma* called Helen.

Since the days of Homer, it is unarguable that Helen is Zeus's daughter, and since Leda is her mother, one can even add with Isocrates that she alone among the children born of the union of Zeus and a mortal has the singularity of being a woman. An instrument of the all-powerful will of the Father, she makes men feel the weight of Eris, just as Hesiod's Pandora, the first woman imagined by Zeus, will rouse humans to the status of sexual beings and to harsh suffering (*ponos*).[39] Night makes her appearance after Zeus, since Eris is her daughter and Ponos the child of this fearsome daughter. There is no doubt about it, woman has the vocation of introducing the dark progeny of Night into the world, but Zeus is responsible. In the *Trojan Women* Euripides, in an immense denial, attempts to exculpate the Father by refusing him any part in the siring of Helen (as if Helen were suddenly endowed with a new catalog of nocturnal relations: daughter of the vengeful Alastor—the familiar of Furies, of Hatred—so close to Nemesis, Murder, Thanatos, but not Zeus).[40] Would Euripides be incapable of breaking with the tradition that associates the children of Night with Zeus's plans concerning Helen? Or, to move ahead and put it differently: insofar as Helen is sexuality, she is the affirmation of the paradoxical solidarity of two modes of procreation deemed contradictory in Hesiod's *Theogony*—the first, occurring under the authority of Eros, operates by the joining of sexes, and the second, under the law of division (Eris is not far), operates by segmentation.

For, it is time to recall, Helen is born from an egg, for the admiration and suffering of mortals, and if Zeus were not her father, perhaps one might be led to interpret this birth from an egg in the cosmogonic mode of the primordial births that color Orphic thought. But Helen has a father and a mother, and while the Greeks display no hesitation concerning her sire's completely divine identity, in this case metamorphosed into a swan, they are divided about her mother. Some say that the royal swan took refuge in Leda's bosom; others, with Sappho, state that Tyndareus's wife simply found the wondrous egg, the product of the rape of Nemesis by the swan Zeus, under a clump of hyacinth.[41] Anyone other than the powerful god would have recoiled before the thought of raping Nemesis, an act fraught with dire consequences. Isn't Nemesis divine Vengeance? But Zeus knows how to force her to submit to his brutal need, for it is precisely the wrath of Nemesis that he needs to set against men: and the "overpowered" goddess will be Helen's mother. Now Nemesis is—no surprise here—a daughter of Night, listed in the Hesiodic catalog after the Keres, the female avengers, before Philotes and Apate (fleshly Love and Deceit), the powers of seduction—then comes Geras, Old Age the harbinger of death, and at last, Eris. Sending Eris into the world, uniting with Nemesis: Zeus's passion to pit the nocturnal lineage against humanity is decidedly consistent.

Nemesis, for instance: Hesiod terms her a *pēma* for mortals;[42] her daughter Helen will have something to emulate, including her submission to Aphrodite accompanied throughout by Philotes and Apate. But in the *Works and Days,* where every dark power is matched with a beneficent figure, Hesiod pairs Nemesis with Aidos, Shame; and when the two divinities wrap their beautiful bodies in white cloaks to quit the earth for the abode of the Immortals, all human hopes for a regulated existence come to an end. Nemesis is dark but necessary, indissociably binding divine power with an ordinary word (*nemesis*). *Nemesis*: the term for fair distribution, proffered before the scandal of outraged justice and which has come to denote indignation,

> And in their ears tell them my dreadful name,
> Revenge, which makes the foul offender quake,[43]

while the phrase *aidōs kai nemesis*, either proclaimed or simply uttered, is enough to remind men of their respect for honor and duty.[44]

The story of Helen's birth, as told in fragment 7 of the *Cypria*, offers a peculiar doubling of Nemesis and *nemesis*, of divine power and word. To get straight to the point: if calling on Nemesis by name is a most efficacious linguistic act, it matters that when the goddess is pursued by the Father in his desire she calls out for what her name means, in the face of Zeus's violence and the world's injustice. But her appeal is also against herself.

Then he sired Helen, the wonder of mortals, she who one day was born of Nemesis of the lovely locks, united in flesh (*philotēti*) to Zeus king of the heavens, out of brutal need. She fled, indeed, and desired no fleshly union with the Father, the god son of Kronos. For, in her soul, she was torn between shame and indignation (*aidōi kai nemesei*).

Aidōs kai nemesis! The solitary daughter of Night protests against the brutal necessity of male desire with her whole being; but tortured by *aidōs kai nemesis*, which is to say, in some respects by herself, [45] Nemesis is the worthy mother of a chaste Helen pitted against the name of Helen.

How is it possible to speak of Helen's chastity after one has trustingly taken the Iliadic Helen at her word when she calls herself *kunōpis*? Is there a way to say that she alone can turn the bitch's *anaideia* against her? Perhaps a palinode is required to compensate for speaking so boldly (*an-aidōs*) of the daughter of Nemesis, as Socrates spoke of Eros in the *Phaedrus*.[46] In any event one should avoid imitating Euripides, whose *Orestes* belatedly attributes an insincere *aidōs* to Helen, only in hopes of later turning divine *nemesis* against her.[47] Perhaps it is better to take note that poetic language from the time of Homer, referring to Helen, accumulates, like so many signs, references to *nemesis*, to *aidōs kai nemesis*, but also, inversely, to *aidōs*, a word for modesty, shame, and even—on two occasions in the *Iliad*—sexual organs.

Helen's fate: Tyndareus, her mortal "father," had already insisted that her suitors swear to cooperate to punish the audacious man who, disregarding all feelings of honor and duty (*aidōs kai nemesis*), would steal the wife with the beautiful tresses from her husband.[48] In the *Iliad* Helen ineffectually sounds the call to order against Paris: "Ah, if I were the wife of a valiant man who respected duty and honor."[49] But Paris is far from internalizing nemesis; he leaves this to the daughter of Zeus. Helen speaks out against Aphrodite, who urges her to join the handsome Paris:

> No! I will not go—it would cause too much indignation (*nemessēton*)—I will not go prepare his bed. Afterward the Trojan women would all blame me.[50]

Then Aphrodite threatens the rebel, who takes fright and, wrapped in her white veil, goes off "in silence, without being seen by any of the Trojan women; the goddess guides her way." Swayed by the violence of Aphrodite's words, readers of the *Iliad* have often not wished to see that only the goddess's act enables Helen to escape the *nemesis* and *mōmos* (blame) of others at this time. For in her divine trickery, Aphrodite knows that Helen has no need of society's judgment since already, in her innermost heart, she has turned the blame against herself—and against

Paris, who does not care. Paris: she will shower him with harsh words but follow him to his bed. From that point on the goddess has no need to intervene. She probably also knows—and the inflamed words of Paris support her—that desire lives on the *aidōs* that is pitted against it.

"It would cause too much indignation," said Helen. "There is no blame," the elders of Troy had answered beforehand. Beyond a doubt, from the *Iliad* onward, Helen has a great deal to do with Nemesis, and ultimately it matters little that Homer gave her mother the fearsome name of the goddess issued from Night. The essential is that here and there Zeus's daughter's brushes with *nemesis* are immediately apparent,[51] which brings us by a circuitous route back to the words of the elders of Troy. *Ou nemesis.* . . : "no blame," the good elders said.

There is no blame . . . since Helen is like the goddesses. But also, there is no blame since Zeus's daughter takes on that responsibility herself. And above all, there is no blame . . . but she is a *pēma*.[52] *Ou nemesis*, "no cause for blame": should this negative be construed as a denial? Commenting on this expression, Benveniste postulates the logical anteriority of a positive exclamation unsupported, it is true, by any textual evidence:

> "Just division" is mentioned in a situation where this division is blocked; therefore "we have a reason to be upset about our fate; we find it undeserved." Then it is easy to understand *the same expression, phrased in the negative*, so that we read it indeed as: *ou nemesis (esti)*: "there is no cause for indignation." Hence, these negatives imply acceptance as a constant: *nemesis*, indignation, anger (at any blow against distributive justice).[53]

Is it impossible to find the "first" statement, that there is cause for blame? One can always imagine that it "appeared" as if by chance in a text, even if it was expressed in a form that has now been lost. One can also take Benveniste's genealogy for what it is: the reassuring reconstruction of an origin expressed in positive terms and not, as so often seems to be the case for the Greeks, given utterance first of all as a negative.[54] Consequently, returning to "what we read indeed," I would wager that the affirmative form of the assertion *nemesis (esti)* is fated to remain hidden, as if lost from the outset. Perhaps because *nemesis*, proclaimed in this way in the face of injustice, carries such forceful indignation that it is always wise to neutralize its effect by employing the negative form.

I will venture no further into the terrain of linguistics-as-fiction, preferring to compare Benveniste—despite his having done so[55]—to Freud, and Benveniste's reconstruction of the meaning of *nemesis* to Freud's comments on negation, where he states that "the content of a repressed image or idea can make its way into consciousness, on condition that it is *negated*."[56] The words of the elders, then: "There is no blame." Yet at the very moment that the elders are speaking, Greeks and Trojans, angry about a war that goes on forever, seek the solution to the conflict in a decisive duel between Paris and Menelaus. "There is no blame." What the elders of Troy say in their denial is that Helen is this beautiful only because she is the daughter of indignation—the daughter, perhaps of a goddess, Nemesis; or a name, *nemesis*; or a cry, *Nemesis!* There is no cause for indignation, because the inclination is to shout "*Nemesis!*"

For if, as I have hypothesized, all the talk about Helen revolves about what "sexuality" means to the Greeks, the lesson can be stated in this way: the act itself is seldom mentioned—by means of an ellipsis in the narrative or, as in Plato's case, the accumulation of small, extremely neutral words[57]—but around it multiple linguistic acts take on the essential, from just division to anger and chastity, this eminently social virtue,[58] to the shame of the *aidoia*: anyone who studies Helen follows the same route, the road between chastity and *anaideia*.

LOSS AND REPLACEMENT

Helen talks about Helen. Others speak of her. There is always a lot of talk around Helen. But speaking of Helen is one thing. What is it like to love her? Without a doubt it means experiencing absence.

Always seen from a distance, from herself, from others, Helen seems to have wings. Ronsard's Helen has wings for dancing ("I lie, you weren't dancing but your foot flew/Over the high ground: so your body was forever/Changed into divine nature"),[59] and the Helen of Greek tradition has wings for escaping. The "winged bird" chased by the young Paris, the soaring phantom pursued by Menelaus, the creature so many others would like to capture: always Helen has already taken flight. A rationalistic reading of this metaphor (as a swan's daughter, Helen is of course a "bird") would quickly bring us to the side of Meilhac and Halévy. It is better to study the Greek sculptors who, when they wished to represent Nemesis, gave her wings "in imitation of Eros."[60] The daughter of Nemesis has wings, like Love whom Plato jokingly speculates that the gods named *Ptēros*, the Feathered One.[61] If Eros proves kind, there is nothing more shared than the "flight" of sexual exaltation: the wings of the beloved, of the lover—those of Sappho, those of the soul in the *Phaedrus*, those again of Ronsard ("And my flighty soul takes off to find yours").[62] The Greek structure of desire dictates that one needs wings to approach what flies and is ever elusive. But the (Greek) structure of desire also dictates that even as one beholds the winged object, one is painfully deprived of it. Loving Helen means experiencing this lack because Eris and all of Night's children have surrounded Zeus's daughter. What lover ever possessed Helen, even when she followed him into his bed, even when she let him carry her away?

As a means of expressing desire for Helen as the experience of a lack, Greek poetic thought oscillates between two figures that I will associate, to be brief, with Aeschylus and Euripides: in *Agamemnon* the fleeing footsteps of Menelaus's wife provoke the irreparable distance of loss while in the *Helen*, Menelaus, caught in the game of being and its double, discovers that the most relentless of wars are those waged for a phantom.

In appearance nothing is simpler than abducting the "flighty" Helen from the man who "holds" her—thus Theseus took her from Tyndareus's keeping and Paris stole her from Menelaus. Except that she who is kidnapped carries herself away. She catches the man she flees, she catches the man she follows. Below the walls of Troy, the Greeks battle for "Helen and treasure." But she has taken a great deal more than treasure from Menelaus. She has dispossessed him of the *agalma* that she is herself. Paris would indeed return the treasure, he who believes that he possesses the woman; he does not guess that Helen is actually taking his life and his city. Helen's lovers see her beauty; they do not hear her name, more truthful[63] than her body, a name in which is written the law that leads the kidnapped woman to steal (*helein*). It is a name that Ronsard, nourished on Greek literature, will alternately derive from the verbs *remove*, *ravish*, and *pillage*, *carry off*, in the midst of which he slips in, like a sinister common denominator, the verb *kill*. This etymology, considered false by philologists, who, all things considered, still prefer to reserve judgment, is nonetheless profoundly true for the Greek poets who, Cratylian before Cratylus, find being in the word.[64] Aeschylus was the first to express it directly:

> Who could give this perfectly truthful name—a person whom we do not see, who, instructed beforehand of fixed destiny, knows how to manage her tongue without missing her goal—the name of Helen, the woman married among the spears, the disputed one? Did she not go off in the name of Helen, the loser of ships, men, and cities, leaving the secret of costly sails, carried by the light breath of a giant zephyr? And so they depart immediately, the large troop of hunters armed with shields, on the trail of those who, manning invisible oars, have landed on the luxuriant shores of the Simois under the effect of bloody Discord.[65]

Helenas, helandros heleptolis, in other words, *Helenē*. The name of Helen is a destiny for others:[66] the taker and loser of ships, men, and cities. Euripides will add that even in direct contact, it is by the seduction of absence that Helen makes off with her lover, who is "seized"—or dispossessed—by *pothos*, "desire," as it is lived out in a modality of loss, since one is dispossessed both of the elusive, ungraspable object and oneself:[67] a desire that nothing can quench, an irreparable loss. But in this case Euripides is content to comment on what Aeschylus brilliantly said in the *Agamemnon*: what reparation can be accomplished by a heavy military operation when the light tracks of the fugitive have already vanished on the mobile surface of the infertile sea?

Stesichorus, making his statement in the form of a palinode, "No, it is not true that you have gone,"[68] confirmed *a contrario* the essence of Helen's fugitive nature. But no one has been better able than Aeschylus to depict the destructive force of this creature of absence. *Bebaken*: she has flown, always, already. Aeschylus's Helen has always swiftly gone beyond, and when, in the dreams of the husband she left behind, she becomes a nocturnal vision, a dream image, already she "has escaped from his hands, in the very instant, on wings that follow the roads of sleep."[69] And in the deserted palace evoked by a famous chorus of the *Agamemnon*, Menelaus sits, a silent and as if empty presence, so accustomed is he to the absence of the departed woman. But what then, in fact, in this first *stasimon* of the tragedy that expresses loss so well, is this phantom that seems to reign over the household? Helen, without a doubt, the critical tradition answered and continues to answer, almost unanimously, strengthened by the knowledge that, from Stesichorus to Euripides, Helen is herself and her double; and, in all serenity (since this translation brings out the well known), the interpretation is offered that it is "the phantom of the woman who has departed on the seas," who through the force of desire (*pothos*) reigns over the household. Another reading is possible, one that is certainly held in less esteem by tradition even though the text supports it as well as the other, one that has more to say about the emptiness caused by the loss:

> Because of the desire for a woman gone beyond the walls, a phantom at last appears to reign over the palace.[70]

In Jean Bollack's French translation, Menelaus is the phantom, who by following the absent woman's traces with his mind has modeled her appearance on that of a ghost. Those accustomed to the usual interpretations invariably resist this reading. And yet, how can one fail to accept it, the moment that one is convinced that Helen knows only how to carry off (or remove, or ravish. . .)? The ghostlike Menelaus is the empty shell, doubly dispossessed since his wife's flight: the one that always projects *pothos* against a backdrop of absence, the one imposed, in essence, by the all-too-aptly named Helen. Helen has taken with her not only Aphrodite and the plenitude of her amorous gaze. More serious is the loss that she has inflicted on Menelaus by stealing his self-possession.

Menelaus's ghostlike vacuity, the effect of Helen as a lack, is the very image—Aeschylean and much more than simply Aeschylean—of sexuality as a relationship to loss.

But simply because Helen's phantom is not to be found in Aeschylus does not mean that we are through with it. For Euripides her deceptive silhouette lends form to the mirage of sexuality. The Greeks and Trojans fought "because they believed that Paris possessed Helen, which he had not," and so, to crown his sufferings, what Menelaus turned out to have reconquered was nothing.[71]

Before Euripides, Stesichorus, then, had created a double of Helen.[72] Meanwhile, as the warriors' melee raged before Troy over an *eidōlon*, the daughter of Zeus, present to herself and her intact body, was far away, in this land of elsewhere that for the Greeks is Egypt.[73] If the *eidōlon*, the ghostly double, is indeed this nonbeing giving the illusion of fullness, this unreality that produces the effect of reality about which Jean-Pierre Vernant speaks,[74] as one reads Homer one would have already been able to suspect that the day would come when Helen would be given the double of her own *eidōlon*: the Helen of the *Iliad*, strained by denunciations of "Helen"; the ambivalent Helen of the *Odyssey* whose manifestations change from one episode to the next, all faithfulness in her memories, all duplicity in those of Menelaus; and above all, the Helen seen in both the *Iliad* and the *Odyssey*—in the *Iliad*, where she is a mirror of Achilles and as such is caught in the demanding preoccupation with the uproar of glory, to the *Odyssey*, where, the mirror of Odysseus, she is conceived of in the universe of appearance.[75] But many other pairings will be added over the centuries to the one that runs through the Homeric poems—on the theme, for example, of a Helen who is at once kindly and malicious, a lucky star for sailors, according to the scholia of Euripides' *Orestes*; but they add that the sailor lost in a storm is better off never seeing Helen's sinister star.[76] To stop with Euripides, I will again mention the astonishment of the reader noting that the adulterous and criminal Helen of the *Orestes* is rewarded with apotheosis, while shame and death surround the irreproachable wife in the *Helen*. This leads to the *eidōlon*, to its seductive force and its misdeeds.

No, you didn't go to Troy, only your double followed Paris. This is the gist of what Stesichorus said. The honor of Zeus's daughter was saved, and sexuality became ghostlike, for the greater joy of the Platos to come. In turn Euripides devotes a tragedy, the *Helen*, to reflect on the *eidōlon*, this imitation (*mimēma*).[77] But its transmutation onto the dramatic stage makes the doubling more complicated, and the uneasiness increases, as if henceforth the proclamation of reality would be insufficient to destroy the illusion.

Of course there is the name Helen, over which men fought, and the woman's body remained in Egypt. What Paris possesses is the name, a vain illusion, and not the body. "Beautiful fatal name/Which caused the sack of all Asia and Europe," glosses Ronsard—Helen's name became a mark of infamy, while her body remained chaste. So be it. Things, however, are not that simple. For the chaste Helen suffers from the shame that clings to her name, and while her body may be pure, she knows that in reality, with the *eidōlon*, the animated ghost who bears an exact resemblance to her woman's body, Paris possessed something more than a name, so that still in Egypt, Menelaus's wife must recognize nonetheless that her body has led two armies to destruction.[78] To put it another way, Helen is an *agalma*—a treasure in the form of a statue—and nothing can be copied more precisely than an *agalma*.[79] Or again, if it is impossible to distinguish between the true Helen and her *eidōlon* by sight, between the true and the false, which vision is the pure one?[80] Such is the frightening question that two Greeks wandering in Egypt will tackle in Helen's presence, one after the other. Teucer will believe he sees the image while he sees the woman, and Menelaus, whose reason wavers at the thought that he is "the husband of two Helens," will not readily abandon the shadow that for so long has given him a reason for living.

Teucer, then, sees the woman and believes he sees a vision (*opsis*), "the bloody image of the woman he has lost, he and all the Achaians." He does not believe he has said it so well; indeed he has lost an image, but not the one he thought.[81] Menelaus's hesitations are more disturbing. Why would he, whose long desire and suffering before Troy are called "Helen," believe this woman, who in his eyes only closely resembles Helen, when she states that he fought for an *eidōlon*? To have labored for a phantom made of mist, labored for wind, labored for nothing, this is more than Helen's husband can bear after ten years of war and long wanderings. And when he cries out,

The immensity of my trials here below alone convinces me, and not you,[82]

the spectator knows full well that this is the last word of the tragedy—the rest is heavenly intervention, that is, drama, even comedy. For left to himself, to the error of his senses and his desire, Menelaus, as Ronsard has him, "embracing as if it were true the idol of the lie,"[83] would again depart, leaving Helen to her fate.

Everything will work out, of course, because, from the *Odyssey* onward, Helen returned to Sparta in the company of her husband, and Euripides could not allow Menelaus to lose his prey in this manner to the shadows. Because above all, it is right that the *eidōlon* pales before its model, for the royal truth to be saved. But it is important to me to go back and remain with Menelaus's cry, because it admirably states that with respect to sexuality, the distinction between "true" and "false" is undoubtedly irrelevant. There are only phantoms, or the truth—what does it matter, since ghosts are true and the truth is ghostlike?

Stopping here, with Menelaus's cry, I am not only ignoring the end of the *Helen* but the Plato of the *Republic*, who makes sexual pleasure a ghost of true pleasure and states that one fights for this *eidōlon* "as one fought below Troy for Helen's ghost, for want of the truth." For want of the truth? Perhaps. But what god could have convinced Menelaus, below the walls of Troy, that his desire was false because he was fighting "for an empty tunic, for a Helen"?[84] All things considered, I prefer to contrast to the Plato of the *Republic* the Plato of the *Sophist* who agrees, willy nilly, that resemblances are "slippery."[85] Stesichorus and Plato are then free to speak of desire only in the mode of the palinode. Euripides is free to save Helen's honor at the last minute, after condemning her wantonness so many times. The evidence remains. Double or single, Helen is never more real than when she is carried off by Paris.[86] If the Trojan war took place for a shadow, is there nothing more true than the Trojan war, nothing more ghostly than a Helen who remained chaste?

Helen. Or, on sexuality as the most real of ghosts.[87]

Chapter 12

WHAT TIRESIAS SAW

> Who can fill in these two precipices with his eyes? One
> is afraid of finding something virgin, untamed. The
> strong woman is best a symbol; in reality she is
> frightening to behold.
> —Balzac, *Beatrice*, Part 1

IMAGINE THE YOUNG TIRESIAS on Mount Helicon. It is midday. His childhood is at an end, his existence as a blind seer already beginning. He saw, he lost his sight.

But what Tiresias beheld on Helicon is not what he saw, in the most common version of the myth, on Mount Cyllene. Tiresias did not see the coupling of two snakes. It follows that he was not transformed into a woman and did not have to become a man once more, before being blinded for incautiously intervening in a dispute between Hera and Zeus concerning the intensity of feminine pleasure.[1]

In the other version of the myth, the only one to be considered here, Tiresias saw and was blinded. And the thing that, in a flash, destroyed his eyes forever is the sight of Athena's body.

Whether a later invention by the Hellenistic poet or an ancient tale,[2] the story is told by Callimachus. Accompanied by the nymph Khariklo, the divine virgin has untied her *peplos* and is bathing in the water of a spring, the midday silence all around her. The adolescent hunter and son of the nymph, Tiresias approaches, led by an unquenchable thirst to the spring. And the unfortunate one, without wishing it, saw what is forbidden to be seen. Full of rage, Athena cries out, and night is already overtaking the child's eyes . . .

If the reader, in search of disquieting oddity, has come upon this tale, there is no doubt that the blinded Tiresias is not in and of himself the main issue. Here we are, as close as we can be, to the "terrifying childhood anxiety" about losing one's sight[3] that Freud detected in "The Sand Man" and which he could have sought in Callimachus's fifth *Hymn*. However, we intend to resist the temptation to fix on the castration complex, and it will not be Tiresias, the voyeur in spite of himself or the

---

*Dedicated to Renate Schlesier.

blind seer, who will retain our interest here,[4] but the blinding flash that shrouded the ephebe with night. In this way we may question the secret law by which seeing Athena's body means losing one's sight but also, perhaps, acquiring the gift of divination. This inquiry leads to Athena alone, the familiar and suddenly unknown goddess, the bearer of this "particular variety of the terrifying that goes back to what has long been known, long familiar": Athena, by whom the strange is nothing else than a type of the well known.[5]

Perhaps because they identify with heroes such as Herakles, Diomedes, or Odysseus, whom the virgin goddess protects with all her solicitude, philologists are apt to highlight the qualities that make Athena the very figure of proximity.[6] For Homer, it is true, as well as for the metopes of Olympia, Athena is *philē*—beloved, loving—and knows how to cultivate the bonds of familiarity that unite her with those under her protection.[7] But the poet is never mistaken. It is a "terrible divinity" (*deinē theos*) who climbs on Diomedes' chariot or who aids Herakles in his Labors.

Philē, deinē: there, in the tension between these two qualifiers, lies the familiar strangeness in the form of a goddess.

SEEING AN IMMORTAL, SEEING ATHENA

Speaking to the blinded Tiresias, Callimachus's Athena—kindly in all ways like the Athena of the philologists—explains that she has nothing to do with this punishment, which is certainly horrible but is a result of the ancient law of Kronos: one cannot behold the gods against their will (*Hymn* 5.101–2).

So, is this general law sufficient to account for Tiresias's story? The lesson is too clear, and the reader resists it, desiring to retain the full meaning of the catastrophe that replaced the light with night and perhaps not fully convinced of Athena's proclaimed innocence. For a moment let us admit that this is indeed a matter of not looking the gods in the face, of not beholding any of them against their will. It is necessary at least to observe that in the time of Callimachus the Homeric epiphanies in which a god only appeared to a mortal of his choice were over (in book 16 of the *Odyssey*, in the case of Eumaios, Athena is visible only to Odysseus, and utterly incapable of contemplating the goddess against her will, Telemachus quite simply saw nothing). To save Tiresias's eyes, couldn't Athena have evaded his sight as she did with the unoffending Telemachus? That was the end, it is true, of the myth—and of its logic in which there is something irremediable about sight.

Therefore, Tiresias saw a god—more exactly, a goddess named Athena. The stubborn reader is not forbidden to wonder about what, in the mythico-religious imagination of the Greeks, is implied for a mortal in the sight of a divine being,[8] particularly one endowed with the name of Athena. In fact, for a human to behold the faces of the gods, even when they are motivated by friendly intentions, is difficult, even dangerous.[9] There, in the *Iliad* Hera fears that Achilles will take fright at the sight of the Immortals in the midst of battle: "The sight of the gods in broad daylight (*enargeis*) can be borne only with difficulty," she explains (22.13).[10] *Enargēs*: a divine means of appearing; etymologically, this word speaks of the white brilliance of lightning, but Homer's commentators readily saw in it—too readily, perhaps—the corporeal presence of the god.[11] One can play at taking yet another step, to focus on the fear generated by the sudden emergence of the god, *enargēs*, and speculate about the terrors accompanying the face-to-face confrontation between man and the divine, those very emotions that the art of the archaic period expressed in the form of frontal representations.[12] But whether they care little for showing their divine bodies or avoid direct contact, the Immortals in Homer rarely appear *enargēs*, preferring to display themselves to humans in multiple forms where humans can recognize—generally, after the fact—that a god was there. As for identifying this apparition by naming the god, that is another matter. In book 13 of the *Iliad*, Poseidon took on the traits of the seer Kalkhas to speak to the Greek warriors. Swift as a falcon, he is already long gone while Ajax is still speculating about the divinity momentarily concealed in human form. And if the hero, proud of having guessed the truth, concludes, "The gods easily let themselves be recognized," one must not be deceived. What Ajax "recognized" is the generality of the divine, deciphered in the "traces left by his footsteps." He no more recognized Poseidon than Aeneas, in book 17, will identify the god that, in the character of a herald, held fast next to him to stimulate his courage as Apollo. By all evidence, since the time of Homer, the gods have been reticent about displaying themselves in person.[13]

Now, with Athena, things are different. Since the initial episode of the *Iliad* (where Achilles instantaneously recognizes the goddess in the two terrible eyes that look at him),[14] up to the Athenian tragedies (where Athena is apt to practice epiphanies for the greater pleasure of her audience of citizens), by way of the *Odyssey* (where, when she pleases, she reveals herself *enargēs* to Odysseus), Athena apparently likes direct contact with mortals, and as accustomed as she is to the game of appearances, she is not above displaying herself in person, even if she intends to be visible only to her favorites. Perhaps this is the warrior-virgin's propensity for epiphany?[15] When, in the works of the poets, the gods cease to appear for a single hero and no longer hesitate to reveal themselves to one and all, the goddess will be all the more dangerous toward those whom she has not chosen.

This brings us back to Tiresias's adventure on Helicon. However, before returning to Callimachus, we will pause a moment to consider a most remarkable Euripidean epiphany, at the end of the *Ion*:

> Ah! to what god belongs this face flashing with light, emerging over the palace rooftop? Let us flee, mother, do not look at the divine except at the time when it is given to us to behold it. (*Ion* 1549–52)

Athena makes haste to stop Ion in his rush by adding that she comes as a friend. However, she does not reject the idea that there is a time for seeing the gods and a time for fleeing contact with them. Callimachus is of the same opinion, and if he insists on the highly involuntary nature of Tiresias's mistake, this attenuating circumstance is not enough to prevent the punishment. But what matters to me in each case is that behind the generality of the warning (not to see the gods against their will), the crucial issue is to avoid the sight of Athena. Without a doubt, there is a considerable difference between seeing Athena and seeing any other god, and to understand this, it is necessary to investigate the specific relationship of the goddess with seeing and being seen. I will return to this point after more details have been resolved concerning the interpretation of Callimachus's text.

Suppose then that Tiresias has been blinded at high noon. Even before Athena takes refuge behind Kronos's harsh law, the reader of the *Hymn* has formed an opinion. The accident ("he saw the forbidden") was included in a warning addressed a few lines earlier to the citizens of Argos ("Whoever sees Pallas nude will behold the city for the last time"),[16] and the nymph Khariklo quickly learned this ominous lesson ("O my poor child! You saw Athena's breasts and flanks; you will not see the sun anymore"). Athena can indeed invoke the general nature of the law; the reader knows that Tiresias was blinded for having set eyes on Athena, and Athena in the nude.[17] For this imprudent male[18] has seen the naked body of the goddess, whose virginal modesty, Callimachus takes care to add, prevented her, in the far-off time of the judgment of Paris and the rivalry of the goddesses, from beholding her own image in a mirror.

At this point in the reading, a few seemingly simple questions need to be asked. The answers, however, are less obvious.

What does *seeing Athena nude* mean? In other words, what does one see when one views the naked body of Athena?

But also (a question we have already foreseen), generally speaking, what does it mean to *see* Athena?

Callimachus's text urges one to begin with the first question. I will heed the suggestion, taking care to remember to return to the second.

The Forbidden Body of the Parthenos

A sharply delineated figure in the Greek imagination, the girl (*parthenos*) is threatened or frightening—which basically amounts to the same thing—and she must be hidden beneath the protective wrapping of clothing, of the veil. No goddess has more right than Athena to the title of *Parthenos*, and Tiresias, for having seen the goddess's breasts and flanks, discovered what no one, god or man, must ever know, so faithful is Athena to her vow of virginity. He saw a forbidden body (and perhaps *the* forbidden body).

There is, to be sure, another virgin goddess whose forbidden body was seen, and, for the imprudent mortal—Callimachus takes pleasure in emphasizing the fact—the result of the adventure was even worse. Athena took only Tiresias's sight; Artemis (the story is well known) pledged Actaeon to death. Actaeon and Tiresias. Or rather, Artemis and Athena. The text takes most of its meaning from the comparison between the two stories, which resemble one another, even though here the only purpose of the second—that of Artemis and Actaeon—is to shed light on the first. However, while Callimachus seems to be making Athena, this friend of manly heroes, into another Artemis by giving her nymphs for companions, the contrast between the two adventures is incontestably greater than the resemblance.[19] If, to punish the same fault, Athena takes away the wrongdoer's sight and Artemis his life, can the difference in their responses be explained only by the different functions assumed by each goddess—the latter as a huntress accustomed to killing and the former as having specific relationship to sight?[20] Another difference comes to mind, concerning the body of each virgin. Artemis loves bathing, and her nudity, which she willingly reveals to the gaze of her nymphs, is fundamental to her provocative chastity, which irresistibly attracts the hunter's desire. On the contrary, even the poets know little about Athena's body, and if Callimachus is to be believed, she is far from any thoughts of seduction when she gives her body an athlete's care. Aware of this discrepancy, Nonnos of Panopolis, the late imitator of Callimachus, will concentrate on the story of Actaeon, which is much more dramatic or explicitly erotic, and, making Artemis into "the goddess that one must not see" and the young hunter into her "insatiable beholder," he will follow the lover's gaze "moving over the chaste body of the virgin whom no one marries." For Artemis is endowed with a body (*demas*) completely exposed to view. In the case of Athena, however, this same Nonnos merely speaks of her "nude forms" (*eidos*, a way of referring to beauty in its immateriality). *Demas, eidos*: two virgin goddesses, two ways of having or not having a body. And, since it is Athena who interests me here, I need to note that she simply does not have a body, not even a body that she keeps to herself in the manner of Artemis. So how can one speak of Athena's naked body?

What did Tiresias see when he startled Athena at her bath? There is a strong temptation to suggest that what he saw had something to do with the discovery of bisexuality. Because first of all, in this version of the myth, Athena's body replaces a pair of snakes, a fairly clear symbol of the revelation of bisexuality, which Tiresias saw—and separated—on Mount Cyllene.[21] But Callimachus himself invites this interpretation, insisting on the virility of the virgin with the muscular arms who when she anoints her body shuns perfumes, unguents, and the mirror in favor of the oil used by athletes (*Hymn* 5.3–21).[22] What is there about the body of a virile virgin? Not surprisingly, a great silence surrounds this question. No Greek—least of all Callimachus—would dare imagine Athena's nudity, much less describe the body of the poliadic goddess in detail. To be sure, in Athens the Parthenos prefers the institutional use of the masculine name, *theos*, barely feminized by the article, to the feminine title of *thea* (goddess). She is *hē theos*, the female divinity. Of course Aristophanes will not miss any opportunity to poke fun at the city of Athens where "a *woman god* (*theos gunēe*) stands fully armed, and Cleisthenes the invert . . . with a shuttle." But even the Athenian comic poet, however eager for gender-derived humor, would probably have rejected a joke made at her expense by a certain Theodoros. When one of Euclid's disciples observed that Athena "is not a god (*theos*) but a goddess (*thea*), because only males can be called gods," the audacious character was supposed to have objected, scandalizing Diogenes Laertes who was telling the story, "How did Stilpon find that out? Did he lift up her dress and look at the garden?"[23] One does not lift up Athena's robe, and Theodorus knows it full well, in the false ingenuousness of the philosopher who pretends not to know that *theos* denotes, beyond the difference of the sexes, the divine itself in its neuter state. But the anecdote is interesting, in what it reveals and in the Greeks' hesitation concerning the Parthenos and their refusal to go any further.

Perhaps the partisans of a bisexual Athena will return to the charge by evoking a late tradition in which what Tiresias really saw was the Palladion.[24] Now, it is known that this famous statue of Athena, with its eminently apotropaic virtues, held a lance in the right hand and in her left, a distaff and spindle (the right, the masculine side, the emblem of virility; the left, the sign of women). But Callimachus's text contains nothing to support this reading. There the myth of Tiresias is certainly the *aition* of the Argive custom of the bathing of Pallas—or, more exactly, of the Palladion—but if the poet, throughout the long description of the rite, confused the goddess and her idol, in the narrative of Tiresias's adventure all references to the Palladion have disappeared, and it is the goddess in person—*sōmatikōs*, a scholiast would say—who blinds the careless one.

When it comes to Athena, it is better not to be too imaginative: one can muse about "the Virgin . . . as a phallic body,"[25] but above all one should temper one's reading of Callimachus by consulting other texts. Athena never looks at herself in a mirror? The reason is that she hated the mirror of the waters. One day, playing the flute, which she had just invented, she beheld her image on the water and saw her face disfigured like the Gorgon.[26] The goddess who enchants the philologists because—they innocently say—"she is a woman and it is as if she were a man"[27] is no stranger to worries about her beauty, she who could not bear to see herself ugly (*amorphos*) and threw far away the instrument that she would henceforth regard as an "outrage to her body" (*sōmati luma*)—for here, on the occasion of this episode, Athena has a body (*sōma*). Her austere admirers protest, of course:

> I cannot believe that the divine Athena, the all-wise . . . was frightened by ugliness painful to the eyes and threw the flute from her hands. For how could the ardent love of appealing beauty have overcome her, she to whom Klotho assigned a virginity without marriage or child?[28]

But this connection suggests it. If the virile virgin hates mirrors, she hates them because she is a woman.

Athena is a woman. It must be repeated, no matter how great the temptation, from Callimachus to modern historians of religion, to erase this fundamental dimension of the figure of the Parthenos (the need for masculine desire to reassure itself about a woman whom one would not fear—in the end—because she was not truly female at all!). That Athena is a woman—and a "large and beautiful woman"—was hardly a matter for doubt to Odysseus in the *Odyssey*. If the hero stresses his difficulty in recognizing the goddess immediately, able as she is to assume all shapes, it was enough, when the body (*demas*) became visible and Athena took on the likeness of a woman,[29] for Odysseus to instantly recognize her. Undoubtedly, reading this passage, it will be suggested that the goddess, always perceived in her appearances, has no body of her own; but the impression persists that Athena can only be identified by Odysseus as the goddess Athena in the form of a woman, and only in that form.

For want of solid evidence for a bisexual Athena, must one then be resigned to conclude with no further questioning that Tiresias indeed discovered that "this virile being is *only* a woman"? That he "caught by surprise this feminine nature that she hides beneath the external characteristics of a function—warfare—reserved for a sex that is not hers"?[30]

It is not evident that this sensible conclusion exhausts the meaning of the story. In search of what Tiresias saw, undoubtedly—I will return to this point—one must go beyond the too simple alternation between the secret virility of the virgin and the warlike appearance that conceals a woman's body. Above all, it is not obvious that a spectacle that the text is so careful not to spell out can be imagined.[31] Therefore, in order to move matters along, let me shift the question a bit. Since, in this attempt to "see Athena," we have gradually lost sight of the role of vision, I will consider for awhile what it is to see the goddess.

THE GODDESS, THE EYE, AND SEEING

The sight of the goddess: an ambiguous formula, but the ambiguity is inherent in Greek thought about vision where, in a complete reciprocity between seeing and being seen, catching sight of the god amounts to catching his eye—as if, in the final analysis, one saw nothing better than the other's eye; as if, with each glance, everything was played out between two gazes. It is for this reason that one recognizes Aphrodite by her delicate neck, her desirable breasts, but also—curiously—by her flashing eyes. It is for this reason that, for Euripides' Hippolytus, not seeing Artemis is the same as not seeing her eye.[32]

The Parthenos is far from breaking this rule. When, in the first book of the *Iliad*, she stays close to Achilles' side, visible only to him, it is by the terrible flash of the goddess's eyes that the hero immediately recognizes *glaukōpis Athēnē*, the virgin with the penetrating gray-eyed gaze.[33] Would it be that seeing Athena is exhausted in the sight of her piercing eye? Returning to a text by Callimachus, one could believe it for a moment:

No mirror either; her eye is still beautiful enough.[34]

Perhaps there is enough terror in the eyes of Athena to make the goddess avoid her own sight. At least, if the game of sight is one of fascination, must one suppose that Athena has no intention of being caught in the trap of seeing, she who reigns as the all-powerful mistress over mortal vision? It is Athena who, in book 5 of the *Iliad*, dissipates the fog from the eyes of Diomedes, and during the battle the hero will be able to distinguish gods from men (what distinction, then, does she wish to prevent Tiresias from making by blinding him?). Once again it is she, "the goddess with the Gorgon's eye, the unconquerable virgin of Zeus," who, in *Ajax*, beclouds the eyes of the hero she wishes to destroy. Finally, it is she, goddess warrior, coming forth "shining with the flashing of her weapons, a bronze brilliance for the eyes," who from birth dazzles even the eyes of the Immortals.[35] How could she fail to punish the eyes of the mortal whose fault it was to see?

But if, as it has already been suggested,[36] it is indeed under the authority of the Athena *Oxuderkēs* (with the penetrating gaze) of Argos that Callimachus places the story of Tiresias, we can bet that the son of Khariklo did not contemplate what was forbidden him for long. The disturbing light from the goddess's eye instantaneously blinded the careless voyeur.

Who has ever beheld Athena with impunity, without her deciding to cast the first glance? When, at the end of the *Ion*, her face, dazzling like the sun, appears before the terrified Ion, the goddess must explain that she is not an enemy, and even this explanation has an ominous sound, as if, in order not to immediately provoke desperate flight—as the aegis did in the *Iliad*—the slayer of the Gorgon, herself clothed in the Medusa's skin, must recall that she can also be kind.

For we must resolve to leave the luminous benefactress of the philologists to speak of the Gorgon, or at least, of this black light that is Athena's Gorgonian aspect. Not only is the goddess the bearer of the aegis, thereby creating "in her opponent a crushing paralysis whose magical efficacy is . . . overdetermined by the Gorgon's mask, with its deathly gaze that freezes all it touches into the immobility of stone"[37] (thus Iodama the priestess was petrified for beholding at night in the temple the goddess covered with the Gorgoneion); but as *Oxuderkēs* or *Glaukōpis*, she has the serpent's piercing stare.[38] Better, the poets aptly name her *Gorgōpis* as if, in her gray eyes, metonymy of the Gorgon, were harbored all the evil power of the chthonian creature that she once had doomed to death. Piercing are the eyes of Athena *Oxuderkēs*, the eyes of the Palladion, the eyes of the cultic or apotropaic statues of the goddess;[39] but piercing too are the eyes of Pallas for the mortal who unexpectedly sees her. And yet, what did Athena fear from Tiresias's gaze? If by undressing her body the goddess abandoned the protection of the aegis, doesn't the Gorgon keep watch in Pallas's eyes?

Unanswerable questions, and perhaps in this case idle ones. For if the myth speaks of the goddess's naked body, that detail alone, when it comes to Athena, is sufficient to alert one to be careful not to neglect it. But this side trip concerning Athena's sight was perhaps not without benefit, in that it has definitely focused our attention on this unknown: the goddess's body. Since the reciprocity between seeing and being seen is itself enough to suggest that the spectacle of Athena is something dangerous, what more does one gain by undressing the goddess? What is it, then, about this body so suddenly glimpsed and then immediately concealed from view?

The Impossible Body of the Parthenos

And if seeing Athena's nudity were seeing an *adunaton*?

Assuredly, this is a bothersome proposition for the one who asks it as well as the reader, and one can attribute it to an immoderate taste for complications. It is included among those statements that one attempts to refute by resorting to the "evidence." Thus, readers hasten to demonstrate that Athena's body was simply that of a beautiful woman. Proof exists—the famous beauty contest of the goddesses judged by the shepherd Paris. A silver Etruscan plate depicts the three Immortal goddesses bathing before the fatal judgment of Paris: to the left and the right, Hera and Aphrodite, bare-breasted; in the center, in the simplest of garments, a beautiful woman, generously proportioned, with long flowing hair; at her feet are carefully arranged a helmet, a lance, a shield, boots, and a dress insistently proclaiming the bather's identity—yes, indeed, it is Athena.[40] But, let us say it outright, because nothing blinds the gaze, the "real" image, despite its realistic intent (and perhaps for that reason alone) does not succeed in convincing us of its reality, any more than does Claude Lorrain's depiction of the judgment of Paris, where Athena is the least clothed of the three goddesses, next to an undraped but modest Aphrodite and a Hera dressed from head to toe.[41] It is better to start over from another angle and note that traditionally the goddesses do not appear nude before Paris but endowed with their functional attributes—and those of Athena, among which are the helmet and breastplate, are part of her garments;[42] the Euripidean theme of the goddesses at their bath (which, in the *Cypria* was reduced to Aphrodite's toilette alone) certainly includes the obligatory reference to the "beauty" of the Immortals, but in the most general of terms and without the slightest detail;[43] and the only representation of Athena at her toilette in fifth-century Greek pottery shows the goddess washing her hands.[44] It certainly can be conceived that, in matters of this beauty competition (*morphē*), the desire to know at last what to believe about the forms of the Parthenos is acute indeed, but it is also a desire that in all likelihood will not be satisfied. There is nothing, in any event, that can prevent me from speaking of an *adunaton*.

Seeing the impossible, then: the body of a goddess who is never reduced to her body alone, because her being is in the multiple appearances that she assumes, in Homer, to deceive Odysseus or to be recognized, in the protective wrappings—breastplate, aegis, *peplos*—that in the minds of the Greeks are indissociably attached to her.

In book 5 of the *Iliad*, according to the scholiasts, Homer would have shown Athena nude; but, more sensibly, with regard to a passage of book 8 in which the same episode is repeated, a scholiast observed that "surprisingly, he does not undress the virgin." And it is perfectly true that the poet does not undress Athena. Of course, when she readies herself for battle, the virgin disrobes; but she slips into another garment without a pause, without a breath in the text. The reader can be the judge, in this passage from Homer:

> Athena, meanwhile, the daughter of Zeus the aegis-bearer, lets slide to her father's floor the supple and embroidered gown (*peplos*) that she has made and worked with her hands. Then, slipping on the tunic (*khitōn*) of Zeus the assembler of clouds, she puts on her armor for battle, the source of tears. Around her shoulders she throws the awesome fringed aegis . . .

The gown has already "slipped" to the floor without the text slowing down to describe the act by which the virgin undoes the fastenings—in the *Hymn* Callimachus will be more eloquent, and the scholiasts as well, who are intrigued by the fluid rapidity of this movement that ends before its beginning has even been mentioned. And, while in book 14 Hera preparing to seduce Zeus is evoked in the desirability of her body, which she bathes and then anoints, here—time, it is true, is pressing since the warrior must reach the battlefield—there is no place for any description at all between the *peplos* that falls to the ground and the *khitōn* that Athena dons. It will be added that *peplos* and *khitōn*, the one a woman's garb meant for inside Zeus's palace and the other a manly tunic for war, are so to speak functional articles. The goddess is not concerned with adornment.[45]

Weapons, aegis, *peplos*: it is worth examining each of Athena's preferred coverings in turn.

The goddess's birth is a warrior's birth. Pallas springs forth from Zeus's august head bearing her bronze weaponry. Moreover, if a more explicit version of this story is to be believed, it is the swallowed Metis who, inside Zeus's body "conceived and wrought as a smith's true masterpiece" these arms from which Athena will not be separated: the bronze breastplate, but also the aegis where the goddess will later attach the Medusa's head.[46] A warrior's array, Athena's weapons are a kind of vestment. In fact, without the complete hoplite's armor with which the goddess was born, the lightly armed soldier is conventionally referred to as "naked" (*gumnos*). But arms clothe a man to such an extent[47] that a paradox claims that a courageous man stripped of his clothing is not really naked if he is armed with a spear and a shield, as the spear serves as his tunic and the shield as his cloak.[48] Athena's garb and weapons are consubstantial with her to such a degree that one sees less and less how the word *gumnos* could be employed to denote Athena's nakedness.

Things are no different with the aegis; for instance, a battle in the Homeric epic: weapons are driven deep into the warriors' bodies

(Homer even attributes to javelins and arrows the desire to bite into men's flesh, indeed, to feed on it). While the gods cannot be killed, they are as vulnerable to wounds as mortals, and Ares, the god of murderous warfare, himself suffered on the day that Athena, fighting at the side of Diomedes, tore open his "beautiful skin" (*khroa kalon*). In book 21 he is engaged in single combat with the goddess on whom he intends to take revenge. He reaches only Athena's "awesome fringed aegis, over which even Zeus's thunder does not triumph," and again it is the goddess who will have the upper hand (398–408). Ares and Athena: between these two warriors is a world. Like human fighters, Ares has a body that can be bruised, soiled with dust and blood, and deeply gashed.[49] Athena cannot be wounded because the aegis protects her, this magic weapon that wards off all blows. But also, Athena cannot be wounded, as if the aegis dispensed her from having a body. Magic invulnerability versus the vulnerability of bodies, aegis versus skin—inevitably the Warrior will triumph over the god of war. Aegis versus skin? While the Homeric aegis sometimes resembles a breastplate, the most traditional depictions of this divine weapon represent it as a skin: a goatskin but also, in a more ominous mode in other versions, the Gorgon's skin that Athena removed, or the skin of a Giant who, like the goddess, was named Pallas—or again Asteros. Therefore, Athena wears this talisman on her body, which cannot be grasped and to which the *Iliad* has not even once given the name of *khrōs* (the Homeric reference to the body by alluding to the envelope of skin surrounding it), and it would be apt to say that, brought back to its original status, the aegis is like the skin of the "artificial goddess."[50]

Last, the *peplos*: a woman's finery, one hopes that it is, all things considered, the most neutral of Athena's clothing, except that once again it is consubstantial with her. This is true not only because the bodies of virgins must be hidden (thus, the *korai* of the Museum of the Acropolis contrast the heavy folds of their *peplos* with the nudity of the *kouroi*). In many respects Athena, who is made up of what clothes her, transcends issues of concealment; in this she resembles the first Hesiodic woman, a bride in the form of a *parthenos*, whose beauty is all exterior, and whom in fact the goddess helped to adorn.[51] Not only can one never see the body of the Parthenos, who removes her *peplos* only to slip into another article of clothing. The important thing is that the connection between the goddess and her clothing seems even closer than usual. Book 5 of the *Iliad* explains that she worked this garment with her own hands and, knowing that Athena presides over the task of weaving, one would not be too surprised to discover that ordinarily a *peplos* served as an object to be circulated, rarely worn by the one who wove it, always given away. Thus, in book 14, Hera will wear a dress that Athena wove for her; the same is true of all clothing, gifts in honor of marriage or engagement, that circulate between the sexes like the very symbol of exchange. Because she refuses this exchange, the Parthenos wears on her body the product of her work, taking back what her hand had made. The autarchic Athena, the goddess seems to live within a closed circuit, and there is no breach giving another access to her. Still—it must never be forgotten— this autarchic weaver needs multiple coverings with which she drapes her body, a body that is unknown to all and perhaps even to herself.[52] Her body is indissociable with what clothes it, to the extent that it lacks any contours except for those traced by the *peplos*.

We must return to our subject, even if we run the risk of discovering that what Tiresias saw remains shrouded in silence. Therefore, for the reader who is becoming impatient, wondering where all these paths away from Athena's body actually lead, and who demands, after all, some certainties (what can one see or say of the goddess's body, whether it be always dressed or not?), I will attempt to focus on the highlights of what can be seen and said about Athena's body. Once again, we will consult the Homeric poems, because they feature Zeus's daughter, to seek some indications on the part of the poet that he at least sees the Parthenos, even while her favorite Odysseus does not recognize her beneath the innumerable manifestations of her artistic performance.

When she appears other than as a tall and beautiful woman, the form well-known by Odysseus, only the poet is able to discern Athena behind Nausicäa's friend, the young shepherd, or the wise Nestor. But the thing that enables Diomedes or Odysseus to identify the goddess is her voice: a sonorous presence, as unfleshly as an untamed *parthenos* would wish it; an opportunity for the reader to note the distance that so often extends between what the epic hero perceives and the vision of Athena that must be attributed to the poet (but at any rate, the reader is not allowed to perceive very much).[53]

Before going into what little can be said about Athena's physical presence, we will focus, as a counterexample, on the footsteps of the goddess who is most present in her own body—Aphrodite, of course. Assuredly, Helen recognizes her by her flashing eyes in book 3 of the *Iliad*, but also by her wondrous throat, her desirable breasts—the very attributes that a man would probably identify with the goddess. But if Aphrodite's beauty is meant to be seen, it also happens, when in book 5 the goddess of pleasure wanders out onto the battlefield, that she painfully experiences her body's vulnerability, in her skin—her flesh (*khrōs*)—where Diomedes' lance penetrated. Then the divine blood spurts forth, "her lovely skin blackens," Aphrodite moans, and in a corner of Olympos, Hera and Athena mock her, thinking that the goddess has cut her hand on a golden clasp while caressing a woman (*Il.* 5.314–425). Aphrodite's body is vividly present, then, in all its corporeal dimensions. Therefore she is disrobed without too much difficulty. And if in the *Homeric Hymn* devoted to her, the goddess takes on the appearance of a virgin ignorant of the yoke in order to seduce Anchises, it is a good tactic for an Immortal who does not wish to frighten the human male she desires—for indeed the text describes Aphrodite's disrobing at length.[54] One even catches a glimpse of the desirable body and fine skin of Hera, the shrewish wife of the father of the gods, when the goddess, bent on seducing Zeus, undertakes a formal toilette, "arranging all her finery about her skin" (*Il.* 14.163–87). But in Athena's case, as we know, the body and its covering are never mentioned.

Based on the poet's depiction of the divine virgin, we will only be able to reconstitute an incomplete view of Athena. There are her eyes, of course, that gazed on Achilles at the beginning of the *Iliad*, her flashing eyes that Athena turns away after having triumphed over Ares (*Il.* 21.415). There is her "beautiful hair"—but in the *Iliad* it belongs to the Trojan statue of the goddess, and on the Achaian side where she has her quarters, the goddess is not characterized by her tresses. But what is mentioned most of all about the goddess's body is what she covers with her aegis or her breastplate—what the warrior protects by donning his armor. In the much-quoted passage in which the goddess prepares for war, before draping the aegis over her shoulders and putting the helmet of invisibility on her head, she dons her armor (*thōrēsseto*). If *thōrax* first refers to the chest before it is used metonymically to refer to the breastplate, in the case of Athena we always have already moved to the second meaning of the word *thōrax*, in which the body is merely implied by the armor that encloses it.[55] Woe to Tiresias, who saw *stēthea*, Athena's breast, which this female warrior never forgets to clad in bronze.

And then, there are Athena's hands—the hands of a weaver who worked her own *peplos*, but above all the powerful hands of the warrior, which protect Diomedes from Ares' lance and are a sufficient weapon against the god of battles and his acolyte Aphrodite. But Athena employs the strength of her hands only on rare occasions—much more rare, in any event, than the translators of the *Iliad* would have it, in their overall wish to provide the goddess with more of a physical nature. Whether it is a god or a man whom she takes by the hand, it is always the other's hand, and not her own, that is mentioned. In fact, Athena has an incorporeal touch, which makes javelins and arrows glance off the heroes, without any movement on her part.[56] At most she resorts to her breath to protect Achilles from Hector's spite, but then we are informed that "she needed a very light breath" (*Il.* 20.439).

A very light breath . . . and then two flashing eyes, often terrible, and powerful hands; and again, a *peplos*, a breastplate, the aegis. This would make up a *parthenos*, the Parthenos. Such at least is the Athena of the *Iliad*. In the *Odyssey*, we have suggested, she is nothing but a voice and semblances, unless she appears *enargēs* (but there the text is astonishingly discreet about what, in this flashing presence, one sees of the goddess).

Let us look no more. Athena's body cannot be encompassed with a description.

There is no hiding the fact that all this adds little definition to what Tiresias saw on Helicon. And, at the end of this survey, the question takes a different form: What, then, did the young Tiresias see, before he became forever old and blind as befits someone who was or will be able to decipher an enigma?

Was what he saw the Gorgon in Athena's eye? The phallic body of the virile virgin? Or the secret of a feminine body, the *heimliche Orte* of a well-hidden woman concealed behind the goddess's warlike wrappings like so many materializations of the forbidden? (in this case, the strangeness of the aegis concealed the familiar; and when it is beheld, the familiar is blinding).

Unless, like Freud on the Acropolis,[57] Tiresias had seen "what cannot be seen," because there would be nothing to see of Athena's body or nothing that can be seen; because perhaps Athena's body, divested of those wrappings that surround the goddess, is nothing. A strange superficiality, the empty presence of the familiar goddess.

Put our minds at ease. To keep Tiresias from dwelling on his lost sight (vision?), as compensation the goddess gave him the superacute hearing of the soothsayer and, in the night of Hades, lucidity among the shades.[58] Since that time, no one has seen Athena's body, but clothed in the *peplos*, armed from head to toe, and equipped with the aegis, the Maiden, her body unapproachably distant but recognizable by her well-known silhouette, still watches over the doors of our modern senates where, as the friend of those men who debate and make war, the goddess of *mētis* appears, for our peace of mind, to incarnate Reason.[59]

Primordial mothers, dispossessed of their original power; Helen, married so many times but whose lovely body is perhaps nothing but a mirage, the immateriality of a ghost; Athena, whose wrappings make up her being. Three feminine figures, three ways of thinking about femininity in a negative register: as privation for the mothers, as illusion itself for Helen—sower of discord—as the mode of nonbeing for Athena.

Would this be the Greek image of femininity in which, if one discounts everything that men appropriate for themselves in their minds, only the negative remains for women? This would amount to restoring Greek women to history, which certainly does not mean abruptly giving them over to "reality" and History with a capital *H*—which facile positivisms liken to the real. But since here it was only a matter of discursive thought, we will focus on the historiographical genre, as a counter-example, to zero in on another(?) discourse on women.

Until now, the texts we have studied are essentially poetic and often marked with a mythico-religious seal. It has not escaped me that there is a great distance between these and the historic prose of a Thucydides, as well as a great risk of a shift in tone. But this is a risk we must accept. At the same time, we must remain open to the possibility that distance does not mean hiatus, and although this shift may restore greater ambivalence to the Greek representation of women, nonetheless the value it places on them is still negative.

FEMININE NATURE IN HISTORY

> "But history, real solemn history, I cannot be
> interested in. Can you?"
>
> "Yes, I am fond of history."
>
> "I wish I were too. I read it a little as a duty; but it
> tells me nothing that does not either vex or weary me.
> The quarrels of popes and kings, with wars or
> pestilences in every page; the men all so good for
> nothing, and hardly any women at all, it is very
> tiresome."
> —Jane Austen, *Northanger Abbey*

WHILE IT IS TRUE that Greek historiography of the classical period is devoted to accounts of wars and assemblies,[1] it is worth taking a moment to consider the part accorded to women in these narratives: a limited part, to be sure, but for that very reason women's role in history as written by the Greeks is all the more remarkable. This is my contention, which does not mean that I will pad my case by noting every single reference to *gunē*. Quite the contrary, I will begin by setting the boundaries of my survey and will confine my choices to certain categories. I will take care to remain within the limits of the *polis* (and the discursive order of the *Hellēnika*). Consequently, I will not consider what Herodotus has to say about barbarian women on the subject of their customs and their relationship to power, whether direct or indirect, nor the suggestions in his work that in barbarian lands a male's access to power is the result of his relationship to certain women.[2] Similarly, I will avoid what the historians say about the wives, mothers, sisters, or daughters of dynasts and tyrants—feminine roles that more than once are superposed, to the extent that incest is almost a tyrant's destiny. Thus, I will not consider either the lives or deaths of these quintessential *femmes fatales*, or their sexuality or childbirth, or even their dreams, which nonetheless play a key role in the unfolding of these narratives. At the same time, I will also disregard the wives of the kings of Sparta and the bitter remarks arising out of conflicts over succession during their pregnancies and at the time of their deliveries.[3]

No deviant customs of barbarian societies or women's roles in the transmission of power: what is left, once these aspects of otherness and *kratos* have been eliminated? What remains is . . . perhaps an *adunaton*: women in the history of the cities and "the actions that they collectively accomplished within it."[4] Studying women only as they act as a group and then noting the rare intrusions of this unthinkable collectivity in the prose of Herodotus, Thucydides, and Xenophon[5] is bound to be a thankless task, since there is no one more faithful than the historian to the orthodoxy of representing the *polis* as a men's club. And yet this is where I will focus my attention, examining narratives whose tightly woven plots allow few women indeed to pass through their mesh. Of course, I will not reject the broader perspectives offered by comparison and more than once will examine the prose of the classical historians side by side with the historic-legendary accounts, rooted in local traditions, developed by a Plutarch or Pausanias in the first and second centuries of our era—late accounts, but incomparably more inclined to treat woman as historical agents.[6] But patience! It is necessary to start at the beginning: with the austere prose of the authors of the *Hellenika*.

THE FATE OF THOSE WHO ARE NOT HISTORICAL AGENTS

Whoever is not an agent of history feels its effects; historians offer ample evidence of this simple statement.

If the history of cities is the history of wars and assemblies, one will not find the slightest mention of women in the domain of politics, which is masculine by necessity.[7] Likewise, it is not surprising that Aristotle, listing all the categories of noncitizens in book 3 of *Politics*, says not a word about women as a group. Since his viewpoint was purely and strictly "political," everything occurs among men.[8] Women, on the other hand, are victims of war. Like all other social groups "incapable" of acting because they are not and never will be, or are no longer or not yet *en hēlikiāi*, of an age to serve alongside the citizen-soldiers, women suffer the consequences. Therefore they unfailingly appear among threatened, displaced, or sheltered populations.

This does not mean that these groups do not form a hierarchy. In fact, when Thucydides takes care to distinguish the lot of the "incapable" or useless (*akhreioi*) from the series including "women, children, and old men," he is perhaps surreptitiously reintroducing the political norm into what is presented as a simple descriptive list. The incapable are certainly useless, but above all—since only citizens are fully qualified for war—it is the noncitizen who is *akhreios*, his "uselessness" being essentially the opposite of the contingent uselessness of men no longer young enough to serve and children not yet ready to do so.[9] And women? As to why they, along with children and old men, are distinct from the *akhreioi*, it will be noted that the historians could indeed be using the word *gunaikes* to refer collectively to the wives of citizens, who are called "women" because there is no feminine form of the word for "citizen," but also because *gunē* is the most common word for "wife."[10] Women are neither citizens nor included among noncitizens, because this composite group is seen as masculine, and one understands how an Aristotle can both exclude women from the list of categories of noncitizens and affirm, as an aside, that they are like "half the city."[11]

As, for example, in the series, "women, children, old men." Or, to cite the combination most widely used by the historians, "women and children." Women and children are seen as precious objects for which men do battle: a treasure "laid down like the stakes of a contest (*athlon*)" when they are being sheltered, and they provide one of the most constant *topoi* of patriotic eloquence. In addition, this group generally appears flanked by the gods of the country in the rhetoric employed by the *stratēgoi* as they exhort their troops not to give up hope.[12] This can be seen as a reminder that in an inextricably political and religious move the city protects its own fecundity, and thus its ongoing survival, by protecting its women and children. Religious is the dreadfully effective law deeming that any serious transgression entails their annihilation;[13] political, or at least civic, is the Greek word order that, instead of putting women first, as I have pretended is the case, more commonly sets children first, since they are the token of its survival—the future already in the present.

Children and women are precious goods to be protected (as the Athenians did at the time of the Persian invasion, when they sent theirs to Salamis) to keep them from being taken hostage. It is true that often it is hard to tell who is being protected and who is a hostage. Thus, when the Plataeans entrusted their children and women to the Athenians in 431, the Plataeans knew full well that there was no reneging on their pledge to the Athenians.[14] But any solution is preferable to the fate befalling a city when the enemy, victorious after a long siege, reduces its women and children to slavery. These are the Greek laws of warfare, which though terrible are tacitly admitted.[15] But when the Thracians indiscriminately massacred the inhabitants of Mykalessos, all of Greece joined Thucydides in recognizing this act as blatant evidence of barbarianism. Therefore, when all is lost, and in the midst of the distress a last opportunity for escape presents itself, one should flee with one's children and women, no matter what the cost, so that the city may continue to live, even if it is "without territory."[16] But when such an escape proves impossible, everything may collapse; then, cornered and in despair, men will kill their children and women, the collectivity's most precious treasure. At least such things come to pass in Herodotus among the Barbarians. The entire group is annihilated and all they possessed destroyed (or else, as in the case of the Babylonians, the women, useless mouths to feed, are killed in a final attempt to sustain the siege). For classical historiography has seen nothing of the sort among the Greeks and in the world of the cities. As reported by Plutarch and Pausanias, the tradition of "Phocidian despair" is as legendary as it is historical, and their annihilation, moreover, was only a plan, since the divinity—Artemis, in this case—saved the women and children from the pyre by giving the *andres* the victory that they despaired of ever achieving.[17]

Whether protected, taken as hostages, reduced to slavery, led far from their homes, or destroyed, women have the same passive role as children.[18] Nonetheless, this statement should be modified. To be sure, the expression *paidas (tekna) kai gunaikas*—always in the accusative as is appropriate for those who are in the position of objects—places the children, the city's hope, ahead of the women. But less formulaic passages prove that women nevertheless have a more active role to play, since they are so intimately associated with the destiny of those who are fighting. Thus women pour libations for the victorious *andres* (as in the case of Philiontes' wives, in Xenophon), and according to Thucydides, women were among those captured in the civil war (*stasis*) and were to accompany the oligarchs of Corcyra into their final entrenchment.[19]

When the role of the women is less passive, the children disappear from the tale. Before leaving the children aside, however, I will mention an episode where, under urgent pressure, the children back the women, who themselves second the *dēmos* of Athens: during the hasty construction of the Long Walls in 478 in which Athenians en masse (*pandēmei*), including women and children, take an active role. But (is this surprising?) because the women are the most effective helpers, this time they are mentioned before the children. Meanwhile, in a situation that is comparable in all respects, the children disappear completely from the account, to be replaced by household slaves (*oiketai*): in this case, it is the city of Argos, at the height of the Peloponnesian War. Allied with Athens, the Argive people decide to build, on the Athenian model, long walls down to the sea, and all work together (*pandēmei*), including women and slaves.[20]

Women and children in Athens, women and slaves in Argos—two alternative groups that give women priority appear in two democracies facing external threats. Perhaps this Thucydidean symmetry brings to mind a passage from Plato on democracy as a paradise for women, slaves, and children. Then one might be led to ponder the divided representations created by the political imagination in historical accounts and that underlie the proclaimed rigor of *logos*. For the moment I will proceed to examine the rare occurrences in which women take a more active role, as men's allies or indeed on their own authority, and play a part in history—or at least in a few of its byways.

A Few Historical Byways

Staying with Thucydides: twice, in the *Peloponnesian War*, women climb on the roofs to fight.[21] To be precise, suddenly they enter the account, at the same time as or alongside the slaves, actively assisting the *andres* engaged in arduous street fighting within the city walls. However, each of these two isolated yet perfectly timed interventions occurs at moments of acute crisis, as if the thread of the narrative, weakened by what it is saying, relaxed for a moment to permit the incursion of an anomaly.

Night, noise, and rain furnish the setting for the first episode. In the town of the Plataeans, which the Thebans have taken by trickery, the *dēmos* leads a nocturnal counterattack. The Thebans struggle to resist:

> but, as soon the Plataeans attacked them, in a terrible tumult, supported by women and slaves who shouted and cried from the houses, at the same time hurling stones and tiles down upon them; and since with that a strong rain began to fall which lasted the whole night, they succumbed to panic.

The luckiest among them owed their salvation to a chance encounter with a woman—again, one woman—who handed them an ax to break the bar on one of the town gates, which allowed them to escape. The others were killed or surrendered.

The second episode occurs at the beginning of the *stasis* in Corcyra. In this case oligarchs and democrats confront one another. As each of the two parties appealed to their slaves by promising them their freedom (which is as it should be), the "servants" (*oiketai*) have allied themselves with the *dēmos* while the oligarchs secure the assistance of mercenaries.

> After a day of rest, the battle began again, and the people carried the day, thanks to the strength of their positions and the superiority of their numbers, all the more because the women boldly assisted them, hurling tiles from the tops of the houses and overcoming their nature to face the tumult.

In this way, for a time, the oligarchs are routed.[22]

The slaves have already dropped out of the account; the women will not reappear either. The fact remains that in Plataea as in Corcyra, their intervention, before a backdrop of noise and fury, brings victory, even if only a provisional one, to the *dēmos*[23] battling a foreign enemy inside the city walls or simply an enemy from within.

Women and slaves: a Greek conjunction representing the disordered city "in tradition, myth, and utopia."[24] It is less well known, perhaps, that this conjunction is found even in the prose of Thucydides, and this merits some attention. Of course historical narratives have a particular style and adopt such expressions only fleetingly and under highly specific conditions. Although the women of Corcyra and Plataea are linked with slaves, as in the tales of gynecocracy or stories of "forced marriage,"[25] they are not engaged in the conquest of exclusively feminine power or forced into servile unions by a tyrant's whim. They simply fight, with the help of slaves, alongside the men for the common salvation of the city or *dēmos*.[26] Of course, the events in Corcyra and Plataea widely diverge from the orthodoxy of the hoplitic battle, in which women do not and cannot have a place. In a mental universe where true warfare takes place outside the city walls, dubious are the tumultuous battles fought within the city, and uncertain the victory, especially when, now and then, the belligerents are fellow citizens. But, in Corcyra as in Plataea, *kratos* remains with the men (who never lost it, not even for an instant), and while the very fact of civil war bodes catastrophe, a city in a state of *stasis* is perhaps less unfaithful to the civic norm than a city where a tyrant flourishes.

In an effort to avoid comparing the incomparable, then, I will consider these two examples from Thucydides in light of the legendary accounts that Plutarch and Pausanias based on local Peloponnesian traditions, and that attribute to women the paradoxical glory of a military victory due solely to their intervention—the stories of the women of Tegea and, above all, the women of Argos.[27]

When the women of Argos undertake the defense of a city in a state of *oligandria*, they are not a mere additional force,[28] like their counterparts in Corcyra in 427, and they do not fight next to slaves, like the women of Plataea do. Instead, full-fledged warriors because they replace men, they leave the slaves far to the rear, posting them at the ramparts "with all of those who, due to their youth or advanced age, were incapable of bearing arms."[29] This takes us far from the norm by which women are both distinct from and associated with the *akhreioi*.[30] Thucydides was more faithful to it when, in one move, he links the women with the slaves and engages them in the service of the men: isn't the *andreia* that Aristotle in his *Politics* discerns in women, utter submissiveness (*hupēretikē*)?[31]

Andreia hupēretikē on the one hand, manly courage of the highest order on the other: there is a clear gap between Thucydides' thinking and manner and the accommodations made by Plutarch and Pausanias. Thus, seeing Plutarch stress the military dimension of the war waged by Telesilla at the head of the women of Argos who are "of an age to serve," the reader is not too surprised to learn that those who fell in combat were buried in a common grave as citizen-soldiers. In Pausanias's account the

Tegean women, who are sometimes associated with the men, sometimes included without further details in the victorious army, and sometimes described specifically in terms of their own actions, will perform a sacrifice to Ares on their own behalf, excluding the *andres* from the feast and taking full credit for the victory.[32]

While for Thucydides women caught in an exceptional emergency behave like the women that they are, the female fighters in Plutarch and Pausanias act as if they were *andres*. It is true that in this instance "as if" is not a negligible phrase; even when the weakness of feminine nature does not end up undermining these impromptu woman-warriors,[33] their actions exhibit a different style than male warfare. They are merely ambushes, followed by sudden appearances, like epiphanies, that "strike the enemy with stupor," thus forcing him to turn tail in a rout (*tropē*).[34] But, on this last point, the women of Plataea or Corcyra have nothing to envy the fighting women of Tegea. As if the very presence of women, this supplementary force, alone could achieve victory, the auxiliaries of the *dēmos* have also seen the routed enemy suddenly turn its back.[35]

Women probably cannot be brought into combat with impunity. Even if the writer is named Thucydides or Pausanias, their inclusion inevitably means a modification of the rules, because endowing women with *andreia* is to commit a serious breach against both language and values. *Andreia* makes women manly—hence Clytemnestra, "with her male plans," the utterly bold woman who boasts of having killed the male *hōsper en makhēs tropēi* ("as in the rout of battle" [*Agamemnon* 1237])— but inversely, women in numerous legendary or edifying accounts resort to ostentatious displays of femininity—to the warriors' shame—and thus are able to provoke a rout. Lifting their robes, they boldly reveal their sex[36] —and the enemy scrambles to flee; unless it is their own men who are in disarray, and they show them their bellies, producers of warriors for the city—and then often the *andres* regain their courage, and with it, victory.[37] It is a way of humiliating males who are not adequate to the task (for example, the words of a Spartan mother to her sons who had survived a defeat: "Do you want to go back to the place out of which you were born?"), but also, perhaps, a way of shocking the men into indignation: scandalous is the behavior of warriors who let their women, whose only war should be childbirth, enter the fray of battle.[38]

Closing this parenthesis in which the striking connections between sexuality and warfare have once again appeared, I would wager that once the war is over these legendary women, like the very real wives of citizens, will once again return to their womanly destinies.[39]

However, one must not be too hasty in hoping to be done with differences between the sexes. From Thucydides to Pausanias, from the deeds of manly women to the historians' accounts, in which women intervene only within the limitations ascribed to their sex, sexual differences never disappear for long, as can be ascertained by investigating the weapons used respectively by the two types of woman fighters.

The women of Plataea send a rain of stones and tiles down on the Theban enemy, and again, the women of Corcyra hurl tiles at the oligarchs. Stones and tiles: these projectiles are the impromptu arms of noncombatants, supplementary forces, or women in the cities—they are also, it is true, weapons of a particularly ominous nature, used by citizens against citizens in times of *stasis*.[40] Stones and tiles: again, these are the weapons of women who, in the mayhem of street fighting, have left their posts as auxiliaries to become the instruments of a type of killing that is not far from murder. Throwing stones turns into stoning,[41] and other "arms" are added to the rebellious women's random array, emblems of feminine life turned to the service of *phonos*, strange and fearsome tokens—mythic as well—as it should be when women's hands toil to shed blood. Thus, the women of Athens, who according to Herodotus turned on the sole Athenian survivor of a battle in which all other citizens perished, stabbed him with the pins that fastened their clothing.[42] But before war definitively topples into *stasis* and murder, I will consider for a moment the stones and tiles of the women of Corcyra and Plataea, just long enough to compare these occasional weapons to the highly regular soldier's gear of the women of Argos or Tegea.

The woman fighters of Tegea don their armor (*hopla endusai*) just as *andres* do, and Telesilla of Argos gives her female troops regular weapons, or almost regular weapons. It should probably be noted that the source of these arms, taken from temples and houses, links them to spheres outside the exclusively military realm of manly warfare. But this is a minor detail, considered from the viewpoint that interests me here. Indeed, in the national traditions of the Peloponnese—which is to say, in accounts governed by the logic of legend—female armies bear *hopla*, not improvised or imitation weapons.

For the moment that the narrative, which in this instance is Pausanias's account of the wars of Messenia, seems inclined to adhere to something resembling a principle based on reality, lo and behold, for a time at least, the improvised weapons mentioned by Thucydides reappear. Thus the women of Messenia, wishing to assist their husbands besieged by the Lacedaemonians in the fortress of Eira, begin by harassing the enemy "with tiles and anything that each could find to throw."[43] But a violent rain begins to fall that prevents them from using the traditional projectiles—a rain that is also legendary, let there be no mistake about it; the rain that fell in Plataea does not seem to have kept anyone from throwing stones and tiles. Then "they dared take up arms" (*hopla*), and the epic battle can begin (anew), the truth being that introducing armed women into a narrative essentially amounts to freeing the text from all concerns with reality. Inversely, a passage by Aeneas Tacticus suggests that, when one argues in terms of "reality"—even if this reality depends on a stratagem—women cannot be given the weapons of the *andres*. The scene takes place in Sinope, during a siege. As there is a shortage of men (*spanis andrōn*),

> for this purpose the women who were best suited physically were given outer clothing and equipment that was as masculine as possible, and as a semblance of weapons and helmets, they were given their bronze pitchers and utensils. They were told to make the tour of the points on the ramparts where the enemy was most likely to see them, but they did not have permission to shoot, for it is easy to see from afar that it is a woman shooting.[44]

While there is a shortage of men, nothing indicates that there is a shortage of weapons—that they had been removed from the temple walls, for example. Therefore it will perhaps be surprising that the women, even disguised as men, had a right only to imitation weapons taken from their kitchens. The reason is that for Aeneas the real never ceases to be a priority, even if, to be sure, in this text the word *real* has more than one meaning. The effect of the real is expected from the account, and the reader is asked to believe that in those days all it took to protect the secret was to keep the forces from deserting; there is the fictional reality of the stratagem, which it is presumed can be imitated—for everywhere women have pitchers; and most important, and all the more constricting because they are "self-evident," there are the rules of sexual division embodied in sexual roles, in which war is "men's business."[45]

WOMEN AND STASIS

War is men's business. This adage perfectly represents the reality of social practices since it requires nothing less than the comic fiction of the Acropolis taken by the women of Athens to refute it. I mean *Lysistrata*, of course. It remains that the political imagination of the Greeks constantly maintains an implicit but strong distinction between "good" (or better, "beautiful") warfare, true warfare, in which the rules of loyal combat are applied, and bad warfare, in which anything is possible and everything permitted. And in bad warfare, which is often called *stasis*, women have a place, be it ever so slight, as Thucydides has indicated. And for that specific reason, Thucydides is of interest here. The fact that the historian's well-knit prose has a place for women, at the heart of *stasis*, may be enough to suggest that there is a necessary and still verifiable link between women and civil war.[46] In fact, the connection between women and conflict is ancient. One only need think of Helen, *eris* incarnated, or

Pandora, who introduced mortals to Ponos, the first child of Eris, herself the daughter of bleak Night. But Pindar also comes to mind, who referred to the hated civil war as *antianeira* ("hostile to *andres*"), a term used in the *Iliad* to describe the Amazons[47] as men's rivals and enemies.[48]

I am probably complicating matters by confining to Thucydides the examples that verify the appropriateness of this association. Street fighting in Plataea, *stasis* in Corcyra—why settle for so little when one could turn elsewhere? There would be no reason at all, in this case, to look beyond fifth-century Athens. All that would be required, for example, in Aeschylus's *Suppliants*, is to bring up everything that makes the Danaid cause into a women's *stasis*.[49] Comedy would be an even simpler matter. The succession of women in *Lysistrata*, which the men of Athens compare to a plot against political power, is an obvious example.[50] Above all, the parabasis of the *Thesmophoriazousae* furnishes decisive evidence. Here, before they turn the theme of the "race of women" (*genos gunaikōn*) against the men, the women ironically lay out its principal argument:

> Of course, everyone vies in condemning the tribe of women: that we are a scourge upon humanity and that everything is our fault: quarrels, discord, ominous civil war, sorrow, war (*eridēs, neikē, stasis argalea, lupē, polemos*).[51]

The meaning could not be more clear. However, if one wished to expand the corpus, it would be possible to plunge into the innumerable accounts treating the theme of women's secession, which the Greek imagination sees as a serious threat to the unity of the *polis*. Moreover, whether this secession is the result of an attack of Dionysian madness, as in the *Bacchae*, or an epidemic, as in many other traditions,[52] matters little in a mental universe in which secession is an equivalent to *stasis* and epidemic is a metaphor for it.[53] And one may divine the specter of other incursions into the divided representations formed by the civic imagination—even in the civic appointments of special magistrates, called *gunaikonomoi*, to oversee women and their conduct. Thus, while commenting on the negligence of the Spartan legislator in this regard, Aristotle arrives at his definition of women as "half" of any city. But, rather than concentrating on this well-known definition, one should consider the statement, central to this development, that the city is "so to speak divided in two," without exception, "between the group of men and that of women." Those familiar with the risks that Aristotle attached to any absolute division might find a great deal to ponder here—it is true that the philosopher was careful to express himself in a hypothetical mode.[54] A long and probably valuable examination could be made of civic institutions designed to face a real or imagined threat, of the stories told within the collectivity of *andres* to stir their anxiety with thrilling episodes. But I said that I would remain with Thucydides' text, even if this entails carefully opening it to what lies beyond. I do not wish to complicate matters for the fun of it but—once again—in order to verify the constrictive power of Greek representations of division and the logic that connects the race of women, who have divided humanity in two, with *stasis*, which cuts the city in two.

For instance, Thucydides' account of the first days of the *stasis* in Corcyra. Now is the time to show that the filter that historiographical reasoning applies to history is not too fine to permit a few figures dear to the imagination to pass through it. By focusing on one paragraph from Thucydides because I see it as a highly significant small unit, I am certainly not unaware that the unique document has a bad press in the world of historians. It is in Corcyra, and Corcyra alone, that Thucydides mentions women taking part in *stasis*. So be it. Yet because Corcyra's civil war is the first *stasis* to be described in the account of the Peloponnesian War, it represents all other such conflicts, and this exemplarity, which the historian himself has been careful to emphasize, is never challenged in the historiographic tradition to follow, where Corcyra endures as the symbol of the horrors of *stasis*.[55]

However, the women's participation is of small enough scope that it does not figure in his account of horrors, and instead Thucydides emphasizes how much violence feminine nature does to itself to be able to face the tumult of war. In fact, from the standpoint of both women and slaves, solidarity with the *dēmos* seems to be paramount, and my point is the same whether the chronology separates the two groups instead of joining them, as happened in Plataea. Like the slaves, the women immediately lapse into obscurity, while the *dēmos*, henceforth identified with the "Corcyreans" because the democrats had the upper hand, is engaged in the violence—and the hypothesis quickly presents itself that Thucydides wishes to remove women from the fray when the fighting turns into *phonos*. True, some women still deserve mention, those who were at the sides of the oligarchs and in Corcyra's second *stasis*, but they are no longer considered to be a group.[56] However, this distance cannot be interpreted as a reflection of the "political involvement" of women who, seen as a potential collectivity, would be more a part of the *dēmos*. The Plataean episode, with its image of a *gunē*[57] who offers the Theban enemies the ax they so greatly need to break down the doors and escape their trap, serves as a reminder that even in a city thought to be unified against the outward enemy the threat is always twofold, be it from two parties—which, in fact, is the case of the Plataeans—or from the women, who may enter the fray in support of either side.

Discreetly, Thucydides says no more about women and *stasis*. But the reader disappointed by the dearth of examples would do well not to lose heart and instead should allow the women to fade into silence and follow the remainder of the historian's account of the *stasis* in Corcyra. Then it will become apparent that in matters of theory, Thucydides does not completely forget that civil war is, so to speak, feminine in essence. Of course, this is a subtle process—as it should be—and the historian does not explicitly link *stasis* with the feminine. Instead he takes pains to emphasize that intestine war falsifies the notion of *andreia*, which is fundamental to the representation of good warfare, in which authentic courage blends with manliness. Although he essentially describes *stasis* as occurring among *andres*, for Thucydides the ideal of *andreia* has been diminished to a word that has been totally usurped.

An example can be found in the famous chapter 82 of book 3, which contains the oft-quoted (and much more rarely discussed) passage treating the pernicious effects of civil war on civic language. It is a remarkable text, representing the height of Thucydidean style, constructed entirely according to the stylistic principle of variation in antithesis, which Adam Parry, among others, sees as the historian's most characteristic trait.[58] However, while the antithesis that turns each expression into its opposite is affected by the asymmetry, the reason for this disequilibrium must be sought—Thucydides invites us to do so—less in stylistic choices external to the object than in the very object of his argument: the gap between the city and its language, a gap that is henceforth irreversible and at work in historical writing itself. Now it so happens that the first set of nouns in which, "when they established a judgment, the factions exchanged the usual evaluations" with respect to actions,[59] includes *andreia*, the word and what it stands for.

What henceforth will be known as *andreia* in partisan speeches is what the historian, from his observation post, characterizes as "reckless audacity" (*tolma alogistos*)—the very same thing that Thucydides will present in chapter 6 as the principal motive (which is not all heroic) of the tyrannicides, whom the Athenian democracy likes to celebrate as heroes. And not content to give this reckless audacity the name of manly courage, the rhetoric of treason adds the qualifier *philetairos* ("friend of his party") to *andreia*. One should not be overly surprised to discover that this is a *hapax* in Thucydides' work. When it comes to political love, the historian only knows the "friend of the city" (*philopolis*), and he uses *philetairos* as if it were in quotation marks, counting on the reader to understand that this simple qualifier is enough to destroy the notion of *andreia* that he is supposed to be describing.[60]

A second shift in meaning is a corollary to the first. There where the historian's cool gaze sees only "prudent hesitation" (*mellēsis promēthēs*), partisan eloquence denounces "cowardice hidden beneath a fine exterior" (*deilia euprepēs*). "Hesitation" is used to describe Lacedaemonian tactics, for example; foresight (*to promēthes*) is too intellectual a quality for Thucydides to fail to appreciate it. However, the discourse of *stasis* has no interest in these values and prefers to use highly marked words, such as *deilia*, which Thucydides reserves for speeches because the highly pejorative connotation of the term is suited to the exaggerations of eloquence. Or he employs the term *euprepēs*, which connotes an extremely negative judgment that the historian, speaking in his own name, generally prefers to apply to the rebels themselves.

The linguistic operation continues with the transformation of wisdom (*to sōphron*) into *proskhēma tou anandrou*, a "mask of cowardice," as the translation goes. But for a rigorous translation of *to anandron*, one would have to read Orwell and master Newspeak, in which "given the word *good*, for example, there was no need for such a word as *bad*, since the required meaning was equally well—indeed better—expressed by *ungood*." *To anandron*, then, would become "unvirility" (and *anandros* would be something like "unmaleness"), because this eminently ideological term refers to a mental system in which, except for the orator's party—likened to the production site of the *andreia*—only "unmen" can be found.[61]

All that is left is to turn "intelligence in everything" (*to xuneton*, a quality highly prized by Thucydides) into "total inertia," and then, tallying the list of new values, one can add "mad impulsiveness" to the lot of the virile man (*andros moira*). For—as already made clear by the use of *andreia* and *anandros*—it is the *anēr* who matters here, both as reality and ideal, and from the vantage point of both the historian and the rebels. But the difference between these two viewpoints is irreconcilable, for in situations where the partisans of *stasis* in each camp herald the arrival of a new man, Thucydides sees only the falsification of words and deeds.

Faced with the general perversion of the meaning of political language, the reader will not be surprised that henceforth careful deliberations are presented as "an orator's trick" or "a pretext for escape" (*apotropē*). And this reflects the essential point of my argument: because *andreia* is the first word to be falsified by the civil war, *stasis* attacks authentic virility, and in a roundabout way this analysis makes the intrusion of the feminine into the historical account possible.

Consoled by this reading, then, I will once again return to what has been said about the women of Corcyra in order to note that, despite its brevity, the passage contains several elements that make it possible to raise the paradoxical question of feminine *andreia*.

At its heart is the tension, which is intense in the text, between their actual boldness and their presumed natural timidity.[62] After stating, as if it were self-evident, that "women boldly assisted the *dēmos*" (*tolmērōs*), why does Thucydides add that "they overcame their nature to face the tumult" (*para phusin hupomenousai ton thorubon*)?[63] Although this question is being asked about a few lines from Thucydides, it could also address larger, recurring issues of the Greek political imagination that tirelessly raise questions about feminine nature: Is it good? Is it bad? Or, to be more precise, is it made of *sōphrosunē* or pure *tolma*?[64]

ON WOMEN AND *PHUSIS*

Thucydides' care not to involve women in the bloodiest episodes of the *stasis* has already led to the supposition that he endowed them (or at least desired to do so) with inherent wisdom and reserve.

To be sure, this postulate should not convince all of Thucydides' readers. Thus—to leave ancient Greece for a moment—shortly after the French Revolution, the idea that women had to overcome their nature to enter the fray must have seemed very strange to a reader such as P.-C. Lévesque. At any rate, this scholar, who at the height of the Thermidorian period had attempted a complete translation of the *Peloponnesian Wars*, comments in his *Etudes d'histoire ancienne*, published in 1811, on the text about the women of Corcyra and attributes to the historian the exact opposite of what he actually said. There is nothing surprising, states Lévesque, about the presence of women at the side of the people; aren't they "always more violent than men in movements of rebellion?"[65] No doubt about it, the overly strong representation of revolutionary women has irreversibly reared up between the text and the reader.[66] But what about a *Greek* reading of this passage?

Closing (not without regret) this postrevolutionary parenthesis to return to the time of the ancient historian, I will wager that, in a mental universe that associates women with *stasis*, Thucydides' statement must have surprised more than one of his contemporaries. In fact, it could be that the historian takes back with one hand what he gives with the other; that even as he permits one element of the traditional "blame against women," in which feminine *phusis* is essentially endowed with boldness, to rise to the surface, he intends all the while to extricate himself by briefly indicating his own criticism or at least keeping his options open. For in book 2, as a conclusion to Pericles' *epitaphios*, the definition of feminine nature that he offers operates on two levels: in the silence that must enshroud women's lives and the paradoxical law that claims that, for women, this natural endowment is at the same time the culmination of the ideal of *sōphrosunē*.[67] And here in Corcyra the nature of women is revealed by its contrary, to be fearful and an enemy of noise—not just any noise, it is true, but *thorubos*.[68]

Thorubos: as if by chance, the word has already provided the frame-work for the women's active role in the events at Plataea, as if women's participation in history only occurred before a background of noise and upheaval.[69] And yet, would this *thorubos* be contrary to feminine nature? Catching a whiff of a meaningful contradiction, the reader is perplexed.[70] And in fact, an examination of Thucydides' other uses of *thorubos* only increases the confusion. For tumult, which is generally characterized by its intensity, is linked to panic, and often to a mixing of the internal and external, or hoplitic tactics with battles at sea—giving rise to something like a naval battle on land, the height of confusion.[71] This amounts to saying that this word describes conditions that, in anyone but Thucyd-ides, portend an explosion of feminine boldness.

In anyone but Thucydides? Not at all. For before mentioning feminine *phusis*, the historian has first, without a hint of reticence, characterized the women's action by its *tolma*. It is true that this does not relieve all the reader's ambivalence, since *tolma*, for Thucydides, is an unstable signifier, which is valorized when used to express the character of the Athenians but which, applied for example to an orator, can just as easily derive from a negative judgment. But one only has to leave Thucydides in order to find abundant evidence of feminine *tolma*, some highly positive and some extremely negative, so that it becomes clear that the ambivalence runs through the entire corpus, not simply individual texts, and is thus split on the question of feminine boldness. If this quality has an eminently positive connotation in the edifying accounts of Plutarch and Pausanias, it seems that from Aristophanes to the tragedians *tolma* is used only in an overtly negative context to refer to women's misdeeds, even crimes.[72]

Leaving Thucydides now and abandoning all thoughts of commenting on his contradictions and calculating his intentions,[73] I will examine what a dualistic tradition has to say on the subject of women's *phusis*:[74] that it is related to fear as well as boldness, to silence as well as *thorubos*.[75] An example, taken this time from Xenophon, will offer an anchorage point among these conflicting images.

For example, after Leuctra: in 369 the Thebans invaded Laconia and ravaged the entire Spartan plain. While the Spartans keep watch, faithful to the adage that in a city without walls, men are the best ramparts, the women succumb to panic. Xenophon, to be sure, mentions it only in passing:

> In town, meanwhile, the women could not bear even the sight of smoke, for they had never seen an enemy army.[76]

Despite its brevity, the sentence says enough. If smoke (*kapnos*) is for Xenophon, as it is for Aristotle, the prototypical example of the sign, the

Spartan women are quick to take fright, since even before they fear the enemy in person, they panic at the smoke that is merely a sign of this presence.[77] Of course, as women living in a land that has never before suffered an invasion, they have some excuse. Nonetheless, this panic singularly contrasts with their reputation for fortitude in the edifying tradition of which Plutarch will be the herald.

Discussing the same episode, one of Xenophon's contemporaries reckons that this attitude, far from belying the reputation of the women of Sparta, is merely a normal reversal that serves to highlight it. I refer to Aristotle, reflecting in a famous passage from book 2 of the *Politics*, upon the fatal consequences of the "slackening" of the women of Sparta (and the gynecocracy that is its corollary). "What is the difference," asks Aristotle, "whether women govern or the governors are ruled by women? The result is the same." And he adds the following, which is of great interest, as it pertains to the question of feminine *andreia*:[78]

> While audacity (*thrasutēs*) has no use in everyday life and has a purpose, if indeed it does, only in times of war, even then the women have done the Laconians the greatest harm (*blaberōtatai*). They certainly did so during the Theban invasion: perfectly useless, as they are in other cities, they caused more trouble (*thorubon*) than did the enemy.[79]

An important passage, in which, as is often the case with Aristotle, the argument, though highly precise, needs to be carefully explicated. The key word, of course, is *thrasutēs*: audacity as considered to be the trait of Spartan women.[80] Audacity is absolutely useless, except perhaps in war—and even then,[81] the philosopher says in substance, in times of war women are useless everywhere; but in addition the Spartan women caused the men trouble, because of their *thrasutēs*. Here things become more complicated, for Aristotle leaves it to the reader to finish the argument and to ask, Did they cause the trouble because they were too daring? Or, on the contrary, as Xenophon has it, because of the emotional nature of their reaction? In this case it would be necessary to admit that their "boldness" has indeed turned into its opposite. To solve matters, let it first be recalled that in Aristotle's eyes *andreia* for a man normally betokens full authority (*arkhikē*), and for a woman, complete submission (*hupēretikē*).[82] Because the women of Spartan exercise *arkhē* in their daily life, boldness is their lot, which clearly means that they do not have the courage of ordinary women. Perhaps, in other words, they have no courage at all (to the extent that they cannot escape their feminine being, this determination of essence, this limitation).[83]

A passage from the *Nicomachean Ethics* devoted to "audacity" as it relates to courage fully confirms this analysis. The definition of *thrasutēs* certainly makes it "resemble" courage, but in the way that a parody resembles the original:

> Therefore boldest men are in reality only cowards playing the brave (*thrasudeiloi*): bold in circumstances where they can imitate the courageous, in frightening conditions they do not hold fast (*oukh hupomeinousin*).[84]

In fact, *thrasutēs* is a form of excess,[85] and it is the nature of excess to turn into its opposite. Thus, not only do Spartan women behave like those of other cities, but since their boldness dissolves into cowardice precisely when it would be necessary to "hold fast," they are more than useless: they are most harmful—and *blaberōtatai* blocks reasoning, which leads to the destructive slackening (*blabera anesis*) of the Lacedaemonian women.

Once again, women enter into men's history against a backdrop of *thorubos*, except that for Aristotle, they provoke it instead of bearing it. Overcoming their natural tendency and steadfastly confronting (*hupomenein*) the tumult, the women of Corcyra behaved with a daring that was close indeed to authentic *andreia*, as if their *phusis*, all moderation, had the potential for transcending itself when an emergency required it. Therefore they were an effective help to the *andres*. Inversely, the Spartan women were ineffective; always excessive and going to extremes, they cause the men additional worry. There where Xenophon saw only an easily explainable weakness, Aristote detects what, for a city, is the most frightening of threats: that its women are an internal enemy worse than any threat posed from outside.

Here this decidedly remarkable passage holds another surprise. For, when he speaks of the "bold" Lacedaemonian women at the time of the Theban invasion, Aristotle seems to borrow his remarks word for word from the imprecations against the race of women that Aeschylus assigned to Eteocles in *Seven against Thebes*.[86] For instance, in the city of Thebes under enemy siege, the women of the chorus cry out their panic. When, after vowing never to "cohabit" with this fatal race, either in happiness or sorrow, Oedipus's son adds:

> Does the woman have the upper hand? It is a rare boldness. Is she afraid?
> For her house and her city, it is a worse evil yet,

how can one fail to see the very words around which the argument of book 2 of the *Politics* is built? *Kratousa gunē*, or the "gynecocracy"; *thrasos*, with its double *thrasutēs*; and this *pleion kakon*, this "worse evil yet," which will become a "tumult" that is even worse (*pleiō thorubon*). Everything is there, even and above all *fear*, the missing word that one would have to know how to detect in Aristotle. But these echoes have yet to come to an end:

Those who stand before our walls thus have the best reinforcements, while
we are destroying ourselves inside,

Eteocles asserts. It may be recalled that Xenophon, after mentioning the
conduct of the Spartan women, evoked the firm attitude of the Lacedaemonian hoplites, standing fast like a human bastion to protect their
rampartless town. Without a doubt, for a city, the Spartan women are
even more frightening than the Theban women of tragedy. Therefore,
while Eteocles only said that they were "harmful," Aristotle employed
the superlative (*blabē*/*blaberōtatai*).

Such is the fate of the race of women, even when they are acclimatized
to living in the city. Pure and simple panic combines with boldness, and
in their excess the Lacedaemonian wives offer nothing new compared to
the very feminine women of Thebes.[87] It is as if excess and lack, these
equivalent evils, replace moderation when feminine *phusis* is characterized
by boldness.

To be sure, the comparison between Thucydides and Aristotle suggests
that one has a choice when one speaks of women. One can either make
the ideal into nature and liken this *phusis* to *sōphrosunē*, women's model
virtue, or one can define feminine nature in terms of excess, and everything becomes possible when women enter into the picture—particularly
the worst, of course. For one suspects that Aristotle, in choosing the
argument based on excess, was content to take the more traveled road, in
a long tradition that, in matters of historiographic prose, goes back to
Herodotus.

Last to be examined here—but chronologically, the first—then, are
the women of Herodotus, whose utterly excessive *phusis* leads to murder.
I cannot decide whether it is by accident or design that on two occasions
Herodotus depicts the women who carry out executions as Athenian.

The first episode functions like the *aition* of a change in the vestimen-
tary customs of the women of Athens. And, as is often the case, this
aition is under the sign of blood and death. The story of the sole Athenian survivor of a battle against the Argives and the Aeginetans is a sorry
one. A messenger with unhappy news, "back in Athens, there he announced the disaster":

> Upon hearing the news, the women whose husbands had left for Aegina,
> angry that he alone of all of them was saved, surrounded the unfortunate
> man from all sides and stabbed him with the clasps of their clothing, each
> one asking him where her husband was. He perished in this fashion (5.88).

Herodotus adds that "the Athenians considered the misdeed of their
women an even more terrible thing than their disaster." And since it was
impossible to find a punishment that fit the crime, they decided to make

them wear clothing without any clasps. The citizens of Argos and Aegina, on the contrary, by lengthening the clasps their women wore, "as a
hostile gesture to the Athenians (*kat'erin tēen Athēnaiōn*)," in fact reflect
the extent of the crime: for what the women of Athens accomplished is
nothing but the extinction, by most un-hoplitic means, of the last soldier
in the Athenian army—in a word, the enemy's dearest wish. But, we
have seen, the most frightening of enemies is sometimes found within
the city walls.[88]

And yet the Athenians did not even dare give a name to the "awful
crime," since they simply referred to it as "the women's *act*" (*to tōn gunaikōn ergon*). In so doing, they were rediscovering a traditional language,
in which *ergon* is used to refer to a "women's crime," especially when the
victim is a male: "the Lemnian crime" (the most famous), the murder of
Itys, the most lamentable[89]—but already, in the *Odyssey*, *ergon* referred to
women's criminal conduct: the *mega ergon* of Melantho, the leader of the
faithless serving women; Clytemnestra's *erga*, the horror of which dooms
the entire female species to shame and casts an unreal light on the
woman of good works (*euergos*).[90] To account for such an expression,
optimists will say that *ergon* is a euphemism; cooler heads will think that
in truth it is the adequate word, for in Greek tradition, on the virile scene
of the action, the only possible act for women matches their boldness and
is thus a crime. Perhaps then one will note that between the "act of
women," generally designated in the singular, as fits a generic action,[91]
and men's lofty deeds in war (*erga*), is the entire gap dividing feminine
nature, forever condemned to excessive boldness, from manly *andreia*,
rich in innumerable accomplishments. Such at least is Herodotus's view,
essentially conforming to the archaic and classical traditions of "feminine
nature," of women's participation in history.[92] Conversely, anyone wishing to object to the issue of *phusis* would have to attribute positive exploits, or *erga*, to women. This is what Plutarch will do much later, and
for him the slaying of the sole survivor of a battle can even pass for proof
of fortitude, on the condition that the scene takes place in Sparta, that
the murderess is a mother killing a survivor who was her son, and that
the action is carried out in the name of the fatherland.[93]

It is time to return to Herodotus, and Athens, where the second episode takes place. The day after the naval battle that saw the Greeks victorious, the Athenians wait for action in Salamis. Brought before the *boulē*,
an envoy from Mardonios delivers the Persian demands, which in essence
require Athens to desert the Greek cause. A councilor named Lykidas
"offers an opinion," in the purest tradition of deliberative action (*eipe
gnōmēn*). In other days this *gnōmē*, duly delivered to the *ekklēsia*, could
have become a decree. But the Athenians are at war with Media, and
Lykidas's statement runs counter to Athenian honor ("it seemed advan-

tageous to him"—*edokee*, another political term—"to welcome the demands and report them to the assembly of the people"). As one might guess, this formal legal procedure will never come to pass. Instead, the angry Athenians listen no further and cease their deliberations,[94] and their wrath abolishing the boundary between politics and what is beyond, the *bouleutai* join in with the other citizens to stone Lykidas, with no other trial. But the story is not over. Here a tumult (*thorubos*) spreads throughout Salamis. A "tumult"? It is time to prick up our ears: the women are not far away. And, in fact, with this *thorubos*, they enter the action:

> The wives of the Athenians learned of what happened; growing excited and egging each other on, they came of their own accord to Lykidas's dwelling and stoned his wife and children.[95]

End of story. Herodotus offers no explicit opinion about the matter, leaving it to the reader to react and interpret it—likewise, he makes no pronouncement on the subject of Lykidas's motives, whether they were the product of base self-interest or pure politics.[96] It is true that his language takes a rhetorical turn, with his use of tmesis and anaphora to describe the women's stoning of the woman and children (*kata men eleusan . . . tēn gunaika, kata de ta tekna*), which the reader probably ought to take as a sign that interpretation is required. As for the Athenians, Herodotus is mute as to whether they condemned their wives' action this time, and Athenian tradition, which justifies the stoning of the *bouleutēs* on the basis of patriotism, will be quick to interpret this silence as consent. In an oratorical flight, Demosthenes will even go so far as to make the women's involvement into a civic act on a par with that of the *andres*, an *exemplum* worthy of the heroes of Salamis.[97] But to carry out this operation, the orator needs to forget that in this instance the women attacked children and not merely another woman. Herodotus, who does not inject any personal comments into the account but is content to slip in an anaphora, was in fact more critical, and the odds are that if the first *kata* introduces the act, the second emphasizes its excess.[98] The notion of excess introduces the specter of feminine nature, which offers the only explanation capable of accounting for such an act.

Attempting in spite of all to make some sense of a story that contains no moral, I will hazard a few remarks. First of all, this "women's act" displays a kind of tension between what is naturally feminine and what mimics the world of men. The feminine group is characterized by a crumbling into individualities—therefore, to form a group, women need to egg each other on (*diakeleusamenē*)—but the involvement is collective and "freely" decided (*autokelees*), as is the case in the masculine universe.

As we have seen, stones are women's weapons, but there is a real gap between the simple throwing of a stone and the collective—not to say civic—practice of lapidation.[99] Only women can go so far as to kill what even the external enemy dares not slay in the city that he has just conquered: a woman and her children. The objection could be raised that since Lykidas was a traitor, the women's act took on a semblance of legitimacy. This would be forgetting that, in the perspective of collective punishment based on the family's "passive" solidarity, as Glotz understood it, the responsibility for extending the punishment to the traitor's kin would rest with the civic body alone.[100] The women took only their own counsel—and that of *thorubos*. One might then suggest that by virtue of the identification—a facile, tempting one—of Mardonios with a "tyrant," Lykidas's behavior was thought to be a collusion with tyranny. And the practice of totally destroying—*uprooting* was the term used at the time—the tyrant's family was widespread.[101] Still, once again, normally women do not act, *andres* do. And furthermore, the women's role in the stoning places this act under the sign of the uncontrollable.[102]

Nothing is to be gained by further argument. It must be recognized that no legal or political explanation can account for the Athenian women's murderous involvement in Herodotus's account. To be sure, their actions echoed those of the men, which were already characterized by immediate violence, but no one had ever consulted the women about the *bouleutēs*'s wife and children. The women listened only to their impulses, and the *autokelees*, in which they went "of their own accord" toward their victims' house, makes it possible to understand that they obeyed only their woman's nature, a thing to be feared once it is unleashed.[103]

This episode from Herodotus brings these pages to a close. It is a reminder that, in Greece, even for historians, there is no collective feminine involvement that does not raise the question—even implicitly—of the much-debated feminine *phusis*. Feminine nature is generally marked by excess/lack[104] and is sometimes contained to the extent dictated by the norm, but every *ergon gunaikōn* unfailingly refers to it. Where the deeds of women are concerned, the feminine seems to be a stronger explanatory principle than the category of action. For all that, it must be added that in the works of the historians of the classical period, women's actions very seldom derive from the discursive nature of the *logos*. When he mentions women, Thucydides outdoes himself to be concise, and given his irrepressible narrative desire, Herodotus's strategy amounts to the same thing. While he is able to recount the murderous episodes of madness of the women of Athens, the Father of History falls silent when it is

time to interpret them, caring little to dignify such episodes with organized commentary—unless he makes the "women's act" into something
like an *aition* designed to explain something other than itself.

Opaque, fleeting, and spotty: such are the acts of women in the historians' accounts, where they appear as self-contained entities within the
overall interpretative grid of the narrative. And the reader wonders what
to do with these aborted narratives, these episodes frozen in time. Confronted with this question, the community of modern historians of
Greece might easily be divided into two clans: the partisans of "reality,"
persuaded that resistance to narrative elaboration is itself sufficient proof
of the historicity of an episode; and those who love narrative for narrative's sake, who would ordinarily treat these episodes as moments of fiction. For my part, I haven't judged it a good idea to take either side
(when the alternatives are each subject to doubt, it is urgent to refuse to
choose). Convinced that in history it is vain to hope to eliminate any
preoccupation with the real, I have chosen, in the epigraph introducing
this section, to break off the quotation from Jane Austen at the very
moment where the speaker was about to assert that "the chief of all this
must be invention."[105] Therefore, it does not seem at all pointless to me
to note that their self-contained status as well as the rarity of these fleeting and opaque narratives reinforce the feeling of anomaly that accompanies women's involvement in the life of the city. But at the same time,
I have made an effort not to forget that the economy of the historical
discourse is subject to the most austere ideal of moderation. In this perspective, it matters that women can be introduced into the account only
when certain conditions—those of Greek political thought—have been
fulfilled. But once feminine nature is allowed to enter the picture, only
the constraints of the historical genre can protect the narrative against
the growing proliferation of representations of a femininity that seems
capable of anything once it is incarnated in actual women. These brief
incursions clearly offer an occasion for the historian, who assigns a *phusis*
to women and women to their *phusis*, to shore up civic identity. In this
manner, the role of historiography in the division of labor that takes
place among literary genres is to reassure the *andres*. But who does not
see that once the normative discourse has played its part, the field is clear
elsewhere, in other genres, for comfortable fantasies about the good femininity that is there for the taking?[106]

NOTES

INTRODUCTION

1. This exclusion, we know, is more radical in Athens than in Sparta. Geneviève Fraisse shows that at other times it is "a structural element of democracy" (1989, 199; see also 14, on the subject of Sylvain Maréchal, the editor of the Babouvist *Manifeste des égaux*). On "the fear of blending the sexes" (ibid., 197).

2. Aristophanes *Clouds* 659–66: it will be noted, moreover, that the rooster only appears on this list because Strepsiades, who is supposed to give examples of quadrupeds, has made an error. The rooster is a biped, which makes it even closer to man. *Alektruaina* is a comic invention, just like *hē alektruōn*, several examples of which are found among the comic poets, or *alektoris*. These terms always serve a comic aim, and thus it makes little sense to write that *alektruōn* is "also used in the feminine in the sense of 'hen'" (Chantraine 1968, s.v. *alexō*). *Alektōr*, the "defender," the "combative," was used "like a kind of nickname to refer to the rooster" (ibid.).

3. See below, chap. 11, p. 203.

4. Brisson 1986, 32 (apropos of *sexus*, derived from the root **sec*, hence *seco*, "to cut, separate, divide"); the need to establish "a healthy distance" between the sexes, 33–35.

5. Foucault 1984, 237.

6. Héritier-Augé 1984–85, 13. On man's "heat," see below, p. 92.

7. See Lloyd 1983, 58–111, and, for Apollo's declaration, Loraux 1981b, 129, 144.

8. "Practices of the Self": Foucault 1984 (18, see also 64: "a question of moderation and control . . . and not interdiction or permission"). Misogyny: whoever wishes to find it goes straight to Aristotle to stress his "prejudices" on the matter (Saïd 1982, 96); see also G. Sissa, in S. Campese, P. Manuli, G. Sissa, *Madre materia. Sociologia e biologia della donna greca* (Turin: Boringhieri, 1983), 83–145, and the highly nuanced article by S. Georgoudi, "Le Masculin, le féminin, le neutre," *Arethusa* (1990).

9. Last, Foucault 1984, 167–83. With Saïd (1982, 99), one will recall that Xenophon, in his *Oikonomikos*, "defined woman solely in negative terms."

10. Vernant 1989, 217.

11. Bouvier 1987, 18–19, 20ff. (developing a suggestion made in Segal 1971).

12. F. Vian, *Les Origines de Thèbes* (Paris: Klincksieck, 1963), 163. Herakles' gowns: see below, chap. 7; his tender skin, see below, chap. 5, 97–99.

13. Fear and trembling: see below, chap. 4; in Aristotle's biological treatises, fear must always be on the female side (Saïd 1982, 96). Tears: Monsacré 1984. Insults: Slatkin 1988.

14. 1) Hippocrates *On Airs, Waters, Places*, and the comments of A. Ballabriga,

"Les Eunuques scythes et leurs femmes. Stérilité des femmes et impuissance des hommes en Scythie selon le traité hippocratique *Des airs*," *Métis* 1, 1 (1986): 121–38; 2) Hippocrates *Regimen* 27–29; 3) Plato, *Laws* 8.836b1.

15. See in general Brisson 1986, 58 ("possession"); Olender 1985, 45 ("pluralism"); Chirassi Colombo 1984, 111.

16. Olender 1985, 51–55; all the quotations are taken from the study on Baubō, the conclusions of which I accept.

17. "Expanding the Concept of Sexuality": Freud's preface to the fourth edition (1920) of *Three Contributions to the Theory of Sex*, in *The Standard Edition of the Complete Psychological Works of Sigmund Freud*, ed. James Strachey, vol. 18 (London: Hogarth Press, 1964), where Freud proposes that "the expanded sexuality of psychoanalysis approaches the Eros of the divine Plato." Bisexuality: "Some Psychical Consequences of the Anatomical Distinction between the Sexes" (1925), in *The Complete Works of Sigmund Freud*, 19: 248–58.

18. On the "danger of simplification" that resides in the strict application of a logic based on polarity, concerning another series of oppositions (youth/adult, savagery/culture): Georgoudi 1986.

19. Zeitlin 1985b, 65.

20. Ibid.

21. Ibid., 80: similar hypotheses in Loraux 1985, 98–102.

22. "Village et forêt dans l'idéologie de l'Inde brahmanique," in Malamoud 1989, 99, 101 (my emphasis).

23. "La Brique percée. Sur le jeu du vide et du plein dans l'Inde brahmanique," in Malamoud 1989, 91.

24. Zeitlin 1985b, 70–71; Fraisse 1989, 82 (quotations). On man-gender, woman-sex, see Loraux 1981b, 80–81.

25. But, in matters of the difference between the sexes and the feminine, it is necessary, at least in the West, to consider a very long period.

26. Detienne 1972. Moreover, observes Chirassi Colombo (1984, 111), Aphrodite reassures men by showing them "the certainty" that when one has the good fortune of being a man "the dimension of *eros* is purely masculine."

27. Experience: *peirasthai*, *expertus esse*; sex: *sexus*; character: *tropos*; nature: *phusis*, *natura*; pleasure: *Venus*; form: *morphē*.

28. Plegon of Thralles (= A1), in Brisson's French translation (1976), upon which I am relying for its precious documentation, on the experience of Tiresias. See also A2 (Hyginus), A3 (Lactantius), A4, A6 (Ovid), A8 (Eusthathius), A11 and 13.

29. For example, Chirassi Colombo 1984, 110 (citing Foucault); Foucault 1984 (98–99) thinks that this opinion is, for a Greek, more fundamental than notions about masculine and feminine. I admit that I am not convinced.

30. See below, chap. 12.

31. Brisson 1976, as well as 1986, 57–59.

32. See below, chaps. 1–2.

33. Thomas 1986, 213.

34. Pouchelle 1986, 319–20.

35. Pausanias 8.26.6. On the root of *lokhos* and *lekho*, see below, chap. 1, pp. 25–27.

36. M. Detienne, "Zeus. L'Autre. Un problème de maïeutique," in Bonnefoy 1981, 2:554; Brisson 1986, 49–50.

37. In the Hippocratic treatise *On Art* (10.1 and 3.12.1), *nēdus* has the very general sense of "the internal cavity of the body." But the equivalence between belly and womb is common.

38. Foucault 1984, 237.

39. Sissa 1987, 181–85.

40. "Lumières indiennes sur la séduction," in Malamoud 1989, 177.

41. M. Detienne, in G. Sissa and M. Detienne, *La Vie quotidienne des dieux grecs* (Paris: Hachette, 1989), 236.

42. From this standpoint, the book by R. Zapperi, *L'Homme enceint* (Paris: Presses Universitaires de France, 1983), seems very reductive.

43. DuBois 1988, 169–71; Burnyeat 1977, 8 (on *Symposium* 206e), 13.

44. See *Phaedrus* 251d–e.

45. DuBois 1988, 183.

46. See below, chaps. 8–9.

47. As DuBois does (1988, 178).

48. Pouchelle 1986, 316, 319–21.

49. Chirassi Colombo 1984, 115.

50. *Republic* 6.490b (*lēgein ōdinos*).

51. *Republic* 3.395d–e (*ōdinousan*).

52. *Republic* 5.462b (the same theme as the *Eumenides* 984–86). The community of women: 446–61. It will be noted that, since the only natural difference is that man begets while woman gives birth (445e), men and women share the same labors. Plato is more complicated than his opponents generally wish to believe!

53. See "Repolitiser la cité," in *Revue L'Homme. Anthropologie: Etat des lieux* (Paris: Navarin/Le Livre de Poche, 1986), 263–83, and Loraux 1987.

54. P. Vidal-Naquet, "Esclavage et gynécocratie dans la tradition, le mythe, l'épopée," in Vidal-Naquet 1981, 267–88.

55. See below, Conclusion.

56. Foucault 1984, 9, 43–44.

57. On this expression, see Pouchelle 1986, 319.

58. On this subject, see the comments made by Marie Moscovici in *Il est arrivé quelque chose. Approches de l'événement psychique* (Paris: Ramsay, 1989), 139.

59. Lou Andréas-Salomé, *L'Amour du narcissisme* (Paris: Gallimard, 1980), 193.

60. Here I have recently come across the discussion of Maurice Olender, in an article that came to my attention only after this preface had been written, concerning the myth of Tiresias and the fact that a woman "melts into a virile cosmogony in which she assumes a position, *in, for,* and *against* the masculine imagination" ("De l'absence du récit," in *Le récit et sa représentation* [Paris: Payot, 1978], 178).

61. The reason is not that the question should not be raised when it is formulated in Greek: see Loraux 1986a. We know from elsewhere that Athena herself was officially "Mother" in Elis. But what are we to conclude from this item of local information?

CHAPTER ONE
BED AND WAR

1. Compare *IG* (*Inscriptiones Graecae*) 5.1.713–14 and 699–712 (numbers 701 and 714 have been quoted here) with Plutarch *Life of Lycurgus* 27.2–3. The corruption in Plutarch's text certainly occurs in an awkward place, but the existence of the inscriptions is enough to support Latte's correction, which R. Flacelière accepts in his edition (Belles Lettres). See R. Flacelière, "Les Funérailles spartiates," *Revue des Etudes grecques* 61 (1948): 403–5.

2. See below, chap. 3. It will be observed that in his *Moralia* (238d) Plutarch reserves the honor of inscriptions only for the tombs of those who have died in battle.

3. For all that, it will be noted that, because they involve the city's fate, the deliveries of the wives of Spartan kings are subjects of narratives: see Herodotus 5.39–41 (the birth of Cleomenes and Dorieus) and 6.63 (the birth of Demaratus), as well as Plutarch *Life of Lycurgus* 3.1–6 and *Life of Agis* 3.7.

4. In Sparta marriage exhibits "negative" traits for men, because it threatens their exclusive relationship to the city and to their companions; for women, on the contrary, it is an initiation into the status of wife and mother of Spartans (A. Paradiso, "Osservazioni sulla cerimonia nuziale spartana," *Quaderni di Storia* 24 (1986): 137–53, 143–44n.

5. Xenophon *Constitution of the Lacedaemonians* 1.3–4 (where the procreation of children is the first point in the exposition); Critias, DK fr. 32; Plutarch *Lycurgus* 14.3. See Napolitano 1985.

6. The words Plutarch uses are significant: *hupomenousai kalōs* evokes the *menein* or the *hupomenein* of the hoplitic imperative (for example, Herodotus 7.104 and 209), and *agōnizesthai pros tas ōdinas* refers to the battle that is childbirth.

7. *Laws* 7.788d–789e. For Plato, exercise does not only prepare women for childbirth but equally for war, for the philosopher wishes to avoid making each city into only half a city (that of men) and instead gives it the value of two: see 804e–805b, 806a (critique of the intermediary regimen of the Spartan women), 813e–814a.

8. Plutarch *Lycurgus* 14.8; cf. *Sayings of Spartans* 227e. On the political dimension of the mother in Sparta, for whom Gorgo is the emblematic figure, see Napolitano 1985, 37–39.

9. On Athenian radicalism on the subject of the beautiful death, see Loraux 1981a, as well as "Mourir devant Troie, tomber pour Athènes. De la gloire du héros à l'idée de la cité," *Information sur les Sciences sociales* 17, 6 (1978): 801–17.

10. See for example D. Kurtz and J. Boardman, *Greek Burial Customs* (London, 1972), 139, as well as P. Devambez, "Le Motif de Phèdre sur une stèle thasienne," *Bulletin de Correspondance hellénique* 79 (1955): 121–34 (130).

11. See H. Riemann, *Kerameikos II. Die Skulpturen* (Berlin, 1940), 24–28; B. Schmaltz, *Untersuchungen zu den attischen Marmorlekythen* (Berlin, 1970), 106–7; and H. Möbius, *Athenische Mitteilungen* 81 (1966), 155. On the exception of depicting a child in its mother's arms, see H. Riemann, *Kerameikos II*, 1–2, and G.M.A. Richter, *Catalogue of Greek Sculptures in the Metropolitan Museum of Art*

(Oxford, 1954), 51–52. See finally U. Vedder, "Frauentod-Kriegestod im Spiegel der attischen Grabkunst," *MDAI* 103 (1988): 161–91.

12. W. Peek, *Griechische Vers-Inschriften*, 1 (Berlin, 1955), no. 548 (=*IG* 2/3^2 [1907]).

13. On the epitaphs in the official cemetery, see Loraux 1975.

14. There are two possibilities that explain the use of Doric: 1) Kratista, with an unlikely name for an Athenian (only one woman named Kratisto in Athens: no. 8773 in J. Kirchner, *Prosopographia attica* [1901–1903]), is a Dorian woman residing in Athens, and the name Damainetos, which could be Spartan, does not weaken this hypothesis; 2) Kratista is Kratiste, the daughter of Demainetos, the wife of Arkhemakhos, both of them Athenians; nothing precludes this hypothesis, for Athenian prosopography of the fourth century is familiar with the names Demainetos and Arkhemakhos (see nos. 3265–67, 3273, 3276, and 2350–52, in Kirchner, as well as nos. 3273 and 3276 in J. K. Davies, *Athenian Propertied Families* [Oxford, 1971]); in this case, must the use of the Doric language be interpreted as bestowing the title of honorary Dorian on the dead woman?

15. J.-P. Vernant, "La Guerre des cités," in Vernant 1974, 38.

16. On the reprobation that weighed on the single male (*agamos*) in Sparta, see Plutarch *Lycurgus* 14–15. It will be observed that the bachelor is called a "trembler" (*tresas*); see below, chap. 3. On the boy and marriage, see P. Schmitt-Pantel, "Histoire de tyran ou comment la cité grecque construit ses marges," in B. Vincent, ed., *Les Marginaux et les exclus dans l'histoire* (Paris, 1979), 217–30, esp. 226–27.

17. See Plato *Laws* 6.779a–e, and among the poets, *Palatine Anthology* 6.276, and Euripides *Iphigenia in Tauris* 204 (Iphigenia unhappy "from the time of her mother's girdle and that night").

18. On the opposition between *numphē* and *gunē*, see Detienne 1972, 157–58, as well as J.-P. Vernant, "Entre bêtes et dieux" (Vernant 1974, 147–48). On continence and reproduction, see Kahn 1978, 100–101. *Alokhos*, the legitimate wife, is contrasted with *akoitis*, the word for the wife as lover (see Chantraine 1946–47, 223–25). Is it by chance that Plato describes Artemis, the chaste goddess superintending childbirth, as *alokhos*, playing on the two values of the prefix *a-* (*sm: "together"; *a-* privative)? Cf. *Theaetetus* 149b.

19. On the bed, *lekhos*, as the symbol for the legitimacy of marriage, see "Le Mariage," in Vernant 1974, 81.

20. In Alipheira, in Arcadia, an altar to Zeus Lekheates indicated, according to Pausanias (8.26.6), the spot where Zeus gave birth to Athena.

21. *Lokhos enedra apo tou lekhous* (ambush, after bed).

22. M. P. Bologna, "In margine all interpretazione di om. *lokhos*," *Studi e Saggi linguistici* 13 (1973): 207–14, who even sees the original meaning of the term in the words "group of armed men."

23. Chantraine 1968, s.v. *lekhetai*.

24. Quotations from C. de Lamberterie, "*Lakheia, lakhainō, lokhos*," *Revue de philologie* 49 (1975): 232–40.

25. See Y. Verdier 1979, 51, 57.

26. Hesiod *Theogony* 158. In his commentary on the *Theogony*, M. L. West

(Oxford, 1971, *ad loc.*) recognizes that the expression can mean that the Titans were shut up in Gaia's womb. If, in spite of all, West doubts the double meaning of *lokhos* in the text, the dual meaning is accepted *in extremis* by R. Arena, "*Ek lokheoio* (Hes. *Th.* 178)," *Mélanges G. Bonfante*, 1 (Brescia, 1976), esp. 38.

27. Laurence Kahn developed this analysis on the subject of *Theogony* 174 and 178 (Kahn 1986, 219).

28. Ibid., 221.

29. *Iliad* 13.277–78 and 285; see below, chap. 4.

30. *Iliad* 6.57–59 (where the child is called *kouros*); Aeschylus, *The Suppliants* 636–702.

31. Euripides *Suppliants* 954, and 963–64 (where sons, future warriors, are termed *kouroi*); see as well 54. On these passages, see Calame 1977, 292–93.

32. Loraux 1981b, 75–117.

33. For example: Aristophanes *Ecclesiazousae* 233–34, 549, *Thesmophoriazousae* 514ff., *Lysistrata* 589–90 and 748; Euripides *Andromache* 24–25 (Andromache is a Greek woman because of her name and her integration into Neoptolemos's *oikos*), *Electra* 652.

34. *Thesmophoriazousae* 830–39. It will be observed that the mother of the good citizen gave birth to a taxiarch or a *stratēgos*, while the mother of a coward brought a trierarch or a pilot into the world, i.e., sailors. Devalorization of the sea is never far away.

35. *Erechtheus*, fr. 5 Austin (quoted by Lycurgus *Contra Leocrates* 100), 22–27.

36. To suffer war "more than doubly" is 1) to give birth; 2) to send one's hoplite sons to war (*Lysistrata* 589–90).

37. On *eranos*, a voluntary tax within an aristocratic system of reciprocity, see Gernet 1968, 185 and 192–99, as well as J. Vondeling, *Eranos* (Utrecht, 1961), and O. Longo, "Eranos," *Mélanges E. Delebecque* (Aix: Université de Provence, 1983), 247–58.

38. The comparison between *Lysistrata* 651–55 and Thucydides 2.43.1–2 (Pericles' *epitaphios*) was made by J. Vondeling (*Eranos*, chap. 7) and more recently, O. Longo has addressed the matter in an article, "La Morte per la patria," in *Studi italiani di Filologia classica* 49 (1977): 5–36, which stresses the beautiful death as an exchange: the citizen's life for glory.

39. Euripides *Medea* 248–51. Medea, the murderous mother striking her husband through her sons: see N. Daladier, "Les Mères aveugles," 229–44, esp. 240.

40. See below, chap. 2, p. 52.

41. Some examples: Euripides *Suppliants* 920, 1135–36; Plutarch *Theseus* 20.5 (*sumponein*); Hippocratic corpus: *On the Nature of the Child* 30, 11, *On the Diseases of Women* (Littré ed.) 1.1, 36, 42, 46, 72.

42. *Regimen* 34.1: the opposition between the males' *epiponōterē diaitē* and the females' *rhaithumoterē diaitē*; see again Hippocrates *On Glands* 573 (Littré). It will be noted that in the treatise *Regimen*, *ponoi* refers to exercises, strengthening, as opposed to *rhaithumiē* (2.2–3; 32.3–6, etc.).

43. For the general meaning, see *Diseases* 4, passim (e.g., 35.4; 36.2; 37.1) and, for childbirth, *On Generation* 18.2 (the primipara: cf. *Nature of the Child* 30.2), as well as *Nature of the Child* 30.11.

44. *On the Fetus at Eight Months* 4.3; for *ponos* as gynecological suffering in this treatise: 3.1; 4.2; 10.3 (labor).

45. Plutarch *Lycurgus* 16.10; Critias, DK, fr. 6.25–27.

46. The *ponos* of the Achaians: for example, *Iliad* 5.567, 12.348 and 356, 13.239 and 344, 14.429, 15.416, 16.568 and 726, 17.41, 82, 158, 401, 718. Cf. Pindar *Isthmians* 6.54. The *ponos* of the Hesiodic peasant, the lot of mortals: *Works and Days* 92 and 113.

47. The labors of Herakles as *ponoi*: e.g., Euripides *Herakles* 22, 357, 388, 427, etc.; Sophocles *Trachiniae* 70, 170, 825, *Philoctetes* 1419. As *athloi*: *Iliad* 8.362–63, 19.133; *Odyssey* 11.618–26; *Homeric Hymn to Herakles* 5; *Theogony* 951, Pindar *Isthmians* 6.49; a few occurrences in Sophocles *Trachiniae* 36 and 80, *Philoctetes* 508–9, and in Euripides *Herakles* 823; for Diodorus and Apollodorus, it is the word used to designate the twelve Labors. On the *ponoi* of Athens in the funeral oration, see Thucydides 2.38.1.

48. I owe this expression to Jean-Pierre Vernant (personal communication).

49. An interesting example is Euripides' mention (*Iphigenia in Tauris* 1464–66) on the dedication to Iphigenia of finely woven fabrics and cloaks left behind by women whose lives ended in childbirth. Fabrics and especially cloaks are symbols of marriage, and it is marriage that death in childbirth exalts in Brauron.

50. On the double connotation, both masculine and feminine, of the girdle, see Schmitt 1977, as well as Detienne 1979, 85.

51. The loosened girdle of women in labor (cf. Pindar *Olympics* 6.39, and Callimachus *Hymn to Delos* 209 and 222; depictions in graphic arts, see P. Devambez, "Le Motif de Phèdre," 124–25) is evidence that the Eileithuias untied it (e.g., Euripides, fr. 696 Nauck², 4–8); Kahn 1978, 103–4.

52. To carry beneath one's girdle: Aeschylus *Choephoroi* 992, *Eumenides* 607, as well as the *Homeric Hymn to Aphrodite* 255 and 282, and Euripides *Hecuba* 762. An inscription from the Asklepeion of Miletus mentions a sacrifice that is to be carried out by women who have given birth and risen from childbed: Th. Wiegand, ed. *Milet. Ergebnisse der Ausgrabungen und Untersuchungen seit dem Jahre 1899* (Berlin, 1899), 1:7, no. 204b9.

53. Schmitt 1977, 1063.

54. Euripides, *Suppliants* 918–20.

55. On the liver as a vital organ, see J.-P. Vernant, "A la table des hommes," in Detienne and Vernant 1979, 87–91, as well as J. Dumortier, *Le Vocabulaire médical d'Eschyle et les écrits hippocratiques*, 2d ed. (Paris, 1975), 18–20. On the liver in female diseases, Hippocrates *Diseases of Women* 1.7, 32, and esp. 43; mortal wounds to the liver: Hippocrates *Epidemics* 5.62 and 7.31; *Aphorisms* 6.18, and *Notions of Cos* 499.

56. Men wounded in the liver: *Iliad* 13.412, and 17.350; Euripides *Phoenician Women* 1422. Men's suicides: Euripides *Herakles* 1149, *Orestes* 1063–64, *Helen* 983; women's suicides: see Loraux 1985, 88–91.

57. Artemis fights on Ares' side during the Trojan war in books 20 and 21 of the *Iliad*; she joins forces with him against the children of Bellerophon (6.200ff.). It will be recalled that Ares, as son of Zeus and Hera, is the brother of Eileithuia and Hebe (Hesiod, *Theogony* 921–23).

58. Angeliki Rovatsou's work in progress on the mythology of childbirth in ancient Greece ought to contribute a great deal concerning the ways in which the Eileithuias intervened.

59. Artemis *Lokhia*: Euripides *Suppliants* 958; *Iphigenia in Tauris* 1097, as well as in a law from Gambreion (*Sylloga*[3] 1219); Artemis Eileithuia: in Boeotia (in Orchomenus: *Athenische Mitteilungen* 7 [1882]: 357), to give only a few examples of these two names.

60. On the unclean nature of pregnant women and women in childbirth, see remarks by L. Moulinier, *Le Pur et l'impur dans la pensée et la sensibilité des Grecs jusqu'à la fin du IVe siècle av. J.-C.* (Paris, 1952), 66–71.

61. Artemis *Sōteira*: Pausanias 2.31.1 (Corinth). *Hagnē*: see, with regard to *hagnos*, on the divine and uncleanness, J.-P. Vernant, "Le Pur et l'impur" (Vernant 1974, 138–39).

62. Callimachus *Hymn to Artemis* 20–22 and 126–27; *Soōdine*; *IG* 7.3407 (Chaeronea).

63. See *Iliad* 6.205; 24.606–9; *Odyssey* 11.324; 15.478; Alcaeus fr. 390 Campbell (regarding Artemis's arrows: "it is you who sheds the blood, *phonos*, of women"). As is the case with the warriors in the *Iliad, phonos* expresses both the idea of murder and blood.

64. A sweet death: *Odyssey* 11.172; 15.410; 17.202; [Callimachus] 60–81— the fear of Artemis's arrows: *Palatine Anthology* 6.271 and 273.

65. *Iliad* 21.483.

66. Stella Georgoudi drew my attention to this point. On the gender of animal names, see her "Le Mâle, la femelle, le neutre. Varations grecques sur le jeu des sexes et ses limites dans la monde animal," *Arethusa* (1990).

67. The lioness as mother: Euripides *Medea* 187–88; the lion and war: see A. Schnapp-Gourbeillon, *Lions, héros, masques* (Paris: Maspero, 1981).

68. The bow, considered a lowly weapon: see P. Vidal-Naquet, "Le Cru, l'enfant grec et le cuit" (in Vidal-Naquet 1981, 193).

69. And in fact, such indeed is war for Artemis, according to Pierre Ellinger: see Ellinger 1978 and now *La Légende nationale phocidienne: Artémis, les situations extrêmes et les récits de guerre d'anéantissement* (Athens: Ecole Française d'Athènes. Boccard, 1993).

70. *Iliad* 17.4–6.

71. Hippocrates *On the Nature of the Child* 18.2.

72. *Iliad* 8.266–72. The comparison of the shield to a belly is only implicit in the text. Homer is not Aristophanes (cf. J. Taillardat, *Les Images d'Aristophane. Etudes de langue et de style*, 2d. ed. [Paris, 1965], 69); but the vocabulary used (*dusken* and above all *kruptaske*, which evokes the use of the word *kruptein* regarding a pregnancy; likewise, during Kronos's "ambush" Gaia "hides" her son [*apokruptaske*]: *Theogony* 157) leaves no uncertainty as to the meaning of the text. It also happens that goddesses behave "like mothers" alongside the heroes in battle. For example, the virgin Athena and Menelaus (*Iliad* 4.130–32) and Odysseus (23.783) and, more normally, since she is really his mother, Aphrodite and Aeneas (5.311–17).

73. Vernant 1982.

74. There would be cause, for example, to compare the image of the knot in a

brutal fight (*Iliad* 13.358–60; 14.389; 17.40) with the sometimes evil bonds of the Eileithuia. The brutal fight is without an outcome when the gods tighten the knot and break men's knees. Need it be recalled that a woman gives birth on her knees (Pausanias 8.48.7–8; *Homeric Hymn to Apollo* 117; the depiction of Eileithuia on her knees: *Enciclopedia dell'arte antica*, s.v. Ilizia; the relationship of the knees to generation: Onians 1951, 174–82), and that the bonds of Eileithuia block childbirth? On the other hand, for a male child (Herakles, in this case), being born amounts to "falling at a woman's feet" (19.110)—an ominous prefiguration of the death of the warrior, who falls at the feet of his opponent?

75. *Mogostokoi*: *Iliad* 11.270; 16.187, and scholia. This word can be compared to *mokhthos*: Euripides *Herakles* 280–81, *Medea* 1261 (the sufferings of motherhood for Megara and Medea). *Mogostokoi*, the Eileithuias (or the Eileithuia) are *polustonoi*, "bringers of groans" (see G. Kaibel, *Epigrammata Graeca* [Berlin, 1878], 241a) but also bear the title of *praumētis*: "kindly deceit" (Pindar *Olympics* 6.43). They are generally presented in this last aspect; see Pindar *Pythians* 2.7–12, for the pairing of Eileithuia the protectress of mothers with Artemis the killer of women.

76. On cries (cf. Plutarch *Theseus* 20.7) see Sophocles *Oedipus Rex* 173 (*iēion kamaton*): *iēios*, which is invoked with the cry of *iē paiōn*, is a term for Apollo and is used as a qualifier for what these cries of pain accompany (cf. J. Carlier, "Apollo" [Bonnefoy 1981, 1:50–55]).

77. Pausanias 7.23.6 (statue of the Eileithuia Purphoros in Aigion).

78. The pains of Leto (Callimachus *Hymn to Delos* 60, 124, 202), because they are pure *amēkhaniē* (ibid., 210–11), are inexpressible in the *Homeric Hymn to Apollo* (91–92).

79. On *ōdis* referring to the child in relation to the mother in Aeschylus while *tokos* refers to him in relation to his father, see J. Dumortier, *Le Vocabulaire médical*, 27–28. Moreover, in the examples cited by Dumortier, *ōdis*, with a doubling of the feminine, describes the girl, while *tokos* applies to the boy.

80. See *Iliad* 11.260ff. and Hippocrates *Diseases of Women* 1.35, 38, 43, 56, 59, 65; 2.113, 139, 144, 172 (delivery, or gynecology).

81. Black pains (*Iliad* 4.19; 15.394); black and shadows are associated with the feminine (for example, Aeschylus *Eumenides* 665); see Ramnoux 1959. *Odunē* and penetration: see the etymology in *Cratylus* 419c (*odunē* as derived from *dunō*, "to penetrate" [Mawet 1979, 43n. 22]).

82. Pain in the liver, in the back: Hippocrates *Diseases* 4.36.2 and 54.6; pain in the belly: Hippocrates *Epidemics* 5.232, 368; *Diseases* 4.54.6; pain in the intestines: Aristophanes *Thesmophoriazousae*, 484; Hippocrates *Regimen* 3.82.1; pain in the kidneys, Aeschylus fr. 361 Nauck². One will add to this list Xenophon *Hellenika* 5.4.58 (pain of an internal hemorrhage).

83. See, for example, *On the Fetus at Eight Months* 3.2, and the innumerable occurrences of the word *odunē* in the treatise *On the Nature of Woman*.

84. A close semantic—and perhaps etymological—relationship (Mawet 1979, 37).

85. *Ponos*: Aeschylus *Agamemnon* 54; Euripides *Phoenician Women* 30. *Ōdis*: Pindar *Olympics* 6.31; Aeschylus *Agamemnon* 1417–18; Euripides *Ion* 45, *Iphigenia in Tauris* 1102.

86. Furthermore, the distance between midwives and women is maintained by the status, which by definition is asexual, of the *maia* (cf. Plato *Thaetetus* 149b–

c). See the comments of N. Daladier, "Les Mères aveugles," 242–44, to which can be added those of Olender 1985, 41–51 (on nurses).

87. On that notion, see Lloyd 1983, 58–111, as well as Manuli 1983, 154–62.

88. On this point the practical wisdom of Phaedra's nurse (who is termed *maia* in lines 243 and 311) matches the thoughts of the author of *Diseases of Women*. See Euripides *Hippolytus* 293–96, and Hippocrates *Diseases of Women* 1.62. The difficulty with women is that they also share all the diseases common to the whole human species (*toisi sumpasin anthrōpoisin*). See Hippocrates *Diseases of Women* and *On the Fetus at Eight Months* 9.1.

89. We refer the reader to a remarkable passage from *On the Fetus at Eight Months* (4.1), where the author speaks of the "victorious proofs" that women give when their bodies and deliveries are involved. Such a statement contrasts with the idea, also a Hippocratic one, that women, out of modesty, know nothing of their bodies. Cf. *Diseases of Women* 1.62 (regarding this text, which she considers to be Hippocratic orthodoxy in matters of gynecology, see the comments of P. Manuli, "Fisiologia e patologia del femminile negli scritti ippocratici dell'antica ginecologia greca," in *Hippocratica. Actes du Colloque hippocratique de Paris* [Paris, 1980], 393–408, esp. 397).

90. A distinction made by the physician, concerned with the diseases of the body, and the legislator, who keeps a watch over the soul's savage tendencies: Demosthenes *Contra Aristogeiton* 2.26.

91. Here Hippocrates *On the Nature of the Child* 13.2 is compared to Aristophanes *Lysistrata* 82. In both cases one must jump so that one's heels reach one's buttocks. See the note by R. Joly (Hippocrates, vol. 12, of the Belles Lettres edition), which points out the comparison without stressing the inversion. On the jump called *bibasis* in Sparta, see Napolitano 1985, 21–22; as an abortive method, see again *Diseases of Women* 1.25.

92. *Nosos*: Euripides *Electra* 656; *anagkē*: Euripides *Bacchae* 88–89; *amēkhania*: *Hippolytus* 163. On *amēkhania* and femininity, see L. Kahn, "Ulysse ou la ruse et la mort," *Critique* 393 (February 1980): 116–34.

93. *Hippolytus* 142; in 143–44 the verb *phoitaō* is found, whose semantic field regards the wanderings of Pan (Borgeaud 1979, 156n.68) as well as sickness. Elsewhere Hesychius gives *phoitos* as a synonym for *mania*.

94. *Hippolytus* 131 and esp. 161–69 (a passage that I have attempted to translate exactly, to match the bitterness of the text). It will be noted that 1) *sunoikein* is the verb for marriage: Hippolytus does not wish to cohabit with any woman (616–50); women, on their part, cohabit with pain; 2) *aura*, the wind in the womb, brings to mind the Hippocratic theory of the breath and its role in generation: see *On the Nature of the Child* 12 and 16–17, and esp. *On the Nature of Woman* 64 (with, concerning *nēdus*, the comments of H. Trapp, *Die hippokratische Schrift De Natura Muliebri. Ausgabe und textkritischer Kommentar* [Hamburg, 1967], 181). More generally, on the "storm" in the female body, see Verdier 1979, 41–46, 73. The theory of "birth winds" in Vedic India is something completely different (Malamoud 1989, 87).

95. See Zeitlin 1985a, 68–74, 77–78.

96. *Choephoroi* 211.

97. Ibid., 204. Orestes, the seed of the house of Agamemnon; see J.-P. Vernant, "Hestia-Hermès. Sur l'expression religieuse de l'espace et du temps chez les Grecs" (Vernant 1971, 1:136).

98. Aeschylus *Prometheus Bound* 683–84, 900 (*ponōn*); *Suppliants* 50 (*ponōn*), and esp. 562–64 (*mainomena ponois atimois odunais te*). This is precisely what the Danaids wish to flee forever: proof *a contrario* is Hypermnestra who spares her husband because of her desire for children (*paidōn himeros* [*Prometheus* 856–66]). On a more general connection between childbirth and madness, see for example Pindar *Prosodies* 1.14 (where Leto, awaiting her upcoming delivery, is a Thyiad).

99. Cf. Hippocrates *Aphorisms* 5.35: "a women is either troubled by hysteria or suffering from the pains of childbirth."

100. Hippocrates *On the Diseases of Girls*. Conception and childbirth as a therapy capable of containing the "female disease": see P. Manuli, "Fisiologia e patologia," 401–2; for the tragic poets (and Plato), childbirth is a disease or its equivalent.

101. See Pausanias 1.18.5 (Phaedra) and *Odyssey* 19.138 (Eileithuia in Amnisos).

102. See P. Devambez, "Le Motif de Phèdre," 123–24 and 126.

103. Plato *Republic* 3.395e.

104. Plato *Phaedrus* 251e (the soul wracked by desire, *oistrāi kai odunatai*, feels the goad and is filled with pain, like Io, and at the sight of the beautiful object, *kentrōn te kai ōdinōn elēxen*; for the soul it is the end of the goad and the pain); *Republic* 6.490b and 9.574a (*ōdisi te kai odunais*), *Timaeus* 86c and esp. *Theaetetus* 148eff., 210b; *Odyssey* 9.415. See again *Hippolytus* 258.

105. *Iliad* 11.264–83 (from the French trans. by P. Mazon [Belles Lettres]).

106. See Hippocrates *Diseases* 4.50.5; on the heating of the blood during childbirth, see *On the Nature of the Child* 18.3.

107. On wounds in the arm, cf. *Iliad* 12.387ff.; 13.538–39, 782; 16.517. On the hero's arm, see N. Loraux, "Héraklès. Le Héros, son bras, son destin" (Bonnefoy 1981, 1:492–98). The warrior's arm: Pindar *Isthmians* 8.38.

108. *Iliad* 11.191.

109. See *Iliad* 4.116–18 (Menelaus, wounded by Pandaros, who shoots an arrow "heavy with black suffering" at him). See also 4.191; 5.397; 11.398 and 846; 15.394; 16.518.

110. *Oxeiai odunai*: 11.268, 272; *belos oxu*: 269; *odunai oxeiai* of women: *On the Nature of Woman* 14.

111. When the first version of this text appeared, Claude Lévi-Strauss drew my attention to the fact that in fifteenth- and sixteenth-century Japan "so-called battle surgeons were also obstetricians for the reason that in both cases the shedding of blood was not caused by disease" (private communication).

112. *Iliad* 11.217: *pikras ōdinas* (cf. Sophocles fr. 846 Nauck[2]: *pikran ōdina*); *pikros oistos*: *Iliad* 4.134 and 216; 5.99 and 110 (cf. Sophocles *Trachiniae* 681: the bitter arrow that strikes the Centaur). Again the arrow is *ōkus* (swift) or *ōkumoros* (which brings quick death), *polustonos* or *stonoeis* (laden with sobs): 5.112; 15.440–41, 451, 590; 17.374, etc.

113. *Iliad* 11.474–84.

114. *Teiromenai*: Callimachus *Hymn to Artemis* 22, *Hymn to Delos* 61, 211;

teiromenon basilēa: *Iliad* 11.283; see as well 11.841 and 15.510 (the wound from an arrow), 13.539 (wound in the arm), 16.60–61 (*odunai*). In the Achaian camp the doctors are especially deft at extracting arrows: 11.507.

115. *Iliad* 11.658–64.

116. *Iliad* 4.116–18: *herma* is a very interesting word, which metaphorically refers to the seed (see Aeschylus *Suppliants* 580). Moreover, at this moment Athena is watching over Menelaus like a mother (130–32) and Menelaus's black blood evokes the image of a woman dyeing cloth purple (140–46).

117. For example, 5.95ff. and 792–99 (Diomedes), 11.810ff. (Eurypylos), 13.538–39 (Deiphobos), 14.437–39 (Hector).

118. See 7.96ff. (in reality the *aneres* are Achaian women, . . . earth and water); 7.236 (the woman, who does not know the labors of war); 8.163–64 (Hector's insults to Diomedes, whom he calls a woman and a doll); 11.389–90 (Paris the archer, likened by Diomedes to a woman); 22.125 (Hector does not wish to be disarmed like a woman before Achilles).

119. Plutarch, *On the Love of Progeny* 192c–d; the "woman who wrote the *Odyssey*": P. Vidal-Naquet, bibliography of M. I. Finley, *Le Monde d'Ulysse*, French trans. C. Vernant-Blanc and M. Alexandre, 2d ed. (Paris: Maspero, 1978).

120. See Monsacré 1984.

121. *Iliad* 12.433–36 ("true worker": see Detienne 1967, 39n. 87); Zeus and scales: 8.68–77; comparison of these texts: Onians 1951, 397–410.

122. Cf. *Odyssey* 19.104ff., with comments by H. Foley, "Reverse Similes and Sex Roles in the *Odyssey*," *Arethusa* 11, 1–2 (1978): 7–26. In Odysseus's mouth, Penelope's *kleos* is to resemble a masculine model; more classically, Penelope answers by stating that a woman's entire value derives from cohabitation with her husband.

123. *Iliad* 9.69: *basileutatos*.

124. Nagy 1979: 69–93.

125. Hesiod *Theogony* 561–612, *Works and Days* 42–105; Semonides fr. 7 (Eng. trans. and commentary: H. Lloyd-Jones, *Females of the Species* [London, 1975]).

126. Loraux 1981a:104–5, as well as "Mourir devant Troie," 808–10.

127. If one accepts the comments of Froma Zeitlin, one would have to attribute this phenomenon to the many links between tragedy and the feminine (Zeitlin 1985b).

128. *Republic* 5.454e; *Laws* 6.785b.

129. Aristotle *On the Generation of Animals* 775a.27–b2; see below, chap. 2, pp. 46, 50.

130. Aeschylus *Choephoroi* 919–21. Line 921 is openly Hesiodic (it is the man's exertion that feeds the women seated inside the house) and places *mokhthos*, like *ponos*, with men. *Eumenides* 625–37 and 658–59 (cf. Euripides *Orestes* 552–55).

131. *Choephoroi* 896–98, as well as 750, 762; N. Daladier, "Les Mères aveugles," 231–32, 241–42.

132. *Choephoroi* 527–33. The snake-nursling is born armed (544).

133. *Eumenides* 606–8.

134. Euripides *Hippolytus* 616–24. On Hippolytus's error, see, for example, C. Segal, "The Tragedy of the *Hippolytus*: The Waters of Ocean and the Untouched Meadow," *Harvard Studies in Classical Philology* 70 (1965): 117–69; Euripides *Medea* 573–75; Aeschylus *Seven Against Thebes* 187–88 and 664 (see P. Vidal-Naquet, "Les Boucliers des héros. Essai sur la scène centrale des *Sept contre Thèbes*," translated by Janet Lloyd in J.-P. Vernant and P. Vidal-Naquet, *Tragedy and Myth in Ancient Greece* [Atlantic Highlands, N.J.: Humanities Press, 1981], 120–49).

135. Compare *Hippolytus* 1392 and 1418 with 131, 175, 198, 204, 1009; see on this subject the comments of C. Segal, "The Tragedy of the *Hippolytus*," 151–52, and "Pentheus and Hippolytus on the Couch and on the Grid: Psychoanalytic and Structuralist Readings of Greek Tragedy," *Classical World* 72 (1978–79): 129–48.

136. *Sphakelos* (spasm, convulsion): 1351; *odunai*: ibid. and 1371. *Mokhthous eponēsa*, Hippolytus says (1367–69).

137. *Hippolytus* 953.

138. Ibid., 1239.

139. In 1238–39 the messenger spoke of *kara* and *sarkas* (the head and the flesh), in 1343–44 the coryphaeus speaks of Hippolytus "disfigured in his young flesh and his blond head" (*sarkas, kara*). Hippolytus himself, after mentioning his head (*kephalē*), says that his skin is also nothing but a wound (1359) and then once again refers to his whole body when Artemis approaches (1392: *demas*).

140. *Kephalē, egkephalos*: 1351–52. Localization of the soul in *kephalē* or *egkephalos* in Alcmeon of Croton and in the *Timaeus* (69c ff.): Onians 1951, 98 and 115–19 (Orphic and Pythagorean influences), as well as Manuli-Vegetti 1977, 29–53.

141. *Hippolytus* 1082.

142. Sophocles, *Trachiniae* 1079 (see 1056). Herakles, hero of strength: on *biē hērakleiē*, Nagy 1979, 318. On the Herakles of *The Trachiniae*, reduced to his broken body, see C. Segal, "Sophocles' *Trachiniae*: Myth, Poetry and Heroic Values," *Yale Classical Studies* 25 (1977): 99–158, esp. 115 and 130.

143. *Trachiniae* 1075; see also 1071–72, lines that the scholiast compares with *Iliad* 16.7 (Patroclus weeping like a little girl).

144. Iole, the legitimate wife: 428 (*damarta*; the same word refers to Deianeira in 406) and 460. Herakles' many marriages: G. Dumézil, *Mariages Indoeuropéens* (Paris, 1979), 61–63.

145. Deianeira: 31–33, see also 54 and 304 (*sperma*); 28, 109 (in 41–42, the translation of *ōdinas* as "torment" or "anguish" weakens the text); 152, 29–30. Iole: 308 (*anandros ē teknoussa*, which is clarified by Hesychius's gloss, "*teknousa*: who is with child"), 315–16, 382, 401, 420; 325: *ōdinousa sumphoras baros*. See C. Segal, "Mariage et sacrifice dans les *Trachiniennes* de Sophocle," *L'Antiquité classique* 44 (1975), as well as "The Hydra's Nursling: Image and Action in the *Trachiniae*," ibid., 612–17.

146. *Trachiniae* 1062–63: Deianeira is *gunē thēlus*, like the Hesiodic women, descendants of the first woman (*Theogony* 590).

147. Herakles and the *nosos* in love: 445, 543–44 (again see 234–35: at the

beginning of the play, Herakles is "in full force, quite alive, flourishing, not weighed down by sickness"); *nosos* referring to the final sufferings of Herakles: 853, 979–80, 1013, 1030, 1084, 1230, 1241, 1260. On the equivalence between *nosos* as the lover's desire and *nosos* as Herakles' suffering, see Segal, "Sophocles' *Trachiniae*," 113–14, and P. Biggs, "The Disease Theme in Sophocles' *Ajax, Philoctetes and Trachiniae*," *Classical Philology* 61 (1966): 223–35, esp. 228.

148. As Herakles observes with increased anger, Deianeira destroyed him "alone, without even a dagger" (1063)—a likely allusion to Clytemnestra, the model for the murderous woman armed with a dagger (*Agamemnon* 1262; see also *Eumenides* 627ff.).

149. Quotation from Dumézil 1969, 97. Ares as the example of the brutal warrior tormented by his lagging strength: Loraux 1986c. Ares destined by his nature to be diminished: Ramnoux 1962, 58.

150. Groaning labors: Hesiod *Theogony* 951 (*stonoenta erga*); ignominious trials: *Iliad* 19.133, *Odyssey* 11.618–26; exhaustion and tears: *Iliad* 8.362–63. Bacchylides will remember, making Herakles weep over Meleager in Hades (*Epinicia* 5.155ff.).

151. *Nosos*: esp. in the tradition exemplified by Diodorus and Apollodorus; see Diodorus 4.31.4 (*nosos* following on Iphitos's murder) and 38.3 (mortal *nosos*); Apollodorus 2.6.2–4 (*nosos* for Iphitos's murder), 2.7.2 (another *nosos*); see also Diodorus 4.11 and Apollodorus 2.4.12 (*mania* and murder of children), 2.6.2 (*mania* provoking Iphitos's murder). Dumézil (1969, 93–94), perhaps too systematically, saw the importance of sickness in Herakles' career. Femininity: see below, chap. 7.

152. Everything happens as if the epic Herakles who weeps and suffers was no longer familiar to Sophocles' audience, or as if Sophocles wished to create a new Herakles, a hero impervious to pain, all the better to highlight his tears of agony (1071–73); the same tendency in Euripides' *Herakles* (1140, 1412, and esp. 1353–56, where the hero is presented at length as having no prior experience with tears). Seneca will develop the theme in detail, from the standpoint of *virtus* (*Hercules on Oeta* 1265–78, 1374ff.). The tears of Herakles' wife are like Deianeira's revenge, characterized by tears (*Trachiniae* 847–49, 919, but also Bacchylides *Dithyramb* 15, 23–26). Like the tears of Deianeira, Herakles' blood will become *khlōron*; inversely, the verb *brukhomai*, which, for Homer, refers to the cries of men who have been fatally wounded, is used to describe Deianeira (904) as well as Herakles (805, 1072).

153. *Ponos* for labors: 21, 70, 118, 170, 356, 825, 830; *ponos* for suffering: 985 (see also 30, regarding Deianeira, and 680, regarding the Centaur); one also finds the synonym *mokhthos* in the *Trachiniae* and in *Herakles* (*Trachiniae* 1101, 1170; cf. 1047).

154. *Odunai*: 777, 959 (*dusapallaktois odunais*; on *dusapallaktos*, see *On the Nature of Woman*, 40, and, concerning the term *aphuktos*, N. Van Brock, *Recherches sur le vocabulaire médical du grec ancien* [Paris, 1961], 220–29), 975, 986, 1021; the sufferings of Herakles will be compared to *On the Nature of Woman*, 38. *Spasmos*: 805, 1082–83; the use of the verb *diaissō* in medical writings: see *Diseases* 1.5, and *Diseases of Women* 1.35; *sparagmos*: 778, 1254; on *spaō, spasmos, sparagmos*, see P. Biggs, "The Disease Theme," 229; A. A. Long, *Language and*

Thought in Sophocles. A Study of Abstract Nouns and Poetic Technique (London, 1968), 131–35; and P. Berrettoni, "Il Lessico tecnico del I e III libro dell'*Epidemie* ippocratiche," *Annali della Scuola Normale Superiore di Pisa* 39 (1970): 241; the intermittent character of the pain totally conforms to the hero's habitus: see N. Loraux, "Héraklès" (Bonnefoy 1981, 1:492–98). *Manias anthos*: 999 (cf. 1089; *anthos* and *anthein* in the medical vocabulary: see Thucydides 2.49.5; Berrettoni, "Il Lessico tecnico," 241). *Therma*: 1046–47, 1082 (and 368: the heat of *pothos*; heat as a characteristic of Herakles' *nosos*: Diodorus 4.38.2, and Apollodorus 2.7.7). Other important words: *phoitada* (980) belongs to the medical vocabulary (see *Nature of Woman* 52: *odunē phoitai*); *brukei*: 987 (cf. *On the Flesh* 19.1, and *Nature of Woman* 35 and 37, where the grinding of teeth [*brugmos*] is associated with sharp and intense pain throughout the belly and lower abdomen).

155. The labored Herakles: in lines 985–86 the use of the perfect passive participle *peponēmenos . . . odunais* will be appreciated, a *hapax* in the tragedy.

156. Far from tragedy and Herakles, medical language, which is not troubled by ambiguities, does not hesitate, on the contrary, to name: see Hippocrates, *On Internal Complaints* 17, where the patient, afflicted by a disease of the kidneys due to sexual excess, suffers pains (*odunai*) in his side and "suffers what a woman in labor suffers." The pains of Herakles and the parturition of the soul: see for example F.H.M. Blaydes, *The Trachiniae of Sophocles* (London, 1871), concerning lines 832ff.

157. *Pleura* is a key word in the *Trachiniae*, used with regard to the Centaur (680), Herakles (768, 833, 1053, 1082), Deianeira (926); see as well 938–39 (Hyllos stretching out alongside the dead Deianeira) and 1225 (Iole sleeping at Herakles' side): cf. P. E. Easterling, "Sophocles' *Trachiniae*," *Bulletin of the Institute of Classical Studies* 15 (1968): 58–69, esp. 65 and 67. It is probably not pure chance that, beginning with line 7, Deianeira's childhood is located in Pleuron (as in Hesiod, fr. 25 MW, 13) and not in Calydon, as the rest of literary tradition has it: I see in this a play on the word *pleura*.

158. *Pleumōn/pleura*: 567–68 (the Centaur) and 1053–54, which can be compared with 777–78 and 1083 (Herakles). *Timaeus* 78c (shared *pleumōn* and *artēria* in the upper and lower cavity) sheds light on 1054. *Pleumonia* as *nosos erotikē*: Onians 1951, 37.

159. *Koiliē*, designating the thorax, stomach, and belly in the Hippocratic texts: see P. Chantraine, "Remarques sur la langue et le vocabulaire du *Corpus hippocratique*," in *La Collection hippocratique et son rôle dans l'histoire de la médecine* (Leiden, 1975), 35–40, and J. Dumortier, *Le Vocabulaire médical*, 12–13 and 17; in the *Timaeus*, the distinction between *anō* and *katō koilia* (69c–73a) should not mask the unity between these two parts as receptacles for the mortal soul; Aristotle, *History of the Animals* 1.15.493b13–14, observes that the ribs (*pleurai*) are shared by the upper and lower parts of the trunk. On the "Sophocles-Hippocrates-Aristotle axis," and Sophocles' privileged relationship with the language of physicians, see N. E. Collinge, "Medical Terms and Clinical Attitudes in the Tragedians," *Bulletin of the Institute of Classical Studies* 9 (1962): 43–55, esp. 47.

160. Devouring: 1055, 1084, 1089, as well as 1056; cf. *Nature of Woman* 10. The net of the Erinyes: 1050–52, if, however, one accepts, with Mazon and Kamerbeek, the translation of *nephelē* as "net"; one can also, with Jebb, under-

stand "a cloud of death," as in *Iliad* 16.350, Pindar *Nemeans* 9.37, Aeschylus *Seven Against Thebes* 228–29, and *Eumenides* 379, and esp. Bacchylides *Dithyrambs* 15, 32. In fact, the polysemy is incontestable.

161. *Iliad* 15.316–17; 21.70, 168.

162. *Oistron: Trachiniae* 1254; see also 840: *phonia kentra*.

163. *Trachiniae* 572–74.

164. If they could, commentators would gladly give the word the single meaning of "poison." But there is line 567, where *ios* irreducibly denotes the arrow. Moreover, it is all the more important to retain the meaning of "arrow" for *ios* because Sophocles, according to C. Dugas, is probably the inventor of the arrow that wounds Nessos, which he uses to replace the bludgeon in earlier visual representations ("La Mort du Centaure Nessos," *Revue des Etudes anciennes* 45 (1943): 18–26). The multiple meanings of *ios* are thus quite real in tragedy and make the translation of all these passages difficult; but outside of tragedy, the multiple values disappear, and *ios* refers only to poison, carefully differentiated from the arrow (cf. Diodorus 4.38.2 and Apollodorus 2.5.2).

165. *Ios*: 567 (arrow), 771 (poison), as well as 716–18 and 832–34. Strictly speaking, it is impossible to make a sharp distinction between the two meanings, as in the *Eumenides* (*ios*, poison and the arrow launched by the Erinyes). On Iole's name, derived from *ios*, see C.A.P. Ruck, "On the Sacred Names of Iamos and Ion," *Classical Journal* 71 (1976): 235–52n. 1.

166. Just like Hippolytus, Herakles begs for the assistance of a helpful blade: a man's death (*Trachiniae* 1014 and *Hippolytus* 1375, where the words used, *egkhos* and *logkhē*, refer to the spear, the virile man's weapon). Both wish to dull their pain, using a word derived from a woman's bed, *eunē: eunasai* (*Trachiniae* 1006; *Hippolytus* 1377).

167. Outside of tragedy the ambiguity disappears, and in Diodorus 4.38.3, it is as a man that Herakles dies, man to the end, surrounded by his warrior's accoutrements.

168. Deianeira dies, like Ajax, from a dagger's blow (*Trachiniae* 930; cf. *Ajax* 834). The text is clear that such a death is a *hubris* for a woman, but by making the nurse into a *parastatis*, a companion of equal rank (889), it also renders this a hoplitic death. Outside tragedy, everything returns to its proper place, and Deianeira meets with a woman's death when she hangs herself (Diodorus 4.38.3; Apollodorus 2.7.7).

169. See below, chap. 6.

170. Euripides *Phoenician Women* 1456–59, 1577–78.

171. *Trachiniae* 913, 915–16, 918, 920 (where the sense is doubly determined: *lekhē*, "bed," institution of reproduction/*numpheia*: the bed of the young bride).

172. Herakles imagines on the contrary that the death inflicted on him is a *lōba* (996), as if his warrior's corpse were insulted while he was still alive.

173. *Trachiniae*, 938–39: *pleurothen/pleuran*. Deianeira wished to die with Herakles (720: *sunthanein*): she dies totally apart from him, and it is for Hyllos that the two dead are joined (see 941 and 1233–35).

174. *Trachiniae* 734–37, 817–18. The nurse's tale explicitly names Hyllos as the cause of Deianeira's suicide (932–33).

175. *Trachiniae* 911. A line with a fine commentary by Kamerbeek: Deianeira's *ousia* amounts to motherhood, and the expression has nothing "illogical" about it, as C. Segal claims ("The Hydra's Nursling," 614).

176. *Trachiniae* 930–31. Despite the difficulty in reconciling the liver with the left side (926), one must be wary of giving *hēpar*, as Kamerbeek does, the broad meaning of "entrails." See Loraux 1985, 90–91.

177. Ajax: Pindar *Nemeans* 7.38 (*phrenōn*); cf. Sophocles *Ajax* 834. Herakles: Euripides *Herakles* 1149.

178. Aristotle *History of the Animals* 1.17.496b11–12: the diaphragm as *diazōma*. On the liver and the diaphragm, see J. Dumortier, *Le Vocabulaire médical*, 18–20.

179. *Trachiniae* 308: *anandros ē teknoussa*, with C. Segal's commentary, "The Hydra's Nursling" (614), and, on *teknou(s)sa*, the comments of V. Schmidt, in *Mélanges R. Keydell* (Berlin, 1978), 38–48.

180. On Deianeira as *numphē*, see *Trachiniae* 527, as well as 104.

181. Hesiod *Theogony* 590 (*gunaikōn thēluteraōn*); Empedocles fr. 616 Bollack (*androdesteroi andres*); Hippocrates *On Regimen* 1.28–29 (the relative virility of men, the relative femininity of women); Plato *Symposium* 191d–e. See above, Introduction.

182. Tiresias, transformed into a woman and back into a man, could attest that out of ten parts of pleasure the woman takes nine.

183. A preliminary version of this chapter appeared in *L'Homme* 21, 1 (1981): 37–67. While preparing these pages, I was able to benefit from the comments of Nathalie Daladier, Hélène Monsacré, Giulia Sissa, and Pierre Vidal-Naquet. Since then I have returned to the issue left open at the end of the chapter (Loraux 1985).

CHAPTER TWO
PONOS

1. Thus, for Herodotus the Trojan War, unlike Marathon, an isolated exploit referred to as *ergon*, is *ponos* (9.27.4); but as a way to stress the length of the fighting at Marathon, the historian calls it *ponos* (7.113–14; the same thing for Thermopylae in 7.224, Salamis in 8.89). *Ponos* is also used to express the extent of great military labors: 7.23ff., 8.74, 9.15.

2. A few examples: *Iliad* 4.26, 57; *Odyssey* 23.250: *ponos* is associated with *telos* or *telein*.

3. "Travail et nature dans Grèce ancienne," in Vernant 1971, 2:17.

4. Herodotus 7.190. Should this use of the word be seen as analogous to our notion of wood that is "worked"? Perhaps, on the condition that we add that for Herodotus a naval battle can be a *trauma* (wound) for ships as well as for a city: once again, the idea of "labor" fades into the background.

5. Thucydides 2.63.1; in 64.3, the great name (*onoma megiston*) of the city is linked to the *ponoi*.

6. For example, Herodotus 1.177.

7. Pindar *Olympians* 6.12, 11.4; *Isthmians* 5.25 (and 1.45: *mokhthoi*); *ponos* of the poet: *Pythians* 9.93, *Paeans* 10.16, as well as *Pythians* 6.52–54 (the poet's

labor like the bees' *ponos*; on this matter, see Svenbro's comments [1976, 175, 187–89], which I will not recapitulate here: *ponos* refers less to the poet as artisan than as someone engaged in a natural process like that of Hesiod's bees, whose fatigue [*kamatos*]) feeds the women-drones [*Theogony* 599, *Works and Days* 305]).

8. See P. Vidal-Naquet, "Une civilisation de la parole politique," in Vidal-Naquet 1981, 21–35.

9. The populace does not understand the value of *ponos*: *Pythians* 8.73; the noble, on the contrary, is distinguished by *ponos kai dapanē*, "effort and expenditure": *Olympians* 5.15, *Isthmians* 1.42 and 6.10 (see Herodotus 2.148).

10. Thucydides 2.64.3.

11. Xenophon *Oikonomikos* 6.7.

12. For example, see Aristophanes *Plutos* 254: the country folk in love with difficulty (*tou ponein erastai*).

13. This perspective receives scant attention in the book by R. Descat, *L'Acte et l'effort. Une idéologie du travail en Grèce ancienne (VIIIe–Ve siècle av. J.-C.)* (Besançon-Lille, 1986); concerned with defining *ponos* within the sphere of need, in this case as "action, taken as reciprocity, because of [bonds] of hospitality," he concludes, "*Ponos* thus logically comes to mean war, viewed as the culmination of these bonds of reciprocity" (125). However, if *ponos* is marked by "a clear predilection . . . for war" ("The warlike meaning concerns more than half the uses" [52]), one would expect a more specific consideration of these instances.

14. *Ponos* of the warrior: on the Homeric epic, see Trümpy, *Kriegerische Fachausdrücke im griechischen Epos* (Basel, 1950), 148; many examples in Aristophanes: *Acharnians*, 694, 1071, *Knights* 579, *Wasps* 685. *Ponos kai kindunos*: Thucydides 1.70.8; Xenophon *Anabasis* 7.3.31 and 6.36, *Cyropaedia* 1.5.12, *Oikonomikos* 21.4. Desire for *ponos*: *Oikonomikos* 21.5–6.

15. Herodotus 9.27.4; Sophocles *Philoctetes* 248; Pindar *Pythians* 1.54; Euripides *Kyklops* 107, 347, 351–52. *Ponos* referring to heroic war: *ponoi Areos* or *Enualios* (e.g., Pindar *Isthmians* 6.54).

16. The *ponoi* of Athens: Euripides *Suppliants* 373 and 577, Thucydides 2.64.3 (as well as 1.70.8 and 2.38.1, 62.1–3, 63.1). A synonym for *ponos*, *mokhthos* also refers to the "labors" of Athens in Pindar (*Paeans* 2.32).

17. Hippocrates *Regimen* 1.34 (*epiponōterē, rhaithumoterē diaitē*); *On the Glands*, vol. 8, Littré, p. 573 (*ponos, argiē*).

18. Sophocles *Oedipus at Colonus* 335–45, with a play on the two senses of the word *ponein*: to "exert oneself"—for a relative/as a manly task.

19. Shadow and softness: Hippocrates *Regimen* 2.49.3; see Xenophon *Oikonomikos* 4.2 (artisans, who have effeminate bodies), Herodotus 6.12 (worn out by *ponos* and the sun, the Ionians *eskiētropheonto*; cf. Athenaeus 12.515, on the Lydians who, in *truphē* and *skiatrophia*, replace the Ionians during the Hellenistic period); Plato *Phaedrus* 239c6–8 (shade/sun, *anandros diaitē*), *Republic* 8.556d–e (*heliōmenos/eskiatrophēkoti*), and *Laws* 6.781a (life in shadow). To this list one will add the youth who, for a short time, has a connection with shade and femininity (Vidal-Naquet 1981, 168). Life in the shade is frequently associated with hot baths, in the definition of a feminine regimen: see *Odyssey* 8.248 (the life-style of the Phaeacians), *Regimen* 66.4 (warm baths and soft beds), Plutarch *Theseus* 23.3

(the regimen that gives two adolescent boys "with manly and ardent hearts" the appearance of girls). Last, the warm bath integrates the stranger into the inner reaches of the house: hence its place in hospitality rites (Bouvier 1987, 12–15).

20. Regimen for the excess of *ponos*: Hippocrates *Regimen* 3.85.2. Because of their softening qualities (Hippocrates *On the Diseases of Women* 3.128 and 220), warm baths cure sickness and fatigue: see Plato *Laws* 6.561c–d and the remarks in Ginouvès 1962, 158–59, 178, 204, 205, 217, 368–71.

21. Aeschylus fr. 99 Nauck[2] (*Europa*), line 7. Apollo and Orestes in the *Oresteia*: *Choephoroi* 919–21, *Eumenides* 631ff.

22. See above, chap. 1, pp. 25–28.

23. Plutarch *Alexander* 40.2 (and 38.3). *Truphē*, however, is a theme that predates the Hellenistic period by some time: see G. Nenci, "*Truphē* e colonizzazione," in *Forme di contatto e processi di trasformazione nelle società antiche* (Pisa-Rome, 1983), 1019–31.

24. Herodotus 6.11–12 (*ponos*, linked with *eleutheriē* and tolerance to the sun's rays, is contrasted with *malakiē*, "softness," with *skiatrophia*, "life in the shade," and slavery).

25. Herodotus 1.126.

26. Here the slave is understood in the Athenian sense of the term, as slave-merchandise. In Xenophon's *Oikonomikos* the slave of a good master has a "will to work" (*ergazesthai*, a neutral term), while the soldier has the "will to exert himself" (*ponein*): 3.4 and 21.4; the slave's work is pure preparation (5.15), directed toward the use that the master will make of the object; in Cyrus's speech against pleasure (Xenophon *Cyropaedia* 7.5.78–80), the slaves who share their masters' *ponoi* are defeated peoples. On the symbolic use of the word *doulos*, see the comments of M.-M. Mactoux, *Douleia* (Paris, 1980), 83–92 (but to cite Herakles' *ponoi* in support of the figure of the slave as a "relative other" [91] is to give short shrift to the complexity of the figure of Herakles).

27. *Ponos/argia*: Aristotle *History of Animals* 6.20.574b29 and Plato *Republic* 8.556c2; *ponos*, contrasted with the sweet life resembling the conviviality of a banquet: Herodotus 7.119, 9.15; *ponos/rhaithumia*: Xenophon *Anabasis* 2.6.6, Aristotle *Nicomachaean Ethics* 1138b31; *ponos/malakia*: Aristotle *History of Animals* 1116a13, Plato *Republic* 8.556c1; *ponos/truphē*: Plato *Republic* 8.556b8, Aristotle *Politics* 2.6.1265a34, etc.

28. See for example *Oikonomikos* 6.10. The question of *skholē* is complicated, and the ambiguity of this concept allows for many twists in meaning, but apparently *skholē* refers to the condition of the free man as opposed to the slave: see J. L. Stocks, "Scholē," *Classical Quarterly* 30 (1936): 177–83.

29. *Ponos* and athletics: besides Xenophon *Cyropaedia* 1.5.10, one would have to cite all of Pindar's work (see A. Szastynska-Scemion, "Le *Ponos* du sportif dans l'épinice grec," *Acta Conventus XI "Erene"* (Warsaw, 1971), 81–85; see Euripides *Alcestis* 1027, Plato *Laws* 1.646c (*gumnasia kai ponoi*), and the remarks of L. Robert concerning the epitaph of a pankratiast, in *Hellenika, Recueil d'epigráphie, de numismatique et d'antiquités qrecs*, vols. 11–12 (Paris, 1960), 345–49. *Ponos* and hunting: see Xenophon *Cynegetica* 12 (in its entirety) and 13.10–14, with commentary by J. Aymard, *Essai sur les chasses romaines* (Paris, 1951), 483–85.

30. Hunting as *paideusis*: *Cynegetica* 12.18 (as well as 1.7 and 12, 6.13 and 19, 13.14 [*philoponia*] and *Cyropaedia* 1.5.9–11 and 1.6.24–26). On the man of *ponos* in Xenophon, see Garlan 1972, 64.

31. On the *athla tōn ponōn*, see *Memorabilia* 2.1.19; theory of effort that is always compensated: *Memorabilia* 2.1.28 (Arete's speech in Prodikos's apology) and *Oikonomikos* 5.1–17 (praise of agriculture).

32. *Memorabilia* 2.1.20–34.

33. *Ponos* as opposed to *hēdonē*, Herakles and the Pythagoreans: see Detienne 1960, and Detienne 1967, 133–35; Herakles the cynic: Diogenes Laertes 6.12, 16, and 18 (Antisthenes), 6.71 (Diogenes modeling himself on Herakles, who had placed nothing above his freedom: see M. Simon, *Hercule et le christianisme* [Strasburg-Paris, 1955], 78–79); Herakles, *ponos*, the Cynics, and the Stoics: see the remarks by Daraki 1982, 167–68. On the intellectual figure of Herakles, see again C. Dugas, "Héraklès mousicos," in *Recueil Charles Dugas* (Paris, 1960), 115–21.

34. *Ponos* associated with Socrates: Xenophon *Apology* 17; Plato *Symposium* 219e8 (as well as comments by Daraki 1982, 167): see below, chap. 9; philosophical *ponein*: Aristotle *Nicomachaean Ethics* 1.13.1102a5 (cf. *Metaphysics* Δ.2.1013b9) and 10.6.1177a33.

35. *Ponos* in the underworld: *Olympians* 1.60 (Tantalus's torment), 2.74 (torments of the "others," opposed to the Royals); same remark concerning *mokhthos*, the poetic term for *ponos*: see *Pythians* 2.30 (Ixion) and Alcaeus fr. 38A Campbell (Sisyphus); *mokhthos* for Pindar also refers to the intolerable trials undergone by Greece during the Persian Wars (*Isthmians* 8.9). *Ponos* and human life: *Pythians* 5.54, and, as opposed to a golden age, *Pythians* 10.41 and *Olympians* 2.68.

36. Demosthenes *Contra Phainippos* 20, 24, and 32.

37. Difficulty of an army: e.g., 1.30.3 and 49.5; 4.36 and 96.5; 5.73.2; 6.67 and 104.2; 7.38.2. The trials of a city: 4.59.1 (*ponoumenē polis tōi polemōi*).

38. *Ponos*, the suffering of the other city: Aeschylus *Persians* 682 and *Agamemnon* 1167. To cause trouble for someone: Herodotus 6.108 (*ekhein ponous*); in the signifier, the Athenians were already able to take advantage of the trial (*ponous anairein*; *anairein* means to win a prize or victory).

39. Thucydides 1.70.8 and 2.38.1.

40. Thucydides 2.39.4 (and 39.1); see Loraux 1981a, 152–55.

41. See L. Robert, *Hellenica*, vols. 11–12 (Paris, 1969), 342–49.

42. Thucydides 2.63 (*ponoi/timas*), 64.6 (*ponoi barunomenoi*).

43. The equivalence between *gumnasia* and *ponoi*: *Regimen* 35.3 and 11; 65.2; 66.6–7; 82.3.

44. *Regimen* 65.2, 78.2; see as well 15.2, 75.1, 81.8, as well as *On Diseases* 4.36.2, 37.1, 38.1–2, etc. Special meaning of medical *ponos*: gynecological suffering, of which childbirth is only one aspect for the doctor (*On the Fetus at Eight Months* 2.2, 3.1, 4.2–3, etc., as well as Aristotle *Generation of Animals* 4.4.773a17).

45. *Ponos* in Sophocles: *Philoctetes* 195, 637–38, 887; *Trachiniae* 680, 985; for Thucydides: 2.49.3, 51.6, 52.1 (description of the plague); for Aristotle: *ponountes* referring to diseases (*Generation of Animals* 1.18.725a17), *ponos* as fatigue (*Physics* 3.195a9, *On Longevity* 5.446b12ff.).

46. *Kamnontes* as a name for diseases: e.g., Hippocrates *Regimen* 2.4, as well as

32.4, 69.2, 71.3; Aristotle *Generation of Animals* 5.7.787a25; *Rhetoric* 2.12.1389a8, etc. An interesting example: *Nicomachaean Ethics* 7.8.1150b4 where the truly sick person is contrasted with one who only feigns sickness to avoid *ponos*-fatigue out of *malakia* and *truphē*.

47. See Aristotle *Generation of Animals* 4.6.775a–27b (concerning the *ethnē*) and *History of Animals* 7.4.584b6–12 (Egypt).

48. Diodorus 4.20.2–3 (emphasis on the absence of *truphē* among the Ligurians) and Strabo 3.4.17 (which contains the history of Poseidonius, quoting it on the subject of people who divide *andreia* between men and women, and even mentioning a kind of "couvade").

49. At an extremely ancient date, the notion of suffering was probably "accidental" (Mawet 1979, 379, on the subject of the *Iliad*); but in the classical period, at least, it had been so acclimatized as to appear innate.

50. However, *ponos* is, as Descat (1986, 63) helpfully recalls, a rare term in Hesiod, unlike *ergon*; but *ergon* denotes chosen work that responds to the demands of *dikē*, while *ponos* expresses the human condition, that a life lived in accordance with justice can attempt to improve.

51. *Works and Days* 91 and 113: see Vernant's two articles on the myth of the races (Vernant 1971, 1:13–79), as well as, by the same author, "A la table des hommes," in Detienne and Vernant 1979, 121–32; see also A. Ballabriga, "L'Equinoxe d'hiver," *Annali della scuola Normale Superiore di Pisa* 11 (1981): 569–603, on the subject of manly *ponos* in Hesiod.

52. For example, Archilochus fr. 15 Edmonds, Euripides *Hippolytus* 189–90, 367; numerous examples in Sophocles: see *Antigone* 1276 and, for the recurring theme of the heaping up of sufferings, *Ajax* 866, 876, 926–27, 1196 and *Philoctetes* 760. Medical version: *Regimen* 61.1, 78.3, 88.3, and Aristotle *Nicomachaean Ethics* 7.15.1154b9 and *On the World* 6.397b23.

53. Egyptians: Herodotus 2.14 (*automatos* evokes *automatē aroura* in *Works and Days* 117, 118); Scythians: Aristotle *Politics* 1.8.1256a31ff., comments by Hartog 1980, 218–19).

54. *Theogony* 226; on the generalizing character of *ponos*, see Ramnoux 1959, 72–73.

55. *Works and Days* 113 and *Theogony* 214. The phrase *ponos kai oizus* is Homeric, evoking war in the *Iliad* (13.2, 14.480), slavery as the reverse of war in the *Odyssey* (8.529). *Oizus* derived from a verb "to cry *oi*," "to lament": Chantraine 1968, s.v.; Mawet 1979, 189 (on *ponos kai oizus*: 190–91).

56. See the remarks by M. Austin and P. Vidal-Naquet, *Economies et sociétés en Grèce ancienne* (Paris, 1972), 27.

57. *Iliad* 11.430; *Odyssey* 23.248–49 (and 306: *oizusas*).

58. *Odyssey* 1.5, with comments on that line by Benveniste 1969, 1:166.

59. *Iliad* 10.244–45, where Odysseus is characterized by *ponos* in the very book where, in line 89, Agamemnon is defined by his vocation for endurance; see again 10.279 and 11.431, as well as *Odyssey* 13.301 and 20.48. Odysseus is the enduring one (*tlēmon, polutlas, talasiphrōn*): see *Iliad* 5.670, 10.231 and 248, 11.466 and *Odyssey*, passim; *tlēnai* as characterizing the human condition: *Iliad* 24.49, *Homeric Hymn to Apollo* 191, with remarks by E. Heitsch, "Tlēmosunē," in *Hermes* 92 (1964): 257–64.

60. On mourning: Nagy 1979, 69–83; on the hero's tears: Monsacré 1984, nn.137–42.

61. Imitated by [Hesiod], *The Shield* 351, in a martial context.

62. E.g., the task: *Iliad* 1.467; the labor of battle: *Iliad* 5.84, 567, 627; 16.568; 21.137 and 249; *Odyssey* 12.117; the trial: *Iliad* 10.89; mourning: *Iliad* 21.525; 22.488.

63. Odysseus's *kamatoi* in the *Odyssey* reflect the tireless tension of his effort: e.g., 5.493 (*dusponos kamatos*); 6.2, 9.75, 10.143 and 363, etc.

64. The warrior's fatigue: *Iliad* 4.26–27 (with *ponos* and *hidrōs*, "sweat"), 13.711, 21.51–52 (broken knees, sweat); see as well 10.312, 399, 471 (where fatigue is *ainōs*, "terrible"). The labor of the artisan: *Iliad* 18.614 (Achilles' weapons, crafted by Hephaistos; see 18.380, where *poneīto* refers to the labor of Hephaistos), *Odyssey* 23.189 (Odysseus's bed, made by the hero), etc. The dead, *kamontes*: *Iliad* 3.278, 23.72; *Odyssey* 11.476 and 24.14; in the classical language, *kekmēkotes*: Aeschylus *Suppliants* 158, 231; Euripides *Suppliants* 756; Aristotle *Nicomachaean Ethics* 1.13.1101b2, 9.

65. See A. Aymard, "L'Idée de travail dans la Grèce archaïque," *Journal de Psychologie* 41 (1948): 29–45, and Finley 1978, 86–87.

66. The maidservant: *Odyssey* 20.118; Eumaios: *Odyssey* 14.65 and 417, and commentary in Svenbro 1976, 62.

67. See Chantraine 1968, s.v. *kamnō*. *Kamnō* and *kamatos* will nonetheless continue to be doublets for *ponos* in poetic language: name for the exploit (Pindar *Nemeans* 1.70, *Pythians* 5.48), for trials (Pindar *Pythians* 3.95), for childbirth (Sophocles *Electra* 530–33, *Oedipus Rex* 174), for the peasant's steadfast labor (Hesiod *Theogony* 599, *Works and Days* 305), *kamatos* again expresses the law of the human condition (Hesiod *Works and Days*, 177; Pindar *Partheneias* 1.19).

68. *Ponēros*, "unhappy": Hesiod fr. 248 and 249 Merkelbach-West (Herakles), Solon fr. 14 West (the mortal species as a whole). *Ponēros*, "scoundrel": the meatseller of Aristophanes' *Knights* is a "scoundrel, born of scoundrels" (*ponēros ek ponērōn* [181–86]); see as well *Wasps* 466 and *Lysistrata* 350 (where the compound *ponōponērōs* refers to the egregious rascal).

69. And for a long time: in the first and second centuries A.D., as Marie-Henriette Quet has pointed out to me, *ponēroi* is the term used to refer to the common people, in opposition to the notables of the cities and the "sage."

70. Xenophon *Oikonomikos* 1.19, where *ponēria* covers *argia* and *malakia*: for Aristophanes, *ponēria* is completely negative, while *ponos* refers to intensive exertion or labor, without any pejorative connotations.

71. See Chantraine 1968, s.v. *penomai*. *Penēs*, the "poor man," is contrasted with *ptōkhos*, the "beggar" and refers to one "who struggles to live by his work, a needy person."

72. L. Febvre, "Travail: Evolution d'un mot et d'une idée," *Journal de Psychologie* 41 (1948): 19–28, nn. 19–22.

73. "Aspects de la personne dans la religion grecque," in Vernant 1971, 2:90.

74. *Mokhthoi* is constantly exchanged with *ponoi* in Euripides' *Herakles*; see also, for example, Theocritus 24.82–83 (twelve *mokhthoi*). *Mokhthos* and *mokhthein* cover all the meanings of *ponos* and *ponein*, from the standpoint of warfare (Sophocles *Ajax* 1188), agricultural labor (Aristophanes *Pluto* 525), childbirth (Eurip-

ides *Medea* 1030 and 1261, *Herakles* 281), and the hero's suffering (in Aeschylus's *Prometheus* 99, etc., and Sophocles' *Oedipus at Colonnus* 105, 437, 1362).

75. A few examples: *ponos* in Euripides' *Herakles*, passim; in the comic writer Kratinos fr. 4 Edmonds (*Omphalos*), and even in Lucian's *Dialogues of the Gods* (13.1.236).

76. *Philoctetes* 1419–20 (in the following lines, Herakles announces to Philoctetes that his *ponoi* will be rewarded with a glorious life); *Trachiniae* 21, 170, 825 (deeds); 70, 356 (servitude); 680, 985 (physical suffering).

77. See C. B. Kritzas, "Héraklès *Pankamès*," *Arkhaiologike Ephemeris* (1973): 107–19, and K. Kerényi, "Hercules fatigatus," in *Mélanges C. J. Burckhardt* (Munich, 1961), 214–20.

78. *Odyssey* 11.618–19 (*kakon moron*); *Iliad* 19.133 (*ergon aeikes*).

79. See esp. Jourdain-Annequin 1985, 496–507, on the distinction between *latreuō*, which refers to work for someone else, if not servile labor, and which can be remunerated by a *misthos* (499–504), and *douleuō*, which implies that Herakles has indeed been sold by Eurytos as a slave (504–7).

80. Sophocles *Trachiniae* 35 (*latreuō*: see also 70, 357, 830; cf. Apollodorus *Library* 2.4.2 and 6.2–4); Aeschylus *Agamemnon* 1040–41 (*doulos*: see Lucian *Dialogue of the Gods* 237). On Herakles enslaved, see Delcourt 1942, 129–30; M. I. Finley, "La Servitude pour dettes," *Revue historique de droit français et étranger* 43 (1965): 159–84 (Herakles as an example of the "real confusion between service and slavery at the prelaw stage": 159–60); Dumézil 1971, 120–26, and G. S. Kirk, "Methodological Reflexions on the Myths of Heracles," in Gentili and Paioni 1977, 291. It will be noted that one etymology, which has been contested but accepted by some philologists, derives Herakles' name from the word *hēra*, "service."

81. E.g., *Iliad* 15.30; [Hesiod] *The Shield* 94, 127; Hesiod fr. 190.12; Pindar *Isthmians* 6.49; Euripides *Herakles* 827. For Diodorus and Apollodorus, everything that is not part of the twelve labors is *parergon* and not *athlos*.

82. Hesiod *Theogony* 951, *Shield* 127 (*stonoentas aethlous*): the same expression in reference to Jason, *Theogony* 994 (and in his *Argonautica* Apollonios of Rhodes will systematically refer to all of Jason's "trials" as *aethloi*. Herakles *athlios*: Euripides *Herakles* 1015 and Dio Chrysostom *On Virtue* 28.

83. *Iliad* 8.362–63; 15.639; 19.133; *Odyssey* 11.618–26.

84. See, for *ponos*: Euripides *Alcestis* 481 and 1149–50, *Herakles* 388; for *mokhthos*: Sophocles *Oedipus at Colonus* 105; Euripides *Herakles* 830. For Sophocles, *ponein tini* can mean "to toil, to labor for someone," in the context of service to a warrior (*Ajax*) or family service (*Antigone*, *Oedipus at Colonus*). Outside the tragic poets, few examples of this meaning can be observed, however: see Xenophon *Symposium* 4.14 (service of the beloved) and the gloss, quoted by Borgeaud 1979, 40, of the proverb "to play the Arcadian" (to act as a mercenary).

85. See, however, some movement back and forth between *ponos* and *athlos*: *Odyssey* 23.248–49; Herodotus 1.126 and 7.26 (*prokeimenos athlos/prokeimenos ponos*).

86. E.g., Pindar *Pythians* 4.165 (the exploit without suffering). During the classical period, the ambiguity of the character of the athlete is nonetheless per-

ceptible, especially when he is heroicized: see the cases cited by Fontenrose 1968, 86–89: Herakles, the model of the hero-athlete. See Gregory Nagy, *Pindar's Homer: The Lyric Possession of an Epic Past* (Baltimore: Johns Hopkins University Press, 1990), 136–45.

87. *Prometheus*, passim (the *athlos* of Io echoes, like his *ponoi* and his *mokhthoi*, those of the Titan); *Theogony* 800 (the forsworn god). Homeric tribulations: *Odyssey* 1.18, 3.262, 4.240–41, 23.248–49, 261, 350; trials undergone on behalf of another: *Iliad* 3.126 (the *aethloi* of the Achaians and Trojans for Helen); *Odyssey* 4.170 (*aethloi* of Odysseus for Menelaus), as well as Hesiod *Theogony* 994–95 (Jason's *aethloi*, ordered by a king). The most interesting passage is *Iliad* 24.734, where Andromache weeps over her son, condemned to carry out ignominious labors (*ergon, aeikes*), *aethleuōn pro anaktos*, "toiling for a master."

88. *Odyssey* 19.572, 576, 584; 21.73, 91, 135, 268; 22.5.

89. H. Trümpy, *Kriegerische Fachausdrücke*, 150, considers suffering to be primary, on the basis of *Odyssey* 4.170 and 241; Chantraine 1968, s.v. *athlos*, contests such an analysis, seeking to preserve the priority of an agonistic meaning (but the funeral games of *Iliad* 23 are *agōnes* and not *aethloi*). In a more measured fashion, the article *aethlos* in the *Lexikon des frühgriechischen Epos*, vol. 1, ed. B. Snell (Göttingen, 1979), considers suffering and peril to be fundamental notions, and its agonistic value only secondary.

90. Herodotus 1.42 and 126; 4.10 and 43; 7.197.

91. This does not involve denying that *athlon* is derived from *athlos*; the view adopted here is not that of philology but of a history that is attentive to the representations that the Greeks associated with a word.

92. *Athlon*, remuneration for a contest as a social service: B. Laum, *Heiliges Geld* (Tübingen, 1924), 57–58: *contra* L. Gernet, "Jeux et droit," in *Droit et société dans la Grèce ancienne* (Paris, 1964), who drops this hypothesis rather quickly (13n.1).

93. *Shield* 305–6 (in *Works and Days* 654, Amphidamas's tournament is denoted by the prizes [*aethla*] that are won there); *Iliad* 23.259, 273, etc. (the *aethla* are mentioned even before the contest is given its name); 22.159–64 (what makes the race both a trial and a contest is the prize, which is Hector's life); *Odyssey* 11.548 (Achilles' weapons) and 21.73, 106 (Penelope).

94. The *athlon* of Herakles: alongside the metaphorical expressions such as *ponōn athla* (Sophocles *Philoctetes* 508–9, Xenophon *Memorabilia* 2.1.19), such a notion is perhaps implicit in a passage from Euripides' *Herakles* (1386–87); there the hero invites Theseus to accompany him to Argos to have confirmed on him the *athliou kunos komistra* (the salary owed the escort of the dog of Hades, named "victory dog" in the French translation by M. Delcourt [Paris: Bibliothèque de la Pléiade]) because his conquest brings to a close the cycle of the Labors and, in terms of the agreement concluded with Eurystheus [lines 15–20], ought to authorize Herakles' return to Argos). But this etymological use of *athlios* would be a *hapax*, and the question remains unanswered, even if it is necessary to refuse to correct the text as Wilamowitz has done, by openly replacing the difficult *athliou* with *agriou* (and making Cerberus into a "wild dog").

95. This is the interpretation of Diodorus (4.8.1: *epathlon*).

96. J.-P. Vernant, "Aspects de la personne," in Vernant 1971, 2:91.

97. On the association between the mercenary worker and the slave (and the distinction between them), see A. Mele, *Società e lavoro nei poemi omericie* (Naples, 1968), 130–33; *drēstēr*: Finley 1978, 63, with Mele's critique, in *Società e lavoro*, 139–40.

98. *Misthos*-"salary," *misthos*-"honor": see Benveniste 1969, 1:163–66; I am not sure that one has to seek, as Benveniste has done, to establish the historical precedence of one meaning over the other: see Ed. Will, "Notes sur *misthos*," in *Mélanges Claire Préaux* (Brussels, 1975), 426–38. The construction of the wall of Troy, by Poseidon and Apollo, for Laomedon, is *aethlos* in 7.452–53, the work of a thete for a *misthos* in 21.444–45 (see Mele's comments, which see this, like all the occurrences of *misthos*, as a later addition: A. Mele, *Società e lavoro*, 37); for the same Laomedon, Herakles will accomplish an *aethlos* with a problematic reward (*Iliad* 5.650).

99. Pindar *Olympians* 10.29 (on the *misthos* of Augeas, see also Pausanias 5.1.9–10, and Athenaeus 10.412e); on the complicated relationship between *misthos* and *athlos*, in the matter of the Augean stables, see Jourdain-Annequin 1985, 500–504.

100. Pindar, *Isthmians* 1.47–53, with the commentary in Svenbro 1976, 175.

101. Aristotle *Rhetoric* 1.9.1367a32.

102. Xenophon *Memorabilia* 2.1.21; see also Diogenes Laertes 6.71 (Herakles, the hero of liberty for Diogenes). An evolution clearly seen by C. B. Kritzas, "Héraklès *Pankamès*," 111–12.

103. On the thete, see A. Aymard, "L'Idée de travail dans la Grèce archaïque," 33; Finley 1978, 87; A. Mele, *Società e lavoro*, 132–33; in the *Eudemean Ethics* (7.2.1245b39), Aristotle makes Herakles a thete.

104. Apollodorus 2.5.5. The power of the new orthodoxy (that dooms Herakles to refusing the *misthos*: see again Diodorus 4.14.1–2): even when the action occurs outside the sphere of *athloi* and could be rewarded, the promised *misthos* is refused: Apollodorus 2.5.9.

105. If he had been, "he is no longer" (Jourdain-Annequin 1985, 517).

106. Diodorus 4.23.1. An element that is important as it is controversial in Greek therapeutics (cf. J. Bertier, *Mnésithée et Dieuchès* [Leiden, 1972], 102–12; for Stoic criticism, see M. Vegetti, "Passioni e bagni caldi. Il Problema del bambino cattivo nell'antropologia stoica," in *Tra Edipo et Euclide. Forme del Sapere antico* [Milan: Il Saggiatore, 1983], 71–90, nn. 28–86): warm baths treat excessive fatigue (*Regimen* 85.2) and are specifically associated with athletics (Pindar *Olympians* 12.18). On Herakles and warm baths, see the documents in Ginouvès 1962, 362–65.

107. *Clouds* 991 and 1044–52; see Ginouvès 1962, 135, 216–17, 362. It will be noted that Prodikos is targeted by name in the *Clouds* (l. 361).

108. An earlier version of this chapter was published in *Annali dell'Istituto Orientale di Napoli. Archeologia e Storia antica* 4 (1982): 171–92. In addition to the thanks that I owe Claude Lévi-Strauss and Maurice Godelier, who invited me to reflect on representations of work in Greece, I wish to express my gratitude to Marie-Henriette Quet and Colette Jourdain-Annequin, who have both read these pages with care.

CHAPTER THREE
THE SPARTANS' "BEAUTIFUL DEATH"

1. I first used this phrase in the original version of this chapter (published in *Ktèma* 2 [1977]: 105–20)—the literal translation of *kalos thanatos*, to be sure, and for this reason it occupies a place in the study of the Athenian funeral oration (Loraux 1981a); however, now it has almost achieved the status of a *topos* in many studies.

2. Loraux 1981a, 98–118.

3. On the paradoxes of "La Traduction de l'hoplite athénien," see Vidal-Naquet 1981, 125–49.

4. Herodotus 7.104 (first dialogue between Xerxes and Demaratus): *menontas en tēi taxei epikrateein ē apollusthai*; see also 9.48.

5. Thucydides 4.40.1.

6. This is the case of Plato in book 1 of *Laws*, as has been observed by E. N. Tigerstedt, *The Legend of Sparta in Classical Antiquity*, vol. 1 (Lund, 1965), 51. For a discussion of the ancient tradition, see C. Prato, *Tyrtaeus* (Rome, 1968), intro., 1–4.

7. Lycurgus *Contra Leocrates* 107.

8. See Detienne 1968.

9. Tyrtaeus 6–7 (Prato), 31; 8.11; 9.33–34; Herodotus 7.209.

10. Tyrtaeus 8.3; Herodotus 7.220. The *Sayings of Spartans* provide a maximalist version of this precept (Plutarch *Moralia* 234e).

11. Tyrtaeus 8.3: Herodotus 7.102, 209, and passim. For a historical application of this precept, see Xenophon *Hellenika* 1, 6, 32–33 (death of Kallikratidas in Arginusae).

12. See Thucydides 4.40.1.

13. Tyrtaeus 6–7, 1–2: "For it is beautiful to die, fallen in the front line as a man of courage, fighting for his country." For the hoplitic interpretation of the Homeric *eni promakhoisi*, see Prato, *Tyrtaeus*, intro., 1–4.

14. My comments pertain to Tyrtaeus 9.23–24. We know that only the Spartans who have died in battle had the right to a stele bearing their name, with the indication "in warfare" (Plutarch *Lycurgus* 27.3); see above, chap. 1.

15. Jeanmaire 1939, 489.

16. Herodotus 7.234: "they all are like those who have fought here" (Demaratus's answer). Perhaps Xerxes' question was intended to emphasize the difference in value between the simple *homoioi* and the chosen corps of *hippeis*: even in exile, Demaratus remains enough of a good Spartan to deny the existence of such a difference.

17. Thucydides 4.40.2: *apistountōn mē einai tous paradontas tois tethneōsin homoious*.

18. Schwartz's correction, accepted by Tigerstedt, *Legend of Sparta*, 147. Ehrenberg (1936, 2295) rightly rejects this reading, which flattens the text. Indeed the context indicates that the problem is that of the beautiful death as a criterion of value in a war of a non-hoplitic type (see the Spartan's answer that Erhenberg [ibid.] wrongly interprets as proof that the Lacedaemonian ideal has weakened). It will be further observed that Thucydides implicitly refers to Hero-

dotus's account of Thermopylae: Sphacteria is a derisive reminder of Thermopylae (4.36.3), and the Spartan's aphorism evokes, in ironic counterpoint, that of Dienekes (Herodotus 7.226).

19. On bravery as a criterion of citizenship, see Thucydides 4.126.1 (Brasidas's speech).

20. I retain the expression but modify it, recalling the complexity of the functioning of *philotēs* within the group of epic fighters: see Slatkin 1988.

21. Cf. Prato, *Tyrtaeus*, 21–22.

22. See ibid., regarding 9.31 (*kleos*); Jeanmaire 1939, 52–53; Finley 1978, 79ff., 112–16; Detienne 1967, 18–24; Nagy 1979, passim.

23. Tyrtaeus 8.5–6: on the maximalism of this formulation, which raises a challenge to the funeral oration, see Loraux 1981a, 99–100. See as well Tyrtaeus 8.5–6 (*mē philopsukheite*) and the *Sayings of Spartans* 210f. (Agesilaos). On the hoplitic *sōphrosunē*, see Detienne 1968, 122–23.

24. Herodotus 9.71: *lussōnta, boulomenon phanerōs apothanein.* Cf. 7.220. It may be compared to the anecdote Plutarch gives in *Agesilaos* 34.

25. Tyrtaeus 6–7, 27–30. See Prato's comments and those of W. J. Verdenius, "Tyrtaeus 6–7D. A Commentary," *Mnemosyne* 22 (1969): 337–55 (and esp. 338ff.), as well as C. R. Dawson, "*Spoudaiogeloion*," *Yale Classical Studies* 19 (1966): 34ff. The two meanings, ethical and aesthetic, are in fact inextricably bound, and *kalon tethnamenai* (l. 1) is echoed by *kalos d'en promakhoisi pesōn* (l. 30). But, as in *Iliad* 22.72–76, which is a model for this development, it is necessary to stress the gap separating the representation of one who has *died beautifully*, whose body is inherently invested with hoplitic, even sexualized values, and the ideology of the beautiful death, where the bodies vanish in a highly elaborate process of abstraction: on this point, Vernant 1982 (= 1989, 41–79) does not sufficiently stress the difference because the "beautiful death" is not an Iliadic concept.

26. Xenophon *The Constitution of Sparta* 9.3; Plutarch *Lycurgus* 21.2 (and 25.3).

27. Tyrtaeus 8, 13–16; Xenophon *The Constitution of Sparta* 9.1 and 6; Plutarch *Lycurgus* 21.2.

28. Herodotus 7.232; 9.71; Xenophon *The Constitution of Sparta* 9.4. See again Tyrtaeus 8.14; Thucydides 5.34.2; Plutarch *Agesilaos* 30.

29. Ehrenberg 1936, 2,292–93.

30. Xenophon *Cyropaedia* 3.3.52–53.

31. The theme of the *despotēs nomos* is the subject of the first conversation between Xerxes and Demaratus (Herodotus 7.102–4).

32. Likewise Ehrenberg 1936, 2296.

33. *Aidōs*: the feeling of one's duty to oneself within a code of values; *aiskhunē*: "shame." On *aidōs* see Tyrtaeus 6–7.12, and the comments by Prato, *Tyrtaeus*, intro., 1–4, as well as Thucydides 1.84 (Arkhidamos's speech). In Sparta *aidōs* is a *habitus*.

34. A Spartan saying makes legislation on courage an unwritten law (*Moralia* 221b–c).

35. Herodotus 7.228. Antiquity clearly understood when the orator Lycurgus glossed *rhēmasi* as *nomimois. Contra Leocrates* 109. W. W. How and J. Wells, *A*

Commentary on Herodotus (Oxford, 1912), gloss *rhēmasi* as *rhētrais*, which would effectively make the hoplitic requirement into a "law," since in Sparta laws are referred to in the form of a *saying*. On *rhēmasi* as "laws" rather than "orders," Ehrenberg 1936, 2292, and Tigerstedt, *Legend of Sparta*, 105 (the latter thinks, however, that the word is deliberately kept ambiguous). It would probably be best, as Pierre Vidal-Naquet has suggested to me, to keep with a translation of the term as "maxims" or "precepts."

36. Loraux 1981a, 105–10.

37. Tyrtaeus 6–7, 29–30; here the beautiful life passes before the beautiful death.

38. Tyrtaeus 9.35–42: the beautiful life of the victor. For these brave fighters' access to *gerousia*, see Prato, *Tyrtaeus*. Prato interprets *en thokoisin* as an allusion to *proedria*. In any event, note should be made of a custom that on the contrary obliges the *tresantes* to yield their places to the younger ones: only a lapse of bravery can overturn the immutable order of age classes.

39. Xenophon *The Constitution of Sparta* 9.6.

40. Tyrtaeus 8.11–14. Here I follow the commentary and translation (slightly modified) of these lines by P. Mourlon-Beernaert, "Tyrtée devant la mort," *Etudes classiques* 29(1961): 391–99.

41. E.g., *Iliad* 5.529–32 (Agamemnon's harangue to his troops): "Friends, be men (*andres*). Have a valiant heart. *Have a sense of shame for each other* (*aidesthe*) in the course of the hard fighting. When warriors have the sense of shame (*aidomenōn andrōn*) among them, many more are saved than are killed. On the contrary, if they flee, there is no glory for them, no help either." See also 15.563–64. On this type of harangue, see Slatkin 1988.

42. Tyrtaeus 9.1–2 [v. n.40, above]. Prato, *Tyrtaeus*, saw the likeness between Tyrtaeus 8.13 and this text.

43. On *xunon esthlon* (9.15), Detienne 1967, 90.

44. Of the type, "Viva la muerte!" The Falangist general Milan Astray addressed in 1936 these frightening words to Miguel de Unamuno. Despite some passing resemblances (in the 1930s), Sparta does not display any of this sort of fascination.

45. Plutarch *Lycurgus* 20.14 (= *Sayings of Spartans* 224c; see also *Sayings of the Kings and Generals* 190b, on the subject of Brasidas).

46. Herodotus 7.104; in fact, it is a question of "winning or disappearing." Cf. *Sayings of Spartans* 218b (Ariston to an orator who was pronouncing the *epitaphios* of the Athenians who died fighting against Lacedaemon: "Which do you think then are ours, who defeated them?").

47. Tyrtaeus 8.9.

48. Tyrtaeus 9.36: *nikēsas*.

49. Cf. Ehrenberg 1936, 2294.

50. Plutarch *Lycurgus* 20.13 (= *Sayings of Spartans* 217f). Tyrtaeus even goes so far as to compare the dead who were wounded in the back to the *tresantes*, a maximalist (or epic) attitude that his followers did not emulate (8.19–20; see the remarks in Ehrenberg 1936, 2294).

51. Lekhaion: Xenophon *Hellenika* 4.5.10 (it will be noted that the relatives behave *hōsper nikēphoroi*: this detail is interesting, for in a competition the essen-

tial is to win); Leuctra: *Hellenika* 6.4.16 (see also 7.1.30). On the particularly "political" behavior of *mothers* in Sparta, see Napolitano 1985, 37–38.

52. Grote thought that this was true in the case of Lekhaion, based on Xenophon *Hellenika* 4.5.14 (Ehrenberg 1936, 2296). But it is not certain that he is not confusing Xenophon's ethical judgment on the behavior of those who flee with the effective reaction of the Spartan city. The case of Leuctra (Plutarch *Agesilaos* 30) is more disturbing: if it were necessary to manipulate the laws to save the survivors from disgrace, wouldn't the inclination toward defeat degrade them all?

53. Cf. Tyrtaeus 8.4 and 24; *Sayings of Spartans* 220a. See Detienne 1968, 119ff.

54. *Sayings of the Spartans* 241f.

55. Ehrenberg 1936, 2294, concerning Thucydides 4.12.1.

56. Ehrenberg 1936, 2296–97.

57. If the analyses of J. Ducat ("Le Mépris des hilotes," *Annales ESC* [Nov.-Dec. 1974]: 1451–64) are correct, the Spartans needed buffoons, and the *tresantes* were likely also to have played this role, with the difference being that even though they are degraded, they are still considered citizens.

58. Cf. G. Busolt, *Griechische Staatskunde* [3rd ed. (Munich: Beck, 1963–72)], 2:659. For integration into the collectivity, it will be recalled that Aristodamos, although degraded, fought in the Spartan contingent in Plataea.

59. Thucydides 4.38.3: *mēden aiskhron poiountes.* Tigerstedt sees in this an exhortation to die in battle (*Legend of Sparta*, 147). If they only wish to incite the hoplites to find an honorable compromise, the Spartans misjudge the Athenians' obstinacy. Perhaps the ambiguity of the answer corresponds to a real hesitation over the meaning of *nomos*?

60. Thucydides 4.41.3; 5.18.7 and 24.2. Why? To recover human capital, essential for Sparta under this circumstance? To cast a shadow over the men who dishonor the city?

61. Diodorus 12.76; Thucydides 5.34.2. As Ehrenberg (1936, 2295) remarks, in Thucydides matters seem to be presented in reverse; ordinarily it is degradation and not fear of degradation that nourishes revolutionary thought (cf. Plutarch *Agesilaos* 30); but in addition to the fact that for Thucydides fear is an essential motive for human actions, the Spartan attitude could be explained by the strength of *aiskhunē* in the Lacedaemonian collectivity (see Xenophon *Hellenika* 3.3.11: Cinadon's plot, motivated by the desire "to be inferior to no one in Lacedaemon"). Therefore it would perhaps be better to sanction an anomaly by tangible punishments than to permit the increase of remorse and shame, fermenters of the dissolution of the social body.

62. Herodotus 9.53ff. Amompharetos refuses to make a strategic retreat in the name of fidelity to the hoplitic commandments, taken in their most narrowly literal sense.

63. In a work of fiction such as the *Cyropaedia* (3.3.44–55), the two reasons are separated, and one is attributed to each camp, with the enemies inheriting the utilitarian version; in reality things are less simple.

64. See for example Thucydides 2.39 (Pericles' *epitaphios*), with the commentary in Vidal-Naquet 1981, 133.

65. Xenophon *The Constitution of Sparta* 13.5: *toi onti tekhnitas tōn polemikōn*.

66. Herodotus 9.62–63 (the Lacedaemonians' *sophiē*).

67. Herodotus 7.211; cf. Plato *Laches* 191c.

68. Cf. How and Wells, *Commentary on Herodotus*, *ad* 9.53–57; A. Dascalakis, "Les Raisons réelles du sacrifice de Léonidas et l'importance historique de la bataille des Thermopyles," *Studi clasice* 6 (1964): 57–82, and esp. 62–63 (many examples of a Spartan army's strategic retreat during the Persian wars); J.A.S. Evans, "The Final Problem at Thermopylae," *Greek, Roman and Byzantine Studies* 5 (1964): 231–37, and esp. 232.

69. Xenophon *Hellenika* 4.8.38–39: death of Anaxibios.

70. Herodotus 7.139; see the comments of Tigerstedt, *Legend of Sparta*, 84.

71. Plutarch *De malignitate Herodoti* 864a–b. Moreover, the pro-Athenian bias is real here, as in 9.54.

72. Cf. Tigerstedt, *Legend of Sparta*, 96, 97, 100, and 105.

73. Herodotus 7.220: *boulomenon kleos katathesthai mounōn Spartiēteōn*.

74. Lysias *Epitaphios* 23–24; see Loraux 1981a, 159, and, on the rivalry between Marathon and Thermopylae, R. W. Macan, *Herodotus. The Seventh, Eighth, and Ninth Books* (London, 1908), regarding 7.224 (*xiphesi*).

75. Herodotus seems moreover to indicate himself that this is the best explanation of the fight (7.220). Perhaps the oracle is, as Dascalakis thinks ("Raisons réelles," 59–61), the *Delphic* version of the matter, but this is not absolutely obvious, and the two explanations—the beautiful death and the royal *devotio*—were not necessarily mutually exclusive.

76. Herodotus 7.209, which here will be compared with Tyrtaeus 8.21–25. See as well 8.202.

77. Herodotus 7.210: Xerxes hopes that the Greeks will flee (*apodresesthai*) without doing battle; on the fifth day, his hopes are dashed; 211: since the first assault of the Medes has failed, the Immortals enter the arena but have no more success; 212: the following day, new Persian hopes, which are answered, on the Greek side, by the most perfect order (*kata taxin*).

78. Herodotus 7.210: *anaidiēi kai abouliēi diakhreōmenoi*; 212: *hate oligon eontōn*. See as well 103–4.

79. Herodotus 7.213.

80. Ephialtes' cupidity: 213; Spartan desire for glory: 220 (*kleos mega eleipeto*).

81. 7.215–17, 223.

82. 7.225.

83. 7.225–26ff.

84. 7.175–77.

85. 7.177.

86. 7.211. This type of calculation is not related to hoplitic morals, to be sure, but it would not be out of place in Homeric epic: e.g., Lycurgus the Arcadian killing Areithoös "by trickery and not by force, in a narrow road where his mass of iron was no help to him against death" (*Iliad* 7.142–44). I owe this comparison to a suggestion made by Marcel Detienne.

87. 7.211.

88. Ibid.

89. The distance can be measured between the Spartan beautiful death and its

Athenian homologue: technicians of war, the Spartans, "strong by nature," display their military knowledge, while throughout their funeral orations, the Athenians show only their bravery (the *topos*: *epideiknusthai tēn aretēn*).

90. The exception is the mention of Leonidas's death, which is perfectly hoplitic: *piptei anēr genomenos aristos* (7.224).

91. 7.223: *hōs tēn epi thanatōi exodon poieumenoi*. See the commentary in Legrand (Hérodote: *Histoires, livres 1–9* [Paris: Les Belles Lettres, 1946–60], 225) and that of Macan, *Herodotus*, which makes a judicious comparison with 3.114, where *exodos* refers to, among other things, a cortege of condemned men led to their execution.

92. 7.223.

93. Ibid.

94. 7.224. For the use of swords as a last resort in hoplitic battle, see Tyrtaeus 8.30 and Prato's commentary, *Tyrtaeus*.

95. 7.225. The sword has already substituted for the lance; fighting with their hands, the Spartans now have only the elementary resources of men in their natural state; finally, reduced to using their teeth, they enter a state of animality. It will be observed that the *agōgē* is not unfamiliar with this type of savage battle, since all holds were permitted to the *agōnes* of the Platanist and the Limnaion altar, including scratches and bites (see Jeanmaire 1939, 514, 518).

96. Cf. Aristophanes *Lysistrata* 1254ff. When he speaks of Leonidas's Spartans as "boars sharpening their defenses," is Aristophanes influenced by Herodotus's account? Or is he thinking of the fights between boars that took place in the Plataniston (Pausanias 3.14.10)?

97. Compared to a boar battling against Polyneices the "lion" (e.g., Euripides *Suppliants* 134–46), in epic as in tragedy Tydeus is the very type of the terrible warrior: cf. Vian 1968, 65ff. and the portrait of Tydeus in Aeschylus's *Seven Against Thebes* (377–94).

98. It is pointless to think that a complement to the verb *parakhreōmenoi* is implied (7.223); used absolutely, this verb indicates much more than indifference to life or death—indifference to *everything* (see comments by Macan, *Herodotus*).

99. *Ateontes* (7.223) is a *hapax* in Herodotus, as it is in Homer, from whom this word is taken (*Iliad* 20.332); in the Homeric context *ateōn* is a synonym for *lussōn*.

100. On the *lussa* of the terrible warrior, Detienne 1968, 121–23.

101. Aristodamos did not flee the beautiful death; he fled *death* (Herodotus 7.229).

102. See Tigerstedt, *Legend of Sparta*, 100 and n. 777.

103. Compare Herodotus 7.225 and *Iliad* 17.274ff.

104. I take this term from Hesiod who, in *Works and Days*, describes the deaths of the men of the Bronze Age in this way (154–55).

105. Are there three hundred or three hundred plus an indeterminate number of chosen men? The text is conjectural (Herodotus 7.205), with several possible interpretations: on the multiple problems that it poses, see Macan's commentary (*Herodotus*), where he cautiously concludes that Herodotus did not understand the phenomenon of the *logades*. If one adopts the lesson of many manuscripts (*epilexamenos andras te tous katesteōtas triēkosious kai toisi etugkhanon paides eontes*),

one is tempted to conclude that Leonidas brought the group of *hippeis* with him, adding to it certain fathers of families. But if one accepts that in 224, when the historian mentions the Three Hundred, he is referring to the entire Spartan corps, one must come back to the correction adopted by Legrand (*epilexamenos andras te tōn katesteōtōn Triēkosiōn*); in this case, Leonidas would have replaced those of the *hippeis* who had no offspring with other Spartan soldiers. But to speak then of a "composite" troop (G. Hoffmann, "Les Choisis: Un ordre dans la cité grecque?" *Droit et cultures* 9–10 [1985]: 17) seems quite exaggerated to me, for the group of the Three Hundred is obviously the vital kernel of the Spartan corps.

106. The Spartans of Thermopylae are fathers of families, and this will doubtless be seen as the sign of close bonds that unite "fatherhood and military value" (see the contribution of A. Aymard, *Revue des Etudes Latines* 33 [1955]: 42–43 and the remarks of Garlan 1972, 65). But this detail is also an integral part of the legend of Thermopylae: can't it be read *after the fact* as the sign of a vocation for death?

107. On the "chosen ones," see the evidence gathered by Detienne 1968, 134ff.

108. In the front lines: in Delion (Diodorus 12.70.1: the Theban chosen ones, Drivers and Soldiers, are *promakhoi*); in a retreat, three hundred elite soldiers with Brasidas (Thucydides 4.125.3).

109. Cf. Pausanias 8.39.3–5 and 41.1 (the chosen Oresthasians doomed to complete extinction for the salvation of Phigalia) and 9.36.2 (the chosen Argives fallen to the last man with their leader while fighting against the Phlegyans).

110. Herodotus 9.64.

111. Herodotus 1.82. On this episode, see Brelich 1961, 22–34 and Detienne 1968, 135–36. On the disdain for life among the chosen ones, another interesting indication will be found in Diodorus 12.79.6–7 (the Thousand of Argos).

112. Unlike the Argive survivors who left the battlefield (which the Lacedaemonians liken to flight), Othryadas remained at his post, and, as Macan observes in his comments on 7.232, he has no reason to reproach himself; but what is true from a hoplitic standpoint is likely not the same from an equestrian perspective, and this is how his shame must be viewed.

113. Isocrates *Peace* 143 believes that this law applies to all Spartans; but see Ehrenberg 1936, 2295.

114. Ehrenberg 1936, 2295 and, on the "warriors' guild," Jeanmaire 1939, 97–107.

115. As in an *agōn*, the mass of the army has withdrawn, leaving only the champions to face the enemy, since 1) reinforcements have not come; 2) the allies have left.

116. Herodotus 7.224–25: the death of Leonidas, perfectly hoplitic to the extent that he embodies the entire city (as H. R. Immerwahr clearly saw in *Form and Thought in Herodotus* [Ann Arbor, Mi., 1966], 260ff.), takes place in the middle of the description of savage battle. After making tribute to civic glory, the historian then continues the narrative of the battle.

117. On "the exceptional situation of the horsemen in the midst of the Spartan *demos* and the type of reserve that set them apart even in death," Jeanmaire 1939, 546 (and, more generally, 542–50).

118. Herodotus 7.208–9; cf. Aristotle *Rhetoric* 1.9.1367a27–31 (in Lacedaemon long hair is a fine thing).

119. According to the expression in How and Wells, *Commentary on Herodotus*.

120. Xenophon *The Constitution of Sparta* 11.3 (and 13.8).

121. Tacitus *Germania* 38.4: *in altitudinem quamdam et terrorem adituri bella*.

122. On the "effects of hair," see Vernant 1985, 42–45, as well as, concerning the hairstyles of the Abantes, D. Fourgous, "Gloire et infamie des seigneurs de l'Eubée," *Métis* 2, 1 (1987): 5–29 nn. 9–13; on the hair of the young and the horse's mane: Georgoudi 1986, 227.

123. On all this, see Detienne 1968, 124, and J. Grüber, *Uber einige abstrakte Begriffe des frühen Griechischen* (Meisenheim, 1963), 15–38.

124. Plutarch *Cleomenes* 8.3.

125. *Iliad* 2.443 and 472; 3.43.

126. Herodotus 1.82; like Xenophon, Plutarch *Lycurgus* 22.2 and *Lysander* 1 attributes the origin of this practice to Lycurgus.

CHAPTER FOUR
THE WARRIOR'S FEAR AND TREMBLING

1. *Iliad* 22.90–375. The quotations are based, occasionally with modifications, on Paul Mazon's French translation [Paris: Belles Lettres, 1937–38] (Budé).

2. *Iliad* 3.33–37.

3. *Iliad* 2.188–270.

4. *Iliad* 11.345.

5. Ajax, the best of the Achaians; after Achilles, of course (*Iliad* 2.768). See Nagy 1979, 26–41.

6. *Iliad* 20.262.

7. *Iliad* 5.859–63. See Loraux 1986c, 349.

8. *Iliad* 24.671–72.

9. *Iliad* 21.281–83.

10. *Iliad* 13.275–86.

11. Regarding the Spartan *tresantes*, see above, chap. 3, pp. 64, 68–69.

12. *Iliad* 14.522.

13. *Iliad* 8.163–64.

14. *Iliad* 11.409–10.

15. *Iliad* 13.222–25, with commentary by Slatkin 1988.

16. *Iliad* 13.470–82.

17. The primary meaning of *phobos* is "flight," "fear" being only a secondary meaning (Chantraine 1968, s.v.).

18. J.-P. Vernant, "L'Autre de l'homme: La Face de Gorgō," in M. Olender, *Le Racisme. Mythes et sciences* (Brussels: Complexe, 1981), 141–55 (quotation, 143); see also Vernant 1985, 39–46.

19. *Iliad* 13.298–300.

20. *Iliad* 5.738–42.

21. The serpent in the simile (called *drakōn*: *Iliad* 22.93) is likewise characterized by its gaze (*smerdaleon dedorke*). It is true that the etymology of the word

drakōn connects it with the verb *derkomai*, which denotes an intense and piercing gaze: see Chantraine 1968, s.v. *derkomai*). On Agamemnon's shield the Gorgon is *deinē derkomenē* (11.36–40).

22. *Iliad* 3.342.

23. *Iliad* 7.206–17.

24. *Iliad* 5.831, 839; see Loraux 1986c, 347–48.

25. *Iliad* 8.349.

26. The figure of the epic warrior has been traced by Dumézil (e.g., 1969); see also Vian 1968, Daraki 1980. On the warrior and fear, hearing and sight, Vernant 1985, 40–43.

27. See below, chap. 5, p. 14.

28. See Loraux 1987, 114–16.

29. *Iliad* 22.123–24.

30. Such a reading, along with its application of psychoanalytic theory, is particularly American: see A. W. Gouldner, *The Hellenic World* (New York: Harper and Row, 1980), 60, using Hector's soliloquy to lead into a discussion of Greek homosexuality; a more nuanced reading in J. M. Redfield, *Nature and Culture in the "Iliad": The Tragedy of Hector* (Chicago: University of Chicago Press, 1975).

31. *Oaros, oaristus* associated with Aphrodite's cortege: *Iliad* 14.216 and Hesiod *Theogony* 205; Hector and Andromache: *Iliad* 6.516; *promakhōn oaristus*: *Iliad* 13.291 (and 17.228). The erotic connotation of these words is primary: Chantraine 1968, s.v. *oar*.

32. *Iliad* 13.291.

33. Hector and Achilles' "rendezvous": there are many more references with multiple textual echoes that, along with *oarizein/oarizemenai*, delicately ally the dreams of encountering the enemy with his tender meeting with Andromache in book 6. See Vermeule 1979, 145–77 ("The Pornography of Death," which did not come to my attention until after I had written this article), and Monsacré 1984, 63–77.

34. *Iliad* 13.131: *menōn*.

35. See for example Nagy 1979, 121–22, 178n. 4.

36. For the condemned hero, it is the fleeting vision of a world that is "normal and full of life" (Segal 1971, 41). It will be added that the brilliant garments, once a symbol of marriage, become in the last lines of book 22 a useless funerary adornment for Hector's body (see Bouvier 1987).

37. *Iliad* 22.157–59.

38. Quotation, taken from J.-P. Vernant [in M. Olender, *Le Racisme*], "Gorgō," 151 (regarding the bond that links the ghost to the murderer).

39. See above, chap. 2, p. 55.

40. *Iliad* 22.189–93.

41. Vidal-Naquet 1981, 167.

42. *Ptōssein* marks a contrast with combat carried on far in front of the lines (*Iliad* 4.370ff. and 5.252).

43. *Iliad* 20.426–27.

44. *Iliad* 22.29.

45. *Iliad* 22.199–201.

46. Swift Achilles: Nagy 1979, 327–30. This gives a better measure of the dimensions of the Eleatic paradox of Achilles and the tortoise.

47. On Ares, the killer of heroes in the last example: Nagy 1979, 294–95.

48. Meaningful like many Homeric names (regarding the name Aeneas, for example, in *Iliad* 13.481–82, the play on the words *ainōs/Aineian* will be noted), the name Deiphobos refers to the one "who routs his enemies" or "routs in battle" (Chantraine 1968, s.v. *phobos*). In 12.94 Deiphobos was "like the gods": expert in disguises, Athena of course has no difficulty taking on his appearance.

49. See Slatkin 1988.

50. *Iliad* 22.282–84.

51. *Iliad* 22.306–11.

52. *Iliad* 16.350.

53. Compare Bacchylides *Epinician* 5.56–85 to *Odyssey* 11.601–2.

54. In an inscription from the fifth century B.C. (R. Meiggs and D. Lewis, *A Selection of Greek Historical Inscriptions to the End of the Fifth Century* [Oxford: Blackwell, 1969], no. 38).

55. Plutarch *Life of Cleomenes* 8.3.

56. The Spartan use of the flute has been amply discussed by the ancients: from a tactical standpoint by Pausanias (4.8.11) but more generally from an ethical perspective (here one sees the search for order and serenity on the part of the attacking army: Plutarch *On the Control of Anger* 458e, Aulus Gelius *Attic Nights* 1.11, who, quoting Thucydides and the *Problemata* of Aristotle, speaks of "musical discipline"). If the flute calms excitement, it can also, in the context of *lussa*, unleash it (Vernant 1985, 55–61), and as always in Sparta, the line between hoplitic order and epic frenzy is maintained.

57. Herodotus's edifying story of Aristodamos will be recalled (see above, chap. 3).

58. Plutarch *Life of Theseus* 27.2.

59. Plutarch *Life of Alexander* 31.9: in the ensuing battle, the terrifying Alexander indeed routs the bravest of his enemies (33.6); another text by Plutarch (*Moralia* 343d–e) compares Alexander to Phoibos, in the context of martial fright: Phoibos-Apollo . . . or Phobos in person?

60. Except for a few slight changes, this chapter is a version of the article published in *Traverses* 25 (1982; issue on fear): 116–27.

CHAPTER FIVE
THE WOUNDS OF VIRILITY

1. On the display of scars as proof of the warrior's valor, see for example Livy 6.14.6, and esp. Cicero *De oratore* 2.124 and 195–96 (trial of M. Aquilius). This action, made illustrious by the orator M. Antonius, is furthermore considered by Quintilian to be ridiculous (*Institutio oratoria* 6.3.100). I am offering a too-brief summary of a rich and complex matter through which Yan Thomas helped to guide me. Concerning the exhibiting of wounds, see his article "Se venger au forum. Solidarité familiale et procès criminel à Rome," in R. Verdier and J.-P. Poly, eds., *La Vengeance*, vol. 3 (Paris: Ed. Cujas, 1984), 71–72.

2. Not only do the dead appear in the *Aeneid*—in dreams (2.278–79) or in the Underworld (e.g., 494–97, as well as 446 and 450)—riddled with wounds, but a reading of Livy shows that scarred wounds are a kind of decoration for the soldier: e.g., 6.14 and 20.7–8, as well as Aulus Gelius 2.11.

3. See J. Boulogne, "Le Sens des *Questions romaines* de Plutarch," *Revue des études grecques* 100 (1987): 471–76.

4. Here I am referring to the analyses made by Georges Dumézil, which have shed considerable light on the figure of the warrior and the second Indo-European function; for more details concerning Coriolanus, see Dumézil, *Mythe et épopée*, vol. 3 (Paris, 1973), 253–56; and, on Indo-European names for the male, *Idées romaines* (Paris, 1969), 225–41; and *La Religion romaine archaïque* (Paris, 1974), 217–18.

5. Plutarch *Life of Coriolanus* 14.2 (on the custom see also, for a more general view, *Roman Questions* no. 49, 276d); 15.1 (Coriolanus's scars). A man of bravery is never "naked" if he is equiped with a spear and a shield (Plutarch *Moralia* 245a), but Coriolanus does not even need weapons, for he is able to make his body into a weapon (*Life of Coriolanus* 2.1), and his scars are yet another weapon.

6. Shakespeare, *Coriolanus* 2.3; on bloodshed "meaning personal value," see *Macbeth* 1.2, with the comments of R. Marienstras, *Le Proche et le lointain* (Paris: Minuit, 1981), 131–32; Coriolanus and virility: see the remarks made by A. Lercercle-Sweet, in *Théâtre public* 49 (1983): 50–55.

7. In the Hellenistic period, the situation is completely different: see for example the inscription made for a physician from Kos who, during a war and a *stasis*, treats the wounded (*traumatiai*) of the city.

8. See Loraux 1981a, 25–26. There is still another difference with respect to Rome, which throughout its history seems to have been concerned with treating the wounded; however, the passages in Livy (2.16 and 47) quoted by G. Majno (*The Healing Hand. Man and Wound in the Ancient World* [Cambridge, Mass., 1975], 381–82) as documentation bear a strong resemblance to edifying anecdotes.

9. Leonidas: Herodotus 7.224 (see as well 6.114; Kallimakhos at Marathon); Plataea: 9.212; Pythia: 7.181 and 8.92.

10. In Greek eyes the inscription on the body can even be a mark of subjugation, as among the Scythians (Herodotus 4.71, with comments in Hartog 1980, 157–61), or an instrument of Pisistratus's tyrannical treachery (1.159).

11. See for example *Iliad* 2.543–44 and 17.363, 497; Pindar *Nemean* 4.33.

12. Ares, the ultimate killer: Nagy 1979, 293–95; Ares among the dead: *Iliad* 15.117–18; Ares wounded by Athena (and Diomedes): 5.855–63 (and Herakles [Hesiod] *Shield* 359–67, 461). See Loraux 1986a.

13. Nevertheless, one time a mortal seems to have wounded Athena in the thigh: see Pausanias 8.28, Clement of Alexandria *Protreptika* 2.36.2; C. Vellay (*Légendes du cycle troyen* [Monaco, 1957], 243) gives all the references concerning this strange story.

14. Pindar *Nemean* 8.28ff. The scholiast thinks that the heat arises from the inflammation of the wounds, but in a Greek tradition of which Aristotle is the spokesman, men's "warm" bodies are frequently contrasted with those of women, which are characterized by coolness: see Lloyd 1983, 100–101, and Héritier 1984–85, 13.

15. Ajax's invulnerability: Pindar *Isthmian* 6.46ff. (and the bibliography in C. Vellay, *Légendes du cycle troyen*, 115 and 265–66; Achilles' invulnerability: ibid., 116); Ajax, the best after Achilles: *Iliad* 2.768–69, *Odyssey* 11.469–70, Alcaeus fr. 387 Campbell, Pindar *Nemean* 7.26–29.

16. See Starobinski 1974, 28; what turns Ajax against himself is *alkē*, the soldier's active strength in action against the enemy (Pindar *Isthmian* 4.35).

17. In suggesting that the soldier sheds others' blood, unlike virgins who hang themselves in order not to shed their own blood (King 1983, 120; see also 1987, 120), one would be forgetting a bit too quickly that the soldier is esteemed because he sheds *his own blood* (Héritier 1984–85, 20).

18. C. Daremberg, *La Médecine dans Homère*, 10–11; G. Majno, *The Healing Hand*, 145; M. D. Grmek, *Les Maladies à l'aube de la civilisation occidentale* (Paris: Payot, 1983), 50–60.

19. *Iliad* 13.322–23; Pindar *Isthmian* 3.18; *Iliad* 21.566–70.

20. *Iliad* 4.539–44. It will be noted that it is precisely Athena who is capable of endowing a man with invulnerability, in fictional time. A comparison with the *Mahābhārata* is tempting, in which the battle is treated as a narrative in book 6.2. The narrator, far from being a fictive character, as in the *Iliad*, is quite real, but he is a *sūta*, a mixture of Brahmin and *kṣatriya*: faced with the blind man Dhṛtārāṣṭra's refusal to accept the gift of "seeing" the battle, Sanjaya becomes the one who will tell the story of the battle; seeing all, even the thoughts of the combatants, he "will not be wounded by weapons and will remain unaffected by fatigue" (from the French trans. by J.-M. Péterfalvi); on the character's invulnerability, see Biardeau 1986, 14.

21. Clement of Alexandria *Protreptika* 2.32.1.

22. It will be recalled that *alkē*, "strength," is first of all "protection": see J. Jouanna, "Sens et étymologie de *alea* and *alkē*," *Revue des études grecques* 95 (1982): 15–36.

23. *Odyssey* 11.506–37. It will be recalled that the warriors of the *Iliad*, beginning with Achilles, weep copiously; see Monsacré 1984, 137–48.

24. *Iliad* 8.533–58; 5.118–20.

25. *Iliad* 12.387–91.

26. Diomedes is struck by an arrow in books 5 and 11, Odysseus in book 11. Glaukos's harsh wound: 16.516–26; it is true that, *karteron*, it exerts a force (*kratos*) on the hero that he would prefer to turn against the enemy (524).

27. On Agamemnon's pains in book 11, see above, chap. 1, pp. 35–36. On the "charged" character of the word *odunē*, see Mawet 1979, 38–54.

28. Daremberg, *La Médecine dans Homère*, 75; this detail also characterizes the paintings of the classical era that were influenced by the epic: see Pausanias 10.25.5–6.

29. *Iliad* 13.291; *oaristus*: see above, chap. 4, p. 81.

30. *Iliad* 24.419–21.

31. *Iliad* 13.339–40, 23.803, 13.499–501, 16.760–61 (to confine ourselves to a few examples).

32. Compare *Iliad* 22.218 and 23.176.

33. *Dateomai*: 22.394 (the body torn apart by the chariot), 23.354 (dogs and birds "dividing" Hector's body).

34. *Iliad* 17.522; note that, in his rage, Achilles even dreams of tearing Hector's body limb from limb: 22.347, 24.409.

35. For Pindar (*Dithyramb* 7), the death of warriors is a sacrificial offering; in Aeschylus's *Agamemnon*, it is a sacrifice without fire to the Erinyes (lines 70–71, with commentary by J. Bollack).

36. On the silence Detienne and Vernant (1979) observe regarding sacrifice and war, I refer the reader to "La Cité comme cuisine et comme partage," *Annales ESC* 36 (1981): 614–22.

37. The verb *epigraphō* is then used: *Iliad* 4.139, 11.387, 13.552–53, 17.599, 21.166.

38. *Iliad* 4.139 (Menelaus's blood as purple dye: 140–47); see also 11.387, 13.552–53, 17.599, 21.166. Note that only *Greek* heroes are grazed in this way by the Trojan warriors, whose insignificance as opponents is thus indicated.

39. *Iliad* 11.348.

40. *Iliad* 4.509–11 (quoted, like other passages from the *Iliad*, from the French translation by P. Mazon, Belles Lettres [1937–38]). *Tameein khroa*: e.g., 16.761; note that for Pindar the enemies' "warm flesh" is, in the Homeric mode, "warm skin."

41. *Iliad* 11.818.

42. Ares: *Iliad* 5.858, 21.398; Hector: 11.352, 22.321; arrows and white skin: 15.313–17; Ajax: 11.573 (white skin), 13.830 (desirable skin, comments by Segal, *The Theme of the Mutilation of the Corpse in the Iliad* [Leiden, 1971], 9 and 22); Monsacré 1984, 60, 65; 14.406 (tender skin).

43. Vermeule 1979, 102–5, as well as Vernant, 1989, 131–52.

44. With Ares, one is convinced this is so (Loraux 1986c).

45. *Iliad* 17.49, 18.177, 22.327.

46. M. D. Grmek, *Les Maladies à l'aube de la civilisation occidentale*, 55.

47. *Iliad* 19.284–85.

48. See below, chap. 6.

49. Lloyd 1983, 63–64.

50. In their way, the Baruya of New Guinea do the same when they tell that the bodies of women were first closed, before the Moon, the Sun's brother, pierced their sex to make menstrual blood flow from the opening: to make the feminine body function, nothing less than surgical intervention is needed: see Godelier 1982, 68.

51. Héritier-Augé 1984–85, 20.

52. Sissa 1987, 181–82; see also Manuli 1983.

53. Vermeule 1979, 119.

54. An earlier version of this chapter appeared in *Le Genre humain* 10 (1984: issue on the masculine): 39–56.

Chapter Six
The Strangled Body

1. Plutarch *Lycurgus* 15, 17–18.

2. *Pasa te idea katesthē thanatou* (death takes all forms), writes Thucydides on the subject of the massacres at Corcyra (3.81.5); therefore not even the horror of

stasis will be depicted in graphic terms, and the fact of death is more important than the explanation of the forms that it takes, even if they are aberrant.

3. See the remarks by Gernet 1917, 112, and Chantraine 1949, 146. As an example, recall that in Athens the function of the Eleven is given simply as to "put to death" (Aristotle *Constitution of Athens* 52.1: *thanatōsontas*).

4. Chantraine 1949, 143, 145–47; other examples of euphemism: "Euphémismes anciens et modernes," in Benveniste 1966, 312–14.

5. Chantraine 1949, 143.

6. Gernet 1917, 232.

7. For example, Plutarch's account of the death of Agis (*Agis* 20): Agis presents his neck to the noose, and then one sees only the corpse stretched out on the ground (20.4); Amphares gives Arkhidamia over to the executioner, thereafter she is referred to only as dead (20.3); the reader sees the two bodies through the eyes of Agesistrata, after which Agis's mother, having paid homage to the dead, "rises to move toward the noose" (20.7), and with this act the scene ends. This concordant series of ellipses is meaningful in an account that claims to be dramatic and detailed. On the subject of all these Greek accounts of death by strangulation, one can make the same comment that J.-L. Voisin made on the subject of Amata's suicide ("Le Suicide d'Amata," *Revue des Etudes latines* 57 [1979], 258): only the preparations for death are mentioned.

8. Cf. Herodotus 4.71–72 (execution of the Scythian king's servants) and 4.60 (Scythian sacrifice): in both cases the verb *apopnigō* is used.

9. Sacrifice presupposes the spurting of blood; lacking which, it must be interpreted as anomalous: see, concerning Hermes' sacrifice in the *Homeric Hymn*, Kahn 1978, 43, 58–59.

10. *Agkhonē* as suicide by hanging: see Euripides *Andromache* 816; *Hippolytus* 777 and 802; *Helen* 200 and 299; as a model for suicide: Semonides of Amorgos 1.18.

11. *Eumenides* 746 (*nun agkhonēs moi termat' ē phaos blepein*); Orestes condemned by the Athenian judges' vote could either kill himself or be put to death. *Oedipus Rex* 1374 (*erg' esti kreisson' agkhonēs eirgasmena*): are these misdeeds for which one hangs oneself, like Jocasta, or for which one is strangled? The first hypothesis is more consistent with the logic of the text (see Loraux 1986b, 37–39), the second is not absolutely impossible.

12. Doubtful case: Aristophanes *Acharnians* 125 ("Isn't there, in truth, something needing hanging?/ Doesn't it deserve the rope?") and Euripides *Heracleidae* 246; sure case: Euripides *Bacchae* 246 (and fr. 1070 Nauck², where *agkhonē* borders on lapidation). *Andragkhos dēmios, ho tous andras agkhōn*: gloss cited by Chantraine 1968, s.v. *agkhō*).

13. D. M. MacDowell, *The Law in Classical Athens* (London, 1978), 254–55; same list, earlier on, in R. J. Bonner and G. Smith, *The Administration of Justice from Homer to Aristotle*, vol. 2 (Chicago, 1938), 278–87.

14. *Kremannumi* (usually employed with regard to hanging) is applied by Aristophanes in a context of *apotumpanismos* (*Thesmophoriazousae* 1028 and 1053); see also Sophocles *Antigone* 309. Bibliography and documents in Bonner and Smith, *The Administration of Justice*, 2:280–82, and M. Hengel, *Crucifixion*, Engl. trans. (London, 1977), 69–73. Strangulation of the condemned by an iron

collar: Bonner and Smith, *The Administration of Justice*, 280–81 (but the authors also speak of "hanging"), as well as MacDowell, *The Law in Classical Athens*, 255, and *Athenian Homicide Law* (Manchester, 1963), 111–13. On execution by asphyxiation in "crucifixion," see also P. Ducrey, *Le Traitement des prisonniers de guerre dans la Grèce antique* (Paris, 1968), 208–13, and "Note sur la crucifixion," *Museum Helveticum* 28 (1971): 183–85.

15. Herodotus 2.169 (Egypt); 3.150 and 159 (Babylon); 4.160 (death of the tyrant Arkesilaos): all examples of the verb *apopnigō*, used in 4.60 to describe the Scythian sacrifice; on this "aberrant" form of execution, Hartog 1980, 194–95.

16. Callisthenes' death by hanging: Plutarch *Life of Alexander* 55.9 and Arrian *Anabasis* 4.14.3 (the alternative: death by hanging/death in shackles could however suggest a type of *apotumpanismos*); the deaths of Indian "philosophers" (Brahmans) by hanging: Plutarch *Life of Alexander* 59.8. Plutarch again: *Demetrios* 33.5 (but this is a swift execution in the context of war). More official evidence is found in Macedonia for lapidation, which is used to punish traitors: cf. P. Ducrey, *Le Traitement des prisonniers de guerre*, 206n.1.

17. Strabo 6.1.8: *estraggalisan*.

18. Demosthenes *Contra Timocrates* 139–41; Diodorus 12.17–18; Polybius 12.16; Stobaeus *Anthology* 4.20–21. See Glotz 1904, 460.

19. Glotz cites only Plutarch's text in support of this statement (s.v. *Poena*, in Daremberg and Saglio, *Dictionnaire des antiquités grecques et romaines*, vol. 4, no. 1 (vol. 7), 535, and K. Latte, s.v. *Todestrafe*, in *Real-Encyclopädie* [Pauly-Wissowa], suppl. 7, 1940, col. 1609.

20. Should the suicide by hanging of Pantites, one of the two survivors of Thermopylae (Herodotus 7.229) be considered a Spartan form of execution by hanging, in which the punishment meted by the city on those it condemns is carried out by the dishonored soldier himself? A vicious circle: the answer to this question presupposes that the data on Spartan executions is not confined to a *hapax*.

21. Here Plutarch takes as his subject the tragic story of Phylarkhos: see E. Gabba, "Studi su Filarco. Le biografie plutarchee di Agide e di Cleomene," *Athenaeum* 35 (1957): 194 and 220, as well as T. W. Africa, *Phylarchus and the Spartan Revolution* (Berkeley and Los Angeles, 1961), 43 and 82n.58. Note that 1) from beginning to end strangulation looms large in the account of Agis's death (19.4 and 8); and 2) Plutarch stresses the disparity between this ignominious death (20.1) and the untouchable status of the king's body (19.9).

22. Voisin 1979, 429.

23. On hanging as a "form of strangulation" among the Germanic tribes, see K. von Amira, "Die germanische Todesstrafen," *Abhandlungen der Bayerischen Akademie des Wissenschaften. Philosophisch-philologische und historische Klasse* 31, 1 (Munich, 1922): 94–98.

24. Hanging: Polybius 12.16 (where the noose is "hung"). Strangulation: Diodorus 12.18 (to die suffocated by the noose); see as well Demosthenes *Contra Timocrates* 139 and Stobaeus *Anthology* 4.44.21: *epipathentos tou brokhou* (the rope that Phaedra used to hang herself is likewise *epispastos*: Euripides *Hippolytus* 783).

25. Suffocation: Plutarch *Agis* 19,9 (*apopnigontes*); strangulation: 20.1 (*strag-*

galēn); the hanged body and how it is treated: 20.4 (*ek tou brokhou kremanenēn sugkatheile*); see also 20.7.

26. Strangulation: K. Latte, "Todesstrafe," col. 1609. P. Cloché, "Remarques sur les règnes d'Agis et de Cléomène," *Revue des Etudes grecques* 56 (1943): 69. Hanging: P. Oliva, *Sparta and Her Social Problems* (Amsterdam-Prague, 1971), 229. G. Glotz ("*Poena,*" 535) speculates that Sparta "strangled or hanged" those it condemned to death. The effort to distinguish between the two practices has a long history, as can be attested by a gloss from the *Suda* which, although lacking a linguistic basis, claimed to establish a distinction between *agkhonē*, "hanging," and *agkhonē, "the noose."

27. Aristophanes is an exception when he adds, in the *Frogs*, the stool (*thranion*) to the ever-present rope: 121–22. Can this detail be explained by the freedom allowed in comedy?

28. Euripides *Hippolytus* 767–71 and 777; Plutarch *Moralia* 253d–e.

29. See Loraux 1985, 52–53.

30. Pausanias 8.23.6, as well as Clement of Alexandria *Protreptika* 2.38.3. However, see King 1983, 118–20, who pleads the case for a "strangled" Artemis but makes this epiclesis into something of a natural epithet for the goddess.

31. Thus Alciphron (*Letters* 3.49) makes no distinction between *kremēsomai* and *straggalisō ton trakhēlon*.

32. See M. Leumann, "Schwer erkennbare griechische Worter im Latein," *Die Sprache*, vol. 1 (1949) [Festschrift Havers], 205.

33. Herakles and the lion of Nemea: Euripides *Herakles* 154 (*agkhonē*; see also Aristophanes *Birds* 1375 and 1378, and *Frogs* 468, where Herakles overpowered Cerberus by grasping his throat, a hold termed *agkhōn*). Sons strangling their fathers: Aristophanes *Clouds* 1385, *Ecclesiazousae* 638–40, *Birds* 1348–52.

34. J. Bayet, "Le Suicide mutuel dans la mentalité des Romains," in *Croyances et rites dans la Rome antique* (Paris, 1971), 135, and n. 4; see also A. Bayet, *Le Suicide et la morale* (Paris, 1922), 297–99.

35. Hippocrates, *On the Diseases of Girls*, Littré 8, 468. *Pnigō* meaning "to drown": see Chantraine 1968, s.v. Recall that *apopnigō* commonly refers to strangulation. Thus, by common reference to suffocation, Greek thought likens two types of death that other civilizations, based on the idea that "likeness creates structure," see as radically distinct: on the opposition between drowning and hanging in the Saga of Hadingus, see G. Dumézil, *Du mythe au roman* (Paris: PUF, 1970), 128 and 136–38.

36. Compare *Aphorisms* 2.43 and *On the Sacred Disease* 1 and 7.

37. *Frogs* 122 and, more generally, 117–25.

38. See the scholia *ad loc.* and *Suda*, s.v. *Pnigos* and heat: see Aristophanes *Clouds* 96, 1054 (Socrates suffocating in the fire of the "thinking-house"), *Wasps* 511, *Birds* 726, 1001, 1091; Plato *Phaedrus* 258c7 and 279b4, *Republic* 10.621a3, *Laws* 11.919a4; Aristotle *Meteorologies* 2.5.316b27 and esp. *On Breathing* 478b (where the link is made between heat and suffocation).

39. See below, chap. 8.

40. See Hippocrates *On Sicknesses* 1.21 and esp. *On Places in Man* 27. Is it by excess of cold and a desire for warmth that young people resort to *agkhonē* during

attacks of melancholy ([Aristotle] *Problemata* 30.1.955a9–10)? See Pigeaud 1988, 126–27 and n. 62.

41. Voisin 1979, 432–35; on prohibiting burial: ibid., 424–27 and "Le Suicide d'Amata," 259–60.

42. *Odyssey* 22.467 and 473.

43. Plutarch *Agis* 20.4.

44. Phaedra has a close relationship with *aiora* (suspension *and* balance): see Pausanias 10.29.3.

45. Euripides *Hippolytus* 780–89. "To stretch": *ekteinō*, twice (786, 789), the meaning of which must be distinguished from *orthoō* ("to straighten out" the body that has been deformed by hanging); note that Plutarch uses the same verb to describe the movement of Agesistrata (*parekteinasa*). "As is due a dead person": in the *hōs nekron* of line 789, note is taken of Phaedra's death; but furthermore one must certainly see it as the recognition of her state in death.

46. For "at least a minimum of rites": L. Gernet, on the subject of those tortured by *apotumpanismos* ("Sur l'exécution capitale," in Gernet 1968, 329).

47. Although the difficult matter of *aiora* deserves its own systematic study, see for the moment R. Martin and H. Metzger, *La Religion grecque* (Paris, 1976), 127–28, and the articles by C. Picard (*Revue archéologique* 28 [1928]: 47–64, B. C. Dietrich (*Hermes* 86 [1961]: 36–50), and J. Hani (*Revue des Etudes grecques* 91 [1978]: 107–22).

48. Chantraine 1968, s.v. *aeirō*. *Artēsai et apartēsai derēn*: for an example, see Euripides *Andromache* 412 and 811.

49. Aeschylus *Agamemnon* 875.

50. Euripides *Helen* 299: *agkhonai metarsioi*; *Alcestis* 229–30: *brokhōi ouraniōi*; *Hippolytus* 769–70: *kremaston brokhon* (see also 779 and 802, and *Orestes* 1305–6), as well as Sophocles *Oedipus Rex* 1266 (*kremastēn artanēn*).

51. Sophocles *Oedipus Rex* 1263–64.

52. See the commentary by Hesychius (s.v. *mē men dē katharōi thanatōi*): "Death by hanging is not pure, but pure is the death that is given by the sword; hence, not even sacrifices for the dead are made for those who are hanged."

53. *Odyssey* 22.443, 462, 472.

54. Plutarch *Agis* 21.1.

55. Rome: Voisin 1979 (426). Greece: Plutarch *Themistocles* 22 (the nooses and clothing of the hanged are thrown into the Barathron), with commentary by J. Bayet, "Le Suicide mutuel," 135n.3.

56. Euripides *Helen* 298–300; Sophocles *Antigone* 54.

57. Epicaste: *Odyssey* 11.279; daughter of Mykerinos: Herodotus 2.131; tragic suicides: *Helen* 200–202 and 686, as well as Neophron, fr. 3 Nauck[2]; Pantites' hanging: Herodotus 7.232; the last resort: Diogenes Laertes 6.86 (Krates).

58. Thucydides 3.81.3 and 4.48.3.

59. See for example Aeschylus *Suppliants* 788; Euripides *Hippolytus* 769–71, 779, 802 (with the gloss by Hesychius: *brokhos-agkhonē*), *Andromache* 844; Neophron, fr. 3 Nauck[2] (*brokhōton agkhonēn*); Plutarch *Agis* 20.1.4.7. In an apocalyptic text, even *brokhisai heauton* is found (*Oxyrhynchus Papyri* 850.6).

60. Quotation from Detienne and Vernant 1974, 49; on the "complicity of the bond and the circle": 290.

61. *Haptō*: *Odyssey* 11.278; Semonides 1.18; Aeschylus in *Oxyrhynchus Papyri* 2161.1.14; Sophocles *Antigone* 1222; Euripides *Hippolytus* 769, 802, *Helen* 136, *Orestes* 1306, *Bacchae* 545, 615.

62. *Odyssey* 11.278 (suicide), 22.472 (execution); Herodotus 4.160 (Scythian sacrifice); Aristophanes *Birds* 572 (bird trap; on *brokhos* in the hunter's vocabulary, see as well Oppian *Cynegetica* 1.151, 2.24, 3.258, 4.448). It is interesting to compare the various uses of the word *brokhos* within one tragedy, ranging from hanging to imprisonment to hunting, whether real or metaphoric: see for example Euripides *Andromache* 844, 502, 506, 720, 996.

63. *Agkhonē* as the trap formed by Herakles' arms: Euripides *Herakles* 151–54; *deragkhē* as a trap for birds: *Palatine Anthology* 6.109.

64. Lasso: Herodotus 7.85 (barbarian's weapon), Thucydides 2.76.4 (weapon of the besieged). Clytemnestra's net of death: Aeschylus *Choephoroi* 557 (cf. Lykophron *Alexandra* 110); in Euripides, three striking instances of *brokhos* as deathtrap: *Andromache* 995–96 (*mēkhanē peplegmenē brokhois*), *Electra* 154 (where the image of the swan weeping for its dead father entangled in the folds of a treacherous net combines with the vocabulary of hunting and an allusion to Agamemnon's death), *Bacchae* 1022.

65. *Odyssey* 22.486–72.

66. F. Robert, "Le Supplice d'Antigone et celui des servantes d'Ulysse," *Bulletin de correspondance hellénique* 70 (1946): 501–5 (quotation, 503).

67. *Hippolytus* 758–63; 828–29.

68. On the bird and aerial themes as metaphors for flight, suicide, and the soul's flight in tragedy, see Aeschylus *Suppliants* 786–803, and Euripides *Andromache* 862 (with comments of H. Parry, "The Second Stasimon of Euripides' *Hippolytus* (732–75)," *Transactions of the American Philological Association* 97 (1966):317–26; in *Helen* hanging is *metarsios* (a doublet for *meteōros*; recall that for Aristophanes *meteōros* denotes the universe of birds: *Birds* 690, 818); the *kremastos* noose and the bird: see R. Padel, "Imagery of the Elsewhere: Two Choral Odes of Euripides," *Classical Quarterly* 24 (1974): 232; last, the *brokhos epispastos* from *Hippolytus* 783 recalls the braided ropes of lines 762–63.

69. A "feminine" death: even when a man hangs himself; in this sense, hanging is a death with feminine overtones. But it is also a woman's death—of adolescent girls and women. There is an obvious distance between the discourse of myth and religion, where it is essentially adolescent girls who hang themselves, and tragedy, where this type of death is first of all that of wives (with the exception, a remarkable one at that, of Antigone: see "La Main d'Antigone," *Métis* 1 [1986]: 165–96). Perhaps it is a sign of the literary elaboration of shared traditional representations.

70. Ariadne: Plutarch *Theseus* 20.1; Kharila: Plutarch *Greek Questions* 293d–f; Erigone, etc. (for other examples, see W. Burkert, *Homo necans* [Berlin, 1972], 77 and n. 26).

71. *On the Diseases of Girls* 8 Littré, p. 466; epidemic of hangings in Miletus: see Plutarch *Virtues of Women* 11.249b–d, with commentary by E. DeMartino, *La Terre du remords*, French trans. (Paris, 1966), 224–26 and 231.

72. See Detienne and Vernant 1974, 279, and E. DeMartino, *La Terre du remords*, 239.

73. On the feminine girdle: Schmitt 1977.

74. Sophocles *Antigone* 1221–22; Aeschylus *Suppliants* 457–65. A functionalist commentary like that of Whittle (*ad* 160: "hanging is particularly easy to a woman, since it requires no more than a normal article of clothing") is a bit abrupt and must be developed by the comments of the same Whittle (*ad* 458) on the transforming of the weapons of weakness into instruments of strength.

75. See Loraux 1985, 31–60.

76. When he learns of Patroclus's death, Achilles must be protected from the temptation to "slit his throat with a blade" (*Iliad* 18.34). The most famous of suicides by the sword is Ajax. Whether chosen (suicide) or accepted (in the beautiful death), this death is always noble: Euripides *Orestes* 1060–61. See as well above, chap. 1, pp. 41–42.

77. For Euripides *brokhos* is usually contrasted with *sphagē* or the verb *thēgō* and its derivatives. See also Plato *Critias* 119e1: the sacrificial hunts carried out by the kings of Atlantis are carried out *aneu sidērou . . . brokhois* (without resorting to iron, with lassos).

78. Plato *Sophist* 220b–c, which can be compared to Euripides *Electra* 154–55 (*doliois brokhōn herkesin*).

79. Plutarch *Agis* 21.1–3.

80. See Oppian *Cynegetica* 4.448–53 (*brokhos* and *dolos* glossed by *anaimōti*, "without shedding blood"). On hanging as a way to avoid bloodshed or the tearing of rape, see Aeschylus *Suppliants* 787–90 (to be compared with 798, where the husband is *daiktōr*, "tearer").

81. Voisin 1979, 428.

82. In a work that remained long unpublished, even when the first version of this study was in preparation, Louis Gernet discusses the matter ("Le Droit pénal de la Grèce ancienne," in Y. Thomas, ed., *Du châtiment dans la cité. Supplices corporels et peine de mort dans le monde antique* [Rome-Paris, 1984], 27), relating this "notable particularity" to "certain very ancient prohibitions." The impressive list of bloody tortures found in the *Eumenides* 186–90 does not derive from a realistic reading but must be seen in light of the nature of the bloodthirsty Erinyes.

83. J. Bayet, "Le Suicide mutuel," 173n.1; see also "Le Rite du fécial et le cornouiller magique" [also in *Croyances et Rites*], 27n.4.

84. Ernout-Meillet, *Dictionnaire étymologique de la langue latine* (Paris: Klincksieck, 1985), s.v. *sanguis* and *cruor*.

85. This involves focusing on a few great strands of an idea and not on the differences and specificities of successive systems, presented with relevance by Manuli and Vegetti 1977.

86. On *haima*, see Chantraine 1968, s.v., and H. Koller, "*Haima*," *Glotta* 15 (1967): 149–55.

87. Plutarch *Moralia* 468c. More complicated, but instructive as well, would be the study of the semantic field of *stragx* (the liquid drop expressed under pressure, with effort), which also gives rise to the vocabulary of strangulation (*straggalē*, *straggalizō*; cf. *strang*, word for "rope" in Old High German), as well as words for the retention of urine (*straggouria*) or the surgical instrument used to draw blood (*straggeion*): see Chantraine 1968, s.v.

88. On *angina* as an ancient borrowing of the Greek *agkhonē*, see Ernout-

Meillet, *Dictionnaire étymologique de la langue latine*, s.v., and M. Leumann, ["Schwer erkennbare griechischer Worter,"] 204–6. In the Hippocratic corpus the word for "angina" is *kunagkhos*.

89. Hippocrates *On Places in Man* 30.

90. See above, chap. 5, 92.

91. The verb *daizō* which, in *Odyssey* 14.434 refers to the division of the meat made at the sacrifice, is frequently used in the *Iliad* to express the tearing inflicted on the warrior's body by bronze.

92. The most powerful example is that of *Ajax*, where after his suicide the hero is termed a "freshly slaughtered victim" (898: *artiōs neosphagēs*); but beforehand he had insisted that his son be able to withstand the sight of the fresh blood of the animals he had just slaughtered without trembling (545–49: *neosphagē phonon*): the animal in place of the man, the sacrifice to express murder (and, more generally, in this passage, the warrior's behavior), the polysemy is at its height.

93. A universe of representations awaiting exploration: it would also be appropriate to question the character of death by the sword (and thus by the shedding of blood) postulated in *Odyssey* 22.462 as "pure" by definition.

94. See Sissa 1987, 180–87.

95. Aristotle *History of Animals* 3.19.520b18–20 and 521a21–23. Perhaps, already in the *Iliad* the "black" blood is contained within the body or considered in its relationship to the body, while shed blood is generally red; thus it is too simple to see *melan haima* as "deep red" blood, which is what F. Rüsche does, on Eustathius's authority, in *Blut, Leben und Seele* (Paderborn, 1930), 42.

96. Aristotle *History of Animals* 7.1.581b1–2 (*haima hoion neosphakton*). On this comparison, which would be a commonplace based on the connections between the first woman and the first sacrifice, see King 1987. It will be observed elsewhere that menstrual blood is sometimes referred to as *katharsis*, and, along with Giulia Sissa who suggested it to me, I am inclined to think that this "purification" is derived, like the "pure" death of the *Odyssey*, from the high value placed on blood that flows.

97. Hippocrates *On the Diseases of Women* 1.72 (Littré 8, p. 152): *khōreei de hoion haima apo hiereiōn*.

98. Hippocrates *On the Diseases of Girls*, Littré 8, pp. 466–67; see King 1983, 177, who, however, emphasizes strangulation and not hanging.

99. The "desire" expressed by the verb *boulomai* (see also *On Places in Man* 39.1 for the desire to hang oneself) is irresistible in that it arises out of shackled nature, and one must take care not to confuse it with "voluntary death by hanging," which in the *Saga of Hadingus* is "the Odinic death *par excellence*" (G. Dumézil, *Du mythe au roman*, 51 and 127).

100. Hippocrates *On the Diseases of Women* 2.177 (Littré 8, p. 360): *kai pnigetai kai thanein eratai*.

101. Uterine suffocation is the principal "disease" of women: see *On the Diseases of Women* 1.2, 3, 7, 8, 32 (*apopnigomai*), 55; 2.124, 125, 126, 128, 130, 177, 200, 201, 202, 203, as well as Aristotle *Generation of Animals* 719a21. See Manuli 1983, 154–62.

102. Giulia Sissa has developed a model for this in *Le Corps virginal* (Sissa 1987).

103. See Hippocrates *On the Diseases of Women* 1.7 (the respiratory tract, which is in the belly); 2.128 (two suffocations: *anō, katō*); 2.169 (*trakhēlos* as the neck of the uterus); 2.202 (postulates direct circulation, from the loins to the head; 3.230 (*stoma, aukhēn* of the womb).

104. The opposition between rope and sword is essentially tragic; but Louis Gernet has taught us how to find the traces of evolving juridical thought in the tragedies.

105. A widespread dichotomy (see Héritier-Augé 1984–85: as well as Godelier 1982, 158, 200, on the hunt of the cassowary, an animal-woman whose blood humans find it repugnant to shed) but one that is not orchestrated in every civilization in the same manner. One only need mention the way that Draupadi's "impure" menstrual blood prefigures the warriors' bloodshed in the "great combat" in the *Mahābhārata* (Biardeau 1985, 220–22).

106. An earlier version of this chapter was presented in November 1982 at a roundtable discussion organized at the Ecole française de Rome by Michel Gras and Yan Thomas and published in Y. Thomas, ed., *Du châtiment dans la cité. Supplices corporels et peine de mort dans le monde antique* (Rome-Paris, 1984), 195–218. The present chapter has benefited from my ongoing dialogue with Yan Thomas concerning the "body of the citizen."

CHAPTER SEVEN
HERAKLES: THE SUPERMALE AND THE FEMININE

1. The quotation from U. von Wilamowitz sums up the meaning of the deeds of Herakles for the Dorian male (*Euripides Herakles* (1888: rpt. Darmstadt, 1969) 2:41; I have utilized the translation from Henri Weil, *Journal des Savants* (1890): 203; the quotation from T. Wiegand, *Didyma* II, Berlin (1958), 301, is a comment on inscription no. 501.

2. See, most recently, W. Burkert, *Structure and History in Greek Mythology and Ritual*, Berkeley and Los Angeles 1979, 79, 83, 96, who refuses to gather under the rubric of "Herkales" the shifting play of differences in the tales of the hero. But the Greek mythographers had already attempted to resolve the difficulty by postulating the existence of several Herakleses: e.g., Pausanias 9.27.8, as well as the description of Elis, where Herakles is often identified as "the Theban" or "the son of Amphitryon" (5.13), in contrast to other Herakleses (5.8, 25; 6.23).

3. Dumézil 1969, 89–94: Dumézil 1971, 117–24, as well as *Mariages indo-européens* (Paris: Payot, 1979), 60–65, and *L'Oubli de l'homme et l'honneur des dieux* (Paris: Gallimard, 1985), 71–79.

4. Starobinski 1974, 26, 17.

5. See above, chap. 2, pp. 53–56.

6. The archaic period does, of course, know of instances of identification with Herakles: this is the case with Milon of Croton (see Detienne 1960); but it is primarily from the time of Alexander that the phenomenon of identification will develop, down to the Roman emperor Commodus, and beyond.

7. Cited from Burkert 1977, 322 ([English trans.]1985, 210); on tears and invincibility: Slater 1971, 342.

8. G. S. Kirk, "Methodological Reflexions on the Myths of Heracles," in Gentili-Paioni 1977, 286.

9. Athenaeus 12.512e, cited by H. Licht, *Sexual Life in Ancient Greece*, 3d ed. (London, 1949), 9–10 (the hot baths connected with his name make Herakles a hero of pleasure). As sire and patron of hot baths at the same time, Herakles is caught in yet another contradiction; the Hippocratic treatise *On Sterile Women* 218 (Littré 8, p. 423) actually proscribes hot baths for the man who wishes to beget a child.

10. *Iliad* 8.362–65; Aeschylus *Prometheus Unbound* fr. 199, Nauck²; Lykophron *Alexandra*, 31ff.

11. Excess of force: Diodorus 4.9.2 (*huperbolē*), discussed by Dumézil 1971: 118; on the *biē hēraklēiē* and the identity of Herakles, see Nagy 1979: 318; ambivalence of force: Nagy 1979: 86.

12. On the melancholy of Herakles: Aristotle *Problemata* 30.1, with the commentary of Pigeaud 1988; Plutarch *Lysander* 2; Lucian, *Dialogues of the Gods* 15.237; see H. Flashar, *Melancholie und Melancholiker in der medizinischen Theorien der Antike* (Berlin, 1966), 37, 63–64, and Pigeaud 1981, 407–9 (on the sickness of Herakles in that it "expresses quite simply the intensity" of the hero who is himself an "allegorical emphasis"). Bile, a manly trait, and women: Aristophanes *Lysistrata*, 463–64.

13. Slater 1971, 339, 377.

14. On the fifty virgins: the daughters of Thespios (or Thestios), deflowered in one, five, or fifty nights (Pausanias 9.27.5–7, Athenaeus 13.556e–f, Diodorus 4.29, Apollodorus 2.4.10 and 2.7.8; *philogunēs*: Athenaeus, ibid.

15. See Athenaeus 6.245d. Play on *Omphale/omphalos*: already in classical literature (Ion *Omphale* fr. 20, Nauck; Kratinos *Omphale* fr. 177, Kock); see the remarks of Delcourt 1955: 149.

16. It is appropriate to recall here that Herakles is *philogunēs*, especially in mythology; in cult he appears "connected much more frequently to youths," and Hellenistic tradition will spell out his homosexual adventures: Jourdain-Annequin 1986 (291–93).

17. Herakles *misogunēs*: Plutarch *On the Oracle of the Pythia* 20; on the exclusion of women in the cult of Herakles, see L. R. Farnell, *Greek Hero Cults and Ideas of Immortality* (Oxford, 1921), 162–63 and on the taboo at Thasos *oude g[u]naiki themis* (*SEG*, II, 505), the remarks of C. Picard, "Un Rituel archaïque du culte d'Héraklès thasien trouvé à Thasos," *Bulletin de correspondance hellénique* 47 (1923): 241–74.

18. Apollonius of Rhodes *Argonautica* 1.853ff. In Apollonius, Herakles is homosexual and the lover of the boy Hylas.

19. The sons of Herakles are listed by Apollodorus (2.7.8); the daughter of Herakles (born to be sacrificed: Pausanias 1.32.6) is mentioned by Aristotle as an oddity (*History of Animals* 7.6585b 22–24), to the greatest joy of Wilamowitz, *Herakles*, 80n.153.

20. Two Herakleses, a misogynist and a husband: M. Launey, "L'Athlète Théogène et le *hieros gamos* d'Héraglès thasien" *Revue archéologique* 18 (1941) 49; the marriage pattern in the life of Herakles: G. Dumézil, *Mariages indo-européens*, 60–

63; thus in Bacchylides (*Dithyramb* 16.29), Iole is designated as *alokhos*, legitimate spouse.

21. On his servitude to Omphale: Sophocles *Trachiniae* 248–57; Plutarch *Theseus* 6.6; Clement of Alexandria, *Protreptika* 2.30. On Herakles as bride (groom): see Pollux 7.40 and the commentary on the comic fragments of Nikokhares, *Hēraklēs gamōn*, in Kock's edition.

22. On Herakles under the yoke: Ovid *Heroides* 9.5–6, 11–12, etc.; Herakles under a gynecocracy: A. B. Cook, "Who Was the Wife of Zeus?" *Classical Review* 20 (1906): 365–78 (gynecocracy of Hera); K. Tümpel, article "Omphale," in W. H. Roscher, *Lexikon der griechischen und römischer Mythologie* (Leipzig, 1902), 3.1. col. 870–87 (on Omphale/Hera).

23. See Plutarch, *Pericles* 24.9, discussed by Tümpel, "Omphale," cols. 876–78.

24. See K. Kerényi, *The Heroes of the Greeks* (London, 1959), 192–201.

25. Delcourt 1955, 139; 1942, 13, 88, 100.

26. On Omphale assimilated to Hera: Tümpel, "Omphale"; to the great chthonic goddess: L. Deroy, "*Omphalos*. Essai de sémantique évolutive," *Ziva Antika* 24 (1974): 3–36, nn. 31–34; to the Asiatic Great Goddess: J. G. Frazer, *Attis and Osiris* (= *The Golden Bough*, 3d ed. [New York and London, 1935], 6:258); to the snake demoness: J. Fontenrose, *Python* (Berkeley and Los Angeles, 1959), 108–10. On Deianeira: Slater 1971, 344; W. Pötscher, "Der Name des Herakles," *Emerita* 39 (1971): 170.

27. Slater 1971, 344. As evidence of the ravages of the impulse to assimilate, see Slater, who legitimates his undertaking by reference to Freud but at this point refers to Graves, who is influenced by Jung.

28. Xenophon *Memorabilia* 2.2.21.

29. On Herakles, youth, and the initiatory passage, see Jourdain-Annequin 1986.

30. See above, chapter 1.

31. On the athletic, rather than the warrior, aspect of the phenomenon, there is also a purely medical interpretation: see G. Maloney, "Contributions hippocratiques à l'étude de l'*Orestie* d'Eschyle," in F. Lasserre and P. Mudry, eds., *Formes de pensée dans la collection hippocratique* (Geneva: Droz, 1983), 71–76, who in commenting on *Agamemnon* 1000–1003 ("Exultant health surpasses its limits, comes so near disease its neighbor so as to breach the wall between them") cites *Aphorisms* 1.3 ("Among athletes, a state of health taken to extremes is dangerous").

32. *Mania/menos*: this association pervades the work of Dumézil, particularly his thoughts on the warrior; on infanticide as a woman's crime: Euripides *Herakles* 1016–24, with the remarks of Daladier 1979.

33. Diodorus 4.11.2; Euripides *Herakles* 1214–15, 1159, 1198, 1205.

34. *Le Surmâle* (Paris: Fasquelle, 1953), chap. 12; in chap. 1, the defloration of the fifty daughters of Thespios is recalled.

35. As André Green observes, "Les Pensées d'Oedipe," *L'Ecrit du temps* 12 (1986): 120.

36. I attempted to demonstrate this with reference to myths of origin (Loraux 1981b).

37. We must distinguish, along with Slater (1971, 289–90), between figures

who, like Dionysos, take refuge in femininity and those who, like Zeus, incorporate the feminine within themselves: Zeus absorbs femininity without ever becoming feminized.

38. This field was opened up by M. Detienne; see "Violentes Eugénies," in Detienne and Vernant 1979.

39. Starobinski 1974, 27.

40. On the qualities of the *gastēr*, see Vernant, "A la table des hommes," in Detienne and Vernant 1979: 94–96, 105. In a wholly different context, Roman law reduces the entire woman to a "belly" (Thomas 1986, 213).

41. Loraux 1981b, 84–86.

42. See esp. Epicharmos *Busiris*, fr. 21 Kock (the spectacle of Herakles dining), as well as *Pholos* fr. 78 Kock; Archippos *Hēraklēs gamōn*, frs. 9–11 Kock; Kratinos *Busiris and Omphale*, frs. 176–77 Kock; Alexis *Linos*, frs. 135, 18 (*boulimos*). A tragic echo of this theme: Euripides fr. incert. 907 Nauck², and *Ion*, fr. 29 Nauck². This gluttony is described at length by Athenaeus (9–10.411a–b).

43. See Athenaeus 10.412a and Pausanias 5.5.4; on Herakles Bouthoinas in Lindos and the story of Theiodamas, see J.-L Durand, "Le Boeuf, le laboureur et le glouton divin," *Recherches et documents du Centre Thomas Moore* 22 (1979): 1–17, and *Sacrifice et labour en Grèce ancienne. Essai d'anthropologie religieuse* (Paris-Rome: La Découverte/Ecole française de Rome, 1986), 149–73.

44. On Olympus, this hunger is paradoxical; in contrast to Herakles, that other bastard son of Zeus, Hermes, gives up eating meat in spite of his hunger for it, in order to secure his place there (Kahn 1978, 64–67).

45. *Ōkimon*: Euboulos *Kerkopes*, fr. 54 Kock. On the aphrodisiac effects of basil, see J. Murr, *Die Pflanzenwelt in der griechischen Mythologie*, Innsbruck, 1890, 199. Aristophanes *Lysistrata*, 928. Appetite and sexuality: see A. Brelich, *Gli eroi greci* (rpt. Rome, 1978), 248–50.

46. Euripides *Autolykos* fr. 282.5 Nauck².

47. Aristophanes *Birds* 1604; *Thesmophoriazousae* 816; *Frogs* 200; *Plutus* 560.

48. See the articles on *gastēr* and *nēdus* in Chantraine 1968, and C. Roura, "Aproximaciones al lenguaje cientifico de la colección hipocrática," *Emerita* 40 (1972): 319–27, esp. 320–21 on the oscillation of these terms in the Hippocratic corpus among the meanings "belly," "loins," "intestine," "stomach," and "womb."

49. It is characterized, for example, by dampness, a feminine element: compare the Hippocratic treatise *On Diet* 60.3 with 34.

50. *Odyssey* 18.2–7; see F. Bader, "Un nom indo-européen de l'homme chez Homère," *Revue de Philologie* 50 (1976): 206–12.

51. *Odyssey* 9.296. Note 1) that in line 415 the Kyklops is prey to the pains of childbirth ("metaphorically," some would say), and 2) that in Euripides' *Alcestis* Herakles is described in terms that evoke the Kyklops of the same author's satyr play, where he likewise has an insatiable *nēdus* (*Kyklops* 244, 547).

52. *Theogony* 460 and 487. See Kahn 1986, 221, 224.

53. See *Theogony* 890, 899; *Bacchae* 527 (to which compare 90, and cf. 99, where Zeus is said to have given birth to Dionysos). For Zeus as for Kronos, swallowing (whether of the baby or of the pregnant mother) is a sort of inversion of giving birth, a birthing upside down.

54. See the brief but thought-provoking comments made by G. Deleuze on the subject of Herakles and surfaces in *Logique du sens* (Paris, 1969), 157–58.

55. The difficult question of the meaning of the lion's skin would require a separate study that I will not undertake here. On the values associated with animal hides, see L. Gernet 1968, 125–26.

56. On the *peplos*: Diodorus 4.14.3; on the *khitōn*: Diodorus 4.38.1–2, as well as Strabo 8.381 and Apollodorus 2.7.7.

57. In his commentary on this exact passage (*Iliad* 5.734ff.), Eustathius defines the *peplos* as a "feminine *khitōn*." But he immediately adds that the *peplos* can be a masculine garment, in Euripides and in the *Trachiniae*, where Sophocles calls the *khitōn* of Nessos a *peplos*. These deviant uses are precisely the ones we ought to take into consideration.

58. See the article *peplos* in Chantraine 1968 and the remarks of M. Bieber, *Griechische Kleidung* (Berlin-Leipzig, 1928), 17–21. S. Marinatos, *Archaeologia homerica*, I.A, Göttingen, claims the word retains the primary sense of "veil." On the *peplos* of the barbarians: e.g., Aeschylus *Persians* 199, 1060, *Suppliants* 720 (all other uses of the word make it a woman's garment). On Athena in the *Iliad*: 5.734, the comments of L. Bonfante, *Etruscan Dress* (Baltimore-London, 1975), 116; on the *Hybristika*: Plutarch *Virtues of Women* 4; on Pentheus: Euripides *Bacchae* 821, 833, 852, 935, 938.

59. On the principle of inversion: Vidal-Naquet 1981, 164–68, and for the case of Herakles, see also Jourdain-Annequin 1985, 505; 1986, 317; on Achilles on Skyros: Jeanmaire 1939, 353–55; on Theseus: Pausanias 1.19.1; on the young man as woman: J. E. Harrison, *Themis*, 2nd ed., rpt. (London, 1977), 507 (on the ritual of Kos).

60. Cf. Farnell, *Greek Hero Cults*, 154, and A. Brelich, *Gli eroi greci*, 126, 195. On Herakles on Thasos and the ephebes: J. Pouilloux, *Recherches sur l'histoire et les cultes de Thasos* (Paris, 1954), 1:369, 377–78.

61. It is true, as Jourdain-Annequin (1986, 314–15), observes (arguing for an initiatory interpretation), that the *peplos* drops out of the story. Nevertheless, I hesitate, and all the more so, to reduce every exchange of clothing between the sexes to a context of initiation.

62. Plutarch *Greek Questions*, no. 58; cf. John Lydus, *De mensibus* 4.46, discussed by J. Bayet, *Les Origines de l'Hercule romain* (Paris, 1926), 314–15 (I am not as convinced as Jourdain-Annequin [1986:316 and n. 226] that Herakles-Melqart is the figure in question there).

63. For the argument that the theme is late, see C. Robert, *Die griechische Heldensage* 2,2 (rpt. Dublin-Zurich, 1967), 593–94; W. R. Halliday, in his commentary on *Greek Question* no. 45 of Plutarch (rpt., New York, 1975), 188; G. Schiassi, "Parodia e travestimento mitico nella commedia attica di mezzo," *Rendiconti dell'Instituto Lombardo* 88 (1955): 108–10, who invokes the authority of Wilamowitz. For the late pictorial evidence, see A. Brandenburg, *Studien zu Mitra* (Münster, 1966), 88–92; and for the classical pictorial evidence, K. Schauenburg, "Herakles und Omphale," *Rheinisches Museum* 103 (1960): 53–76, esp. 73. Note that this disguise is the model for many future transvestisms; on Statius, see N.J.H. Sturt, "Four Sexual Similes in Statius," *Latomus* 41 (1982): 833–40.

64. Or does not know: hence, in the matter of feminine garments, the *Ma-hābhārata* presents a feminized Arjuna, a eunuch in Virata, about whom Dumézil (1968, 72) rightly observes that "the appearance he assumes does not conform any the less with his own or his father's nature" (Indra). The representation of the *Mahābhārata* in Peter Brooks' production (1985/1986) did an admirable job of showing the highly virile warrior's complicity with the feminine.

65. On servitude, see Brandenburg, *Mitra*, 92; Farnell, *Greek Hero Cults*, 141. On Herakles made effeminate by love, see John Lydus, *De magistratibus* 3.64.

66. On the *krokotos* and wool-working, see, e.g., Lucian *Dialogues of the Gods* 15.237 and *How to Write History* 10; Plutarch *Moralia* 785e; Dio Chrysostom 32.94; see also Ovid *Fasti* 2.318ff. On the mitra and tambourine: Ovid *Heroides* 9.63; Seneca *Hercules Furens* 469–71, *Hercules on Oeta* 375, *Phaedra* 317ff.; for Greek allusions to the connections of Herakles with Phrygian or Lydian music (the furthest removed from manliness), see Pausanias 5.17.9 and Ion *Omphale* fr. 22, 23, 39, Nauck[2].

67. For the *krokotos*, see, e.g., Athenaeus 4.155c and 12.519c. For elaborate dress: Artemidorus (2.3) lists young men of marrying age, priests, musicians, actors, and devotees of Dionysos. On the flowery robe, see again Clement of Alexandria, *Paidagogos*, with Marrou's note, *ad loc*.

68. On the *mitra*, see Brandenburg, *Mitra*. On its association with women, see, e.g., Aristophanes *Thesmophoriazousae* 257; with barbarians: ibid. 163 as well as Herodotus 1.195, 7.62, and 90; Athenaeus 12.535–36; with Lydia: Pindar *Nemeans* 7.15 (and on the Lydian way of life, Athenaeus 12.515–16 and 15.690b–c). On the *mitra* of athletes, see Pindar *Olympians* 9.82–84, *Isthmians* 5.62.

69. Frazer, *Attis*, 6.258.

70. A. van Gennep, *Les Rites de passage* (1909, rpt. Paris-The Hague, 1969), 245.

71. In Apollonius of Rhodes and Theocritus, Herakles is the lover of the boy Hylas. An aberrant Hellenistic version makes him the lover of Eurystheus (Athenaeus 13.603d), but this is a matter of displacement of the theme of erotic servitude that is well attested in the heterosexual career of the hero.

72. M. Delcourt, *Hermaphrodite* (Paris, 1958), 10, 23, and on Herakles, 33–39. Also to be noted are the penetrating remarks D. Fernandez has made on the femininity of figures like Achilles and Herakles in a study entirely devoted to the confusion of the sexes: *Porporino ou les mystères de Naples* [Paris: Grasset, 1974], part 3, "Achille à Skyros."

73. On transvestism and marriage: M. Delcourt, *Hermaphrodite*, 27, 34. On the Koan ritual: see Halliday, *Greek Questions*, 216–19; Cook, *Classical Review*, 1906, 377; M. P. Nilsson, *Griechische Feste von religiöser Bedeutung* (Leipzig, 1906), 453; L. R. Farnell, "Sociological Hypotheses Concerning the Position of Women in Ancient Religion," *Archiv für Religionswissenschaft* 7 (1904): 90, and *Hero Cults*, 165–66; R. Vallois, "Les Origines des jeux olympiques," *Revue des Etudes anciennes*, 28 (1926): 305–22; M. Launey, "L'Athlète Théogène et le *hieros gamos* d'Heraklès thasien." *Revue Archéologique* 18.2 (1941): 46–47, and *Le Sanctuaire et le culte d'Héraklès à Thasos* (Paris, 1944), 134–35, 203–5, etc.

74. See Athenaeus 5.198c–d as well as Sophocles *Oedipus the King* 209–12; Euripides *Bacchae* 822, 828, 833; Diodorus 4.4.4; Lucian *Dionysos* 2; Strabo 15.1038; Seneca *Oedipus* 405f.

75. On Dionysos feminized: Euripides *Bacchae* 150, 233–36, 353, 453–59, 464; see M. Delcourt, *Hermaphrodite*, 39, and also the reservations of C. Picard, "Dionysos *mitrēphoros*," *Mélanges Gustave Glotz* (Paris, 1932), 2:707–21. For Roman representations of a bearded Dionysos in women's clothes, see R. Turcan, "Dionysos *dimorphos*," *Mélanges d'Archéologie et d'Histoire* 70 (1958): 243–93. On transvestism in Dionysiac ritual, see Philostratus *Imagines* 1.3; see C. Gallini, "Il Travestismo rituale di Penteo," *Studi e Materiali di Storia delle Religioni* 34 (1963): 211–28.

76. On Herakles and Dionysos, see, e.g., Sophocles *Trachiniae* 510–11, and Strabo 15.1.6 and 8 (where the flowered dress is Dionysiac); also C. Robert, *Heldensage*, 2:2, 647; M. Launey, *Héraklès à Thasos*, 153–57; M. Delcourt, *Hermaphrodite*, chap. 2; as well as G. K. Galinsky 1972, 81–82.

77. Aristophanes *Frogs* 45–47, 108–9.

78. Dionysos, however, is not lacking in contacts with war but thereby declares his singularity: see F. Lissarrague, "Dionysos s'en va-t-en à la guerre," in C. Bérard, C. Bron, A. Pomari, *Images et société en Grèce ancienne* (Lausanne, 1987), 111–20.

79. See above, chaps. 1 and 2. On hot baths to soothe the exertions made at the *gumnasia*, see Hippocrates *Regimen*, 2.66.4. On Herakles the hero of polarity, see N. Loraux, "Héraklès. Le héros, son bras, son destin," in Bonnefoy 1981, 1:495–96.

80. On this garment (and in particular the combinations *peplos*/ crown and *peplos*/ribbon) as wedding presents, see Gernet 1968, 107. On the cloak as *peplos*, see Sophocles *Trachiniae* 602, 613, 674, 758, 774; as *khitōn*, 580, 612, 769.

81. As winding sheet, the *peplos* evokes the one used by Clytemnestra in the *Oresteia* of Aeschylus to trap Agamemnon: see *Agamemnon* 1126, 1580 and Sophocles *Trachiniae* 1051–52. Herakles as a woman: *Trachiniae* 1075.

82. G. Dumézil 1971, 129.

83. If, with M. Delcourt in the Pléiade *Euripides*, we accept the manuscript reading of *Herakles* 1304, Hera's dance takes on an unavoidably gynecocratic significance: "To pound out the message on the floor of Olympus that she is putting on Zeus's shoes."

84. Herakles and Ares: linked with the god in the oath of the Athenian ephebes and in the *kosmos* ([Aristotle] *De mundo* 2.392a.26–27); the hero attacks Ares directly (in the Hesiodic *Shield*) or indirectly, through adversaries who are his allies (Pausanias 6.19.12) or through his children (Euripides *Alcestis* 498–504, where this confrontation takes the form of a *daimōn*). See J. Fontenrose, *Python*, 32, 34 and n. 6.

85. Eileithuia, goddess of childbirth and daughter of Hera, prolonged Alcmene's labor to please her mother (Diodorus 4.9.4). It may be recalled that in certain traditions Hebe, like Ares, is a parthenogenetic child of Hera.

86. Callimachus *Hymn to Artemis* 148–51; Diodorus 4.39.2–3.

87. On *Trachiniae* 1105, see, e.g., J. Bollack, "Vie et mort, malheurs absolus," *Revue de philologie* 44 (1970): 46–47.

88. For the literary tradition concerning the infant Herakles, see Lykophron *Alexandra* 39, 1326; Diodorus 4.9.7; Pausanias 9.25.2. For pictorial evidence see A. B. Cook, *Zeus*, III,1 (Cambridge, 1940), 89–94; J. Bayet, *Herclé. Etude critique des principaux monuments relatifs à l'Hercule étrusque* (Paris, 1926), 150–54; W. Déonna, "La Légende de Pero et de Micon et l'allaitement symbolique," *Latomus* 13 (1954): 140–66, 356–75; M. Renard, "Hercule allaité par Junon," in *Mélanges J. Bayet* (Paris, 1964), 611–18; K. Schauenburg, "Herakles unter Göttern," *Gymnasium* 70, 128–30, observes that in large part the pictorial tradition may be older than the earliest literary sources.

89. Diodorus 4.9.8.

90. Slater 1971, 345 (see also 338–40, 342).

91. See M. Delcourt, *Hermaphroditea* (Brussels, 1966), 22 (adoption, not physical motherhood). On the prohibition associated with the physical relationship of mother and infant, see Daladier, 1979.

92. A. B. Cook (*Classical Review*, [1906]: 366–69) goes so far as to deny that Hera ever conceived any child of Zeus; on Hera, divine matron and dubious mother, see W. Pötscher, "Hera und Heros," *Rheinisches Museum* 104 (1961): 320; Slater 1971, 202; and Burkert 1977, 211.

93. See M. Detienne, "Puissances du mariage," in Bonnefoy 1981, 2.67–69.

94. The first translation is put forward by Wilamowitz, Farnell, and Pötscher, among others; the second by Kretschmer and Kerényi.

95. See, e.g., A. B. Cook, *Classical Review* (1906): 373; Farnell, *Greek Hero Cults*, 100; Slater 1971, 343.

96. J. E. Harrison, "Primitive Hera-Worship Illustrated from the Excavations at Argos," *Classical Review* 7 (1893): 74–78; A. B. Cook, *Classical Review* (1906): 371–73; Benveniste 1969, 219–20.

97. For the etymological link *Hera/hero*: see F. W. Householder and G. Nagy, "Greek" in *Current Trends in Linguistics*, 9, ed. T. A. Sebeok (The Hague-Paris, 1972), 770–71. The most important article on the subject is W. Pötscher, "Der Name des Herakles," *Emerita* 39 (1971): 169–84.

98. On this "religious misinterpretation" see Pötscher, "Name," 181.

99. I am indebted for this analysis to Nagy 1979, 302–3, 318.

100. This is noted by Pötscher, "Name," 182.

101. On Hera's glory as detrimental to Zeus, see J. E. Harrison, *Classical Review* (1893): 75.

102. The story also occurs in the *Herakleid* of Panyassis, cited by Clement of Alexandria *Protreptika* 2.36.2

103. The connection is made by C. Robert, *Heldensage*, 2.2, 426–27. For the suckling Herakles: Lykophron *Alexandra* 1326; Diodorus 4.9.7; Achilles Tatius [astronomer] *In Aratum* 146; Hyginus *Astronomica* 2.43 (*boulimia*); Eratosthenes (*Catasterisms*, 44) has Hera reject the infant but gives no reason. In these last three authors, the episode produces the Milky Way.

104. Lykophron *Alexandra* (with scholia *ad loc.*, and compare those on *Iliad* 5.395.

105. Slater (1971, 347–50) develops the fantasy of the breast poisoned by the arrow dipped in the Hydra's venom and ignores the fact that in Homer, Hades is similarly wounded and the wound is in fact curable. But it is just too good an

opportunity for him to make Hera into a snake and Herakles, compared to the serpent Orestes (*Choephoroi*, 530–33), a counter-snake. . . .

106. See above, chap. 1, p. 31, and esp. J. Le Goff and P. Vidal-Naquet, "Lévi-Strauss en Brocéliande" in R. Bellour and C. Clément, *Claude Lévi-Strauss* (Paris, 1979), 273–75.

107. On this whole question, see Loraux 1986a, 96–101.

108. Slater (1971, 351) notes it but offers only dubious comparisons. Strangely insensitive to matters of the orientation of the body, J. Chellandre misses this passage in a work devoted to *La Droite et la gauche dans les poèmes homériques* (Paris 1944).

109. See Hippocrates *Epidemics* 2.6.15, 6.2.25, and 6.4.21; *Aphorisms*, 5.38, 48. For commentary on these texts, see G.E.R. Lloyd, "Right and Left in Greek Philosophy," in R. Needham, ed., *Right and Left. Essays on Dual Symbolic Classification* (Chicago, 1973), 167–88. According to Galen *On the Epidemics of Hippocrates*, 6.48, this opinion is both old and widely shared; thus Parmenides said, "On the right, boys, on the left, girls."

110. Conversely, it is always the left breast of Hermaphrodite that is exposed in the statues, to emphasize his/her femininity: M. Delcourt, *Hermaphroditea*, 32. But it is on the masculine side that the Sauromatian warrior women destroy every sign of femininity by cauterizing the right breast (Hippocrates *Airs, Waters, Places* 17).

111. Daremberg (1865, 67–68) affirms the "predilection" of the Homeric texts for the wounds on the right side. For men wounded on the right: e.g., *Iliad* 4.481 and 11.507. Hera is a warrior when she faces Artemis in book 21. One cannot simply explain the wound in the right breast in book 5 by pointing out that the right side is not protected by the shield and so is the only part exposed. There is nothing in the passage in question that specifies that Hera was in the position of a combatant against Herakles (and it is Panyassis, not Homer, who placed the action at Pylos).

112. In any case, the use in 5.393 of the form *dexiteron* (*dexiteron kata mazon*) singles out Hera in her specific role, since the separative suffix *-tero-* always contains a differential value: since the feminine breast is the left one, *dexiteron* emphasizes the presence (problematic, to be sure) of a masculine dimension in Hera. On *-tero-*, see Benveniste 1948, 116–19.

113. Herakles is nursed at Hera's right breast in all depictions, and this is all the more striking because *kourotrophoi* divinities generally give the left breast to the child they hold (see T. Hadzisteliou-Price, *Kourotrophos* [Leiden, 1978], 18–19). It remains unclear whether this fact is to be interpreted in isolation, as derived from an independent tradition, or seen as based on *Iliad* 5.393.

114. The phrase ("parti pris de narration") is from Kahn 1978, 175.

115. Quotation from A. Green, "Le Mythe: Un objet transitionnel collectif," *Le Temps de la réflexion* 1 (1980).

116. This essay is a revised version of an article published in the *Revue Française de Psychanalyse* 26 (1982): 697–729, proceedings of the Colloque de Deauville (1981) on myth. In reworking these pages, I must acknowedge my debt to Laurence Kahn, Gregory Nagy, and Maurice Olender. The translation of the original essay (with some minor omissions) was first published in *Before Sexuality:*

The Construction of Erotic Experience in the Ancient Greek World, ed. David M. Halperin, John J. Winkler, and Froma Zeitlin (Princeton, N.J., 1990), 21–52, Robert Lamberton, trans.

INTRODUCTION TO PART THREE

1. Still it is in death that this inventory is most effectively accomplished: on the abstract bodies of the Athenian dead in public funerals, see Loraux 1982, 34–36.

2. Loraux 1981a, 105; see also "Un absent de l'histoire? Le corps dans l'oeuvre de Thucydide," in N. Loraux and Y. Thomas, eds., *Le Corps du citoyen* (Editions de l'Ecole des Hautes Etudes en Sciences sociales, forthcoming).

3. *Theaetetus* 149a–151d.

4. *Phaedrus* 251a ff.

5. *Phaedo* 66b, 79c, 81c–d.

6. On the exclusions repeated throughout the *Phaedo*, see below, chap. 8 and n. 7.

CHAPTER EIGHT
THEREFORE, SOCRATES IS IMMORTAL

1. In this study I shall be considering the *Phaedo* insofar as it established a new tradition. I am, of course, well aware that, set in the context of the evolution of Platonic thought as a whole, this text simply marks a particular stage in Plato's treatment of the subject of the soul. Nevertheless, in this paper I shall be considering only the new departures that it introduced. The history of the tradition from mid- to neo-Platonism has already been studied: see, for example, P. Courcelle, "L'Ame fixée au corps," in *Connais-toi-même: De Socrate à Saint Bernard* (Paris, 1875), vol. 2, ch. 3, 325–414. The history of the *Phaedo* in university circles during the nineteenth and twentieth centuries essentially remains to be written.

2. These are the three disciplines sanctioned as a means of approaching the dialogue by R. Schaerer in his much-quoted article, "La Composition du *Phédon*," *Revue des Etudes grecques* 53 (1940), 7.

3. On the prehistory of the immortality of the soul: see, for example, M. Detienne, *La Notion de Daimon dans le pythagorisme ancien* (Paris, 1963), 69–85 [Pythagoreanism]; J.C.G. Strachan, "What Did Forbid Suicide at *Phaedo* 62b," *Classical Quarterly* 20 (1970): 216–20 [Orphism]; also, more generally, Rohde 1928; F. Sarri, *Socrate e la genesi storica dell'idea occidentale di anima* (Rome, 1975); and J. Bremmer, *The Early Greek Concept of the Soul* (Princeton, 1983).

4. On the funerary ritual in epic literature, see Vernant 1982; also, more generally, Vermeule 1979, 83–116.

5. Plato *Phaedo*, trans. with intro. and commentary by R. Hackforth (Cambridge, 1955), 77d–e. On the reality of the body in Homer, see Vermeule 1979, 97; in Homer *psukhē* is the vehicle of a man's identity but does not in itself constitute that identity; G. Nagy, "Patroklos, Concepts of Afterlife and the Indic Triple Fire," *Arethusa* 13 (1980): 162.

6. See Loraux 1981a; also Loraux 1982.

7. Xanthippe taken home: Plato *Phaedo* 60a; Crito told to pay no attention to the servant and his advice: 63e; the multitude dismissed by philosophers: 64c: the soul takes leave of the body: 81e; discourse on material things left behind: 100d, 101c–d; the man who bids farewell to the pleasures of the body: 114e; the servant to the Eleven bids farewell to Socrates, who reciprocates: 116c–d; why the women were sent away: 117d.

8. In that he locates souls in Hades, Plato is faithful to normative Greek representations; but when he ascribes *phronēsis* to those who philosophize, he takes a decisive step forward. What he thereby does is extend to philosophers in general the fate that, in Homer, was reserved for Tiresias alone: in the *Odyssey* 10.492–95, the diviner preserved his consciousness (*phrenes*) and his reason (*nous*) in Hades. On *phrēn* (clearly connected with *phronēsis*) and *nous*, see Nagy, "Patroklos," 165. *Phronēsis*, which in the fifth century meant the activity of thought, seems to have been a key word in Socrates' thought, to judge from Aristophanes' *Clouds*: E. A. Havelock, "The Socratic Self as Parodied in Aristophanes' *Clouds*," *Yale Classical Studies* 22 (1972): 1–18.

9. I have borrowed this expression from J. Le Goff, *La Naissance de Purgatoire* (Paris, 1981), 14. The question of place pervades the *Phaedo*, culminating in the mythical geography of the underworld, because what is at stake is the posthumous existence of the soul: to exist means to exist somewhere. Epicurus was to be the first Greek philosopher to conceive of the destiny of the soul in terms of time rather than space: see D. Lanza, "La Massima epicurea 'Nulla è per noi la morte,'" in *Democrito e l'atomismo antico*, ed. I. Romano (Catania, 1980), 357–65.

10. Vernant 1982, 65; Vermeule 1979, 12; S. Humphreys, "Death and Time," in *Mortality and Immortality: The Anthropology and Archaeology of Death*, ed. S. C. Humphreys and H. King (London, 1981), 263.

11. In this respect the philosopher's behavior has some analogies to that of the renunciates of ancient India: see C. Malamoud, "Les morts sans visage: Remarque sur l'idéologie funéraire dans le Brahmanisme," in G. Gnoli and J.-P. Vernant, eds., *La Mort, les morts dans les sociétés anciennes*, (Cambridge-Paris, 1982), 447–49.

12. Plato *Phaedo* 80c–d. It is interesting to note that what Plato does in the interests of his demonstration is to cut short the ritual, immobilizing the body at the point when it is put on show, at the *prothesis* (the laying out); as he sums up Cebes' thoughts, Socrates "forgets" the cremation that brings the ritual to a close and essentially annihilates the body: it is a typically Platonic ploy.

13. In agreement with W.J. Verdenius ("Notes on Plato's *Phaedo*," *Mnemosyne* 11 [1958]: 242) and against L. Robin (the Belles-Lettres edition), I think the perfect participle *leloumenos* should be restored at 116b7, for it makes an important point.

14. Orphism: D. J. Stewart, "Socrates' Last Bath," *Journal of the History of Philosophy* 10 (1972): 253–59; Socrates already dead: P. Trotignon, "Sur la mort de Socrate," *Revue de métaphysique et de morale* 81 (1976): 1–10; the women and their care of the dead body: Vermeule 1979, 14.

15. See Daraki 1982, 159–60.

16. In *De rerum natura* 3.870–93, Lucretius was to introduce a similar argument concerning the idea that the soul *is not* immortal: since there is no life after death, why lament over the destiny of one's own body?

17. Hesiod *Works and Days* 164–73, and Pindar *Olympians* 2:66–89.

18. On the authentic Aristotelian view of death, see D. Lanza, "La Morte esclusa," *Quaderni di storia* 11 (1980): 157–72.

19. Socrates as a poet, and Aesop: 60b–61c; Socrates as the servant of Apollo: 84a–85b. On Aesop, Apollo, and the heroic cult of the poet, see Nagy 1979, 315–16. I have also borrowed from Nagy the idea of the model or "generic poet" as the epitome of a poet (by which it is not necessarily intended to suggest that Hesiod and Aesop are themselves fictitious figures).

20. Or even ghosts, according to E. A. Havelock's commentary on line 94 of *Clouds* (*psukhōn sophōn*: "The Socratic Self," 13–16), where he detects a play on words involving, on the one hand, the Homeric meaning, on the other the truly Socratic meaning of *psukhē*.

21. Daraki's expression (1982, 164–65).

22. See Loraux 1981a, 101–4.

23. On the *Menexenus* see Loraux 1981a, 268–74 and 315–32.

24. A whole study would be needed for a detailed commentary on this list. We should, for example, note with K. Dorter ("The Dramatic Aspect of Plato's *Phaedo*" *Dialogue* 8 [1969–70]) that the number of individuals named tallies with that of Theseus's companions on his Cretan expedition: it is a way of reminding us that the initiatory myth of Theseus mentioned at 58a–b gives the *Phaedo* its meaning.

25. For another modality of the same process of appropriating *andreia*, see pp. 171–74.

26. A series of comparisons have been made: *Phaedo* 68a1–2 and 6; Thucydides 2.43.1 and *Symposium* 208c; *Phaedo* 68b9–c1 and Lysias *Epitaphios* 25; *Phaedo* 114e and Lysias *Epitaphios* 24.

27. *Phaedo* 68b–69b; on the exchange involved in a beautiful death, see O. Longo, "La Morte per la patria," *Studi Italiani di Filologia Classica* 49 (1977): 5–36.

28. See for example R. Loriaux, "Note sur la *phrourá* platonicienne (*Phédon* 62b–c), *Les Etudes classiques* 36 (1968): 28–36.

29. *Phroura*, a noun denoting an action: F. Bader, "Ephore, pylore, théore: Les composés grecs en -*oros, ouros, -ōros*," *Revue de philologie* 46 (1972): 202; the body as a prison: P. Courcelle, "La Prison de l'âme," in *Connais-toi toi-même* 2: 345–80, and P. Boyancé, "Note sur la *phroura* platonicienne," *Revue de philologie* 20 (1963): 7–11; the Platonic reversal of the traditional representation of Hades as a prison: see also the *Cratylus* 403a–404b; the jail, the animal pen: P. Chantraine, "Sur l'emploi de *ktēmata au sers de bétail, cheptel*," *Revue de philologie* 20 (1946): 5–11; the guard post: J. Roux and G. Roux, "A propos de Platon. Réflexions en marge du *Phédon* b2b et du *Banquet*," *Revue de philologie* 35 (1961): 207–11. We should also note that there may well be an ironic reference to the military sense of this word in *Clouds*: at 716–21, Strepsiades, the ordinary man who tries to become initiated to philosophy, finds himself worn out "from mounting guard and singing [*phrouras aidōn*]"—yet another (particularly bold) example of the systematic reversal of the *Clouds* in the *Phaedo*.

30. Plato *Phaedo* 117b3–5, which may be compared to the *Illiad* 13.278–86.

31. This dimension is not considered in Dumézil's article on Socrates' final words and in which he criticizes readings referring to this passage as the healing of the sickness that is life ("Divertissement sur les dernières paroles de Socrates," in ". . . *Le Moyne noir et gris dedans Varennes*," Paris [Gallimard], 1984).

32. See A. Brelich, 22–34.

33. See below, chap. 9.

34. Cf. P. Louis, *Les Métaphores de Platon*, Rennes, 1945, 57–63.

35. It is significant that *menein*, a verb associated with hoplites, and its compounds appear over and over again in the *Phaedo* (see esp. 62a–e, 98e, 102e–107e2, and 115a–16a).

36. *Autos* is a word used by the historians to lend veracity to what they are saying. See, for example, Thucydides 1.22.1 and 2.48.3.

37. Rather than "Plato was unwell," might this "weakness" have something to do with the human weakness referred to in 107b (which is characterized by insufficient faith in the immortality of the soul)?

38. On the importance of the theme of persuasion in the *Phaedo*, see Dorter, "The Dramatic Aspect," 574.

39. J. Moreau, "La Leçon du *Phédon*," *Archives de philosophie* 41 (1978): 81–92; in a famous article ("La Méditation de l'âme sur l'âme dans le *Phédon*," *Revue de métaphysique et de morale* 33 [1926]: 469–91), M. Gueroult tries to show that one should get over one's first impression that "the entire conversation is aimed solely at persuading us to share a *belief*" (471).

40. Among the countless interpretations of the dedication of a cock to Asclepius, it is worth noting that of R. Minadeo, "Socrates' Debt to Asclepius" (*Classical Journal* 66 [1971]: 293–97), who compares 118a with 89a–b, regarding it as "an expression of gratitude for the success of the dialectical discussion." That success matters as much to the disciples as to Socrates, hence the "we" ("we owe a cock"). Asclepius, the doctor-god, was believed to have brought human beings back to life: in the *Phaedo*, saving the life of the *logos*—even ensuring its immortality—is of even greater importance.

41. *Misologia* (hatred of discourse) is coined by analogy with *misanthrōpia* and is based on the idea that "there is a similarity between *logoi* and human beings." Instances where Socrates and the *logos* are treated as interchangeable: at 102, the verbs *hupomenein* and *ethelein*, which serve to describe the behavior of a hoplite, are transferred from Socrates to the *logos*, then applied once again to Socrates.

42. M. Detienne points out that in passing from Homer (*Odyssey* 11.602) to Plato (*Laws* 12.959b) we move on from the body, which is the basis of Herakles' personality, to the soul, which constitutes the self in any person ("Ebauches de la personne dans la Grèce archaïque," in *Problèmes de la personne*, ed. I. Meyerson [Paris, 1973], 46–52).

43. See V. Goldschmidt, "La Religion de Platon," in *Platonisme et pensée contemporaine* (Paris, 1970), esp. 68–71.

44. Plato, *Phaedo* 79c, 81d. The soul too much attached to the body evokes the *psukhē* of the Homeric poems and lyric poetry. There, it is an *eidōlon* which, as Vermeule points out (1979), 29, cannot really be separated from the body.

45. Plato, *Phaedo* 82d–83a: see J. P. Vernant, "Le Fleuve *amélès* et la *mélétè thanatou*," in Vernant 1971, 1.108–23; also M. Daraki (1982), 161–65.

46. Detienne, "Ebauches de la personne," 49; see also, on 67e, 70a, 80e, 81b–c, and 83a, M. Detienne, *La Notion de Daimon*, 71–85.

47. Cf. L. Gernet, "Quelques rapports entre la pénalité et la religion dans la Grèce ancienne" in Gernet 1968, 295–99.

48. *Thermos* and its derivatives occur sixteen times in the dialogue; in interpreting Socrates' reaction to the advice "not to become heated," we should bear in mind that *thermos* can also mean "courageous": Crito is inadvertently advising his friend to forswear his dialectical courage.

49. It is still perfectly possible for a recalcitrant reader on the contrary to use this description to attack the thesis of the immortality of the soul, as does Lucretius who, without actually naming Socrates, certainly appears to be thinking of the *Phaedo* in *De rerum natura* 3. 526–32.

50. On the ambiguity of *pharmakon* (poison/remedy), see Derrida 1972, chap. 1.

51. Socrates' acceptance of death is in line with the theme of the dialogue, and we should not seek to term it a suicide even if tradition has interpreted it this way. Indeed, by introducing this type of execution, the Thirty injected a sinister parody of freedom into the iniquity; probably the fictitiously suicidal aspect of such executions (Gernet, 1968, 307–8) is what led the Athenians to institutionalize the use of hemlock as the penalty for political crimes. Thus, not only is no blood shed (see above, chap. 6), but the condemned individual agrees to his own end. Can we imagine a more effective way of drawing all responsibility away from the city?

52. The Platonic tradition regards the *atrapos* of the *Phaedo* (66b) as the straight and narrow path of virtue, as mentioned by Hesiod and Pythagoras; cf. A. Festugière, *Les Trois protreptiques de Platon* (Paris, 1973), 79–80, and P. Courcelle, *Connais-toi toi-même*, vol. 3, 625–45. Without seeking to contradict the tradition that consistently adopts this particular view, I would compare this passage to line 123 of Aristophanes' *Frogs* (where the effects of hemlock are described in the same terms as those used by Plato); it is furthermore worth noting that *atrapos* is not a common word in Plato's works (only one other occurrence). Yet again, Plato here twists Aristophanes' words, or turns them around, in order to make a serious point.

53. On hemlock, see Aristophanes *Frogs* 123–26; Theophrastus *Historia plantarum* 9.8.3, 16.8–9; Nicander *Alexipharmaka* 186–94 (hemlock and madness: see also Galen, *Quod animi mores corporis temperamenta sequantur* 3.775–77 and *Etymologicum Magnum*, s.v. *kōneion*). Of the many Greek euphemisms for hemlock, it is worth drawing attention to the term *aphrōn* (the "mad" drink, the drink that destroys *phronēsis*): cf. A. Carnoy, "Les Noms grecs de la ciguë," *Les Etudes classiques* 28 (1960): 369–74.

54. This point has already been made, for example by C. Gill, "The Death of Socrates," *Classical Quarterly* 23 (1973): 25–28.

55. I owe this idea to a suggestion made by J. P. Vernant. See "Figuration de l'invisible et catégorie psychologique du double" (Vernant 1971), 2.65–78. On the interplay between the sign and the tomb in the word *sēma*, see G. Nagy, "*Sēma* and *Noēsis*: Some illustrations," *Arethusa* 16 (1983): 35–55.

56. See Plato *Phaedo* 99d–100a, an impressive passage on this image.

57. From the church fathers onward. Perhaps the reason is that the *Phaedo* frees the pure soul definitively from the body, delivering it forever from the cycle of reincarnation. In any event Gregory of Nazianzus and Saint Ambrose develop the metaphor of the body-prison at considerable length, which is all the more remarkable in that, by proclaiming the resurrection of the body, Christian thought from the outset avoids the pitfalls of the spiritualistic approach.

58. This chapter was first published in *Le Temps de la réflexion*, vol. 3 (Paris: Gallimard, 1982), 19–46. My debt to Gregory Nagy and Jean-Pierre Vernant is obvious. Marcel Detienne and Gulia Sissa aided me in developing the comments on hemlock. Translated by Janet Lloyd. [ZONE 4: *Fragments for a History of the Human Body, part 2*. Copyright © 1989 Zone Books. Reprinted with permission].

CHAPTER NINE
SOCRATES, PLATO, HERAKLES

1. On this subject see Pigeaud 1988.

2. Plutarch *Life of Lysander* 2.5. This text condenses [Aristotle's] *Problemata* 30 (953a10–18), which investigates the reasons why remarkable men, whether in philosophy, politics, theory, or the *tekhnai*, are melancholy like Herakles; in 26–27 Plato and Socrates are quoted, with Empedocles. On the erroneous correction of Herakles into "Heraclitus" in Plutarch's text, see remarks by R. Flacelière, *ad loc.* (Belles Lettres) and "Héraclès ou Héraclite?" in *Hommages à Marie Delcourt* (Brussels, 1970), 207–10.

3. On "Herakles' sickness," see for example Hippocrates *Diseases of Women* 1.7 (Littré, p. 33); melancholy and philosophy: Pigeaud 1981, 124, 308, 407; and 1988, 10–14 and 108–9n.4.

4. The expression is from V. Goldschmidt, *Essai sur le Cratyle. Contribution à l'histoire de la pensée de Platon* (Paris, 1940), 114n.2.

5. *Symposium* 221c–d.

6. V. Goldschmidt, "Le Paradigme dans la théorie platonicienne de l'action," in *Questions platoniciennes* (Paris, 1970), 92–93n.

7. V. Goldschmidt, "Theologia," in *Questions platoniciennes*, 141–72.

8. Here I will mention neither the abundant literature concerning the relationship between cultural and epic heroes, nor the tension within each heroic figure between the human and the more-than-human. On the subject of Plato, it should be recalled that in *Hippias Major* 293a9 Socrates contrasts ordinary *andres* with "heroes who have gods as fathers." The model for this is Herakles, but Achilles is also mentioned (see also *Apology* 28c, where he is the representative of the "demigods who died in front of Troy"). The disparity between Achilles and Herakles is nonetheless real in practice: Herakles is the *hērōs-theos* (Pindar *Nemeans* 3.22), while Achilles is not.

9. Plato's Phaedrus is able to recognize Gorgias behind Nestor, Thrasymachus or Theodorus behind Odysseus (*Phaedrus* 261b–c); on the social importance of this practice of comparison, see M. Detienne, *Homère, Hésiode et Pythagore* (Brussels, 1962), 41, and, regarding the *Symposium* 221c6, A. Rivier, *Un Emploi*

archaïque de l'analogie chez Héraclite et Thucydide (Lausanne, 1952), 20–21 and n. 23.

10. See M. Detienne, *Homère, Hésiode et Pythagore*, 54 (on *Hippias Minor* as a critique of the use of comparison).

11. A. Rivier, *Un Emploi archaïque de l'analogie*, 20–21, 46–48, 52–53; see also E. Fraenkel, *Plautinisches im Plautus* (Berlin, 1922), 171–74.

12. Quotations from A. Rivier, *Un Emploi archaïque de l'analogie*, 20, 53, 50; on *eikazō*, see also, by the same author, "Remarques sur les fragments 34 et 35 de Xénophane," *Revue de philologie* 30 (1956): 37–61, nn. 46–48.

13. *Republic* 3.396c; refer to J. Brunschwig's remarks in "*Diēgēsis* et *Mimēsis* dans l'oeuvre de Platon," *Revue des Etudes grecques* 37 (1974): xvii–xix.

14. *Phaedo* 99d–100a.

15. V. Goldschmidt demonstrated this (*Le Paradigme dans la dialectique platonicienne* [Paris, 1947], 103–11n.104, with the reference to the passage in the *Republic*).

16. On traditional but also philosophical *paideia*, M. Detienne, *Homère, Hésiode et Pythagore*, 37–60.

17. *Symposium* 220b–d; in c2 Alcibiades quotes *Odyssey* 4.242 but takes the line out of context to eliminate all references to the "treachery" of Odysseus the spy. On Plato's reduction of the ambiguities found in the epic, see C. P. Segal, "The Myth Was Saved: Reflections on Homer and the Mythology of Plato's *Republic*," *Hermes* 106 (1978): 315–36, n.323.

18. *Phaedo* 94d and *Republic* 3.390d quote *Odyssey* 20.17 (where the *Republic* sees a paradigm of *karteria* worth retaining). In this quotation as in the one made in *Symposium*, the verb *tlaō* is found.

19. See P. Pucci, *Odysseus Polutropos. Intertextual Readings in the Odyssey and the Iliad* (Ithaca, N.Y., 1987).

20. *Republic* 10.620c. Note that Odysseus's soul chooses "the life of a private person unfamiliar with business" (the very same that, in the *Gorgias*, is identified by the multitude with the philosopher), because it retains the memory of his past trials (*ponōn*): *polutlas* has prevailed over *polutropos*, and wisdom replaces *mētis*.

21. On *Apology* 28a–d and *Crito* 44a–b, see N. A. Greenberg, "Socrates' Choice in the Crito," *Harvard Studies in Classical Philology* 70 (1965): 45–82, as well as C. P. Segal, "The Myth Was Saved," 320–21.

22. On the name of Phthia and the paradox of the heroic condition in *Iliad* 9.363 (line altered by Plato) and 19.328–30, see Nagy 1979, 184–85.

23. See, for example, *Gorgias* 526d1 (*hōs phēsin Odusseus ho Homērou*).

24. For the overall outline of this history, Galinsky 1972, 9–100 (Herakles in literature, from Homer to comedy).

25. For Herodotus, Herakles is the progenitor of several royal genealogies, those of the kings of Lydia down to Candaules (1.7), that of the Scythian kings (4.8–10), and of course that of the kings of Sparta (7.204), to which Plato alludes in the first *Alcibiades* (120e) and in *Laws* 3.685d, as if to a well-established *topos*—which does not necessarily mean that he is using tradition for his own ends. But Platonic criticism deliberately attacks the genealogical claims of the aristocratic *genē* in the cities: see *Theaetetus* 175a6–7 and *Lysis* 205c–d (where

the ancestor is Herakles). The notion of the "rumor" of the city comes from M. Detienne, *L'Invention de la mythologie* (Paris, 1981), 155–89.

26. *Symposium* 177b2–3; *Gorgias* 484b; *Theaetetus* 169b.

27. *Cratylus* 398d–e, with commentary by V. Goldschmidt, *Essai sur le Cratyle*, 113–14.

28. Aristophanes *Clouds* 1044–54; on the variant made by Unjust Speech on the subject of Herakles and warm baths, see above, chap. 2, pp. 57–58.

29. Cf. the parabasis in *Peace* (esp. 741–60), where Aristophanes repeats nearly verbatim the praise that he made of his poetic art in the parabasis of the *Wasps* (esp. 1031–43).

30. *Theaetetus* 169b; *Euthydemus* 297b–98e.

31. Xenophon *Banquet* 8.28–29, which should be compared to *Memorabilia* 2.1.20–34 (Prodikos's apology).

32. See, for example, *Clouds* 184 (Strepsiades catching sight of the disciples: "Herakles! what kind of animals do you have here?") and *Frogs* 298 (Xanthias in a panicked move upon seeing an infernal monster: "That's the end for us. Ah, Lord Herakles!").

33. Oath of Hippias (*Hippias Major* 290d10), of Thrasymachus (*Republic* 1.337a4), of Socrates (*Euthyphro* 4a11, *Charmides* 154d7, *Lysis* 208e2; cf. Xenophon *Banquet* 4.53); see also *Symposium* 213b8 (Herakles invoked by Alcibiades upon seeing Socrates) and *Meno* 91c3 (Herakles invoked by Anytos against the Sophists and Socrates); particularly interesting is *Euthydemus* 303a6 (which must be compared to 297b–d).

34. *Apology* 22a6–8; allusion to Herakles: see, for example, R. Höistad, *Cynic Hero and Cynic King. Studies in the Cynic Conception of Man* (Uppsala, 1948), 34, and Galinsky 1972, 78n.36, as well as the note by L. Robin *ad loc.* (Pléiade).

35. *Symposium* 219e8 (*ponois*). Odysseus, another hero of endurance, will be mentioned in an allusive but clear way in 220c2, in a passage devoted, it is true, not to physical but mental endurance. Diogenes: Diogenes Laertes 6.34.

36. *Cratylus* 411a6–b1.

37. L. Robin (*ad loc.* CUF) mentions Aesop's fable (279) where the ass, dressed in a lion's skin, terrorizes shepherds and flocks until the wind lifts up his skin and everyone beats him with sticks and *clubs* (Herakles' other emblem, turned against the impostor). Disguised as Herakles, the Dionysos of the *Frogs* quickly displays his cowardice (45–47; 495–500). The Cynic posterity of this theme: Diogenes will be presented as saying to the one who was puffed up about the lion's skin covering him: "Stop dishonoring the garment of courage" (or "valor": *aretē*, Diogenes Laertes 6.45). The ironic-serious use of the vocabulary of courage is constant in *Cratylus* beginning with 411a: see 411b, 415a, 421c1, 426b, 440d (*skopeisthai andreiōs*, an expression that suggests that *skopein* refers to courageous activity itself).

38. *Euthydemus* 297b7–d2: *Phaedo* 89c4–7; *Theaetetus* 169b1–c2.

39. Simultaneously confronted with the Hydra of Lerna and a monstrous crab Hera sent as reinforcements, Herakles can win only with the help of Iolaos; Socrates is forced to do without help (which, in the *Euthydemus*, makes his strength) or to go to the aid of Iolaos-Phaedo.

40. *Euthydemus* 297d1: *ho d'emos Ioleōs*; in *Phaedo* 89c6–7 the namesake of the dialogue *compares* himself to Iolaos but *identifies* Socrates with Herakles.

41. *Theaetetus* 169b6; on the classificatory role and Platonic use of adjectives ending in *-ikos* in the service of "a sort of dialectic humor," see P. Chantraine, *Etudes sur le vocabulaire grec* (Paris, 1956), 132–42, 147 (*iskhurikos*), 151–52.

42. *Karteria*, a preeminently hoplitic virtue (*Laches* 193a), represents Socrates' nature for the comic writers as for Xenophon (see Ameipsias *Konnos* fr. 9 Kock [*karterikos*], as well as Xenophon *Memorabilia* 1.2.1 [*karterikōtatos*]; on *katerikos*, cf. Chantraine, *Etudes sur le vocabulaire grec*, 147); Plato shifts it to the realm of thought, and the strength of soul becomes the dialectician's virtue: see for example *Sophist* 241c9 (*iskhuros logos*); recall that Socrates is *iskhuros* (*Hippias Major* 303b2).

43. As Giulia Sissa once remarked to me, in practical terms, Herakles has an intellectual dimension, represented from an early date by the theme of the theft of the Delphic tripod, by which Herakles becomes Apollo's rival.

44. In their considerations of Herakles, the Stoics will also be more Socratic than Platonic: V. Goldschmidt, *Le Système stoïcien et l'idée du temps* (Paris, 1953), 152.

45. Diogenes Laertes 6.4 (*palaistikos eimi*, which can be compared to *Theaetetus* 169b4).

46. Diogenes Laertes 6.11, with commentary in Daraki 1982, 167.

47. Diogenes Laertes 6.5; recall that in the *Phaedo* Antisthenes is among the friends present at Socrates' side.

48. Diogenes Laertes 6.16 and 18; I will not enter into the dispute between R. Höistad ("Was Antisthenes an Allegorist?" *Eranos* 49 [1951]: 16–30) and J. Tate ("Antisthenes Was Not an Allegorist" *Eranos* 51 [1953]: 14–22, nn. 15–18) as to whether the interpretation of this Herakles is moral or allegorical. The incarnation of endurance, Odysseus is, with Herakles, one of the great heroes of the Cynics (before becoming the hero of Stoicism): see R. Höistad, *Cynic Hero and Cynic King*, 97–100; W. B. Stanford, *The Ulysses Theme* (Oxford, 1954), 96–98 (Antisthenes) and 121–22 (the Stoics), as well as L. Paquet, *Les Cyniques grecs* (Ottawa, 1975), 19. On the Cynic Herakles, see also D. R. Dudley, *A History of Cynicism* (London, 1937; rept. Hildesheim, 1967), 13 and 43.

49. Diogenes imitating Socrates: see also Dudley, *A History of Cynicism*, 27; Diogenes and Herakles: Diogenes Laertes 6.71 (quoted in L. Paquet's French translation), as well as 6.40 (Diogenes swearing by Herakles).

50. Diogenes Laertes 6.2 and 104–5; Höistad (*Cynic Hero and Cynic King*, 36 and 42) rightly compares the *iskhus sōkratikē* (Diogenes Laertes 6.11) and the Strength of Herakles (Diogenes Laertes 6.16 and 18).

51. See Detienne 1960.

52. See Galinsky 1972, 101–3.

53. On the modalities of this operation in the *Phaedo*, see above, chap. 8.

54. In this respect, from the fifth to the fourth century it underwent an evolution parallel to that of *ponos*, which is so closely connected with it.

55. As has been rightly observed by Höistad, *Cynic Hero and Cynic King*, 53.

56. See, for example, Höistad, *Cynic Hero and Cynic King*, 33 and 48, and, in a more nuanced way, Galinsky 1972, 101–7.

57. *Republic* 3.388a–b and 390d.

58. *Republic* 3.396d. There is a great temptation to place Herakles' name beneath the description of a hero who joins "sickness" with love, evoked in the *Trachiniae*, drunkenness, as in *Alcestis*, and "unhappiness," which in the tradition more than once brings down Zeus's son.

59. This chapter first appeared in *Histoire et structure. A la mémoire de Victor Goldschmidt*, ed. Jacques Brunschwig, Claude Imbert, and Alain Roger (Paris, 1985), 93–105. I am grateful to the editors of this festschrift, who have generously authorized the re-publication of this text and contributed a few modifications.

CHAPTER TEN
THE MOTHERS' CASE DISMISSED

1. Sissa 1987.

2. On the designation of the Athenians as "sons of Hephaistos," see Loraux 1981b, 132.

3. Delcourt 1955, 19–36; G. Roux, *Delphes, son oracle et ses dieux* (Paris: Belles Lettres, 1976), 19–51.

4. G. Roux, *Delphes, son oracle*, 34.

5. See Godelier 1982.

6. Hesiod *Theogony* 420–28.

7. *Teleios* and all the derivations of *telos* certainly form one of the dominant semantic fields of the *Oresteia*; nevertheless, in the specific context of the prayer to the Pythia, this term is singularly apt.

8. *Homeric Hymn to Apollo* 420–28; Euripides *Iphigenia in Tauris* 1235–83. See A. Iriarte, "La Terre de Delphes," *Sources* 14 (1988): 3–15, nn. 12–13.

9. On this phrase of Freud's concerning the Medusa's head, see the comments by L. Kahn, "Le Monde serein des dieux d'Homère," *L'Ecrit du temps* 2 (1982): 117–20.

10. Concerned with presenting a continuous genealogy, Hesiod makes Phoibe into the daughter of Ouranos and Gaia and the mother of Leto, mother of Apollo and Artemis (*Theogony* 404–8): as it should be in the world of the gods, the succession of powers is a family affair. Preoccupied with the clash between the feminine and the male principle, Aeschylus knows only feminine divinities at the beginning and then refers Apollo to Zeus alone.

11. Loraux 1981b.

12. This analysis is influenced by the argument of Monique Schneider: see *Freud et le plaisir* (Paris, 1980), 44–51, as well as "Visages du matricide," in *La Femme et la mort* (Toulouse: Grief, 1984), 19–29.

13. Or that of Zeus, the son of Kronos, against the Giants, the sons of the Earth: it is for a reason that in the archaic Attic vases studied by F. Vian (*La Guerre des Géants* [Paris: Klincksieck, 1952], 96), Ge turns her back on Athena.

14. Varro, in Saint Augustine *City of God* 18.9.

15. *Mutterrecht und Urreligion* is available in the English translation by R. Mannheim, *Myth, Religion and Mother Right* (New York, 1967); on history and

myth, see the introduction, 69–75; on Athenian myth, 157–58 (note that, in the analysis of this tale, Bachofen links it to that of the *Eumenides*).

16. In a trial—unlike what happens in the assembly of the people where a majority is absolutely required—the rule is that "the party carrying the majority is the victor; *but if the votes are equal, the defendant wins*" (Aristotle *Constitution of Athens* 69.1). This probably means that, since the accuser has the initiative, if he does not obtain the majority that he sought against his opponent, he has not won.

17. Is this asymmetry encompassed by the statement of the rule? Is it an interpretation? Or a specious argument, based on pure *peithō*? Note at least that in the absence of explicit confirmation, the first possibility is still hypothetical.

18. *Eumenides* 972–75. On *kratos*, which in Homer refers to "the superiority of a man, whether he deploys his strength among those of his own camp or against his enemies," see Benveniste 1969, 2:75.

19. For example, much could be said about the way in which "in their minds, the Baruya attribute women with powers that the mind immediately takes away from them to add them to those of men" (Godelier 1982).

20. See Loraux, *Les Mères en deuil* (Paris: Seuil, 1990).

21. Aeschylus *Agamemnon* 1415–18, 1433, 1524–29 (Clytemnestra); 155 (the chorus).

22. On the etymology of *mēnis* and the prohibition concerning this word, see C. Watkins, "A propos de *mēnis*," *Bulletin de la société de linguistique* 72 (1977): 187–209.

23. In the *Eumenides* 314, the Erinyes say "our wrath," within, it is true, a negative phrase that weakens the force of the word in advance; but in any event, because they are the incarnation of wrath, the Erinyes are the only ones who can use this word in their own name without fearing its redoubtable strength.

24. See "De l'amnistie et de son contraire," in Y. Yerushalmi et al., *Usages de l'oubli* (Paris: Seuil, 1988), 34–39, and Loraux, *Les Mères en deuil*.

25. *Eumenides* 889. On the couplet, "fear the other's *mēnis*/ abandon one's own *mēnis*," see Watkins, "A propos de *mēnis*."

26. Euripides *Iphigenia in Tauris* 1273; *Homeric Hymn to Demeter*.

27. See the speech of Phoenix in book 9 of the *Iliad*; on the mourning of the Achaians conveyed by Achilles' name, Nagy 1979.

28. See Laura Slatkin's article "The Wrath of Thetis," *Transactions of the American Philological Association* 116 (1986): 1–24, as well as, more recently, *The Power of Thetis: Allusion and Interpretation in the Iliad* (Berkeley and Los Angeles: University of California Press, 1991).

29. On Greek mythology as a "language with no synonyms," see M. Delcourt, *L'Oracle de Delphes*, 139 (specifically concerning a comparison between the female Dragon of Delphi and the Erinyes).

30. This chapter originally appeared in *Psychanalystes* 13 (1984): 3–15, in response to an invitation by Monique Schneider, in an issue entitled "Le Politique et l'exclusion du féminin"; except for slight modifications and the addition of several notes, I have adhered to the original.

31. These two points are developed in Loraux, *Les Mères en deuil*.

32. I am thinking principally of Slater 1971.

CHAPTER ELEVEN
THE PHANTOM OF SEXUALITY

1. Or again, as has already been mentioned, to give men the feelings that women are denied.

2. Plato *Phaedrus* 242e–243b (as well as 244a, in which Socrates makes Stesichorus the author of his speech on Eros); Helen and Stesichorus: again, see Isocrates *Praise of Helen* 64.

3. Helen haunts Socrates' second speech: 248c2 (allusion to Adrasteia, epithet for her mother, Nemesis); 251a (the beautiful face of the young boy is, like that of Helen, of divine aspect and, like her face, makes one shudder); 252a (leave everything for the beautiful object, as Helen in Sappho fr. 16 Campbell); 252d (make the beloved into an *agalma*), etc.

4. It is of little importance to my argument whether or not Helen's name, from the standpoint of a supposedly authentic etymology, denotes her as the "Greek Venus" (H. Grégoire, "L'Etymologie du nom d'Hélène," *Bulletin de l'Académie royale de Belgique* 32 [1946]: 255–65).

5. Abductions of women at the dawn of history: Herodotus 1.1–5 (who attributes this sort of remark to the Persians); the power and fear that she inspires, causes of the Trojan War and the Peloponnesian War: Thucydides 1.9.1–3 (and 23.6); the Helen-Aspasia of the comedies appeared in the lost plays of Kratinos and Eupolis: see esp. Aristophanes *Acharnians* 524–29.

6. *Iliad* 3.125–28.

7. This is Helen's introduction of Odysseus (3.200–202); she is also found speaking in 3.173–80, 229–42, 399–412, 428–36; 6.344–58; 24.762–75.

8. "Bitchiness": 3.180, 6.344 and 356. In Giraudoux's *La Guerre de Troie n'aura pas lieu*, "animal names" are reserved for the erotic partner, in a tender way of switching sexual roles (2.12).

9. *Agalma*: Aeschylus *Agamemnon* 740; *kallisteuma*: Euripides *Orestes* 1639 (Helen as the instrument of the gods to drive away *hubrisma*, the insolence of mortals; the echo of the two neuters is everything, except lacking in meaning); *teras*: Euripides *Helen* 256 (it is Helen who speaks, distant from herself as in Homer). *Thauma*: *Cypria* fr. 7 Allen, 1; *pēma*: *Iliad* 3.48–50 and 160 (*pēma* is the "cause or subject of pain . . . a harmful thing as the origin, agent, or bearer of a process, and not as the outcome of a process": Mawet 1979, 101).

10. Stylistic innovations aside, Sappho's Helen, depicted both as she who loves and who is loved, also derives from this fluctuation: see C. Calame, "Sappho et Hélène. Le Mythe comme argumentation narrative et parabolique," in J. Delorme, ed., *Parole-figure-parabole. Recherches autour du discours parabolique* (Lyon: Presses Universitaires de Lyon, 1987), 209–29, n.219.

11. Helen's tears: e.g., *Iliad* 3.142, 176, *Odyssey* 4.184; see Monsacré 1984, 158–60. Ares and *polemos*: *Iliad* 3.132, 165; Helen, tears and blood: Euripides *Helen* 364–65 (and 199, 213); cf. *Orestes* 56–57, 1363.

12. *Iliad* 2.356 and 590; the scholiasts propose both interpretations.

13. Here I will stop distinguishing between Helen and "Helen," while waiting for a new pairing to emerge in the opposition between Helen and her phantom.

14. See below, chap. 12.

15. *Iliad* 3.396–97; quotation from Otto 1981, 118; on Aphrodite and blissful sexuality, see also W. Burkert, "Afrodite e il fondamento della sessualità," in Calame 1983, 135, 139 (Greek sexuality as unproblematic).

16. *Himeros*: Hesiod *Theogony* 200. Paris and Helen: *Iliad* 3.437–47; Zeus and Hera: 14.314–28. Note with A. Bergren that these two realized desires make sexuality into the truth of the war ("Helen's Web: Time and Tableau in the *Iliad*," *Helios* 7 (1980): 19–34, nn.28–31.

17. The suitors' desires: Hesiod fr. 199.2 Merkelbach-West (*himeirōn Helenēs posis emmenai ēukomoio*); note that in the *Iliad* Helen in effect bestows an identity on Paris, who is referred to several times as "Helen's husband with the fine hair." Paris's desire: *Iliad* 3.442–46; Helen's obedient silence: 447.

18. Helen's white veil: 3.141, 419–20; Aidos's and Nemesis's white veil: Hesiod *Works and Days* 198–200.

19. Which does not exclude the possibility that words pertaining to sexuality may also refer to battle: see above, chap. 4, pp. 81–82.

20. Isocrates *Praise of Helen* 50; Ronsard, *Sonnets pour Hélène*, 1.38.11 and 2.66.

21. *Iliad* 3.156–60.

22. Hence Aristotle's extrapolation of a view of pleasure based on Helen (*Nicomachean Ethics* 2.9.1109b9ff.): "The feelings of old men regarding Helen are what we ourselves ought to feel in the place of pleasure, and we must always repeat their words, and it is *by thus bidding farewell to pleasure* that we commit the fewest errors."

23. In this passage, the strong meaning of *ainōs*: see A. Amory, "The Gates of Horn and Ivory," *Yale Classical Studies* 20 (1966): 20n. *Phōs ainolampes*: Aeschylus *Agamemnon* 389 (with the commentary in Bollack and Judet de la Combe 1981, 1:2, 415). Since Alcman (fr. 27 Page: *ainoparis*), tradition has generally displaced the sense of the ominous to associate it with Paris (see Euripides *Hecuba* 944, *Helen* 1120, as well as Aeschylus *Agamemnon* 713). In Euripides *Electra* 1062, there is perhaps a play upon *ainos* (fatal)/ *aînos* (praise), concerning Helen's beauty and that of her sister Clytemnestra.

24. See below, chap. 12.

25. *Iliad* 3.180; *Odyssey* 4. 145 (Helen); *Odyssey* 8.139 (Aphrodite) and 11.20 (Clytemnestra); Kratinos *Khirones* fr. 241 Kock (Aspasia).

26. *Kakai kunes*: *Iliad* 13.620–39; the bitch and *anaideia*: see M. Faust, "Die künstlerische Verwendung von *kuōn* (Hund) in den homerischen Epen," *Glotta* 48 (1970): 25–27; S. Lilja, *Dogs in Ancient Greek Poetry* (Helsinki, 1976), 21–22; and C. Mainoldi, *L'Image du loup et du chien dans la Grèce ancienne* (Paris: Ophrys, 1984), 107–8.

27. A woman with more than one man: Aeschylus *Agamemnon* 62; Euripides *Kyklops* 181. Helen as "bitch": Euripides *Andromache* 630; see also Lykophron *Alexandra* 87 and 850. Helen's immodesty in Euripides: see esp. *Trojan Women* 989–92 and 1027; Helen, virtuous but likened to a Nymph who has been violated: Euripides *Helen* 184–90.

28. Aeschylus *Choephoroi* 594–601; Clytemnestra-bitch: Aeschylus *Agamemnon* 607, 1228 (see *Choephoroi* 621). Helen-Erinyes: Aeschylus *Agamemnon* 749; Euripides *Orestes* 1386–89. The Furies are bitches in Aeschylus (*Choephoroi, Eu-*

menides), in Sophocles (*Electra* 1388), in Euripides (see esp. *Orestes* 260–61: *kunōpides Gorgōpes*), and even in Aristophanes (*Frogs* 472); on the Furies as bitches: C. Mainoldi, *L'Image du loup*, 47.

29. *Stugerē* (same root as *Styx*, the river of the underworld, and of the verb *stugeō*, "to hold in horror," which Euripides uses abundantly with respect to Helen): *Iliad* 3.404; see *Iliad* 9.454 (the Erinyes), 8.368 (Hades), 2.385 and 18.209 (Ares; three examples with *polemos*); Hesiod *Theogony* 226 (Eris). *Kunos kakomēkhanou okruoessēs*: *Iliad* 6.344; see *Iliad* 9.257 (Eris, *kakomēkhanos*) and 9.64 (civil war, *okruoessē*), as well as 13.48, 24.524, and Hesiod *Theogony* 936 (*kruoeros*: "terror," "moaning," "war").

30. *Iliad* 19.325: *rhigedanē*, which will be compared to 24.775. On this matter, see L. L. Clader, *Helen* (Leiden, 1976), 18–22. Quotation from Ronsard, *Sonnets pour Hélène*, 1, 2.5–6.

31. *Odyssey* 14.69; Aeschylus *Agamemnon* 63–64.

32. Theognis 1231–32. Eros *lusimelēs*: Hesiod *Theogony* 121, 911; Alcman fr. 3.61 Page; Sappho fr. 44a Campbell. See also Archilochus fr. 85 Edmonds (*lusimelēs pothos*) and Hesiod *Works and Days* 66 (Aphrodite gives Pandora "painful desire and the cares that crush one's limbs").

33. The cursed wife: Aeschylus *Agamemnon* 406, as well as Euripides *Hecuba* 948–49, *Andromache* 103–4, *Trojan Women* 357, *Helen* 687–90. Ares is *miaiphonos* (murderous scoundrel), as will be Helen's beautiful hair in Euripides (*Trojan Women* 881–82).

34. *Iliad* 24.30: *makhlosunē alegeinē*; note that one of the possible etymologies of *algos* links this word with the Latin *algeo*, "to be cold": Helen *rhigedanē* is never far away.

35. Plato *Republic* 9.586b–c; Plato only mentions Helen in this passage and once in the *Phaedrus*—but what texts!

36. Hideous Eris: Pausanias 5.19.2; Helen-Eris: Aeschylus *Agamemnon* 1454–61, as well as Euripides *Helen* 246–49, 1134–36, 1156–57, and 1160. See Ramnoux 1959, 134–35.

37. Eris the founder of the human order: Nagy 1979, 218–20.

38. Aeschylus *Agamemnon* 355, with commentary in J. Bollack (Bollack and Judet de la Combe 1981, 1:2, 380–82).

39. The first woman and Zeus's *boulē*: Hesiod *Theogony* 572; see Loraux 1981b, 75–117; Helen and Pandora: Ramnoux 1959, 71–72. Ronsard had made the comparison, evoking Pandora with regard to his Helen (1.18, l. 8). Eris and *ponos*: *Theogony* 225–26.

40. Euripides *Trojan Women* 765–69. On Helen, the object of inextricable hate and love, Cassin 1985.

41. On the Orphic egg, see M. Detienne, "Les Chemins de la déviance," in *Orfismo in Magna Grecia* (Naples, 1979), 72–74n. Helen, daughter of Leda/ Nemesis: Apollodorus 3.10.6–7, Pausanias 1.33.7, as well as Sappho fr. 166 Campbell. On Helen's egg, see also A. Ruiz de Elvira, "Helena. Mito y etopeya," *Cuadernos de filologia classica* 6 (1974): 99–109n.

42. *Theogony* 223–24; in 592 it is the turn for the "race of women" to be a *pēma* for mortals, who find themselves to be male, sexual beings: Loraux 1981b,

80–81. Philotes and Apate are part of Aphrodite's train (*Theogony* 224; 205–6). Aidos and Nemesis: *Works and Days* 198–200.

43. Quotation from Shakespeare, *Titus Andronicus* (5.2.39–40).

44. *Nemesis*: here I am relying on Benveniste 1948, 79–80; *aidōs kai nemesis*: directly influenced by Benveniste, see J.-C. Turpin, "L'Expression *aidōs kai nemesis* et les actes de langage," *Revue des études grecques* 93 (1980): 352–67.

45. Which Kérenyi, a Jungian and fine reader of texts, clearly saw (1945, 14–15). In the passage of *Titus Andronicus* quoted in n. 43, aside from the needs of the plot, a similar logic impels Tamora, disguised as Revenge, to proffer the name of Revenge.

46. *Anaidōs*: *Phaedrus* 243c1.

47. Euripides *Orestes* 98–102 and 1361–62. This is the most classical Euripidean viewpoint, but not the only one: on Euripides' *Helen* interpreted in Aristophanes' *Thesmophoriazousae* as a "palinode," see Zeitlin 1982a, 201.

48. Hesiod fr. 203 Merkelbach-West, 81–82.

49. *Iliad* 6.351: *nemesis kai aiskhea polla*; more concrete than *aidōs*, *aiskhea* can, however, be considered as a synonym: see C. E. von Erffa, *Aidōs und verwandte Begriffe* . . . (Leipzig, 1937), 20.

50. *Iliad* 3.410–12 (same formula spoken by Hera in book 14).

51. What Kérenyi did not fail to point out concerning 3.156 (1945, 26–27).

52. On Helen, at once blamed and praised, Cassin 1985, 162.

53. Benveniste 1948, 80. My emphasis.

54. See N. Loraux, "Sur un non-sens grec. Oedipe, Théognis, Freud," *L'Ecrit du temps* 19 (1988): 19–36, n. 23.

55. I am thinking of the article "Remarques sur la fonction du langage dans la découverte freudienne" (Benveniste 1966, 75–87), which criticizes in particular Freud's article "On Opposite Meanings in Primitive Words" (1910); on this article, see J.-C. Milner, "Sens opposés et noms indiscernables: K. Abel comme refoulé d'E. Benveniste," in S. Auraux, ed., *La Linguistique fantastique* (Paris: Clims-Denoël, 1985), 300–310.

56. Freud 1964b, 235. Benveniste's postulation in 1948 of an earlier positive form is retrospectively clarified in 1966, 84 (remarks on *linguistic* negation: "The characteristic of linguistic negation is that it can only annul what has been stated, which it must explicitly posit in order to suppress it").

57. Neuter from the standpoint of gender as much as meaning: see *Phaedrus* 225e5 (*poiei ta meta touto takhu tauta*: "He quickly does this, which follows that") and 256c3–4 ("they get down to business. And, the business concluded . . .").

58. See, for example, Benveniste 1969, 340.

59. *Sonnets pour Hélène* 2.48.12–14.

60. The bird and its wings: Aeschylus *Agamemnon* 394 (and 691–92); see also Euripides *Helen* 606, 618–19, 666–68, 1516, as well as Lykophron *Alexandra* 822. Helen as "bird": Lykophron *Alexandra* 87, 131, 513; Meilhac and Halévy, *La belle Hélène* 1.5. In the *Cypria* Nemesis's ultimate metamorphosis makes her into a goose. Winged Nemesis: Pausanias 1.33.7.

61. Plato *Phaedrus* 252b.

62. Taking flight: Plato *Laws* 738c10–d1 (*aphrodisiōn tina diaptoēsin*). Wings: Sappho fr. 22 Campbell, 14; Plato *Phaedrus* 246d, 249d, 251a–252b; Ronsard, *Sonnets pour Hélène* 1.17.8.

63. *Agamemnon* 682: *etētumōs*.

64. For Chantraine 1968, s.v. *Helenē*, "one seeks in vain for an etymology." On the Greek poetic practice of forging etymologies as signifiers, see "*Poluneikēs epōnumos*. Le Nom des fils d'Oedipe entre épopée et tragédie," in C. Calame, ed., *Métamorphoses du mythe en Grèce antique* (Geneva: Labor et Fides, 1988), 151–66.

65. Aeschylus *Agamemnon* 681–98 (based on the French trans. by P. Judet de la Combe). See Ramnoux 1959, 131, as well as "De la légende à la sagesse à travers le jeu des mots," in Gentili and Paioni 1977, 195–96.

66. As Judet de la Combe observes (Bollack and Judet de la Combe 1982, 2:21–22); with him (31–32), it will also be noted that in this text the name Helen also "negates" that of Menelaus (*Helenas*/Menelaus) as well as that of Paris-Alexander (*Helandros*/Alexandros). I would add that in line 685 *nemōn* is perhaps an indirect reference to Nemesis.

67. Euripides *Trojan Women* 981–83.

68. Negation, once again . . .

69. Stesichorus, quoted by Plato *Phaedrus* 243a (*oud' ebas*); Aeschylus *Agamemnon* 406–7 (*bebaken*) and 424–46 (*bebaken*), with comments by Bollack (Bollack and Judet de la Combe 1981, 1:2, 440–42). According to Isocrates (*Praise of Helen* 65), Helen appeared before Stesichorus as an image in a dream. Lykophron will develop the image of a fleeting Helen (*Alexandra* 110–14 and 130–31) and that of the beloved Helen in a dream—this time dreamed by Achilles (*Alexandra* 171–73). Helen as a dream image: see Ronsard once more, *Sonnets pour Hélène* 1.60 and 2.41.

70. Aeschylus *Agamemnon* 414–15, with commentary by Bollack (1981, 1:2, 426–32).

71. Euripides *Helen* 611 and 718.

72. Stesichorus and sight: G. Nagy, *Pindar's Homer* (Baltimore, 1990); Helen and her double: Zeitlin 1982a, 202.

73. *Eidōlon*: Stesichorus fr. 63 Page (which will be recalled by Lykophron *Alexandra* 141–43); another version of the Egyptian story of Helen is found in Herodotus 2.113–20.

74. *Annuaire du Collège de France* (1976–77), 426–27.

75. The Iliadic Helen, the mirror of Achilles: L. L. Clader, *Helen*, 5ff.; on Helen in book 4 of the *Odyssey*, see R. Dupont-Roc and A. Le Boulluec, "Le Charme du récit," in *Ecriture et théorie poétique* (Paris, 1976), 30–39.

76. Euripides *Orestes* 1629, 1684, with scholia. On the Euripidean paradox of Helen, see Jouan 1966, 52–53, and Zeitlin 1985b, 81–82.

77. Helen, mistress of *mimēsis*: Zeitlin 1982a, 204.

78. Euripides *Helen* 33–36, 42–43, 65–66, 588, 1100 (name/body), and esp. 383–84; Ronsard, *Sonnets pour Hélène*, 2.9.13–14 (and 2.54).

79. Euripides *Helen* 262–63; 704–5; 1219 (*nephelēs agalma*).

80. *Opsis* and *prosopsis*: 577 (559), 569–70, 636.

81. Euripides *Helen* 72–77 (and 118–19, 121, 160–61). Helen, *opsis* and *erōs*

in the *Praise of Helen* by Gorgias: F. Donadi, "Gorgia, *Elena* 16," *Bolletino dell'Istituto di Filologia greca (Padova)* 4 (1977–78): 48–77, nn. 50–52.

82. See esp. line 593, with the commentary by M. Delcourt (*Euripide. Théâtre complet* [Paris: Pléiade], 928) and the remarks E. Bloch (*Le Principe d'espérance*, French trans. [Paris, 1976], 222–25) devotes to the "reality" of the Helen-*eidōlon*. War for nothing: 603, 751; for a cloud: 707, 750; for a gust of wind: 32.

83. Ronsard, *Sonnets pour Hélène*, 1.60.11.

84. Séféris, "Hélène," ll. 50 and 68 (*Poèmes*, French trans. J. Lacarrière).

85. Helen, need it be recalled, is dear to the Sophists: see Cassin 1985.

86. This is why I have focused on this Helen and not on the one who is considered a goddess and is the object of a cult in Sparta or elsewhere. But—as the reader may have surmised—my intention here was not to present an exhaustive monograph on Helen.

87. The original version of this chapter was published in *Nouvelle revue de psychanalyse* 29 (1984; issue on sexuality): 11–31.

CHAPTER TWELVE
WHAT TIRESIAS SAW

1. On the canonical version of the story, see the material gathered by Brisson 1976.

2. In lines 55–56 of *Hymn VI* (*Bath of Pallas*), Callimachus asserts that others have told the story before him; this statement is taken seriously by K. J. McKay, *The Poet at Play. Kallimachos, The Bath of Pallas* (Leiden [*Mnemosyne*, supp. 6], 1962).

3. Freud 1964a, 231.

4. This does not mean that Tiresias as a figure was not utterly marked for this adventure: see above, Introduction.

5. Freud 1964a, 220, 222–26 (*Unheimlich/Heimlich*).

6. Athena and Herakles: *Iliad* 8.362–69; and Diomedes: *Iliad* 5.116–17 and 809, 10.283–91; and Odysseus: *Iliad* 10.278–80; *Odyssey* 3.218–24, 378–80, 13.372. Athena, goddess of proximity: Otto 1981, 65, 71, 78.

7. See E. R. Dodds, *The Greeks and the Irrational* (Berkeley, 1951), 35. To be sure, in Greek, "as in many languages, the word that would convey this particular nuance of the frightening is lacking," but in the word *philos* there is virtually much more disturbing unfamiliarity (see Slatkin 1988) than in *xenos*, the word for "foreigner" that Freud mentions ([1964a], 221), on the authority of Reik.

8. On this question, see particularly Buxton 1980, 30–32, and A.-F. Laurens and H. Gallet de Santerre, "Des hommes aux dieux en Grèce: Droit de regard?" in *Hommages à François Daumas* (Montpelier, 1986), 463–81.

9. E.g., *Homeric Hymn to Demeter* 105ff.

10. Or, to follow Pucci's translation (1985, 171 and 1986, 8): "The gods are terrible in their fully blazing appearance."

11. Thus, to comment on *Odyssey* 3.420 (where Athena has appeared *enargēs*), Eustathius says that "she has appeared *corporeally*" (*sōmatikōs*). On the difficulties involved with understanding the word *enargēs*, see Pucci 1986, 21–22.

12. On the terror of the face-to-face confrontation and the Gorgon's mask that graphically embodies it, see Schlesier 1982, 23ff., Vernant 1985 (and 1989, 119–20).

13. From the *Iliad* to the *Odyssey*, the textual strategy of the epiphany is of course quite different, as Pucci noted (1986, 8), but this is not my point.

14. Despite Pucci's arguments (1985, 176) in favor of maintaining the ambiguity (Achilles' eyes/Athena's eyes), I have made a choice: see n. 33 below.

15. Otto 1981, 61.

16. H. Kleinknecht, "*Loutra tēs Pallados*," *Hermes* 74 (1939): 301–30, n. 316 (rpt. in *Wege der Forschung: Kallimachos*, ed. A. D. Skiadas [Darmstadt, 1975], 207–75) is interested in this echo from the sole perspective of the relationship between myth and rite.

17. According to Apollodorus, the version in which Tiresias "was blinded for having seen Athena totally naked" dates back to Pherecydes (3.6.7).

18. Note that the prohibition against seeing Pallas in the nude is addressed to men (lines 51–54) and comes after a prohibition aimed specifically at women (lines 45–48). On the ritual dimension of the hymn and the question of bathing statues, see L. Deubner, *Attische Feste*[2] (Berlin, 1956); and Ginouvès 1962, 283–84, 292–94.

19. In Nonnos's *Dionysiaka* (4.337–45), the dying Actaeon expounds on the theme, suggested in Callimachus, of Athena's gentleness compared to Artemis's cruelty ("Happy Tiresias! For you have seen Athena's nude form without perishing").

20. Such is the interpretation of K. J. McKay, *Poet at Play*, 27.

21. The pair of snakes and bisexuality: Brisson 1976, 55–56. Whatever Athena's affinities with the snake, one still cannot assert with Brisson (66) that "Athena can be likened to a serpent." It is better to base one's reasoning on the terms of the mythic sequences and observe 1) that, in this version, it is seeing— Athena equals seeing—snakes copulating; 2) that, in the best logic, for Tiresias seeing Athena is also equivalent to the two other sequences preceding his punishment (his experience of femininity, his role in the argument between Zeus and Hera): if one compares the two versions of the myth and reckons that Callimachus's version is a "condensed" version of the other, one has to take the method to its conclusion.

22. According to Jouan 1966, 101, Callimachus would be alluding here to Sophocles' *Judgment*, where Athena was satisfied with oil while Aphrodite used a perfumed unguent.

23. Athena is *hē theos* in the Athenian inscriptions; *theos gunē*: Aristophanes *Birds* 829–31; Theodorus's joke: Diogenes Laertes 2.116, where the garden is a startling metaphor in the context of the Parthenos's sexuality—mention is made of Aphrodite's "cleft meadows." *Theos* as a neuter designation for the divine per se: in book 20 of the *Odyssey*, Athena, speaking to Odysseus or seated at his side, is the goddess with the blue-grey eyes (*thea glaukōpis*: 44, 393), but when she wishes to assert her divine essence, she states, "I am *theos*" (47).

24. See Frontisi 1975, 104–6 and 110 (see the discussion about Palladion); description of the Palladion: Apollodorus 3.12.3.

25. Quotation by G. Rosolato, who is asking, "What was Freud contemplating on the Acropolis?" *Nouvelle Revue de Psychanalyse* 15 (1977): 135.

26. To play the flute is to make the face of the Gorgon; see Schlesier 1982 and Vernant 1985, 56–58.

27. Quotation in Otto 1981, 72.

28. Account of the adventure and commentary in Athenaeus 14.616; see also Plutarch *Moralia* 456b (*amorphia*), Apollodorus 1.4.2 (*amorphon*), Clement of Alexandria *Paedagogos* 2.31.1 (*aprepes*), and Ovid's Latin variations (*Art of Love* 3.505; *Fasti* 6.699). Concerning the notion of *amorphia*, I am greatly indebted to the ongoing research of Maurice Olender.

29. Even if it is not necessarily Athena's "true" face but one that she might adopt (Pucci 1986, 14–15). *Odyssey* 13.287–319 (and 16.157–64); in line 288 (*demas d'ēikto gunaiki*), however, it would be forcing the text to translate it, as V. Bérard and P. Jaccottet have done, "She *resumed* the form of a woman," which amounts to prejudging Athena's "ordinary" form; at the most, the text permits one to understand, "She had taken on the form of a woman for a body."

30. Brisson 1976, 34, my emphasis. More subtly, Buxton, who accepts the basic premises of Brisson's argument, observes that to move from apparent masculinity to latent femininity "means a more radical transgression of the divine identity than would be the case with Aphrodite's 'transparent' femininity" (1980, 31).

31. In l. 88 *stēthea kai lagonas* (breast and flanks) has nothing descriptive about it; these terms simply situate parts of the human body, male or female.

32. *Iliad* 3.396–97 (Helen and Aphrodite), *Homeric Hymn to Aphrodite* 181 (Anchises and Aphrodite), Euripides *Hippolytus* 86. On the reciprocity of sight, Frontisi 1975, 110.

33. *Iliad* 1.197–205; in l. 201, with Otto and McKay and against Mazon (who sees Achilles' eyes there), I interpret *deinō osse* to refer to the eyes of the goddess; on *osse* as expressing the fiery gaze, see A. Prévot, "Verbes grecs relatifs à la vision et noms de l'oeil," *Revue de philologie* (1935): 271.

34. *Hymn* 5.17, passage that McKay rightly views as important. On the mirror (where one looks straight at oneself, in the form of a simple face), cf. J.-P. Vernant, "Résumé des cours et travaux," *Annuaire du Collège de France, 1979–80*, 453–59, and Vernant 1989, 117–29.

35. *Iliad* 5. 127–28 (Diomedes); Sophocles *Ajax* 450 (*hē Dios gorgōpis adamatos thea*) and 51–52, 83–85 (Athena and Ajax); Orphic fragment 174 (O. Kern, ed.), with commentary by Detienne and Vernant 1974, 172.

36. This hypothesis underlies the interpretation of *Hymn 5* by K. J. McKay; on Athena *Oxuderkēs* in Argos (Pausanias 2.24.2) and *Ophthalmitis* in Sparta, see the remarks of L. R. Farnell, *The Cults of the Greek States*, vol. 1 (Oxford, 1896), 279.

37. Quotation from Detienne and Vernant 1974, 173; story of Iodama: Pausanias 9.34.2.

38. *Oxuderkēs*: it will be recalled that the root of *derkomai*, which expresses the intensity of the gaze, furnishes one of the words for snake, *drakōn* (cf. A. Prévot, "Verbes grecs relatifs à la vision," 233–35); *glaukōpis*: in Pindar's eighth *Olympian*, snakes are *glaukoi*, which the scholiast glosses as "terrifying."

39. On the efficacy of the archaic statue's gaze: Frontisi 1975, 108–10; Plutarch *Moralia* 309f, quoting the historian Derkyllos, tells of the adventure of the

Trojan Ilos, blinded for having saved the Palladion from a blazing temple and who recovered his vision after appeasing the goddess's anger; recall the prohibition made to the men of Argos against seeing Pallas (i.e., according to the scholia to Callimachus's *Hymn 5*, the Palladion that the Argive women bathe each year).

40. See C. Calvi, "Il Piatto d'argento di Castelvint," *Aquileia Nostra* 50 (1979): 355–56, fig. 1. I thank Claude Bérard for having sent me, at François Lissarrague's request, a photocopy of this document "to show [me] what Tiresias saw."

41. *Landscape with Judgment of Paris*, National Gallery of Art, Washington, D.C. (no. 2355).

42. For Dumézil, Paris did not choose among three types of beauty but the three functions.

43. The three goddesses bathing: Euripides *Andromache* 284–86, *Helen* 676–78; they wash their gleaming bodies (*aiglanta sōmata*) or simply their beauty (*morphan*); *morphē*, "form" as a word for "beauty": again, see *Trojan Women* 975 and *Iphigenia in Aulis* 183–84. On all of this, see Jouan 1966, 95–99.

44. See C. Dugas, "Tradition littéraire et tradition graphique dans l'Antiquité grecque," *L'Antiquité classique* 6 (1937): 13 and fig. 6 (krater from the Bibliothèque Nationale, Paris). The opposition that provides the structure for the image, as in the case of Sophocles (n. 22), contrasts Athena, who is washing (content with water from a fountain), and her rivals, who adorn themselves.

45. *Iliad* 5.733–38. Scholia to line 734 (*katekheuen*) first mention the detached clasps in terms analogous to those used by Callimachus (*Hymn 5* 70), then the disrobed goddess; see also the scholia to 8.385. On Athena in this passage from the *Iliad*, see Loraux 1981b, 142–43.

46. Athena born armed: Stesichorus fr. 62 Bergk, *Homeric Hymn to Athena* 4–5, Callimachus fr. 37 Pfeiffer. Metis forging Athena's weapons: Chrysippus fr. 908 von Arnim. Cf. Detienne and Vernant 1974, 172 (quotation).

47. "The weapons, the garment of an individual are connected to the individual and cannot be seen as abstract" (Gernet 1917, 222n.103).

48. Plutarch *Moralia* 245a (*Virtues of Women*), with commentary by Ellinger 1978, 23.

49. See Loraux 1986c, and above, chap. 5, 92–99.

50. The aegis as the Gorgon's skin: Euripides *Ion* 987–97; as the skin of Pallas the Giant, or the Giant Asteros: Clement of Alexandria *Protreptika* 2.28.2, with commentary by F. Vian, *La Guerre des géants* (Paris, 1952), 198 and 267 (where the Palladion of Ilion is covered with a man's skin); L. Koenen, R. Merkelbach, "Apollodorus (*Peri theōn*), Epicharm und die *Meropis*," *Papyrologische Texte und Abhandlungen* 19 (1976): 3–26. *Khrōs* referring to the flesh penetrated by the weapon and pain: e.g., *Iliad* 11.398. The "artificial goddess": I have borrowed this expression from G. Dumézil (in *Le Festin d'immortalité*).

51. Loraux 1981b, 84–86.

52. To wit, the multiple occurrences of the verb *dunō* (to dig into, to slide into) concerning Athena: see for example *Iliad* 5.845; 8.378 and 387; 17.551.

53. Pucci 1986, 9 stresses the difficulty of perceiving the gods' bodies, and especially, in the case of Achilles, of seeing Athena, this "white figure."

54. *Homeric Hymn to Aphrodite* 161–67; however, the ellipsis of the very *instant* of disrobing invites further development of the point advanced by P.

Friedrich (*The Meaning of Aphrodite* [Chicago and London, 1978], 136–37) concerning nudity as a constitutive element of this goddess.

55. *Iliad* 5.737; cf. 8.376 and Euripides *Ion* 993; *stēthos* is, for the warrior, what covers the breastplate (*thōrēx*): see *Iliad* 16.133 and 17.606; in *Ion* 995, Athena wears the Gorgon's skin on her chest (*epi sternois*); shoulders: see *Iliad* 5.738 and *Homeric Hymn to Athena* 14–15.

56. Artisan's hand: *Iliad* 5.735; female warrior's hand: 5.836 and 853, 21.403 and 424; man's or god's hand, not hers: 4.541, 5.29–30 (except 21.286, where she acts with Poseidon); supplement on the body added by P. Mazon: translation of 1.197, 5.799, 21.397; Athena's incorporeal intervention: 11.437–38.

57. According to Rosolato, "Que contemplait Freud?" 138.

58. Callimachus *Hymn 5* 119–30; Apollodorus 3.6.7.

59. This article was originally published in *L'Ecrit du temps* 2 (1982): 99–116 and has benefited from the comments of Luc Brisson, Claude Calame, and Claude Bérard concerning the "reality" of what Tiresias saw. I am grateful to each of them for the time they devoted to this discussion and have attempted to explain here why I persist in my view. Last, I owe much to my conversations with Piero Pucci on the question of epiphanies.

CONCLUSION
FEMININE NATURE IN HISTORY

1. This phrase is based on a remark made by A. Momigliano concerning wars and constitutions as the privileged objects of ancient historiography ("Some Observations of Causes of War in Ancient Historiography," *Studies in Historiography* [London, 1966], 112–16); with Herodotus, Thucydides, and Xenophon, "historiography" is understood in the sense of *Hellenika*.

2. M. Rosellini and S. Saïd, "Usages de femmes et autres *nomoi* chez les 'sauvages' d'Hérodote," *Annali della Scuola Normale Superiore di Pisa* 8, 3 (1978): 949–1005; A. Tourraix, "La Femme et le pouvoir chez Hérodote," *Dialogues d'Histoire ancienne* 2(1976): 369–86; the essential study remains the article by S. Pembroke, "Women in Charge: The Function of Alternatives in Early Greek Tradition and the Ancient Idea of Matriarchy," *Journal of the Warburg and Courtauld Institute* 30 (1967): 1–35.

3. Herodotus 5.39–42, 6.61–66; Xenophon *Hellenika* 3.3.2–4. See also Pausanias 3.4.3–4, 7.7, and 8.7, as well as Plutarch *Lycurgus* 3.1–6.

4. To borrow Plutarch's expression (*Virtues of Women* [*Moralia* 253e]).

5. I will focus on these three great works of classical historiography because they have come down to us in their entirety and their full development can be followed, something that would be impossible with textual fragments.

The attention to historical *narrative* and what it accepts or rejects sets this study apart from three articles devoted to closely related subjects: Schaps 1982 (who is primarily concerned with establishing women's *real* attitude toward war), Graf 1984 (who is especially interested in stories of women warriors, who in his view are the *aitia* for cults or rituals that invert the normal distribution of roles), and Napolitano 1987 (who focuses solely on the tensions within the Spartan tradition).

6. Thus Plutarch writes his treatise on *The Virtues of Women* to refute the famous assertion in the *epitaphios* of Pericles (Thucydides 2.45.2) that women have a specific "virtue"; just like Antisthenes (Diogenes Laertes 6.12), Plutarch believes that women and men have a single *aretē*; from this he deduces that feminine exploits are an adornment to historical exposition (*ton historikon apodeiktikon*: *Moralia* 243a).

7. In his account of the "Phocidian despair," Plutarch will give the mouthpiece to women; but here they are choosing their death, and even under these circumstances they hold their own assembly, carefully distinguished from that of the men and doubled by a children's assembly (*Virtues of Women* 2 = *Moralia* 244c–d).

8. Aristotle *Politics* 3.1274b38–1275a23; in 1.1260b15–20 the distinction is made between women, "half of the free population," and children, future members of the community.

9. Thucydides 2.6.4 and 78.3; among the *akhreioi* evacuated by the Athenians are slaves, as can be deduced from 2.78.4; on *akhreios* in a political context, see 2.40.2, where some have seen an echo of the use of the word *khrēstos* to refer to the citizen (cf. Loraux 1981a, 414n.17). On "not again" and "never again": Lysias *Epitaphios* 50–53 (Loraux 1981a, 126–27); women, children, old men: e.g., Xenophon *Hellenika* 6.5.12.

10. Women, wives of citizens: Chantraine 1946–47, 219, 250; the asymmetry between the "people of Athenians" and the "people of women" in the *Thesmophoriazousae*: Loraux 1981b, 126–27. In Lysias (*Epitaphios* 34), *gunaikes* specifically denotes the wives of Athenian men.

11. Aristotle *Politics* 2.1269b12ff. (Aristotelian commentary on a page from Plato *Laws* 6.780d–781b; see also *Laws* 7.806c). Practical application: e.g., Herodotus 7.120, where "the entire people" includes citizens and women.

12. *Athlon*: Lysias *Epitaphios* 39 (in the development on Salamis, entirely focused on this *topos* of official rhetoric); women, children, gods (or statues of gods): e.g., Thucydides 7.69.2, as well as Herodotus 2.30. On the concrete reality of this *topos*, see Y. Garlan, *Recherches de poliorcétique grecque* (Paris, 1974), 70.

13. See Herodotus 3.65 and 6.139, where, as in the imprecations contained in oaths, human fecundity is linked with the fecundity of the flocks and the earth: cf. M. Delcourt, *Stérilités mystérieuses et naissances maléfiques dans l'antiquité classique* (Paris, 1938).

14. Salamis: Herodotus 8.40 and 60, Thucydides 1.89.3; by sheltering women and children within the walls, the Periclean strategy reversed the habitual tactic, which was to move them outside the territory: Thucydides 2.14.1. Hostages: Herodotus 7.52.2 (see also 3.45.5 and Aeneas Tacticus *Poliorcetica* 5). Held hostage/protected: compare Thucydides 2.6.4 (and 78.3) with 2.72.2.

15. E.g., Herodotus 6.19.3; Thucydides 3.68.3 (and 36.2), 4.48.4 (where it is a matter of *stasis*), 5.32 and 116.4. Thracians in Mykalessos: Thucydides 7.29.4 (as well as Pausanias 1.23.3).

16. Herodotus 1.164 and 166 (the Phocians), Thucydides 1.103.3 (the Messanians of Ithome); see also Thucydides 2.27.1 and 70.3.

17. Herodotus 1.176 (the Lycians), 7.107.2 (a Persian dignitary), 3.150 and 159. On "Phocidian despair," *aition* of the feast of the Elaphebolia in Hyampolis, see Plutarch *Virtues* 2 (= *Moralia* 244b–e) and Pausanias 10.1.6–7; concerning

this episode, see also Pierre Ellinger on Artemis and wars of annihilation, *La Légende nationale phocidienne: Artémis, les situations extrêmes et les récits de guerre d'anéantissement* (Athens: Ecole française d'Athènes, 1993).

18. This statement makes it possible to clarify the remarks made by C. Dewald ("Women and Culture in Herodotus' *Histories*," in H. P. Foley, ed., *Reflections of Women in Antiquity* [New York, 1981], 93n.) on the privileged role of women as the mirror of civilization in Herodotus's account; in this role, in fact, women are not alone, as they are closely linked with children.

19. Xenophon *Hellenika* 7.2.9; Thucydides 4.48.4 (these women will be reduced to slavery, as if by an external enemy; were they *sitopoioi*, as in Herodotus 3.150 or in Thucydides himself [2.78.3]? The account does not say).

20. Thucydides 1.90.3 (Athens); 5.82.6 (Argos). As the presence of children in the first passage seems strange, some editors, on the basis of a scholia, have considered the mention of women and children to be a simple gloss of *pandēmei*; since no one has judged it appropriate to consider "women and slaves" to be a gloss of the same word, *pandēmei*, in the second text, I will not accord this careless correction of Thucydides 1.90.3 the same attention that Schaps gives it (1982, 195n.1).

21. An abnormal post, to be sure, even for men: in book 4 (48.2) the democrats will climb on a roof to massacre their opponents, using the same weapons that the women did in book 3—tiles. Women on the roof, in another context, licentious this time: Detienne 1972, 187–88.

22. Thucydides 2.4.2–7 (Plataea); 3.73–74.2 (Corcyra). In Corcyra the people took their position on the Acropolis, while the oligarchs occupied the Agora (72.3): these recall the respective positions of the women and old men in *Lysistrata* (the dramatization of a kind of *stasis*).

23. During the second *stasis* in Corcyra, many women are with the oligarchs (4.48.4), but no slaves are mentioned.

24. See P. Vidal-Naquet, "Esclavage et gynécocratie dans la tradition, le mythe, l'épopée" (Vidal-Naquet 1981, 267–88).

25. Cf. D. Asheri, "Tyrannie et mariage forcé," *Annales ESC* (Jan.-Feb. 1977): 21–48.

26. Plutarch links this theme with that of forced marriage in his account of the lofty deeds of the women of Khios who, assisted by slaves, helped the men to carry out the siege of Philip, son of Demetrios (*Virtues* 3 = *Moralia* 245b–c).

27. Pausanias 8.5.9 (Tegea); 2.20.8–10 (Argos), to which Plutarch can be added: *Moralia* 245d (= *Virtues* 4). Again see Pausanias 4.21.6–11 (Messenia).

28. Thucydides 3.74.1: *xunepelabonto*. Note that before they decided to fight alongside the men and with the same weapons, the women in Pausanias's account of the Messenians first acted as a supplemental force (4.21.6).

29. Pausanias 2.20.9; on this point I am further developing the work of P. Vidal-Naquet 1981, 175.

30. This begins in the *Iliad* where, in the war-torn city represented on Achilles' shield, "women and their young children, standing on the ramparts, defend it with the help of men whom old age kept back" (18.514–15).

31. *Politics* 1.1260a20–24; thus women share *andreia* with men, but, like the slave's virtue, this courage is characterized by *hupēresia* (see 1295b26).

32. Pausanias 8.5.9 (Tegeans and women), 8.45.3 (the Tegeans); 8.48.4–6

(women); sacrifice to Ares Gunaikothoinas: ibid.; likewise, the women of Argos sacrifice to Ares: Plutarch *Moralia* 245e. It goes without saying that in ordinary times, the *nikētēria*, victory feasts with sacrifices and banquets, were carried out only by men (Graf 1984, 246).

33. Pausanias 4.21.9 (Messenian women).

34. Ambush: Pausanias 8.48.4 (Tegea); *epiphanēnai*: ibid., 5; *thaumazein*: Plutarch *Moralia* 245e (Argos); *tropē*: Pausanias 8.48.5 (Tegea).

35. Thucydides 2.4.2: *trapomenoi*; 3.74.2: *tropē*. The fact that these victories are provisional is not sufficient to invalidate them, despite the pedestrian conditions mentioned by Schaps 1982, 195. It will be observed that in the Thucydidean corpus *tropē* often has its place in an uncertain battle (against a backdrop of *thorubos*) or naval combat.

36. On women's *anasurma* in war, see Zeitlin 1982b, 144–45, for whom such displays of female genitalia are entirely apotropaic, since the desired effect, as it is in the case of the Gorgon's head on the shields, is to repulse the enemy (the Gorgon: Apollodorus 2.7.3).

37. See Plutarch *Sayings of Spartans* 241a–b and *Virtues of Women* 246a. Helen King, "Agnodike and the Profession of Medicine," *Proceedings of the Cambridge Philological Society* 32 (1986): 53–75 (nn.61–68), does not believe in the apotropaic virtue of this gesture, which she sees everywhere as the display of the part of the female body devoted to reproduction. But it is not clear that the two acts are mutually exclusive; they could overdetermine each other, and if the surname of Marpessa, the heroine of Tegea also called Khoira (Pausanias 8.47.2; 48.6), indeed contains, as Graf (1984, 248n. 25) and I have each supposed, an allusion to the female organ, for which one of the surnames is *khoiros*, the two readings, as in Pausanias (8.47.2: Khoira; 47.5: the Gorgon), reinforce rather than exclude one another. On all these matters, see "Les Guerriers et les femmes impudiques" (J. Moreau, in *Mélanges H. Grégoire* [Brussels, 1981], 283–300), as well as F. Le Roux, "La Mort de Cuchulainn," *Ogam: Tradition Celtique* 18 (1966): 365–99; and Olender 1985, 34–38.

38. See above, chap. 1.

39. After Plataea was taken by the Peloponnesians, the women who remained in the town were of course destined for slavery: Thucydides 3.68.2; on a less dramatic mode (and to cite a late source), see Plutarch *Pyrrhus* 29.12, where the Spartan women returned to their homes the moment the reinforcements arrived, "having no further wish to be involved with the war."

40. E.g., Plutarch *Moralia* 245b–c (the women of Khios): *lithous kai belē*, "stones and projectiles"; for Rome, Dionysius of Halicarnassus 6.92.6 (the women of Corioli defend the city against the Roman enemy by throwing tiles from the rooftops). There is also the tradition concerning the death of Pyrrhus, killed in Argos by a missile—a stone or a tile, depending on the version (e.g., Pausanias 1.13.8)—thrown by a woman; other accounts speak of women throwing darts from the rooftops: see the remarks by P. Lévêque, *Pyrrhos* (Paris, 1957), 625. *Stasis*: Thucydides 4.48.2.

41. Herodotus 9.5: lapidation of Lykidas's wife and children by the Athenian women; cf. Plutarch *Moralia* 241b (*Sayings of Spartans*): the woman who uses a tile to kill her son, the sole survivor of a war.

42. Herodotus 5.87; also, in Euripides' *Hecuba*, the Trojan captives blind Polymester with an "unwarlike hand," using clasps from their clothing (1169–71). Pins and femininity: Verdier 1979, 238–53. Along with fasteners one should add the shuttle used by a stepmother in the myth of Phineas to put out her stepson's eyes: see D. Bouvier and P. Moreau, "Phinée ou le père aveugle et la marâtre aveuglante," *Revue belge de philologie et d'histoire* 61 (1983): 5–19. As Stella Georgoudi has pointed out to me, while already in Herodotus the clasp is the instrument of collective murder, it is also a weapon that isolates each woman in her bloody act (*hekastēn*): even in a group, each of the women of Athens acts on her own.

43. Pausanias 4.21.6; note the *hekastē* (see n. 42 above).

44. Aeneas Tacticus 40.4–5.

45. The opinion of Lysistrata's husband (*Lysistrata* 520), who quotes Hector's words to Andromache (*Iliad* 6.492).

46. Far indeed from ancient Greece, the social practices of the Baruya of New Guinea suggest such a link, since the rare women warriors of this utterly masculine society take part only in internal conflicts and against other women (Godelier 1982, 132 and 219).

47. The conjunction between civil war and the Amazons seems to reflect a transhistoric logic: roaming far afield from Pindar and Homer, one need only think of the figure of Théroigne de Méricourt, an Amazon at the time of the French Revolution (E. Roudinesco, *Théroigne de Méricourt. Une femme mélancolique sous la Révolution* [Paris: Seuil, 1989], 104–12).

48. Homer *Iliad* 3.189; Pindar *Olympians* 12.15–16.

49. In line 13 of the *Suppliants*, Danaos is referred to as *stasiarkhos*; the rest of the text contrasts the *kratos* of women (1069–70) with that of *andres* (393, 951); see also 645: *eris gunaikōn*, which Mazon translates as "the women's cause."

50. It is not at all surprising that in the Athens of 412–11 men speak of *stasis* in the language of tyranny (*Lysistrata* 619, 630–34); beginning in 415, accusations of tyranny were the order of the day (see Thucydides 6.53 and esp. 60.1), and in 409 the decree of Demophantos (quoted by Andocides *Mysteries* 97) will identify the factions with the instigators of tyranny.

51. Aristophanes *Thesmophoriazousae* 786–88; see Loraux 1981b, 75–117 (on the race of women).

52. Dionysiac madness: e.g., in the *Bacchae*; cf. 35–36 (*mania* of the female people in Thebes) and 1295 (*mania* of the whole city, *pasa polis*, as if the "madness" of women caused the madness of the city at large); on the theme of the warlike Maenads, cf. *Bacchae* 52 and the Argive accounts (Pausanias 2.20.4). "Epidemic," *loimos* or *nosos*: e.g., the epidemic of hanging among the girls of Miletus (Plutarch *Moralia* 249b–d = *Virtues* 11).

53. Secession/sedition: this theme is at the center of *Lysistrata*; see also Dionysius of Halicarnassus 6.45.1 (*apostasis*) and 83.4 (*stasis*). Sedition and epidemic: the association is obvious in Aeschylus (see *Suppliants* 635–91 and *Eumenides* 782–87); see again, for example, Pausanias 5.4.6, as well as F. Frontisi, "Artémis bucolique," *Revue de l'histoire des religions* 198 (1981): 46–47nn. and 48n. 59 (*stasis* in the Greek text, epidemic in the Latin).

54. Aristotle *Politics* 2.1269b12–19.

55. See Thucydides 3.82.1 and, for example, Dionysius of Halicarnassus 7.66.5.

56. Compare Thucydides 3.74.1 (*hai gunaikes*) and 4.48.4 (*tas gunaikas, hosai*).

57. Ibid., 2.4.4; this *gunē*, the discrete incarnation of the treacherous woman (for a different example, see Aeneas Tacticus 31.7) only deserves a fleeting mention. Note however that there is a perceptible disparity between the *hai gunaikes*, fighting alongside the Plataeans (in fact the pro-Athenian *dēmos*), and an isolated *gunē* who helps the Thebans.

58. A. Parry, "Thucydides' Use of Abstract Language," *Yale French Studies* 45 (1970): 3–20, n. 7.

59. Thucydides 3.82.4; see N. Loraux, "Thucydide et la sédition dans les mots," *Quaderni di storia* 23 (1986): 95–134.

60. For Thucydides, *tolma* is an unstable signifier, sometimes positive, sometimes used in a negative context: thus the accent is placed on the qualifier: *tolma alogistos* of the Tyrant Killers: 6.59.1; on *tolma* (or *thrasutēs*) as a word for feminine boldness, see below, 242 and n. 72. *Andreia* is always positive in Thucydides' language, except when paired with *philetairos*: *philopolis*, four examples.

61. Quotation from G. Orwell, *Orwell's 1984: Text, Sources, Criticism*, ed. Irving Howe (New York: Harcourt Brace Jovanovich, 1963), 199. *Sophrōn* of course has a positive value for Thucydides, and during the debate on Mytilene in book 3, Diodotos associates *agathos politēs* with *sophrōn polis*.

62. Women's "virtue" is just as problematic for Livy, since the action of the Roman matrons against Coriolanus's mother and wife can be attributed to *muliebris timor* (2.40.1).

63. Graf 1984, 245 simply lists this passage of Thucydides among the series of traditional declarations on the subject of women's ineptitude for war.

64. This question provides the structure of the *Bacchae*, in which one of the two sides of feminine nature is *sōphronein* (Euripides *Bacchae* 314–16), and the other corresponds to *tolma* (1222 *tolmēmata*).

65. P.-C. Lévesque, *Etudes d'histoire ancienne*, vol. 3 (Paris, 1811), 54–55; see on this point N. Loraux and P. Vidal-Naquet, "La Formation de l'Athènes bourgeoise. Etude d'historiographie 1750–1850," in R. R. Bolgar, ed., *Classical Influences on Western Thought A.D. 1650–1870* (Cambridge, 1978), esp. 206.

66. Which today's historiography of the French Revolution enshrouds in silence. Note that for Michelet women oscillated between pity and violence (E. Roudinesco, *Théroigne de Méricourt*, 203–10; see also Fraisse 1989, 138, and, regarding Legouvé, 48–50). On the contrary, the tradition of the Paris Commune, lyrical about its relationship to the Revolution of 1789, makes revolutionary women into total heroines: see for example P.-O. Lissagaray, *Histoire de la Commune de 1871* (Paris: La Découverte-Maspero, 1983), 110, 187, 216–17, 322, 326, 353.

67. Thucydides 2.45.2.

68. Note that *thorubos*, according to Aristophanes, is already an obligatory component of women's daily life: see *Lysistrata* 329 (*thorubos* at the fountain); it is true that, seeing themselves as "citizens" (333), the women of Athens make the "maidservants and slaves branded with iron" responsible for the uproar (330–31).

69. To which, in Thucydides 2.4.2, are added the shouts and cries of victory from the women and slaves (*kraugē, ololugē*). Recall that *ololugē* is the feminine version of the highly masculine and warlike paean; a victory cry, *ololugē* accompanies the Athenian women's taking of the Acropolis (*Lysistrata* 240) or in tragic Argos marks the appearance of the luminous signal of the beacon fire: see Aeschylus *Agamemnon* 28 (as well as 587: Clytemnestra's *ololugē*; 595: the slaves' *ololugmos* "like that of women"). In a similar context, the women's *alalagmos* blends with the soldiers' cry (*kraugē*) during a street battle: Plutarch *Pyrrhus* 29.8.

70. *Hupomenein*, verb of hoplitic resistance, normally is complemented by *kindunos*; in this case *thorubos* would only be what *kindunos* is for men: what "nature" wishes one to endure without weakening. Cf. a similar use of this verb in Plato (*Laws* 6.781c5) concerning women.

71. See 1.49.4; 2.94.2; 2.104.1, 113.1 (besieged city); 3.77 (Corcyra); 4.68.4 (taking of a city by betrayal); 4.94 (confusion of earth/sea); 4.127 (the barbarians' *thorubos*); 7.40.3 and 44.4; 8.10.9; 8.92.7 (situation of *stasis*).

72. Used by Thucydides with regard to the actions of the Corcyrean women, *tolmēros* is found a few chapters later, in the development on the *stasis*, with a connotation that has nothing positive about it (3.83.3). Women's *tolma*, positive: Pausanias 4.21.6 (the women of Messenia), 8.47.5 (women of Tegea); Plutarch *Moralia* (= *Virtues*) 245d (and 245b, where women's *thumos* is involved). Negative *tolma*: *Lysistrata* 284 (the taking of the Acropolis is a *tolmēma* for the old men); Aeschylus *Choephoroi* 596–97 (women's loves as *pantolmoi*). The "crime of the Lemnian women" mentioned by the chorus of *Choephoroi* was described as *tolmēma* by later tradition (see Photius *Lexicon*, s.v. *Kabeiroi*).

73. I do not, however, overlook the importance of A. Parry's remark ("The Language of Thucydides' Description of the Plague," *Bulletin of the Institute of Classical Studies* 16 [1969]: 108) that *phusis* figures among the "scientific" words that the historian uses when he intends for his narrative to have an emotional impact.

74. Leaving aside the theoretical contribution that a Plato can bring to the debate by challenging the existence of such a *phusis* or reducing it to the biological difference between the sexes (*Republic* 5.453b, e, 454e, 455d–e, 456a), I will confine myself to the remarks of those who accept "feminine nature" as a fact.

75. A similar duality is found in *Lysistrata* between *thrasos*, which is negative when applied to old men and positive for women (545), and "wisdom" (473–508, 546); see again 545 (for *phusis*) and 549 (for *andreia*).

76. Xenophon *Hellenika* 6.5.28. Although he does nothing to contradict this detail, Plutarch amplifies it and imperceptibly modifies it (*Agesilaos* 31, 33–34); but he catches himself by telling of the Spartan women's proud behavior, under like circumstances, during Pyrrhus's attack (*Pyrrhus* 27.4–8, 28.5 and 29.5–12).

77. It is true that "even signs of things to be feared (*phobera*) make one fear," as Aristotle observes, reflecting on the role of *sēmeia* in fear (*Rhetoric* 2.1382a30).

78. Women's *andreia*: an oxymoron that fascinated the Greeks; the matter of Spartan women, in whom all the contradictions of such a notion are condensed, did not escape Aristotle's sharp eye. To give this development its full importance in the *Politics*, one must nevertheless treat Aristotle as a philosopher and not

merely as a "sociologist," as P. Cartledge does ("Spartan Wives: Liberation or Licence?" *Classical Quarterly* 31 [1981]: esp. 86–88), which leads him to miss the direction of Aristotle's demonstration. Napolitano (1987, 131) sees "una dialettica delle tradizioni" but diminishes the meaning of the text by speaking only of Spartan traditions (135–42).

79. Aristotle *Politics* 2.1269b32–39.

80. Plutarch *Numa* 25.9 will likewise say that their regimen led them to "become bold" (*thrasuterai genesthai*), first of all by acting in a manly way (*andrōdeis*) toward the *andres*.

81. An important reservation, which must not be minimized, as J. Redfield does in his translation of this passage ("The Women of Sparta," *Classical Journal* 73 [1978]: 149), at the cost of treating *thrasutēs* as a positive virtue, which is not at all the case here.

82. *Politics* 1.1260a23.

83. On this limit that is feminine nature for Aristotle, see G. Sissa, "Il corpo della donna: Lineamenti di una ginecologia filosofica," in S. Campese, P. Manuli, G. Sissa, *Madre Materia* (Turin, 1983), 83–145, and S. Georgoudi, "Le Mâle, la femelle, le neutre. Variations grecques sur le jeu des sexes et ses limites dans le monde animal," *Arethusa* (1990).

84. *Nicomachean Ethics* 3.1115b32–33; cf. 2.1107b3 and 1108b31, as well as 7.1151b7; in 3.1115a14–16, Aristotle observes that the impudent man is called courageous "metaphorically; for he resembles the courageous man." Note that since the time of the *Iliad* and Thersites, the connotations of *thrasos* are passably ambiguous: distinguishing, after Pollux, *tharsos* (courage) and the phonetic variant *thrasos* (effrontery, impudence), P. Chantraine ("A propos de Thersite," *Antiquité classique* 32 [1963]: 18–27) believes that the name Thersites must be seen as having a largely positive connotation, but on several occasions he refers to the character's cowardice, as when, for example, he states that "this 'all-courageous' Thersites is a coward"; for another interpretation of the name Thersites, Nagy 1979, 259–62.

85. From this standpoint, it is entirely bad. Thucydides associates *thrasos* with ignorance (*amathia*: 2.40.3, as well as 61.4), while, in the same passage *tolma* can be associated with *logos*. It will take civil war for boldness to truly become *alogistos*. Note that, in *Eumenides* 863, mutual boldness (*thrasus*) is a way of referring to civil war.

86. Aeschylus *Seven Against Thebes* 187–94 and 201 (*blabē*).

87. Ibid., 792 ("Be reassured, women who are too much your mothers' daughters").

88. This analysis contrasts with the argument proposed by C. Dewald ("Women and Culture in Herodotus' *Histories*," 98), for whom the women's actions show that in Herodotus's eyes "men and women share equally in the interplay of social values."

89. *Ergon*, to refer to the "Lemnian crime" (on the subject of which, consult G. Dumézil, *Le Crime des Lemniennes* [Paris, 1924]): Herodotus 6.138, Philostratus *Heroicus* 19; to refer to the murder of Itys: Thucydides 2.29.3.

90. Melantho: *Odyssey* 191.91–92; Clytemnestra: *Odyssey* 11.424–34 and 24.191–202, where the thrust is the same as in the diatribe against women of

Semonides of Amorgos: even the virtuous woman is part of a cursed race (Loraux 1981b, 108–11).

91. Inversely, typical women's activities, such as weaving, are easily expressed in the plural: e.g., Herodotus 4.114 (*erga gunaikēia*). On *ergatis* or *erganē* as qualifiers for women, see A.-M. Vérilhac, "L'Image de la femme dans les épigrammes funéraires grecques," in *La Femme dans le monde méditérranéen* (Lyons, 1985), 91–96n.

92. Concerning Artemis herself, whose manly courage (*andreiē*) is a *thōma* for Herodotus (7.99), the word *ergon* is not used unambiguously (8.88; cf. 87, where *ergazomai* suggests that Artemis works only for her own interest).

93. *Moralia* (= *Sayings of Spartans*) 241b.

94. *Deinon poiēsamenoi*: Athenian men react as emotionally as the women in 5.87 (*deinon poiēsamenas*).

95. Herodotus 9.5.

96. Note the verb *hēandane*, an archaizing variant of *edokee*.

97. Demosthenes *Crown* 204; Lycurgus *Contra Leocrates* 122 only mentions the masculine side of history.

98. I owe this analysis to remarks of Catherine Peschanski.

99. See M. Gras, "Cité grecque et lapidation," in Y. Thomas, ed., *Du châtiment dans la cité. Supplices corporels et peine de mort dans le monde antique* (Rome-Paris, 1984), 75–88.

100. Glotz 1904 (457 and 467), discussing this affair in the framework of collective executions, consistently "forgets" women's involvement in history; on the quasi-legality of this type of execution: 458–59.

101. See Dionysius of Halicarnassus *Roman Antiquities* 7.9 (family of Aristodemos, tyrant of Cumae), as well as Strabo 7.1.8 and Athenaeus 12.541d–e (the Locrians' revenge on the wife and children of Dionysius of Syracuse).

102. M. Gras, "Cité grecque et lapidation," 86.

103. This interpretation is markedly different from that of C. Dewald ("Women and Culture," 98); cf. Schaps 1982, 195 ("The women, at any rate, were no appeasers").

104. Striking formulations of this idea in the *Oresteia*: Aeschylus *Agamemnon* 485–86 (taking the *horos* reading of the manuscripts), and esp. *Choephoroi* 596–601.

105. *Northanger Abbey*, chap. 14. Original quotation: *Northanger Abbey and Persuasion* (New York: E. P. Dutton, 1906), 101.

106. This is a revised edition of an article called "La Cité, l'historien, les femmes," published in *Pallas* 32 (1985): 8–39.

SELECTED BIBLIOGRAPHY

THIS SELECTIVE bibliography contains only works that have been frequently mentioned or that are essential to the development of my argument. Please consult the footnotes for other references that appear throughout the text.

Benveniste, Emile. 1948. *Noms d'agent et noms d'action en indo-européen*. Paris: A. Maisonneuve.

———. 1966. *Problèmes de linguistique général*. Paris: Gallimard.

———. 1969. *Vocabulaire des institutions indo-européennes*. Vols. 1–2. Paris: Editions de Minuit.

Biardeau, Madeleine. 1985–86. *Le Mahābhārata*. Vols. 1–2. Excerpts translated from the Sanskrit by Jean-Michel Péterfalvi. Introduction and commentary by Madeleine Biardeau. Paris: GF-Flammarion.

Bollack, Jean, and Pierre Judet de la Combe. 1981–82. *L' "Agamemnon" d'Eschyle*. Vols. 1–2. Lille-Paris: Presses universitaires de Lille-Editions de la Maison des Sciences de l'Homme.

Bonnefoy, Yves. 1981. (Ed.) *Dictionnaire des mythologies*. Vols. 1–2. Paris: Flammarion.

Borgeaud, Philippe. 1979. *Recherches sur le dieu Pan*. Rome-Geneva. Institut Suisse de Rome.

Bouvier, David. 1987. "Mourir près des fontaines de Troie. Remarques sur le problème de la toilette funéraire d'Hector dans l'*Iliade*." *Euphrosyne* 15: 9–29.

Brelich, Angelo. 1961. *Guerre, agoni e culti nella Grecia arcaica*. Bonn. Habelt.

Brisson, Luc. 1976. *Le Mythe de Tirésias. Essai d'analyse structurale*. Leiden: Brill.

———. 1986. "*Neutrum utrumque*. La Bisexualité dans l'Antiquité gréco-romaine." *L'Androgyne*. Les Cahiers de l'hermétisme. Paris: Albin Michel. Pp. 31–61.

Burkert, Walter. 1977. *Griechische Religion der archaischen und klassichen Epoche*. Stuttgart: W. Kohlhammer. English trans. by John Raffan, *Greek Religion*. Cambridge: Harvard University Press. 1985.

Burnyeat, Miles F. 1977. "Socratic Midwifery, Platonic Inspiration." *Bulletin of the Institute of Classical Studies* 24: 7–13.

Buxton, Richard. 1980. "Blindness and Limits: Sophocles and the Logic of Myth." *Journal of Hellenic Studies* 100: 22–37.

Calame, Claude. 1977. *Les Choeurs de jeunes filles en Grèce archaïque*. Vol. 1. Rome: Ateneo.

———. 1983. (Ed.) *L'Amore in Grecia*. Rome-Bari: Laterza.

Cassin, Barbara. 1985. "Encore Hélène: Une sophistique de la jouissance." *Littoral* 15–16: 161–76.

Chantraine, Pierre. 1946–47. "Les Noms du mari et de la femme, du père et de la mère en grec." *Revue des Etudes grecques* 59–60: 219–50.

———. 1949. "Les Verbes grecs signifiant tuer." *Die Sprache* 1: 143–49.

———. 1968. *Dictionnaire étymologique de la langue grecque. Histoire des mots*. Paris: Klincksieck.

Chirassi Colombo, Ileana. 1984. "L'Inganno di Afrodite." *I labirinti dell'Eros*. Florence: Libreria delle Donne. Pp. 109–21.

Daladier, Nathalie. 1979. "Les Mères aveugles." *Nouvelle Revue de Psychanalyse* 19: 229–44.

Daraki, Maria. 1980. "Le Guerrier à *ménos* et le héros *daimoni isos*." *Annali della Scoula Normale Superiore di Pisa* 10: 1–24.

———. 1982. "Les Fils de la mort." In *La Mort, les morts dans les sociétés anciennes*. Ed. G. Gnoli and J.-P. Vernant. Cambridge-Paris: Cambridge University Press-Editions de la Maison des Sciences de l'Homme. Pp. 155–76.

Daremberg, Charles. 1865. *La Médecine dans Homère ou Etude d'Archéologie sur les médecins, l'anatomie, la physiologie, la chirurgie et la médecine dans les poèmes homériques*. Paris: Librairie académique Didier et Cie.

Delcourt, Marie. 1942. *Légendes et cultes de héros en Grèce*. Paris: Presses Universitaires de France.

———. 1955. *L'Oracle de Delphes*. Paris: Payot.

Derrida, Jacques. 1972. "La Pharmacie de Platon." In *La Dissémination*. Paris: Seuil. Pp. 71–197.

Descat, Raymond. 1986. *L'Acte et l'effort. Une idéologie du travail en Grèce ancienne (VIIe–Ve siècle av. J.-C.)*. Besançon-Lille: Les Belles Lettres.

Detienne, Marcel. 1960. "Héraklès, héros pythagoricien." *Revue de l'Histoire des Religions* 158: 19–53.

———. 1967. *Les Maîtres de la vérité dans la Grèce archaïque*. Paris: Maspero.

———. 1968. "La Phalange. Problèmes de méthode." In *Problèmes de la guerre en Grèce ancienne*. Ed. J.-P. Vernant. Paris-The Hague: Mouton-Edition de l'Ecole des Hautes Etudes en Sciences sociales. Pp. 119–42.

———. 1972. *Les Jardins d'Adonis*. Paris: Gallimard.

———. 1977. *Dionysos mis à mort*. Paris: Gallimard.

Detienne, Marcel, and Jean-Pierre Vernant. 1974. *Les Ruses de l'intelligence. La Mètis des Grecs*. Paris: Flammarion.

———. 1979. (Eds.). *La Cuisine du sacrifice en Grèce ancienne*. Paris: Gallimard.

DuBois, Page. 1988. *Sowing the Body. Psychoanalysis and Ancient Representations of Women*. Chicago: University of Chicago Press.

Dumézil, Georges. 1968. *Mythe et épopée I. L'Idéologie des trois fonctions dans les épopées des peuples indo-européens*. Paris: Gallimard.

———. 1969. *Heur et malheur du guerrier*. Paris: Presses Universitaires de France.

———. 1971. *Mythe et épopée II*. Paris: Gallimard.

Ehrenberg, Victor. 1936. *"Tresantes," Paulys Real-Encyclopädie der Altertumswissenschaft*. Stuttgart/Munich: Metzler, then Druckenmüller, 1894–1980. Vol. VIa2, col. 2292–97.

Ellinger, Pierre. 1978. "Le Gypse et la boue. I. Sur les mythes de la guerre d'anéantissement." *Quaderni Urbinati di Cultura Classica* 29: 7–35.

Finley, Moses I. 1978. *Le Monde d'Ulysse*. 2nd ed. French translation by C. Vernant-Blanc and M. Alexandre. Paris: Maspero.

Fontenrose, Joseph. 1968. "The Hero as Athlete." *California Studies in Classical Antiquity* 1: 73–104.

Foucault, Michel. 1984. *Histoire de la sexualité*. Vol. 2. *L'Usage des plaisirs*. Paris: Gallimard.

Fraisse, Geneviève. 1989. *Muse de la raison. La Démocratie exclusive et la différence des sexes*. Aix-en-Provence: Alinéa.

Freud, Sigmund. 1964a. "The Uncanny" (1919). *The Standard Edition of the Complete Psychological Works of Sigmund Freud*. Vol. 17 (1917–19). Translated and edited by James Strachey. London: Hogarth Press. Pp. 219–52.

———. 1964b. "Negation" (1925). *The Standard Edition of the Complete Psychological Works of Sigmund Freud*. Vol. 19 (1923–25). Translated and edited by James Strachey. London: Hogarth Press. Pp. 235–39.

Frontisi-Ducroux, Françoise. 1975. *Dédale. Mythologie de l'artisan en Grèce ancienne*. Paris: Maspero.

Galinsky, G. K. 1972. *The Herakles Theme*. Oxford.

Garlan, Yvon. 1972. *La Guerre dans l'Antiquité*. Paris: Fernand Nathan.

Gentili, Bruno, and Giuseppe Paioni (eds.) 1977. *Il Mito greco*. Rome: Ateneo.

Georgoudi, Stella. 1986. "Les Jeunes et le monde animal: Éléments du discours grec ancien sur la jeunesse." In *Historicité de l'enfance et de la jeunesse*. Actes du Colloque international. Athens. Pp. 223–29.

Gernet, Louis. 1917. *Recherches sur le développement de la pensée juridique et morale en Grèce*. Paris: Leroux.

———. 1968. *Anthropologie de la Grèce antique*. Paris: Maspero.

Ginouvès, René. 1962. *Balaneutikè. Recherches sur le bain dans l'Antiquité grecque*. Paris: De Boccard.

Glotz, Gustave. 1904. *La Solidarité de la famille dans le droit criminel en Grèce*. Paris. Rpt. 1973. New York: Arno Press.

Godelier, Maurice. 1982. *La Production des grands hommes*. Paris: Fayard.

Graf, Fritz. 1984. "Women, War and Warlike Divinities." *Zeitschrift für Papyrologie und Epigraphik* 55: 245–54.

Hartog, François. 1980. *Le Miroir d'Hérodote. Essai sur la représentation de l'autre*. Paris: Gallimard.

Héritier-Augé, Françoise. 1984–85. "Le Sang du guerrier et le sang des femmes. Notes anthropologiques sur le rapport des sexes." *Cahiers du GRIF* 29 (Winter: *L'Africaine: Sexes et signes*): 7–21.

Jeanmaire, Henri. 1939. *Couroi et courètes. Essai sur l'éducation spartiate*. Lille: Bibliothèque universitaire. Rpt. 1973. New York: Arno Press.

Jouan, François. 1966. *Euripide et les légendes des Chants cypriens*. Paris: Les Belles Lettres.

Jourdain-Annequin, Colette. 1985. "Héraklès *latris* et *doulos*. Sur quelques aspects du travail dans le mythe héroïque." *Dialogues d'Histoire ancienne* 11: 487–538.

———. 1986. "Héraclès Parastatès." In *Les Grandes figures religieuses*. Lire les polythéismes. Vol. 1. Besançon-Paris: Annales littéraires de l'Université de Besançon 329/Les Belles Lettres. Pp. 283–331.

Kahn, Laurence. 1978. *Hermès passe ou les ambiguïtés de la communication*. Paris: Maspero.

———. 1986. "Un père, un fils, on mange. Une version mythique de la dévoration." *Lieux de l'enfant* 6–7: 209–41.

Kerényi, Karl. 1945. *Die Geburt der Helena*. Zurich: Rhein-Verlag.

King, Helen. 1983. "Bound to Bleed: Artemis and the Greek Women." In *Images of Women in Greek Antiquity*. Ed. A. Cameron and A. Kuhrt. London: Croom Helm. Pp. 109–27.

———. 1987. "Sacrificial Blood: The Role of *Amnion* in Ancient Gynecology." *Helios* 13: 117–26.

Lloyd, Geoffrey E. R. 1983. *Science, Folklore and Ideology. Studies in the Life Science in Ancient Greece*. Cambridge: Cambridge University Press.

Loraux, Nicole. 1975. "*Hēbē* et *andreia*. Deux versions de la mort du combattant athénien." *Ancient Society* 6: 1–31.

———. 1981a. *L'Invention d'Athènes. Histoire de l'oraison funèbre dans la "cité classique."* Paris-The Hague: Editions de l'Ecole des Hautes Etudes en Sciences Sociales/Mouton.

———. 1981b. *Les Enfants d'Athéna. Idées athéniennes sur la citoyenneté et la division des sexes*. Paris: Maspero.

———. 1982. "Mourir devant Troie, tomber pour Athènes." In *Information sur les sciences sociales* 17, 6 (1978): 801–17.

———. 1985. *Façons tragiques de tuer une femme*. Paris: Hachette.

———. 1986a. "*Matrem nudam:* Quelques versions grecques." *L'Ecrit du temps* 11 (*Destins de mythes*): 90–102.

———. 1986b. "L'Empreinte de Jocaste." *L'Ecrit du temps* 12 (*Oedipe*): 34–54.

———. 1986c. "Le Corps vulnérable d'Arès." *Le Temps de la réflexion* 7 (*Corps des dieux*): 335–54.

———. 1987. "Le Lien de la division." *Le Cahier du Collège international de Philosophie* 4: 101–24.

Malamoud, Charles. 1989. *Cuire le monde. Rite et pensée dans l'Inde ancienne*. Paris: La Découverte.

Manuli, Paola. 1983. "Donne masculine, femmine sterili, vergini perpetue. La ginecologia greca tra Ippocrate e Sorano." In Silvia Campese, Paola Manuli, Giulia Sissa, *Madre Materia. Sociologia e biologia della donna greca*. Turin: Boringhieri. Pp. 149–92.

Manuli, Paola, and Mario Vegetti. 1977. *Cuore, sangue e cervello. Biologia e antropologia nel pensiero antico*. Milan: Episteme Editrice.

Mawet, Francine. 1979. *Recherches sur les oppositions fonctionnelles dans le vocabulaire homérique de la douleur*. Brussels: Académie royale de Belgique, Mémoires de la Classe des Lettres.

Monsacré, Hélène. 1984. *Les Larmes d'Achille. Le Héros, la femme et la souffrance dans la poésie d'Homère*. Paris: Albin Michel.

Nagy, Gregory. 1979. *The Best of the Achaeans. Concepts of the Hero in Archaic Greek Poetry*. Baltimore: Johns Hopkins University Press.

Napolitano, Maria-Luisa. 1985. "Donne spartane e *teknopoiia*." *Annali dell'Istituto Orientale di Napoli. Archeologia e storia antica* 7: 19–50.

———. 1987. "Le Donne spartane e la guerra. Problemi di tradizione." *Annali dell'Istituto Orientale di Napoli. Archeologia e storia antica* 9: 127–44.

Olender, Maurice. 1985. "Aspects de Baubō. Textes et contextes antiques." *Revue de l'Histoire des Religions* 202, 1: 3–55.

Onians, Richard B. 1951. *The Origins of European Thought*. Cambridge: Cambridge University Press.

Otto, Walter F. 1981. *Les Dieux de la Grèce*. French trans. Paris: Payot.

Pigeaud, Jackie. 1981. *La Maladie de l'âme. Etude sur la relation de l'âme et du corps dans la tradition médico-philosophique antique*. Paris: Les Belles Lettres.

————. 1988. *Aristote. L'Homme de génie et la mélancolie*. Translation, presentation, and notes by Jackie Pigeaud. Marseilles: Rivages.

Pouchelle, Marie-Christine. 1986. "Le Corps féminin et ses paradoxes: L'Imaginaire de l'intériorité dans les écrits médicaux et religieux (XII–XIVe s.). In *La Condición de la mujer en la Edad Media*. Madrid: Ed. Universidad Complutense. Pp. 316–31.

Pucci, Pietro. 1985. "Epifanie testuali nell'*Iliade*." *Studi Italiani di Filologia Classica* 3: 170–83.

————. 1986. "Les Figures de la *mētis* dans l'*Odyssée*." *Mētis* 1: 7–28.

Ramnoux, Clémence. 1959. *La Nuit et les enfants de la Nuit dans la tradition grecque*. Paris: Flammarion.

————. 1962. *Mythologie ou la famille olympienne*. Paris: Presses Universitaires de la France.

Rohde, Erwin. 1925. *Psyche: The Cult of Souls and Belief in Immortality among the Greeks*. New York: Harcourt, Brace.

Saïd, Suzanne. 1982. "Féminin, femme et femelle dans les grands traités biologiques d'Aristote." In *La femme dans les sociétés antiques*. Ed. E. Lévy. Actes des colloques de Strasbourg. May 1980 and March 1981. Pp. 93–123.

Schaps, David. 1982. "The Women of Greece in Wartime." *Classical Philology* 77: 193–213.

Schlesier, Renate. 1982. "Das Flötenspiel des Gorgo." *Notizbuch* 5–6: 11–57.

Schmitt, Pauline. 1977. "Athéna Apatouria et la ceinture. Les Aspects féminins des Apatouries à Athènes." *Annales ESC* (Nov.-Dec.): 1059–73.

Segal, Charles P. 1971. "Andromache's *Anagnorisis*." *Harvard Studies in Classical Philology* 75: 33–57.

Sissa, Giulia. 1987. *Le Corps virginal. La Virginité féminine en Grèce ancienne*. Paris: Vrin.

Slater, Philip E. 1971. *The Glory of Hera*. Boston: Beacon Press.

Slatkin, Laura. 1988. "Les Amis mortels. A propos des insultes dans les combats de l'*Iliade*." French trans. by N. Loraux. *L'Ecrit du temps* 19 (*Négations*): 119–32.

Starobinski, Jean. 1974. "L'Epée d'Ajax." In *Trois fureurs*. Paris: Gallimard. Pp. 11–71.

Svenbro, Jesper. 1976. *La Parole et le marbre. Aux origines de la poétique grecque*. Lund.

Thomas, Yan. 1986. "Le 'Ventre.' Corps maternel, droit paternel." *Le genre humain* 14 (*La valeur*): 211–36.

Verdier, Yvonne. 1979. *Façons de dire, façons de faire*. Paris: Gallimard.

Vermeule, Emily. 1979. *Aspects of Death in Greek Art and Poetry*. Berkeley and Los Angeles: University of California Press.

Vernant, Jean-Pierre. 1971. *Mythe et pensée chez les Grecs*. 2 vols. 4th ed. Paris: Maspero.

————. 1974. *Mythe et société en Grèce ancienne*. Paris: Maspero.

————. 1982. "La Belle mort et le cadavre outragé." In *La Mort, les morts dans les sociétés anciennes*. Ed. G. Gnoli and J.-P. Vernant. Cambridge-Paris. Pp. 45–76. (= Vernant 1989: 41–79).

————. 1985. *La Mort dans les yeux. Figures de l'Autre en Grèce ancienne*. Paris: Hachette.

————. 1989. *L'Individu, la mort, l'amour. Soi-même et l'autre en Grèce ancienne*. Paris: Gallimard.

Vian, Francis. 1968. "La Fonction guerrière dans la mythologie grecque." In *Problèmes de la guerre en Grèce ancienne*. Ed. J.-P. Vernant. Paris-The Hague: Edition de l'Ecole des Hautes Etudes Supérieures/Mouton. Pp. 53–68.

Vidal-Naquet, Pierre. 1981. *Le Chasseur noir. Formes de pensée, formes de société en Grèce ancienne*. Paris: Maspero.

Voisin, Jean-Louis. 1979. "Pendus, crucifiés, oscilla dans la Rome païenne." *Latomus* 38: 422–50.

Zeitlin, Froma. 1982a. "Travesties of Gender and Genre in Aristophanes' *Thesmophoriazousae*." In *Reflections of Women in Antiquity*. Ed. Helene Foley. London-New York: Gordon and Breach. Pp. 169–217.

————. 1982b. "Cultic Models of the Female: Rites of Dionysos and Demeter." *Arethusa* 15: 129–57.

————. 1985a. "The Power of Aphrodite: Eros and the Boundaries of the Self in the *Hippolytus*." In *Directions in Euripidean Criticism*. Ed. P. Burian. Durham, N.C.: Duke University Press. Pp. 52–110 and 189–207.

————. 1985b. "Playing the Other: Theater, Theatricality, and the Feminine in Greek Drama." *Representations* 11: 63–94.

GLOSSARY OF ESSENTIAL TERMS AND NAMES

ACHILLES — The "best" (i.e., the bravest) of the Achaians (Nagy 1979). Warrior hero of the *Iliad*, in many respects close to Ares: he is "gigantic, furious, swift" like Ares, and to his enemies his sinister brightness flashes like fire. The son of a goddess and a mortal, he chose immortal glory and a short life, a condensed version of mortality. The hero is so multidimensional that Achilles can weep copious tears, withdraw into himself like a Mother in anger (*mēnis*), or, when mourning Patroclus, fast like Niobe grieving for her children. All such conduct serves only to authenticate his manly strength.

AGAMEMNON — King of kings, husband of Clytemnestra (who will kill him), the brother-in-law of Helen. In book 11 of the *Iliad*, wounded by an arrow, he suffers sharp pains like those of a woman in childbirth.

Agkhonē — Strangling or hanging. In both cases, this death by suffocation is without honor because blood is retained inside the body instead of being spilled. A woman's punishment or suicide.

Aidōs — The feeling of what one owes to another or to oneself. Its only sphere of action is society and, within it, hierarchical relationships (e.g., in Sparta, pertaining to all who are not *homoioi* toward the "Like Ones"). When referring to women, this word has another tonality, referring to reserve but also modesty (its opposite is *anaideia*, a mixture of impudence and immodesty), which can quickly turn into shame (it will be recalled that *aidoia* denotes the sexual organs as "shameful parts").

Anēr, pl. *andres*; *andreia* — *Anēr*: man in his virility; hence, in his bravery or as a citizen. Opposed to *gunē*, woman (in a particular case of this opposition, *anēr* can refer to the husband and *gunē* the wife). *Andres* refers to the collectivity of men as males-citizens-fighters, to the extent that one can posit an equivalence between *andres* and *polis* (the city means the men of the city). Hence *andres* is frequently used in the present work to refer to the collective Greek speaker on the subject of the standard views about the difference between the sexes, with the understanding that this speaker is at the same time the audience. *Andreia*: denotes manly courage; both descriptive (it belongs to men) and prescriptive (it should belong to men).

APHRODITE — Refers here less to the cosmic force presiding over love among all living creatures (gods, men, and animals) than the mistress of pleasure and desire among humankind. In this respect the city limits as much as possible the role of *hēdonē* in marriage, with Hera ensuring that moderation is observed. Because Aphrodite, unlike Athena, whose body is impossible to perceive, is the goddess most present in her lovely body, historians of religion see her as the incarnation of the immediacy of realized desire.

ARES — God of war as manifested in brutal and murderous carnage. "Scourge of mortals," he gorges himself on the blood of warriors and serves as their ultimate killer. However, he too is subject to the action that he unleashes and is vulnerable and sometimes wounded like any human fighter. Athena, with her wily cunning, excels at cutting him down to size.

Aretē — From epic to civic ideology, the term for "value" or "virtue," understood in the sense of *virtus* or *virtu*. The history of the word— with the active intervention of the philosophers—reflects its transformation into the more edifying connotation of the word *virtue*.

ARTEMIS — Divine virgin, seen here in her relationship to women, for whom she is both a protectress and a scourge. *Lokhia*, she is the divinity who presides over childbirth but also, manifested in the form of blood, she kills women in childbirth. *Apakhomenē*, she is hanged or strangled, and this epiclesis calls to mind the notion that blood usually strangles women. Also mentioned in the sad story of Actaeon the hunter, who was devoured by his dogs because he saw her at her bath. Artemis is to be feared.

ATHENA — Another divine virgin, perhaps the first to deserve this title, in that she is the daughter of the Father. A warlike divinity endowed with *mētis*. In this respect, as the only one capable of getting the best of Ares, she is always able to overcome brute force. A fearsome magician, she is the possessor of an (almost) invulnerable body, and her eye blinds the careless, such as Tiresias, who saw her unclothed body, which is known only by its wrappings (the *peplos* of the virgin, the warrior's shield, the aegis that, in the *Iliad*, she receives from Zeus).

Athlos (Hom. *aethlos*) — Trial accompanied by suffering, heroic (Herakles) or athletic exploit. *Athlon* is the prize awarded for an *athlos* and the object for which one surpasses oneself.

Brokhos — A hunter's snare, the knot that women tie around their necks in order to hang themselves.

CLYTEMNESTRA — Wife and murderess of Agamemnon, lover of Aegisthus. But above all, the mother of Iphigenia (for whose death she will never forgive Agamemnon), Electra, and Orestes, who will kill her. Helen's sister. A wife with "manly plans," the tyrant of the city of Argos, she often embodies the idea of gynecocracy, that maximum form of subversion. But all in all, it may be that this feminine form of power is still more acceptable (because it is so clearly negative) than a mother's rage, so disquieting, even frightening, in its intransigency.

DIONYSOS — Present in this book as the god of theater. In addition to his connections with the feminine, note also his relationship with Herakles (in Aristophanes' *Frogs*, Dionysos dons a lion's skin to pass himself off as the hero).

Gastēr — Belly. Stomach. Like *nēdus*, but in more formulaic expressions it can also refer to the belly as the container for a child.

GORGON — Not mentioned in this book in person but metonymically, as the sign of what fascinates, terrifies, and paralyzes. In this respect, she is located in Athena's eyes, and when her skin is not the goddess's aegis, it is her head that adorns the shield that Athena possesses from Zeus. Not surprisingly, she can be seen in the warrior's eye and on his shield.

Gunē, pl. *gunaikes* — Woman, women. The Other, for men, generally domesticated under the heading of wife; in this case, this means being the reproducer, for the *anēr* and for the city. In the plural it refers to the female sex considered as a species (Hesiod speaks of the "race of women"). By definition not a political group except when it is said, along with Aristotle speaking of Sparta, that they are "half" of the city (but the Lacedaemonian women behaved badly indeed, according to the philosopher); they can also serve as abnormal fighters in civil wars or legendary tales.

Haima — Blood. Originally, blood spilled (outside the body). In fantasies of heroic virility, it is more likely to flow from the wounded warrior's body than from the bodies of women, who are, however, destined to bleed. In hanging or strangling, blood is contained within the body, as in the case of certain "women's diseases," which makes this type of death into primarily a feminine fate, as if the female body were naturally blocked.

Hēdonē — Pleasure. Not defined, except by its opposite, as pain's successor and accomplice (this is Socrates speaking). Tiresias knows of its intensity because he had been a woman.

HELEN — The most beautiful of women as a sexual being, cause of the Trojan war. Daughter of Zeus and Nemesis, or the sister of Clytemnestra, her beauty is supernatural, and her body, which is the glory and misfortune of Troy, is as superb as it is unreal or ghostlike.

HERA — Zeus's irascible wife, the protectress of marriage and, in this respect, the enemy of Aphrodite. Her hatred of Herakles leads her to pursue him and subject him to Eurytheus and his "groaning" Labors, before she becomes his divine "mother," either suckling him to immortalize him or adopting him. In the *Iliad* the hero carries out at least one act of aggression against the goddess when he wounds her in the right breast.

HERAKLES — "Hera's Glory" and "Glorious by Hera." The hero of manhood, caught in the epico-heroic contradictions of the status of *anēr*: strong and suffering, misogynist and lover of women, fond of hot baths but committed to *ponos*. From the Pythagoreans to the Stoics, via Plato and the Cynics, the apologia of Prodikos is repeated, attributing to him the free choice of a life of *ponos*. As a result, he benefits by being naturalized as a philosopher. After reckoning the multiple signs of his intimate relationship with the feminine, we are not too surprised that he dies at the hands of a woman—his wife Deianeira. His body wracked with intense pain, he suffers like a woman but dies like a man. Heroic honor is saved, *in extremis*.

Homoioi — The "Like Ones." The official designation in Sparta of full-fledged citizens. In any city the implicit definition of the *andres* in opposition to all others.

Kalos thanatos — The "beautiful death." From Sparta to Athens, the death of the citizen-soldier fallen for the city. The model for *andreia* and *aretē*, for "courage" and "valor," characterized, especially in Athens, by its abstract dimension. Once the syntagma has been formed, *kalos* loses its aesthetic connotations and suggests a purely civic form of beauty.

Kamatos, verb *kamnō* — See *ponos*.

Khrōs — Skin as it is the surface of the human body, assuming that the thickness of the flesh beneath the skin is indissociable with the surface. "Flesh" and "skin" reveal the body in its living density, and in the case of the warrior it is both enclosed and barely protected by this envelope, which can be deeply pierced by arrows.

Kuōn — Dog. A word with a masculine *form*, but when preceded by the feminine article (*hē kuōn*), it refers to the bitch, frequently considered the emblem of a totally feminine, impudent lubricity.

LEONIDAS — King of Sparta, who died a brave death at Thermopylae (480 B.C.), at the head of a contingent of three hundred elite soldiers, all *homoioi*. The battle over his body evokes the melees of the *Iliad* over the hero's body.

Lokhos — (same root as *lekhō*, the "woman in childbirth," *lekhos*, "the marriage bed," *Lekheatēs*, epiclesis for Zeus as he gave birth to Athena). Term denoting childbirth and ambush. It is uncertain whether the term derives from one root or two. The hypothesis has been made that only one root is involved, or at least that the Greeks understood it in this way. *Lokhia*, the "woman in childbirth," is the epiclesis of Artemis, who is both helpful and terrifying to women.

Mokhthos — See *ponos*.

Mēnis — Black rage that is not forgotten and feeds on itself. The anger of the dispossessed mother, always appeased in the end—and, behind the founding *mēnis* of Achilles, one can perceive "Thetis's wrath" (Slatkin).

Mētis — The wily intelligence of the Greeks (Detienne and Vernant 1974). With a capital letter, the divinity first loved and then swallowed by Zeus, the engulfed "mother" of Athena.

Nēdus — The inside of the body considered as a cavity. Hence, the belly, the stomach, the womb. Poets are fond of playing on the last two meanings on the subject of Kronos swallowing his children, Zeus absorbing Metis, or Herakles the glutton.

Ōdis, ōdines — The pains of childbirth. Used metaphorically by Plato, it refers not to the "agonies" of the soul but to the pains caused by the exertion required in approaching the beautiful or in the act of thinking.

Odunē — Any penetrating, piercing pain, that of a wound, that which is typically referred to as *ōdis*. This last use is fairly common, especially since the plural *odunai* is phonetically close to *ōdines*.

Peplos — A piece of cloth, a veil, or garment. A barbarian's or woman's garment (in this respect *peplos* serves to indicate femininity). Athena is ritually clothed in a *peplos*, and over the course of his busy history, Herakles will wear more than one of them.

PHAEDRA — Theseus's wife, the plaything of Aphrodite, who inspired in her a violent passion for the headstrong youth Hippolytus. Her lovesickness reveals the "nonviable constitution" of women, for whom sickness, love, madness, and childbirth present the same physical signs of derangement. Blood tends to choke the bodies of women afflicted with "women's diseases," and Phaedra will find her death in the mortal suffocation of the noose.

PLATO — The well-known Athenian philosopher. For Plutarch he figures in the list of melancholy geniuses, along with Herakles and Socrates. He does not merely put Socrates onstage as the protagonist of his dialogues and use him as a complex indicator of strength and weakness. In this book he is considered one of the identifiable agents in Greek speculations about the difference between the sexes.

Polemos — War. Still considered beautiful during the classical period, because the enemy is a foreigner. Declared to be hateful and yet still dearly loved in the *Iliad*. Transforms an *anēr* into a man. Thus it has the reputation for "not being the business of women."

Polis — The city. Both as reality and as ideal, the *deus ex machina* of official Greek parlance and of modern historians of ancient Greece concerned with the shared representations of the archaic and classical periods.

Ponos, verb *ponein* — Work as a trial, both exploit and suffering: the manly *ponos* of war, the *ponos* of childbirth for women. *Ponos* also is used in the plural (*ponoi*) in classical texts to refer to the deeds of Herakles, which in the epic are designated as *aethloi* (see *athlos*). As a term denoting pain or fatigue, it is synonymous with *mokhthos* and *kamatos*.

Psukhē — Life, the breath of life: in this use, it is allied with *sōma* (body) in the Athenian funeral oration. The soul: like the Orphics, Plato separates it from and opposes it to the body. The body's other.

SOCRATES — His name alone suffices, I think. But he is also formed of his body and soul. It will be added that in extreme cases he is stronger than Herakles. In Aristophanic comedy he takes an interest in questions of gender and sex.

Sōma — The body. In a civic perspective, not truly the property of the citizen but instead belonging to the city, which, expending *sōmata kai ponous*, spends "bodies" and suffering, which boils down to an accounting of human losses and wasted efforts. For Plato (via Socrates), it is not the property of the philosopher, whose entire being is supposed to reside in the *psukhē*. So Socrates wages a long battle against the body, which must be dispensed with but returns in the form of Plato's language.

Stasis — Treason, hence civil war. The (poorly) hidden face of Greek politics. It is *antianeira* (hostile to the *andres*), just as the Amazons are in Homer. Therefore all the most horrible types of death find their place there, beginning with the hanging of male citizens.

TIRESIAS — Blinded by Hera for revealing that pleasure is essentially feminine, or by Athena, who caught him in the intimacy of her bath. In the first version of the tale, he knew of what he spoke because he (she?) experienced it while in a woman's body. Here he is considered in the part of his story that precedes his career as a seer.

Tresantes — The Tremblers. Homeric heroes may occasionally tremble (*trein*), since by definition the hero feels, has felt, or will one day feel fear. In Sparta this term officially designates fighters who have fled the battlefield and whose status as citizens is thereby degraded.

Tropē — The turnabout to flee that gives its name to the Greek term for defeat. To be provoked among the enemy, when one is a man—above all, to avoid succumbing to it oneself! Paradoxically, women warriors provoke it on all accounts.

Truphē — The sweet life, softness, luxury. Opposed in every term to *ponos*.

ZEUS — Father of gods and men. Father, too, of paradigmatic women; while he merely created Pandora, the first woman, in the form of a virgin, he gives birth to Athena and engenders Helen. Decidedly, the supreme god wanted the difference between the sexes to divide humanity in two. The fact that he began by subverting it to his own ends is not a completely separate story.

INDEX

Nicole Loraux is Director of Studies at the
Ecole des Hautes Etudes en Sciences
Sociales in Paris.